IN PURSUIT OF BILL

IN PURSUIT OF BILL

A Comprehensive History of
the Rugby World Cup

BOXSTAR MEDIA

First published in the United Kingdom in 2007 by
Boxstar Media Ltd

All imagery supplied by Action Images Ltd (Reuters)

ISBN 978-0-9556411-0-7

Designed and produced by
Action Publishing Technology Ltd, Gloucester

Printed and bound in Great Britain

This book is dedicated to my courageous grandmother
Maria Emily Ilkiw – the rock upon which my magnificent family was built.

Contents

Acknowledgements

WHERE DO I START? Much the same question I asked myself when I first took this project on in 2002, but it didn't take long to find direction after hundreds of interviews with key figures in the game – both past and present. To pick up on a comment John Eales made to me many years ago: 'Rugby people are generally good people.' It really is a very simple assessment, yet so applicable on many different levels when referring to the international rugby family.

Many good rugby people have made this project possible and my gratitude to all of them cannot be justified by merely a few words on this page, not to mention the list that would probably amount to an extra 300 pages if I was to thank them all individually. You know who you are, and I know who you are, and I'm forever grateful for your support. From legendary players and captains of Rugby World Cups right through to the archive assistants from various unions around the world, my sincerest thank you to everyone within the international rugby family and across the media who has helped this project come to fruition.

I must also thank my family and friends for their unwavering support, and the great team at Action Publishing Technology for their tremendous efficiency and professional guidance. Finally, a massive thank you to my dearest fiancée Katherine, who has been so understanding and offered many words of encouragement while also making a large contribution to the following pages.

Despite many long nights tapping away on the keyboard until the early hours, forgoing multiple social events and wondering if a normal life will ever return, it really has been an absolute pleasure to write this book. My passion for this great game is channelled through these words and I hope and trust you will enjoy reading how this amazing tournament has developed into the powerhouse that it is today from very humble beginnings back in 1987. Enjoy!

Lance Peatey

Foreword

MOST PEOPLE KNOW a person named Bill; it's a reasonably common name. What is not so well known is the origin of this abbreviation in reference to The Webb Ellis Cup – the symbol of world rugby supremacy named after the student William Webb Ellis of Rugby College in England, who is so famously attributed with creating the distinctive feature of the rugby game when he first took the ball and ran with it.

The tale of Webb Ellis is well known to many in the rugby world, but the story of how the piece of silverware named after him became known as 'Bill' can be traced back to the victorious Wallabies team of 1991. Having just defeated England in a tense final at Twickenham, we were enjoying the warmth of the claw-foot baths deep under the Twickenham grandstand when one of our team members asked for a sip from 'Bill' – an obvious reference to The Webb Ellis Cup. At the time it was filled with XXXX beer and various other liquid refreshments. The nickname stuck and has since become ingrained in the Australian rugby vernacular, while also developing as a pet name internationally for rugby's ultimate prize.

As one of the younger members of the squad on that occasion I didn't realise the enormity of our accomplishment. Looking back it's now apparent that winning a Rugby World Cup is something only a select group of players are privileged enough to experience during their career. Fortunately I experienced it twice – 1991 and 1999.

While the on-field achievements will always provide fantastic memories, the greatest moments were in the dressing rooms after we'd won. These are the very rare moments where you can spend time with your team-mates and truly enjoy the spoils of victory while reflecting on the sacrifices and hard work that brought you there.

In 1991, I remember soaking in the bathtubs at Twickenham with the likes of Phil Kearns, Simon Poidevin and Michael Lynagh. In 1999, I was one of the last players to leave the change room, but not before singing the national anthem with my team-mates and enjoying a cigar with Joe Roff, Ben Tune and Matt Burke. These are the moments you wish would last forever.

In 1995 it was a vastly different experience as we were bundled out by England in the quarter-final stages courtesy of a Rob Andrew drop goal. One of the lasting memories of that campaign was the looks of disappointment on the faces of the Australian supporters we crossed paths with in Perth airport as they were heading to South Africa in anticipation of seeing us play in the semi-finals. If looks could kill!

However, the disappointment of 1995 was a major contributor to our success in 1999 as the core group of senior players had learned a great deal from that experience and we were determined not to suffer the same fate.

In 2003 I experienced the Rugby World Cup in Australia not as a player but rather a commentator for one of the local television broad-casters. It provided a different perspective to my previous Rugby World Cup experiences, but it was just as enjoyable – and far more relaxing!

While each of my Rugby World Cup experiences has been memo-rable for different reasons and moments, the one constant factor has been the quest for 'Bill'. It never ceases to amaze me how one small trophy can unite a group of individuals to surge towards one common goal. While we may not have always achieved the desired result, the quest for 'Bill' symbolises all the great things about rugby.

Tim Horan
Dual Rugby World Cup winner – 1991 & 1999
Player of the Tournament – 1999

1

From obscure origins to international showpiece

THE WHISTLE SOUNDS, the village crowd roars and chaos ensues. The sound of the whistle is hardly crisp – more likely a local shepherd able to generate the sound from days spent herding his flock. Team colours have little part. The players do resemble fine-looking athletes and they are dressed in nothing but ancient headwear and a skimpy piece of leather covering their private parts, if that (some primeval writings suggest the Greeks played totally nude). There is limited structure to the game and team tactics are not a high priority. Two teams are opposing, but such is the anarchy surrounding the ball, it looks a lot more like every man for himself.

The year is somewhere just after 146 BC. The Roman Empire has conquered Greece and with it adopted a series of Greco cultural traditions before applying its own imperial stamp. The game being played is Harpastum – the Roman version of Episkyros (also known as Phaininda), an ancient ball game that dates back to 2000 BC. The Romans called Harpastum 'the small ball game' because the ball used was a lot smaller than any used for other games of that era. It was around eight inches in diameter and made from stitched leather that was usually stuffed with animal skin or chopped up cloth. Inflated pig bladders were later used, which resulted in many balls coming in different sizes.

There is no clear account of what the rules were, but it was played on a rectangular field and the number of players varied from game to game. Certain records suggest there were most likely 8–12 players on each side. However, some ancient Greek and medieval records point to hundreds of players involved on a much larger playing surface that sometimes spread throughout parks and villages. The playing field was split by what we now commonly know as the halfway line, and the idea of the game was for a team to keep the ball on their own side for as long as possible, using both their hands and feet. Some ancient Roman leaders even helped dignify the game. Emperor Julius Caesar and his generals were apparently so convinced of its combative conditioning benefit they made it part of military training for the Roman Army.

When the Roman conquerors first came to the British Isles, they brought with them Harpastum and it was very popular among the local inhabitants. Legend has it the Romans even played and defeated a British Isles team. There were ball games already present in the region, but Harpastum continued to be played, and rule variations from village to village were commonplace. Throughout the centuries, various ball games came and went. There is no clear evidence to suggest that Harpastum evolved into any form of modern football, but the ancient game in part certainly resembled the modern games of rugby and American football.

To suggest that rugby evolved from an ancient Greco-Roman ball game may knot the stomach of many purists, but it would be naive to think the renowned institutional story of William Webb Ellis is the sole event that contributed to the formation of the game.

On the now famous strip called The Close at Rugby College in England between 1749 and 1823, there was a style of football played that had limited rules. One distinctive feature was that a player could catch the ball and punt to another player, but they could not run with it. There was a student by the name of William Webb Ellis who defied this rule by catching the ball and running with it, instead of kicking it, during a game on The Close in the autumn of 1823. As a plaque at Rugby College now reads.

> This stone commemorates the exploit of William Webb Ellis who with a fine disregard for the rules of football, as played in his time, first took the ball in his arms and ran with it, thus originating the distinctive feature of the rugby game. AD 1823

The event involving Webb Ellis occurred on The Close under those circumstances, though some aspects have become blurred over time.

One romantic account to evolve in more recent years is that Webb Ellis picked up the ball and ran with it, suggesting that the game being played on The Close was something more similar to soccer, but that version of events more likely evolved over a few post-match pints coupled with some misinterpretation of the actual event.

Some sceptics even suggest that the story of Webb Ellis was not true at all and it was an official move by the first administrative body – the Rugby Football Union (RFU) in England – to give the game an international identity that originated in Britain. Like most historical accounts, there is one for the conspiracy theorists in rugby too, but so obvious are the early ties to Rugby College that there is little weight to the anti-RFU argument.

Rugby has preserved a distinct identity ever since that landmark occasion with William Webb Ellis on The Close. The game maintained a strictly amateur existence until 1995, and prior to that its survival as a sport relied heavily on an affiliation with the wealthier classes of society. That allegiance was also vital for the game's survival amid a century-old threat of extinction, largely posed by two rival professional codes – American football and rugby league. Quite ironically, rugby was the predecessor to both of those games, and now the forefather has emerged as a truly international sport with more potential to grow. Unlike its twentieth-century adversaries, rugby is not geographically confined to a presence in only a handful of countries and the onset of professionalism since 1995 has brought a renewed existence for the code.

As Australia's 1991 Rugby World Cup-winning coach Bob Dwyer explained: 'The game has achieved an amazing amount in a very short time. What it has taken other sports 100 years to achieve, rugby has achieved in a decade. It's freakish. We've had the example of soccer before us to see what worked for them and what didn't, but it has been amazing growth. The game's organisation and presentation is unrecognisable from when the first Rugby World Cup was played in 1987 to now.'

Rugby is now played in more than 100 countries and the flagship event at the forefront of the renaissance – the Rugby World Cup – is the third largest sporting event in the world behind the Olympic Games and the FIFA World Cup. Most encouraging of all for the game is the potential it has to develop while maturing as a professional sport. The dual impact of having the first Rugby World Cup in 1987 and the advent of professionalism in 1995 ensured the game's future as one of the world's biggest winter codes. But what also suggests that the game is perhaps destined for even greater success, is the resilience it has shown throughout history. This hardiness is best illustrated by the way rugby maintained a distinct identity, while effectively providing the foundation on which two professional rival codes were built on opposite sides of the Atlantic – American football in the United States and rugby league in the British Isles.

Rugby's relationship with American football is fascinating. During the middle part of the nineteenth century, not long after the event involving Webb Ellis at Rugby College in England, some students at Princeton University in New Jersey started playing a game called 'ballown'. The aim of the game was for a team to advance the ball past their opponents using their fists and feet. A similar form was later adopted at Harvard University, with the sophomore class and freshman class opposing in a game played on the first Monday of every school year. The event was aptly named 'Bloody Monday' because of how rough and violent it was.

The American version was a far different take to what had eventuated at Rugby College in England, and it was perhaps a sign of the times that such a violent offshoot evolved while the country was gripped by a bloody Civil War from 1861–1865. Popularity of the game spread rapidly following the Civil War, and most institutions adopted some form, but wide disparity of rules from college to college eventually stemmed the rapid growth.

Princeton was one of the first to establish a set of rules, which were almost identical to those of soccer – as established by the Football Association in Britain around the same time. Soon after that Yale, Columbia and Rutgers joined the fold to form the first Intercollegiate Football Association (IFA) in 1873. A notable absentee from this group was Harvard University, which became isolated because it did not play soccer and instead pursued the 'Boston Game', which had hybrid rules more closely aligned with rugby. In 1874, Harvard hosted McGill University of Montreal in two games – one for each set of different rules the two colleges played under. The rules that McGill played under were those of rugby, which they had learned from the British Army garrison in Montreal. Within a year, Harvard had adopted the same rules and in 1875 they played Yale in the very first edition of 'The Game' – now the oldest, and one of the most renowned, College Football rivalries in the United States.

On November 23, 1876 – one year after The Game first took place – representatives from Harvard, Princeton, Columbia and Yale held a convention in Springfield, Massachusetts to standardise the American rules. They adopted the rules of rugby in their entirety and in the immediate years that followed the newly reformed IFA ensured the rules remained the same for all games played within the Association. But it wasn't long before changes were introduced. Walter Camp, former medical undergraduate and later the head coach at Yale, was the main man who opposed many IFA rules and his desire to have only 11 players per team was the forerunner to a system of rule changes that slowly saw the game distance itself from rugby. Player numbers were reduced in 1880 and the system of downs was introduced in 1882. The game of American football was beginning to take shape, but not without widespread criticism for its violent nature.

During The Game between Harvard and Yale in 1892, Harvard introduced the 'flying wedge' – an offensive formation developed by a chess master that involved players interlocking their arms and charging at the opposition to make way for a score. It was virtually impossible for Yale to defend against and resulted in so many injuries that it was banned the following year. The banning only seemed to make the annual grudge match even more bitter and in 1894 newspapers reported that seven players were carried off 'in dying condition'. Following that, both Yale and Harvard broke off all sporting contact for two years.

Though the rules had been altered, the game still resembled rugby more than any other code of the time and it was not looked upon favourably by many influential people in American society. By the turn of the century, many colleges felt compelled to ban the game for its increasing brutality. Certain records suggest that in 1905 alone, 18 players died and another 159 suffered severe injuries. Something had to be done for the game to maintain existence and it came from the highest level, with the then President of the United States, Theodore Roosevelt, summoning a group of representatives from Princeton, Yale and Harvard to review the game entirely or see it banned by edict. Roosevelt had a soft spot for the sport and did not want to see it abolished completely, but the social responsibility of his position forced his hand to resolve widespread condemnation of its brutality. What resulted from the summit was the formation of a body that eventually became the National Collegiate Athletic Association (NCAA) – now the largest collegiate sports body in the world.

The NCAA introduced the forward pass in 1906, which finally saw the end of rugby's continued association with American football. The onset of rule changes that began in 1880 had slowly distanced the sport from its forefather, and the introduction of the forward pass ultimately ended rugby's place as a major winter sport in North America. For the early part of the twentieth century, rugby still maintained some presence in the region. The United States can even lay claim to being the current Olympic champions in rugby after winning the gold medal at Paris in 1924, when rugby last featured as an Olympic sport. But the days of rugby playing a major part in the American winter are all but a distant memory now, with American football the number one spectator sport in the United States.

Rugby may have lost the battle to become the main winter code in North America, but history shows it has left a legacy in the region as the forefather to American football and Canadian football. The main trophy played for in the Canadian Football League (CFL) – the Grey Cup – to this day has a reference to rugby inscribed on it. The game is still widely played throughout North America at club level – and the United States and Canada regularly field teams in the Rugby World Cup – but rugby's capacity to grow in the region is largely stemmed by the dominance of fully professional national football codes in both countries. For now, rugby remains the poor relation in the region, but some enthusiasts are optimistic it is more of a sleeping giant ready to rise when professionalism properly infiltrates the playing ranks.

Around the same time that American football established its own identity with the introduction of rule changes that culminated in the forward pass, rugby was fighting a separate battle in its British homeland. Unlike the divergence in North America, this conflict was bitter and evolved from a clash of working-class values in the north of England and the higher socio-economic classes aligned with the RFU in the south.

During most of the nineteenth century, rugby enjoyed a growth in popularity throughout the British Isles, but by the 1890s tensions were growing at the administrative level. Established in 1871, the RFU largely controlled the game in Britain through its many member clubs scattered across the country. Always closely aligned with the higher socio-economic classes in society, the RFU maintained a long-standing ban on professional players. This move frustrated the northern England working class, who could not afford time off work for travelling, training and playing on a regular basis. Tensions mounted and a split was inevitable. It came in 1895, when the Northern Rugby Football Union (NRFU) was formed in Huddersfield after a group of clubs agreed that broken time payments, which accounted for lost time at work, could be paid to their players. This effectively brought about the great rugby divide that saw the birth of rugby league and rugby union as separate entities. Within five years, the NRFU started altering their rules in an attempt to make their game more spectator-friendly. First the lineout was abolished, then the play-the-ball ruck was introduced – ending the ruck and maul contest – and eventually the number of players on a team was reduced from 15 to 13.

Rugby league formally established its own identity in 1901, when the separate Yorkshire and Lancashire NRFU competitions merged to form the Northern Rugby League. While the RFU did not approve of how the original rugby game was bastardised into a different form, the great divide from the northern working class ensured the traditional game remained one for the higher social classes. Less than two decades earlier in the 1880s, soccer had faced a similar transformation in Britain and the game was eventually dominated by the working classes. The RFU administration was determined to ensure rugby would not follow a similar path and they were successful in alienating the working-class north.

Rugby's relationship with rugby league was born to a bitter beginning and has never really been amicable. It was particularly tense for the best part of a century following the great rugby divide in 1895, and the hostility has only been partially relieved since rugby turned professional in 1995. Now it is very common for players to change between the two codes, particularly in Australia, and in more recent times England, where both sports enjoy a large professional presence. Right up until the early 1980s though, it was common for rugby players who made the switch to rugby league not to be invited to team reunions and to be ostracised by the rugby community. Thankfully for both codes this behaviour has subsided, but many older heads in rugby circles are not so forgiving of league for how it pillaged some of the finest rugby talent for 100 years.

'For love, not money' was a common catch-cry used among the largely white-collar rugby union population. The players involved did not consciously adopt that line; it was a subconscious path forged by how the administrative ranks wished to define the sport. The RFU and the later International Rugby Football Board (now simply known as the IRB), founded in 1896, wanted rugby to be known as 'the gentlemen's game', where solicitors, accountants and the like could vent controlled aggression at the weekend, then don their suits and ties for the courtroom or boardroom on Monday. The game's alliance with the higher social classes also ensured this prophecy. It was a vision that did not sit well with the largely blue-collar rugby league population, who wore the criticism of being uncivilised working-class thugs, frowned upon for profiting from a game of sport.

Even more unacceptable to the rugby fold was that rugby league was derived from rugby itself. The working-class population was seen to have bastardised a primarily higher-class sport and they were profiting from it, but now it is a far more level playing field. The tide has changed to such an extent that rugby has become even more lucrative to players at the highest level, with corporate dollars boosting playing contracts beyond what most rugby league franchises can offer.

In the 40 years that followed the end of the American Civil War in 1865, rugby provided the foundation for what is now the number one spectator sport in the United States. Around the same time, on the opposite side of the Atlantic, in Britain and throughout her colonies, the game also braved a bitter century-long struggle with rugby league amid a strictly amateur existence until 1995. Rugby truly has endured its fair share of ups and downs since William Webb Ellis performed *that* deed on The Close in 1828, yet its distinctive style remains and the game's future is now assured. The two descendants that once threatened rugby's survival for more than a century will always uphold a solid existence in their own popular territories, but the forefather has one key quality that will always set him apart – a rapidly growing international presence.

During the same period that rugby had a marked influence on American society in the post-Civil War years, the game made its way to the British colonies in Australia, New Zealand and South Africa. These three southern hemisphere countries are now major power-houses within the world fold. Along with England and France in the northern hemisphere, they form the Big Five challengers for Rugby World Cup superiority.

Ireland, Wales, Scotland and Argentina are also strong contenders for the most sought-after prize in world rugby – The Webb Ellis Cup. More affectionately referred to as 'Bill' by the victorious Australia team from Rugby World Cup 1999, this coveted trophy has become the target of every nation seeking rugby supremacy and the showpiece surrounding it brings an atmosphere of Olympic proportions for every host nation. The passionate Pacific Island nations bring their deft skills and running flair to threaten a major upset, and like an athlete from Uganda lining up in an Olympic 100m freestyle heat, the lower-ranked countries simply savour the experience. For the Big Five and their closest rivals though, it is all or nothing. Their goal is plain and simple. They have come to reach the pinnacle of a four-year quest. They have come to lay their claim for the ultimate prize in world rugby. They have come *In Pursuit Of Bill*.

2

Birth of a sporting powerhouse

RUGBY WORLD CUP is a modern-day sport phenomenon. From humble amateur beginnings, it is now the third biggest sporting event in the world behind the Olympic Games and Football World Cup. Even more promising for this now-powerful institution is the major potential for future development. Rugby World Cup is a mere greenhorn in comparison to the Olympic movement and FIFA, but unprecedented growth since the first tournament in 1987 suggests the event has a very prosperous future – a future that may only be limited by a reluctance to discard traditional amateur roots and take the game beyond its comfort zone, beyond the confines of major rugby-playing nations.

Tracing the roots of how this sporting powerhouse emerged is a short journey back to the late 1970s and early 1980s, when the strictly amateur code was a sitting duck just waiting for an entrepreneur to pick up and cash in for a healthy pay day. The sports world had just witnessed the transformation of cricket when Australian media mogul, the late Kerry Packer, transformed the game and left purists of the sport in his wake with the introduction of One-Day International cricket. Rugby presented a similar opportunity, but thankfully two passionate men from the southern hemisphere did everything they could to thwart the threat and ensure the game would stay under the jurisdiction of genuine rugby people who governed it from the very beginning.

Sir Nicholas Shehadie – a highly regarded lock, prop forward and captain of Australia in the post-war years from 1947–1956 – as President of the Australian Rugby Union (ARU) during the early 1980s, teamed up with former New Zealand All Blacks manager Dick Littlejohn to become the driving force behind the formation of the inaugural Rugby World Cup in 1987. The pair formed a durable partnership that battled against the wishes of the traditional Home Unions – England, Ireland, Scotland and Wales – to effectively save rugby from the threat of money-hungry entrepreneurs.

'The home unions always thought it was their game and ridiculed us badly. They really didn't care too much at all about the colonies,' Shehadie explains. 'But what they didn't seem to realise was people in the colonies could easily pick up a sport and run with it, like Kerry Packer did with cricket. It was a great opportunity that we [the rugby community] could take the game a step further and keep it under the control of rugby people.'

The concept of having a Rugby World Cup was first introduced to the ARU in the late 1950s, when Jock Kelleher and Harold Tolhurst from the Manly club in Sydney proposed the idea. They were quickly dismissed by the administration. The idea was said to have been floated again by some Sydney businessmen forming a syndicate in the late 1970s to provide financial support if the board liked it, but Shehadie's predecessor as President at the ARU, Bill McLaughlin, didn't receive backing from his board and the idea was quashed again.

Momentum for the campaign increased in the background though, and in 1982 a promoter from London representing International Sports Marketing (ISM) – Neil Durden-Smith – came to meet Shehadie, John Dedrick (ARU secretary) and John Howard (treasurer) in Sydney. Durden-Smith needed someone to raise it to the IRB and the ARU supported the idea. It was the first time Shehadie had been introduced to the concept of a Rugby World Cup. He originally began pushing for 1988 – the bicentenary of the first settlement in Australia – as a year to celebrate by having England come out and play. That vision soon grew into hosting the very first Rugby World Cup.

Meanwhile, there were other movements around that were pointing towards developing an international showpiece for the game. A Sydney-based sports writer at the time, David Lord, was proposing the idea of a World Rugby circus that would travel the globe with some of the world's top players. His idea never actually launched, but Lord had secured a commitment from 208 of the best players from the world's top rugby nations to take part in a world professional rugby circuit.

There was lots of talk of rebel tours to South Africa, and entrepreneurs were putting the idea out that players could actually make money from the game. During Alan Jones' period as Australia coach – around 1984–85 – there was certainly a 'rebel tour' being promoted by David Lord and there was a fair amount of acceptance from the team to the concept. It was enough to kick Shehadie into overdrive on the organising front.

'I called an unofficial meeting of my executive – John Howard, Norbert Byrne, Ross Turnbull and John Dedrick,' Shehadie, also a former Lord Mayor of Sydney (1973–75), explains in his autobiography – *A Life Worth Living* (2002). 'I stressed to them that if we were to save our game and not lose it to some entrepreneur, we would have to act promptly and organise a World Cup.'

Shehadie stressed that rugby people had to be involved in the formation and ongoing management of the event and his executive agreed. Across the Tasman, New Zealand was also facing a similar dilemma with talk of a rebel tour to South Africa for which the players would be paid. The New Zealand Rugby Union (NZRU) was also talking Rugby World Cup and they were thinking 1987.

Shehadie flew to New Zealand for a meeting with his New Zealand counterpart Cec Blazey – a highly respected man who was also on the International Rugby Board (IRB). From that meeting, four representatives from each union were elected to a special committee to prepare a submission for the IRB's consideration. Shehadie and Littlejohn were elected joint committee chairmen, although it was not exactly smooth sailing at the start.

'He and I didn't get on very well,' Shehadie reflects. 'Prior to us being made co-chairmen, he was manager of the All Blacks and he thought I was a bit of a stand-over man, trying to take control of everything. It didn't take long though for us to become the best of friends and there really couldn't be a better guy to work with.'

The committee worked out that 1987 would be the best year because it didn't have any other major world sporting event like the

Olympic or Commonwealth Games, or FIFA World Cup, to compete with. Shehadie and Littlejohn formed what soon became known as 'The Nick and Dick Show' and what followed was a barnstorming tour of the Home Unions throughout the UK to promote the idea of a Rugby World Cup.

The Home Unions comprised half of the IRB delegates who would eventually decide the fate of the Rugby World Cup idea. England, Ireland, Scotland and Wales all had two representatives (two votes) each on the international board. Australia, New Zealand, France and South Africa also had two representatives each. South Africa's situation proved a tricky one though because their apartheid policy would prevent them taking part in the proposed 1987 tournament. Australia and New Zealand would not allow South African players into their countries due to political sanctions.

The South Africa Rugby Union (SARU) President at the time, Danie Craven, had been misled by some opponents of the idea and blamed Shehadie and Littlejohn for Australia and New Zealand's stance until he became aware of the real reason. Losing South Africa's vote would have made it hard for the idea to be approved by the IRB, but a saving grace for The Nick and Dick Show came by the way of Dr Roger Vanderfield, who made a private visit at his own expense to South Africa, where he was highly regarded by many South African officials, particularly Danie Craven. Vanderfield visited several unions across South Africa and he finally spoke at the SARU board meeting in Cape Town, where he was given a very warm reception after making an address that would later play a crucial part in the final vote. It planted the seed that eventually made South Africa decide not to vote at all.

South Africa's stance favoured no side and it was the most politically correct decision for a country that was isolated from the world fold and in no need of any more political barriers on the international scene. The decision ultimately left the Home Unions with a majority of the vote that would eventually decide the fate of the proposal.

In the UK, meanwhile, The Nick and Dick Show received a cold reception from a lot of the media. Traditionalists from the top down ridiculed the idea. As Shehadie recalls, 'We even offered [the television and marketing rights] to the BBC for US$6 million. They laughed at us and said it would never work and that we would never get it through the international board. We received a lot of criticism, but the English press really underestimated how determined we were to see this work.

'We carried out meetings with the various councils and we were hoping that the different unions would then instruct their [IRB] delegates to vote in favour of it. The first committee we met was the Welsh and the meeting wasn't going particularly well. It was over dinner and they'd had a bit to drink. I was copping a lot of flack.'

One hour into the meal, Shehadie became restless and set the conversation straight.

'I'd had enough and I eventually said, "Are you in, or are you not? Let us know now." There was a complete hush around the room and Ken Harris, who was the esteemed President of the Welsh Rugby Union stood up and said, "I am behind it 100 per cent", and the rest of the table echoed his stance.'

It was a positive start for The Nick and Dick Show, but the road ahead was a much tougher one. After meeting the Welsh, a meeting was scheduled in Dublin with the Irish board. Word from the Emerald Isle was that they would be opposed to any World Cup movement. Shehadie and Littlejohn arrived at Dublin airport at 2am amidst one of heaviest snowstorms the region has ever experienced. The meeting was planned for the next day prior to the Ireland v England Test match, but the snow was so heavy the match was cancelled and so too the meeting because many of the Irish board could not make it to the city. It was rescheduled for the following week in Edinburgh ahead of the Scotland game, and the reception The Nick and Dick Show received there was equally as cold as the snowstorm they had endured a week earlier.

'We had dinner with some of the Scottish executives and their wives on the evening prior to our meeting with their full board. We were given a really hard time by their treasurer, Gordon Masson, who went about telling us we were not needed and rugby was *their* game ... that a World Cup would be staged over his dead body.'

Shehadie did not stand down and told Masson not to come when the World Cup was held. A satisfying irony for Shehadie came some seven years later in the Rugby World Cup tournament of 1991 to see Masson as president of the Scotland Rugby Union escorting Princess Anne on to the field at several games. 'When he saw me, I confronted him and pinched him to see if he was still alive!' Shehadie later wrote in his autobiography.

After meeting with the Scottish board the morning of the match day, The Nick and Dick Show endured another battering from the Irish board. The solid start with the Welsh was a distant memory after Scotland and Ireland gave the new movement nothing to cheer about. It was then on to England, where Shehadie and Littlejohn addressed some 30+ delegates from the Rugby Football Union (RFU). Both men walked away from that address unsure of which way the English delegates would vote.

The tour had been successful insofar as briefing the relevant unions, but it left a relatively unclear account of where the vote would go. The biggest confrontation of all came for the duo when they were to meet with the game's governing body – the IRB. Before the meeting, Shehadie and Littlejohn reaffirmed their commitment to the cause with each other and pledged not to take a backward step after coming so far with the concept.

Then it was to the East India Club in St James Square in London, where the pair would face their sternest opposition so far. Shehadie came under massive fire in the meeting from Hermes Evans, the Welsh delegate, who accused Australia of turning the game professional by paying players' expenses up front. This was a reference to an Australia team that had done this at the Hong Kong Sevens the year before. Shehadie was caught in an unfortunate situation, but yet another saving grace for the campaign came from the then secretary of the IRB, Bob Weighill.

'They had me over a barrel but Bob Weighill nudged me under the table and gave me a note saying that England had done the same thing two years previously, when they went to America. Hermes Evans finished the blast and I stood up and said, "You're quite correct sir, but my people are doing the right thing. We simply followed England on everything they did."'

Shehadie thanked God for old friends after it put a sudden halt to the conversation. The next thing asked was whether, if the IRB decision went against having the tournament, Australia and New Zealand would go it alone.

'I said we would answer that question after they made their decision, and I said it with a look in my eyes as to say "just try us", knowing full well we could go it alone if we had to. But that would have brought too much damage to the game and we really didn't want to do that.'

The meeting was a sour note to end on for The Nick and Dick Show, but a back-up plan was on standby for Australia and New Zealand to go it alone if the proposal was rejected – a move that would have no doubt put the international game in turmoil and potentially split the two hemispheres.

The final vote was taken in Paris on March 20, 1985. The pair had done all they could and now it was up to the 14 delegates left to vote. The Rugby World Cup needed eight of those 14 votes to go ahead and the movement was only guaranteed six votes through Australia, New Zealand and France. France were a great ally for the movement through the strong hand of Albert Ferrasse, then president of the French Rugby Union, who was described by many as a real dictator and a good person to have on side.

The four Home Unions still held the power though, with eight remaining votes after South Africa decided not to take part in the ballot at all. It was still up in the air as to which way it would go.

'You couldn't really tell which way it was going to go with [England], but one of their delegates – John Kendall-Carpenter – was a very close friend,' Shehadie explains. 'We first met in 1947 when I toured over there. He was a boy from Penzance and we were training there for three weeks during that tour. I trusted Kendall-Carpenter, but we still couldn't work out which way England was going to go.'

Shehadie and Littlejohn were sitting in a Paris bar enjoying a Guinness when the final ballot took place. A journey that would have taken most 5 10 years had taken them a little more than two. It was all about to come to a head, and the duo had done all they could. The voting results finally came through and it was 8–6 in favour of having a Rugby World Cup in New Zealand and Australia during May and June of 1987. The two deciding votes had come from England and Wales: Kendall-Carpenter from England and Keith Rowlands from Wales broke rank with the other six delegates from the Home Unions to vote in favour of the concept. The final tally in favour was two votes from New Zealand, two votes from France, two votes from Australia, one vote from Wales and one vote from England. Ireland and Scotland remained steadfast against the concept, and the other English and Welsh delegates went against the idea too.

It was a huge triumph for The Nick and Dick Show, and an important decision for world rugby, but the hard work had only just begun.

The IRB established a Rugby World Cup committee, with Shehadie, Kendall-Carpenter and Littlejohn made joint chairmen, but a power struggle soon emerged between the establishment and the maverick duo from Australasia. The IRB rejected the World Cup name and tried to call the event the William Webb Ellis Tournament, but first points went to The Nick and Dick Show. World Cup Pty Ltd became the main vehicle by which the committee would pursue all marketing and commercial negotiations, and that company name laid the foundation for what has become Rugby World Cup as we know it today.

The marketing and commercial value for the Rugby World Cup was always going to be a hard sell for the inaugural tournament. Commercial professionals had to be engaged, but there was simply no budget to cater for a top-line marketing agency. It was back to the old boys' club, and the reliable network of contacts within the rugby community came through for the movement once again. Shehadie convinced a highly respected entrepreneur in sports marketing – Wilf Barker – to take on the role of representing World Cup Pty Ltd, and selling the marketing rights. They negotiated a relatively small fee of US$50,000 and Barker committed to seeing it through for the love of the game – the same commitment much of the movement had been built on.

'We weren't getting paid. None of us were getting any money for this. We had up to nearly 1,000 volunteers across Queensland, New South Wales and New Zealand,' Shehadie explains. 'Securing a good sponsor and selling the marketing rights was vital to the success of it all and we found it tough trying to find a sponsor because of the state South Africa was in [with apartheid] and knowing they wouldn't be able to take part.

'The late Mark McCormack [IMG founder and Chairman], regarded as the godfather of sports marketing, rang me personally and they wanted to get involved. They had to put in a proposal like everyone else, but we finally gave [the marketing rights] to Westnally – an organisation from England who set up a branch in New Zealand. They won it for around US$5million. They had to pay US$1million straight up. We sat up until 6am in the morning with the solicitors at the Travelodge in Sydney to sign the final agreement. It had to be paid in instalments and by the time the first game started it was completely paid off. In those days we were getting something like 21 per cent interest, which covered a lot of the travel expenses. After paying everyone back, we made about US$2.5million profit.'

The marketing deal with Westnally was the first of some key signings that ensured World Cup Pty Ltd would bring the tournament to fruition. A logo was registered in New Zealand and it is the same Rugby World Cup logo that stands today, with the shape of a rugby ball distinguished by 16 bars representing the number of teams to compete in the inaugural tournament. The next piece of the commercial puzzle was to secure a major sponsor and it finally came when Japanese communications company K.D.D. committed to the tune of US$3.25million.

But as the commercial side gathered momentum, The Nick and Dick Show continued to endure pressure from the IRB and Home Unions. The final attempt to overthrow Shehadie and Littlejohn came in Los Angeles at the Beverley Wiltshire Hotel. John Kendall-Carpenter remained loyal to his co-chairmen and informed Shehadie of what was awaiting the pair in Los Angeles. The IRB had formed a sub-committee of five people, headed by Kendall-Carpenter, who were observing the organisation of the tournament. There was a motion to have those five people put on the board of World Cup Pty Ltd, effectively taking control of the board away from Australia and New Zealand. Shehadie and Littlejohn were having none of it.

'Dick and I were asked to remain outside while they discussed certain matters. It was schoolboy stuff,' Shehadie reflects in his autobiography. 'They had no idea we knew what they were debating. When we were allowed into the room, some people had their heads lowered. I emphatically rejected the proposal, stating that they needed a two-thirds majority by the existing board. Dick's union also gave him the authority to stand fast, so he didn't mince his words either. They were flabbergasted. We then walked out. The matter was never raised again.'

Thankfully that was the end to what was an unwelcome power struggle that threatened to derail the tournament, but one final political hurdle came unexpectedly with a military coup in Fiji on May 14, 1987. It was one week before the start of the tournament, and there were concerns as to whether Fiji would be able to take part. Western Samoa were on standby if required, but Fiji made it to their first pool match 10 days later and unexpectedly cruised to a 28–9 victory over a quality Argentina side that included Hugo Porta at fly-half. It was quite a remarkable maiden Rugby World Cup victory.

The Nick and Dick Show had endured just about everything en route to organising the inaugural tournament, but the final piece of the puzzle was something that had escaped the attention of all amidst the turmoil of bringing this massive event together.

'John Kendall-Carpenter rang me just prior to the World Cup starting and he said, "Son, we have a problem ... we haven't got a trophy." I never thought about it too much and it seems nobody else did either,' Shehadie recalls. 'John then went down to Garrards [the Crown jewellers] in London and found this cup. He rang me and he said he could buy it for £6,000. I had no hesitation in telling him to buy it.'

The trophy was made of silver gilt and it was a copy of an original piece by Carrington & Co. of London, made in 1906 and designed by England's famous Huguenot silversmith Paul de Lamerie (1688–1751). That trophy is now the ultimate prize in world rugby – The Webb Ellis Cup.

3

Rugby World Cup 1987: the tournament

WHAT SEEMED LIKE a long and winding road to Rugby World Cup 1987 was a rapid journey with a series of turns that threatened to prevent the event from coming to fruition. The organising committee had a little more than two years to set everything in place from when the IRB first decided to stage the event, and boardroom politics between the international governing body and the host unions might well have derailed everything had it not been for the steadfast approach of The Nick and Dick Show. Shehadie and Littlejohn were just two passionate rugby men, who wanted to ensure the flagship event for rugby was not exploited by entrepreneurial greed and remained in the control of the people who treasured it most – rugby people. Their noble and selfless journey for the code was complete when the opening game between New Zealand and Italy kicked off in Auckland on May 22, 1987.

'Dick looked across at me straight after that first ball was kicked off and we both smiled. We had made it against the odds,' Shehadie reflects. 'I retired [as President of the ARU] straight after that tournament, and remain thankful for everything rugby has done for me. I'm just glad we could give something back to the game.'

More than just giving something back to the game, The Nick and Dick Show effectively saved it from the looming clutches of money-hungry entrepreneurs and ensured control of the Rugby World Cup would remain firmly with the IRB after the 1987 event. In an ironic twist, the same administrative body that had been so strongly opposed to the Rugby World Cup concept is now the ultimate bene-ficiary thanks to the determination of Shehadie and Littlejohn. The legacy of The Nick and Dick Show will remain the cornerstone of Rugby World Cup history, but the groundswell of support since the first event and the move to professionalism have transformed the game in an unprecedented manner.

The first tournament was played in 1987 amid a strictly amateur existence. While a select few European clubs were giving leading players under-the-table payments much earlier, it was certainly not a major earner for any player involved. The 16 competing unions were to receive a small allocation of money after the tournament, but it would do little more than cover some travel costs and team clothing.

There was not enough time to hold any qualifying matches, and with all else that needed to fall in place it was agreed that the 16 teams participating in the inaugural tournament would be by invita-tion only. One of the biggest issues to arise from this was whether to include South Africa. Some time had passed since South Africa decided not to vote on the Rugby World Cup, but unfortunately the apartheid political landscape in the country remained unchanged. Host nations New Zealand and Australia would still not allow South Africa players into their countries, and their opposition was echoed by other unions who threatened to boycott the event if the Springboks were allowed to compete.

Worldwide political opposition to South Africa had denied the 1987 tournament one of its main contenders, and one week out from the event a military coup in Fiji also threatened to destabilise the competition. Thankfully the latter did not prevent Fiji from taking part, but co-host New Zealand were still healing wounds from the great rugby divide across the country caused by the 1986 Cavaliers rebel tour to South Africa. The Cavaliers were effectively an All Blacks team forced to establish a separate identity after the New Zealand Rugby Union (NZRU) would not sanction the 1985 tour to South Africa. Two Auckland lawyers, who were members of rugby clubs and well supported by the anti-apartheid Labour government of the time, forced an interim injunction in the High Court to stop the tour five days before it was scheduled to depart. There was no time for the ruling to be challenged in 1985, meaning that tour was cancelled, but the drive among a select group of New Zealand players and officials ensured the Cavaliers tour went ahead the following year.

The Cavaliers were not aligned to any organisation, despite the complete makeup of the team being active or fringe All Blacks at the time, and they played in black and gold colours. Reaction from a majority of the public was very hostile towards the rebel tourists, partly driven by a negative media campaign that never viewed the concept as beneficial to the greater cause of the game in New Zealand. The Cavaliers were also paid for the tour, which defied the amateur rules at the time and portrayed the players as selfish. Lack of match coverage contributed to a blurred public perspective and players who had been idolised by many New Zealand fans were suddenly frowned upon for being disloyal to their country. A young Auckland reserve at the time by the name of Sean Fitzpatrick recounts one of the darkest periods in New Zealand rugby history:

'It definitely split the country. Some players on the Auckland team were coming and going a bit to what we suspect was Cavaliers training or meetings,' Fitzpatrick recalls. 'I was in the Auckland reserves and I remember us going to play at Canterbury. We played the game and then came back into the change room. All of a sudden the older guys were showered and dressed, and before we knew it they had gone. They went to Christchurch, and from there on to the UK and down to South Africa.

'I can remember coming back that night from Canterbury to Auckland and people at the airport spitting on us as we were waiting to get our bags off the carousel. All of these protestors were shouting "How dare you associate with those bastards!" It was terrible.'

So disenchanted was the New Zealand rugby public that players who were in no way associated with the Cavaliers tour still bore the brunt of widespread criticism. Two respected frontline players at the time – John Kirwan and David Kirk – were notable absentees from the Cavaliers squad. Kirwan was playing in Italy and declined to tour because his father was ill, but Kirk withdrew on moral grounds. His decision commanded respect from many fans and administrators of the establishment, and later played a part in his being handed the All Blacks captaincy when regular skipper Andy Dalton was forced to withdraw from the 1987 tournament after a training injury.

When the Cavaliers returned from what was largely an unsuccessful tour in terms of results – having lost three of four matches against the Springboks – they received a hostile homecoming. Players who were in contention for the All Blacks were suspended for two Test matches and an unlucky few who worked in government jobs suddenly found themselves unemployed. The New Zealand rugby fold was divided like never before and some serious reparations were required with the inaugural Rugby World Cup scheduled to kick off in Auckland a little more than one year later.

New Zealand faced a touring French side in June of 1986, and with the suspended Cavaliers not available the selectors were forced to pick a young and inexperienced team later dubbed the 'Baby Blacks'. Against the odds, the young side scored a famous 18–9 victory over a star-studded France team in Christchurch. Unbeknown to all involved, that victory began a much-needed period of restoration for New Zealand rugby prior to Rugby World Cup 1987. The rebel players returned to the selection fold after the Baby Blacks suffered a narrow defeat to Australia following the unexpected victory over France, and divisions within the team were rife. David Kirk, who had withdrawn from the Cavaliers on moral grounds, was the newly appointed captain of the Baby Blacks and he and John Kirwan endured a lot of criticism from the Cavaliers contingent.

'It was fairly hostile among some players when the Cavaliers rejoined the team and David Kirk was still captain,' recalls Sean Fitzpatrick. 'You could sense there was a real rift within the team. The old guys came back and were hell bent on controlling the team again. They tried to make out that Kirk and Kirwan had made the wrong decision [in not touring with the Cavaliers] and the selectors should get rid of them.

'The New Zealand public were not very forgiving of the Cavaliers either. I can remember on the Friday night before we played the third [1986] Test against Australia in Auckland, all of us players were sitting on the roof of our hotel at 11 o'clock at night watching a heap of protesters outside throwing things at the hotel.'

The division within the New Zealand playing ranks looked unlikely to heal in time for the Rugby World Cup less than 12 months later. It was also reported that the All Blacks were split across two separate after-match functions at Eden Park the following day – one in the car park for the Cavaliers and one in the stadium for those players aligned with the establishment. Not only had New Zealand suffered a series loss to their trans-Tasman rivals Australia and surrendered the Bledisloe Cup, but a seemingly immovable wedge remained between the two sets of players and a period of uncertainty followed.

Thankfully for New Zealand rugby and Rugby World Cup 1987, this unwelcome issue did not spiral any further downwards during the off-season and a tour of France at the end of 1986 went a long way to restoring some of the damage. Ironically though, what was perceived as an event that would cause irreparable damage to New Zealand rugby at the time was in fact a blessing in disguise. The All Blacks were able to blood a significant portion of their younger players following the fallout from the Cavaliers tour, which effectively provided the perfect foundation for ultimate success at the inaugural Rugby World Cup.

Australia went into the tournament as equal favourites with New Zealand on the back of an outstanding 1986 season. France were the early pick of the northern hemisphere nations after finishing on top of the Five Nations Championship in 1986 and 1987. Scotland were also travelling well after a strong year in 1986 that saw them finish on equal points with France, but their team was thought to be partially on the wane. In contrast, Wales were on the rise with a group of young players starting to gel nicely. Their commendable performance in the inaugural tournament was indicative of a team almost fulfilling their potential, but not quite there – befitting of their Triple Crown success in the Five Nations a year later.

The pool stage

There were 16 teams from six continents contesting the 1987 tournament. Zimbabwe was the only representative from Africa, Japan the sole country from Asia, and Argentina the only country from South America. Europe had the most countries involved – England, Ireland, Scotland, Wales, France, Italy and Romania – while North America was represented by the United States and Canada. Oceania had the smallest population of any continent to pull from, but it was well represented by joint tournament favourites New Zealand and Australia, as well as the traditionally entertaining Pacific Island nations of Fiji and Tonga. All participating countries were invited by the IRB, and Western Samoa was on standby if any nation pulled out at the last minute. There was continued disappointment that South Africa was not competing, and dispute over whether the eventual winner could genuinely claim world champion status without the Springboks present, but the show had to go on and Argentina were invited to take their place.

The 16 teams were split across four pools. Pool 1 contested all of their pool matches in Australia between the Concord Oval in Sydney and Ballymore in Brisbane, while the 12 other countries played all their pool matches throughout New Zealand. For the knockout stage of the tournament, it was agreed between the host nations to split the quarter-finals, before both semi-finals were played in Australia, and then New Zealand would host the third place play-off and the final.

Rugby World Cup 1987: the pools and order they finished

Pool 1	Pool 2	Pool 3	Pool 4
Australia	Wales	New Zealand	France
England	Ireland	Fiji	Scotland
United States	Canada	Italy	Romania
Japan	Tonga	Argentina	Zimbabwe

The spread of countries from across the world ensured the 1987 tournament was a genuine global event, but many people were still unsure of what to expect. The Home Unions had been steadfast against the Rugby World Cup concept for the most part, and they were still treading cautiously. It is widely rumoured that those same administrations who so strongly opposed the event early on were pleased it was being staged far away from the United Kingdom, so that if it happened to fail they could easily distance themselves.

Australia struggled to capture as much attention for the event as it would have liked, competing for ticket sales against the professional mainstream winter codes – rugby league and Australian Rules football. In New Zealand there was more of a sense of excitement as the rugby world gathered as one for the very first time, but the stadiums were far from overflowing in the early part of the tournament. There had been very little budget to market the event, and ticket sales were largely reliant on a passionate rugby population simply turning out for the love of their national game.

When it finally came to game day for the opening match on May 22, 1987, host nation New Zealand came up against Italy at Eden Park in Auckland in what was eventually a lopsided affair. Had it not been for an outstanding second half from the All Blacks, where they scored 53 unanswered points before handing Italy a record 70–6 defeat, the match might well have brought dire consequences for the tournament. The New Zealand rugby public was still deeply scarred from the fallout of the Cavaliers tour and a loss to a minnow would have been unbearable for the host nation's fans, with ticket sales across the board plummeting. As it turned out, crowd figures improved as the event progressed and by the time New Zealand played their final pool game at Athletic Park in Wellington, a sell-out crowd of 35,000+ watched as the host nation handed out another heavy defeat (46–15) of Argentina before finishing top of Pool 3.

New Zealand's other pool match, between the victories over Italy and Argentina, was against their Pacific Island neighbours Fiji. It was another record defeat (74–13), but Fiji was hard done by with the schedule, having to face the might of the All Blacks only three days after their memorable victory over Argentina. All of Fiji's three pool games were played across seven days – hardly accommodating for a team that had endured the most difficult preparation of any ahead of the tournament – yet they still managed to finish second in Pool 3 and advance to the quarter-finals – an outstanding feat given the circumstances.

Pool 1 had taken a predictable shape with Australia finishing on top and England second. The opening pool match between those two nations turned out to be much closer than many expected. The Wallabies were tipped to beat England comfortably on the back of what was considered the biggest forward pack Australia had ever fielded, but the less-fancied England rose to the challenge. Had it not been for New Zealand referee Keith Lawrence controversially penalising England 18 times compared to Australia's six, and awarding David Campese a try after he appeared to have knocked on, the score might have been very different. Nonetheless it was a commendable opening performance from England, and it did enough to make the tournament co-favourites realise that the northern hemisphere nations were not going to lie down and let it be the predictable Australia v New Zealand final everyone was expecting.

Australia had an unconvincing performance against the United States one week after the England match before eventually emerging comfortable winners, but they were given a major wake-up call in the first half against Japan four days later. On the back of outstanding performances from their captain and lock Toshiyuki Hayashi and fly-half Seiji Hirao, Japan sent shockwaves through the Brisbane crowd when they trailed the Wallabies by just three points (13–16) at half time. Australia eventually found their way in the second half before going on to win 42–23, but their performances in the pool matches were hardly befitting of a team considered equal favourites to claim the tournament crown. Australia fly-half Michael Lynagh remembers all too well Australia's relatively average form during the 1987 pool stages.

'We had a great year in 1986 after beating New Zealand on their home soil to win the Bledisloe Cup series. A lot of media thought we were a good chance to go on and do it again, but the team just didn't feel the same,' Lynagh recalls. 'The writing was probably on the wall after unconvincing performances in all of our pool games. Japan turned out to be a particularly tough match. They played really well and we played very poorly, particularly in the first half.'

The match to command most attention in Pool 2 was between Wales and Ireland at Athletic Park in Wellington on the Monday after the first weekend of fixtures. The picturesque New Zealand capital is surrounded by rolling hills and sits on a natural harbour, which creates a seemingly permanent blustery effect that sees it more commonly referred to as 'windy Wellington'. Match day for Wales against Ireland was no exception, with a howling gale favouring one direction.

Ireland captain Donal Lenihan chose to run with the wind in the first half after winning the toss, but fly-half Paul Dean struggled to utilise the advantage for the men in green and a meagre six points from two Michael Kiernan penalty goals was all Ireland mustered from the first half. Wales fly-half Jonathan Davies used the wind more precisely in the second term, landing two decisive field goals to steer his team to a 13–6 victory that avenged the Five Nations loss to Ireland in Cardiff earlier that year. Wales played a better strategy in the windy conditions, but Ireland did miss some tactical influence after their coach Mick Doyle was rushed to Auckland hospital with a suspected heart attack. Doyle was eventually given the all-clear, but the game against Wales was gone with the wind and a quarter-final showdown with co-favourites Australia was the price Ireland eventually paid for coming second in Pool 2.

One of the more enthralling pool matches at the 1987 tournament was the Pool 4 clash between France and Scotland, which resulted in a draw, but a noticeable trend was starting to take shape across three of the four pools. Seven of the eight member nations that made up the IRB – England, Ireland, Scotland, Wales, France, New Zealand and Australia (South Africa was the eighth member) – were sitting well clear of the minnows in their respective pools. The only exception was Pool 3, where it was a three-way battle for second place between Fiji, Argentina and Italy. Each had won a game and were sitting equal on two points, and Argentina were left in the unfortunate position of needing to score three tries in their last pool match against New Zealand to advance. Unfortunately for the Pumas they could only manage one try, which meant Fiji defied the odds and went on to qualify for the quarter-finals after scoring more tries than Italy and Argentina.

The quarter-finals

After an intense schedule of 24 matches played over two weeks, the pool stage drew to a close. Rugby had never seen so many Test matches played in such a short period and interest in the tournament was gaining more momentum as it unfolded. Now it was time for the highly anticipated knockout phase to take centre stage.

Australia's charismatic coach at the time – Alan Jones – was always good for a colourful comment that defied the clichés so commonplace at post-match media conferences. Trying to deflect criticism directed at his team for their obvious lack of form coming into the quarter-finals, Jones fittingly called on a war metaphor to sum up the transition from the pool stage to the knockout stage of the tournament: 'So far it's been bows and arrows. This is hand grenades time.'

It was a concise and accurate assessment. Up to that point, teams had been able to slip up in the pool stage and still qualify – as did all the quarter-finalists except for Australia, New Zealand and Wales.

Now they simply had to win or pack their bags for home. New Zealand clearly had their artillery firing at the right time ahead of the quarter-finals, racking up 190 points in their pool matches (including 30 tries) while conceding only 34 points. In contrast, for all the words their coach could muster, co-favourites Australia were far from finding their target. France were also not as convincing as their Five Nations Grand Slam status from months before attested to.

The 1987 quarter-finals were played over three days across Australia and New Zealand. The All Blacks were the first team to advance after a clinical performance against Scotland at Lancaster Park in Christchurch. Unlike their pool matches though, where tries flowed freely, New Zealand employed a more traditional approach tailored for the finals phase. Their tactics were simple – sustained possession through brute force up front. The likes of the Whetton brothers and Buck Shelford, combined with the polish and panache of ball-playing forwards such as Michael Jones and Sean Fitzpatrick, were always going to be a tough ask for Scotland to defend against.

'We had fun in the pool games, but when it came to the finals it was a different story,' Fitzpatrick recalls. 'Our coach Brian Lochore called it the death or glory time, and from the top down there was a different attitude across the squad. We were clearly the best team to that point, but we had to make sure we followed it through in the finals.'

New Zealand went on to defeat Scotland comfortably (30–3), but a large portion of that tally came from the boot of reliable fly-half Grant Fox, who slotted six penalty goals and two conversions for a personal haul of 22 points. The All Blacks scored only two tries, which was a credit to the Scottish defence in the end.

The pick of the quarter-finals from a spectator perspective was the match between France and Fiji. The French are widely recognised as one of the more spontaneous and unpredictable of rugby nations, but on this occasion they defied that entirely with a very structured gameplan. It ultimately saw them triumph 31–16 to advance to the final four, and a few glimpses of backline magic were a welcomed variation. However, it was Fiji that won the hearts of the Auckland crowd with some of the most enterprising play of the tournament.

Despite unconvincing form through their pool matches, Australia produced a fine opening period against Ireland in their quarter-final at the Concord Oval in Sydney. By the 25th minute the home team had scored three tries, with fly-half Michael Lynagh converting them all and adding two penalty goals. As though a challenge had been thrown his way via Grant Fox playing such a significant role in New Zealand's advance to the semi-finals, so too Lynagh made the game his own and directed a superlative opening spell that never saw Ireland recover.

'We knew that our form had not been great, and we needed a good performance,' Lynagh recalls. 'You could tell from the tension in the dressing room before kick-off that we were ready for a better showing, and the first half really felt like the wheels were back in motion for our campaign.'

Despite the loss of scrum-half Nick Farr-Jones, who was flattened by Ireland flanker Phil Matthews in the third minute after launching a high ball from a lineout, Australia went on to win 33–15. The Farr-Jones incident only destabilised the team temporarily, and provided good impetus for the forward pack to lead the first-half onslaught.

Wales were statistically the best placed northern hemisphere team going into the knockout stage, but they had not really been tested by any opposition to that point. Victory over a disjointed Ireland team in windy Wellington was hardly a performance to hang their hat on, so it came as no surprise that England started favourites in the quarter-final match between the two old rivals. It was the last of the four quarter-finals, and it is rated by many as the worst game of the 1987 tournament.

For all the confidence England had gained from a commendable match against Australia, their run was quickly halted by a Welsh team determined to spoil any chance of fluid ball movement. Wales had a massive 25–9 penalty count against them from French referee René Hourquet, but their stalling was an effective tactic, strangling England into error-ridden play that allowed Wales to capitalise with three tries while conceding just one penalty goal for a 16–3 victory. Needless to say it was an anti-climax to an otherwise exciting quarter-final round, and the joy was short-lived for Wales with a semi-final against New Zealand awaiting them six days later.

The semi-finals

With the stage set for two semi-finals that each pitted a northern hemisphere team against a southern hemisphere team (France v

Australia and Wales v New Zealand), the 1987 tournament entered its final two weeks with high anticipation across Europe and Australasia. The Home Unions had one flag left flying with Wales still alive. France had quietly progressed well despite a draw with Scotland, but neither was expected to pose any major threat against their more fancied southern hemisphere opponents. Most of the rugby world was already talking up the New Zealand v Australia final that many had expected from the very start, but someone forgot to tell France to follow the script.

The semi-final between Australia and France at the Concord Oval in Sydney was easily the match of the tournament, and is still widely regarded as one of the best matches in the history of the game. The match seemed destined for extra time until Lynagh and Campese decided to run the ball from their own half. It was a bad option and France came up with the ball before putting it through many sets of hands for Serge Blanco to score the match-winning try in the corner. Against the odds, France sealed a remarkable victory and Australia were relegated to the third place play-off.

Australia were absolutely gutted by the loss to France in the semi-final. From the lofty heights of a series triumph over the All Blacks on New Zealand soil one year before, it was a harsh reality check. The players sat silent in the dressing room after the match and their coach Alan Jones is widely reported to have yelled, 'Would someone turn the god damn showers on to make some noise in here!' The whole squad was simply drained and lost for words – emotionally and physically.

For all the outstanding attributes the semi-final between France and Australia had, the other semi-final between Wales and New Zealand at Ballymore in Brisbane was a more lopsided result. If New Zealand were considered to be clinical in their pool matches, their form in the knockout stage could be described as surgical to say the least. The All Blacks had stepped up another gear for what their coach Brian Lochore had termed the 'death or glory' phase, and glory now seemed inevitable. They showed no remorse for a disjointed Wales team that had perhaps punched above its weight to reach the semi-finals. New Zealand scored eight tries to one before sealing a record 49-6 victory. Their triumph came off the back of a near flawless first-half performance that saw them take a 27–0 lead into the break.

Wales were first to score in the second half, but their resurgence was short-lived and the only record that would come their way was for lock Huw Richards becoming the first ever player to be dealt a red card and sent off in a Rugby World Cup. New Zealand enforcer Buck Shelford was lucky not to follow after miraculously escaping the same penalty for putting a clean punch on Richards. Some luck did obviously go the All Blacks' way, but for the most part they were deserving of the record score line that would see them enter the inaugural Rugby World Cup final as clear favourites.

Third place play-off

The penultimate match of the Rugby World Cup seems destined to remain criticised as a meaningless fixture, but the inaugural third place play-off was surprisingly entertaining and unpredictable. For all the bruised and battered bodies within the Wales team, they did exceptionally well to lift their injury-depleted squad up for the clash against Australia four days after absorbing a heavy defeat to the All Blacks. The Red Dragons were given no chance against a Wallabies team expected to win easily at Rotorua International Stadium, but it was another that would defy the script. Australia were reduced to 14 players just four minutes in when flanker David Codey was sent off by English referee Fred Howard. The remaining Australia forwards rose to the challenge of having one less player up front, and did exceptionally well to lead what looked a probable victory, but for the second time in less than a week the Wallabies would endure another loss in injury time. Wales wing Adrian Hadley crossed in the corner in the dying seconds before fullback Paul Thorburn converted from the sideline to give the Red Dragons a one-point victory and third place overall.

The course of results hit many on the Australia team very hard. Talented fullback Roger Gould walked away from a training session one day before the team was due to depart for the third place play-off in New Zealand and never again played for the Wallabies. In his 2003 pictorial publication *Story of the Rugby World Cup*, Nick Farr-Jones described Australia's 1987 Rugby World Cup experience as so bad he too almost contemplated early retirement.

'We really had gone from the heights of world rugby to its absolute

depths,' Farr-Jones lamented. 'At 25 I was contemplating early retirement and for the first time understood why the great Mark Ella had
given the game away at a similar age. Quite simply, it was no longer
pleasurable.'

Thankfully the rugby world did not see the last of Nick Farr-Jones.
The talented scrum-half bounced back from what was also a bad run
of form personally, and he later avenged the 1987 disappointment by
leading Australia to success at the second Rugby World Cup in the
United Kingdom and France during 1991.

The final

In striking contrast to Australia, New Zealand were in the highest
possible spirits ahead of a home final against France at Eden Park in
Auckland to decide the first ever Rugby World Cup champion. Aside
from a slow start in the first half of their first pool match against
Italy, the All Blacks had been ruthless in their march to the final.
Their opponents had endured a lot more to that point – a hard-fought
draw with Scotland in the pool rounds, an energy-sapping quarter-
final showdown with Fiji, and an exhausting victory over Australia in
the semi-finals – and player fatigue was surely a major factor in the
final result. Fullback Serge Blanco and lock Alain Lorieux, two
players who had been so crucial to France's semi-final success over
Australia, took their place in the starting side but neither was
anywhere near full fitness.

With the benefit of hindsight it is fair to say France had peaked and
used all their energy reserves in the semi-final against Australia. The
final against New Zealand was one challenge too many for the then
champions of Europe to capture another prized southern hemisphere
scalp. The All Blacks forward pack laid the foundation for another
methodical performance, with outstanding ball control from the
outset.

France had done well to be trailing only 9–0 at half time. A penalty
goal straight after the interval narrowed the score to 9–3, but that
would be as close as they would come to New Zealand. Grant Fox
landed four quick penalty goals for the home side, and when skipper
David Kirk crossed for a try before putting John Kirwan over for
another try two minutes later it was 29–3 and all but over.

France did have one last say when scrum-half Pierre Berbizier capped off a fantastic tournament with a sensational try that saw him handle the ball four times. The try to Berbizier was in itself a magnificent score, but no person in the world rugby fraternity could deny the All Blacks were the masters of their own destiny and deserving champions of the inaugural Rugby World Cup – the final score 29–9.

'At the end of the day the All Blacks ran first ... and daylight came second,' Farr-Jones recalls. 'I am still not sure what they did in the off-season to improve so quickly but a combination of exceptional new playing talent, shrewd coaching and strategies, and a total commitment to the job at hand laid the foundations for this great team that would go on to dominate world rugby for almost four years.'

The 1987 triumph for the All Blacks was not only one of sheer dominance and precision, it was a remarkable turnaround from one year earlier when New Zealand rugby lay in ruins following the infamous Cavaliers debacle. In effect though, the Cavaliers episode may have been a blessing in disguise. It allowed younger players to be blooded in the 'Baby Blacks' of 1986 and galvanised a large squad capable of beating any team in the world. Along the way, the bitter schism between those aligned to the Cavaliers and those aligned to the establishment was quickly filled by the shared undying loyalty of wearing the black jersey and a vision to put New Zealand at the top of world rugby. With all of that was instilled the most fundamental of all rugby rules – to enjoy the game.

New Zealand's positive display on the field was the result of players enjoying a relaxed and fun environment, which broke new ground and brought them closer to the fans. It was the first time the All Blacks had properly toured their own country, and it was the first time they performed the famous Haka on New Zealand soil – something previously reserved for touring overseas. Sean Fitzpatrick fondly reflects back on a time when the players were billeted in the Wairarapa region during the finals:

'We went to a place where [All Blacks coach] Brian Lochore was from and we were all billeted out for the night,' Fitzpatrick recalls. 'It was like being back at school. We all went into this pub called The Lake and there were all these families having dinner. The team manager gathered us all and would yell out our names before introducing us to the family we were staying with. We then grabbed our bags and jumped in the family truck before staying the night at their farms.'

The simple things were done well by New Zealand from the playing field to the public arena, and they were now at the forefront of an exciting new era for world rugby. Rugby World Cup 1987 was the birth of a new generation of the game, which would eventually see it evolve into a professional sport. While the tournament forged a path that still made rugby purists cringe about the introduction of a global showpiece, what was equally clear to the public eye were those most admirable amateur roots and values upon which the sport was built – camaraderie, courage and enjoyment. New Zealand embraced those values, and in the years that followed they became the benchmark for all nations aspiring to win The Webb Ellis Cup.

FIVE MAGIC MEMORIES

Opening shot from Kirwan restored All Black faith

When the first whistle blew for kick-off in the opening match of the inaugural Rugby World Cup at Eden Park in Auckland on May 22, 1987, there was a collective sigh of relief from rugby's visionaries of the latter twentieth century. The immovable view of an established few among the Home Unions, who persisted to scrutinise the tournament as scornful to the greater cause, was quite literally a distant thought for a moment. Sir Nick Shehadie and Dick Littlejohn – The Nick and Dick Show – had reached the climax of their epic preliminary act with assistance from John Kendall-Carpenter of England, and now the main performance was set to take centre stage.

Eden Park could hold 46,000 spectators at the time, but the stadium was only half full – perhaps reflective of a lack of marketing budget combined with the damage done by the Cavaliers tour one year earlier. Light rain fell throughout the afternoon, but that had never kept New Zealand fans away before. What some later believed to be a big factor was the decision to stage the opening ceremony and first match when many people were still at work on a Friday afternoon – something that had never been done before in New Zealand. The organising committee claimed the Friday afternoon timing would allow the opening match to command all the attention it deserved and permit a full programme of matches on the ensuing weekend.

Perhaps it was a costly commercial decision in hindsight, but it fulfilled a purpose nonetheless in putting the host nation and rugby icon – the All Blacks – at the forefront of what was now the showcase event for the sport. Predictably the result was an easy victory for the All Blacks as they scored 12 tries (one a penalty try) to none, but most importantly it brought a positive start for a demanding rugby public. Zinzan Brooke – a rookie among an All Blacks squad riddled with great names before him – fondly recalls the opening match.

'New Zealand rugby needed a good lift and the floodgates opened with the John Kirwan try off the kick-off that took the [New Zealand] score over 50 points,' Brooke said. 'It brought the crowd to their feet and with it came this big shot of momentum for the All Blacks, and that seemed to carry over to the rest of the tournament.'

The Kirwan try that gave the opening match the ingredient it required came from an Italy restart, which had resulted from his first try straight after the half-time break. The ball was caught by New Zealand captain and scrum-half David Kirk, who passed it on to fly-half Grant fox, and he in turn distributed to Kirwan. With blatant disregard for every attempt made to tackle him, the burly All Blacks wing carved his way through the whole Italy team *en route* to a length-of-the-field try under the posts. It not only lifted everyone in the stadium to their feet, but also sent a clear and positive message out to rugby's emerging generation tuned in around the globe.

'That was my first real taste of rugby as a spectator,' dual Rugby World Cup champion Tim Horan recalls of his schoolboy days at Downlands College in Queensland, Australia. 'We were all watching it on television. It was my last year at school, and I was playing in the First XV, running out on weekends to 4,000 people watching our games. I used to try my best to imitate that try in training and in games at school. It certainly made rugby capture my imagination.'

The opening match was not the commercial success the 1987 tournament organisers would have hoped for, but recollections of half empty stands were quickly overridden by the Kirwan try that became the trademark memory. Not only did that try inspire a victory that crucially restored New Zealand's faith in their beloved All Blacks after a year of turmoil, it sowed the seeds for a new rugby generation and brought a previously insular game on to the global sporting landscape.

Military coup cast no restriction on fabulous Fiji flair

There were only eight days remaining to the opening match at the inaugural Rugby World Cup when the Pacific Island nation of Fiji was at the centre of a military coup led by Lieutenant Colonel Sitiveni Rabuka, who was then third in command of the Royal Fiji Military Forces. Rabuka was part of the indigenous Fijian community, who have had ongoing tensions with Indo-Fijian ethnic groups ever since Fiji became independent from the United Kingdom in 1970. The sitting government at the time of the coup was Indo-Fijian, and they had only just come to power in the general elections held one month earlier. Rabuka claimed to the world that he was leading the coup on the grounds of racial discrimination from the Indo-Fijian community. The two conflicting groups have roughly the same percentage population in Fiji and tensions have always been high.

The event cast doubt on whether Fiji would be ready to take part in the tournament, and organisers had Western Samoa on standby. Having defied so much to that point, Sir Nick Shehadie and his organising committee were determined not to have any last-minute hitches that would destabilise the event.

'We had Western Samoa ready to fill in if the [Fiji] players couldn't get out of the country,' Shehadie said. 'It was good that it didn't come to that though, because Fiji turned out to be a very popular team at the tournament.'

Fiji took the field against Argentina for their debut Rugby World Cup appearance and very few observers had high expectations for the Pacific Islanders following their unstable preparation. Eighty minutes later they walked away from a four tries to one (28–9) victory over an Argentina team that included the famous Hugo Porta at fly-half. The result gave Fiji a promising start to claiming the second quarter-final place in Pool 3 behind New Zealand.

It then became a battle of tactics, and Fiji decided to put an under-strength team out against the All Blacks with a view to saving their stronger players for the final pool match against Italy. The plan succumbed to a predictable start – a thrashing at the hands of New Zealand (74–13), and then it backfired with a narrow loss to Italy (18–15). The three-way battle for second place was ultimately determined by the most number of tries scored, and Fiji came through with one more try than Italy to advance to a quarter-final showdown with France.

It was in that 1987 quarter-final against France at Eden Park in Auckland that the true essence of Fiji rugby was first introduced to the international sporting world. Standing opposite a heavyweight opponent and strong title contender, Fiji won the hearts of many with a glittering display against an unusually methodical France team. It was the French who usually enjoyed notoriety as the exponents of flamboyant rugby, but on this occasion Fiji stole the limelight.

The quick feet of fly-half Severo Koroduadua, and midfield pairing of Tomasi Cama and Kaiava Salusalu, totally mesmerised the French defence. High-risk tactics rarely work during finals though, and it was only a matter of time before Fiji were exposed through the error count. They had enjoyed an early lead after a memorable try to flanker Manasa Qoro – a score that inspired a very creative opening period – but when Koroduadua later dropped the ball cold in open space, Fiji's confidence also took a dive and France pounced. Koroduadua had a tendency to hold the ball in one hand and wave his hands around, but his colourful ways were eventually exposed by tight tactics from France.

Les Bleus eventually triumphed 31–16 to set up a semi-final against Australia, but the efforts of Fiji deserved high praise. The military coup by Rabuka may have claimed most of Fiji's spotlight on the world stage, but a very determined squad of players also put their mark on history, firmly establishing their country as a proud rugby nation.

Scotland the brave contained France for memorable draw

One of the most exciting pool matches at the inaugural Rugby World Cup was the Pool 4 clash between France and Scotland at Lancaster Park in Christchurch. Unlike the other lopsided matches of the opening weekend, this clash put two of the stronger contenders against each other and fans were treated to an enthralling clash that eventually saw the teams finish locked together (20–20) at full time. Sadly for Scotland they lost their outstanding fly-half John Rutherford to a knee injury very early on, but the team held its nerve and enjoyed an early lead after lock Derek White scored a try.

Such was the damage to ligaments and cartilage in his knee that Rutherford never played for Scotland again. Most observers thought the loss of Rutherford was too much for Scotland to overcome against France, but Douglas Wyllie moved from centre to fly-half and Alan Tait came on at centre to fill the void. More than fill the void, both were vital in marshalling a solid defensive effort from the backline. It was then left to Gavin Hastings to kick the points, and his four penalty goals saw Scotland enjoy a 16–6 lead at one stage. Then came a remarkable final period slightly tarnished by some dubious refereeing.

France played their way back into the match with tries to scrum-half Pierre Berbizier and outside centre Philippe Sella to bring the score to 16–14. Then a controversial moment in the 79th minute saw referee Fred Howard from England permit a try to France fullback Serge Blanco that perhaps should not have been allowed. Much to the dismay of Scotland captain Colin Deans, who thought along with many of his team-mates that an injury stoppage was imminent after wing Matt Duncan and Berbizier were both down, France were awarded a penalty. Blanco took a quick tap from the penalty before running half the length of the field to score the try that would put France in front for the first time.

'It was strange how fast this try came,' France centre Philippe Sella recalls. 'Lucky he could run all the way and score this himself because players from both side did not know what he does.'

Scotland was caught napping and Blanco made them suffer, but the match was far from over. With four minutes of injury time added, Scotland spread the ball wide and ironically it was wing Matt Duncan who recovered from his previous injury and crossed in the corner to draw the scores level with a kick to come. Gavin Hastings then lined up for the conversion that would have given Scotland a memorable victory, but his attempt missed by the barest of margins and the score remained 20–20.

'Scotland played very well,' Sella said. 'It was good for our team because it wake them up for the bigger matches later in the tournament.'

Scotland the brave defied the loss of their influential fly-half Rutherford and provided very stiff opposition to France. It was a match that illustrated how closely contested the tournament could be among the top nations in world rugby. It was the first ever draw in Rugby World Cup history and one of the most memorable matches of the pool stage in 1987.

Semi-final showdown brought best of rugby theatre

There are those games that command strong recognition for years after they have been played, and the 1987 semi-final between Australia and France is definitely one. Some still regard it as one of the best games of rugby ever. The enduring image of fullback Serge Blanco scoring the decisive try in the dying moments, as Australia hooker Tom Lawton dives desperately and unsuccessfully to stop him, is a lasting memory for those who watched it.

Australia capitalised on the indiscipline of France to take an early 9–0 lead with three penalty goals from Michael Lynagh, but France refused to lie down. When Troy Coker easily won a lineout close to Australia's line, his team-mates stood by expecting the ball to come out for Lynagh to make the clearance, but France lock Alain Lorieux had other ideas. Lorieux ripped the ball off Coker and from within the middle of a maul somehow made his way through the whole Australia forward pack for a memorable score in the corner. A young Martin Johnson watching the Lorieux try was left in awe as he observed a fellow lock forward enjoy the limelight in a crucial match.

'I remember as a young lad watching that ... you just saw Lorieux get in, rip the ball out, go down the blindside and just stuff the ball over the line. It was one of those great tries from nothing,' recalls Johnson. 'I was sitting there and thinking that was an amazing try to score in a Rugby World Cup semi-final.'

It was that same doggedness in Lorieux's try that saw France recover three times when Australia had gone into the lead. The match had all the names – Lynagh, Campese, Farr-Jones, Sella, Blanco – and the quality of play was befitting of those names. Fatigue also played a part, with exhausted and injured players littered all over the field through the dying minutes. The scores were level at 21–21 with only three minutes of regulation time left when Lynagh stepped up to kick another penalty goal after a further infringement from France to take Australia to a 24–21 lead. Many spectators were left gasping, thinking the match could not take another turn, but France bounced straight back with a penalty goal to Didier Camberabero to level the scores again at 24–24.

Then there was an inexplicable moment where Lynagh and Campese tried to run the ball from their own half. It came at a price as they lost possession. France then spread the ball wide and Blanco scored the final try that broke Australian hearts and put *Les Bleus* into the inaugural Rugby World Cup final.

It came as a pleasant surprise to the New Zealand players watching from afar that France had eliminated Australia. The All Blacks had been troubled by the Wallabies the year before, losing a Test series on home soil, and many of the New Zealand players were happy with the prospect of playing France in the final instead of Australia.

'It was very interesting when France scored that final try. It was very obvious who our players wanted to play in the final – not Australia,' All Blacks coach Brian Lochore was later quoted as saying in *The Rise & Rise of Australian Rugby* by Philip Derriman. 'They saw Australia as a very strong opponent. The French side is always very fickle, and we reckoned they'd had their big game. It would have been a tougher game in the final if we'd played Australia.'

Regardless of the form guide, France had played a very significant part in showcasing the Rugby World Cup to the world and deserved their place in the final: the draw against Scotland; the running spectacle against Fiji; and a shock semi-final result that gave the tournament the element of surprise it needed. Unfortunately for *Les Bleus* however, the final would prove to be one game too many as they fell victim to a well-oiled All Black machine that only knew one direction – forward at pace.

The final say was All Black

While the opening match played out on a relatively tame level of enthusiasm from the public, the final in Auckland was a very different story. The city was alive with rugby. All of the hotels were full of rugby people on an international scale and finally it felt like a Rugby World Cup tournament was on. Former Australia coach Bob Dwyer, who was only months away from returning to the post of national coach, fondly recalls his time as a touring spectator:

'We were used to having tours and one or two hotels with teams staying in them, but nothing on this scale,' Dwyer said. 'Every restaurant, every café, every bar and every hotel – it was all rugby. To see people that we had last seen while we were on tour – our liaison manager from Ireland, our bus driver from France – and bump into them going down the street was absolutely fantastic.'

The game itself was a letdown in comparison to the Australia v France game a week earlier. New Zealand dominated from the opening exchanges, and through a ruthless pack of forwards they ground down a tired France unit from tighthead prop to fullback. As quickly as *Les Bleus* would find some intermittent spark to stall New Zealand's domination in the possession stakes, the dynamic back row of Buck Shelford, Michael Jones and Alan Whetton would snuff it out. Jones also made his mark in attack, scoring the opening try after pouncing on a loose ball that resulted from Patrice Lagisquet charging down a Grant Fox field goal attempt. France scrapped well for the first half and drew to within six points at one stage early in the second half, but most of the final 30 minutes was dominated by the All Blacks and they eventually won easily (29–9).

It was an emphatic victory, indicative of a fine mix of players that consisted of the more established names like Shelford, Whetton and Fox, combined with talented youth that would eventually develop their own legendary status. Rookie hooker Sean Fitzpatrick had staved off a comeback attempt from New Zealand's original tournament captain Andy Dalton to keep his place in the side, and it was plenty to savour for a young player on the world stage.

'We didn't really know how big the Rugby World Cup would be. Even after the final we were sort of like, 'Ah well, that's that done ... what now?' Fitzpatrick reflects. 'Craig Green [New Zealand wing] tells a great story about how we won the Rugby World Cup on the Saturday and 5am on Monday morning he was standing on a corner in Christchurch with his packed lunchbox waiting to go roofing. There was no real big party or no parade. It was just another win for the All Blacks really.'

Another win for the All Blacks and the status of rugby world champions for the next four years – a standing they richly deserved after establishing a team that would dominate the world stage through the interim years of 1987 to 1991. The game may not have been a spectacle, but the Rugby World Cup final was a groundbreaking event for the international focus it brought to the sport. Commercial interest would only increase from that point and, as former Australia coach Bob Dwyer later described, 'It was a village market back in 1987 compared to what it is now.'

4

The interim years: 1987–1991

THE CHAMPION ALL BLACKS of 1987 had only just started to peak when they triumphed over France in the final. What followed was a three-year domination of the sport, which saw New Zealand maintain a record unbeaten run of 17 consecutive Test matches from 1987–1990. The team was built around the same nucleus that made up the 1987 squad: however one noticeable change was at scrum-half when 1987 tournament captain David Kirk retired to take up a Rhodes scholarship at Oxford University in England. Kirk was only 26 at the time, and a stubborn hamstring injury sustained in the one-off Bledisloe Cup match against Australia in 1987 ultimately ended a short yet very distinguished international career. Kirk played just 17 Tests, but 14 of those resulted in victories, and for 11 of them he was captain during a tumultuous time for New Zealand rugby.

'I really enjoyed playing under David Kirk. He was a fantastic captain,' recalls Sean Fitzpatrick. 'I thought he did really well, and I was really pleased for him after all the shit he went through with the Cavaliers the year before the 1987 tournament.'

Kirk made an unpopular late withdrawal, on moral grounds, from the 1986 Cavaliers tour and it took a while for him to regain respect from many of the older Cavaliers players who returned to the All Blacks fold after their ensuing suspension. He was in many ways fortunate to become New Zealand captain only by political circumstances following the Cavaliers tour and injury to two senior players – Jock Hobbs in 1986 and then Andy Dalton just prior to the 1987 tournament – but Kirk had a fine vision for how the game was played, and a successful corporate career post-rugby is indicative of his outstanding leadership qualities.

Following the retirement of Kirk, it was the dynamic Number 8 and team enforcer Wayne 'Buck' Shelford who was charged with leading the All Blacks through one of the finest periods of their impressive rugby history. Australia were the closest any team came to the All Blacks during 1987–1989, with a 19–19 draw in Brisbane during the 1988 Bledisloe Cup series. Wales, France, Argentina, Ireland and Scotland were all put to the sword during that time – some of them on consecutive occasions – but it was Australia who finally broke the All Blacks' dominance with a comfortable 22–9 victory in a Bledisloe Cup dead-rubber in Wellington at the end of the 1990 southern hemisphere international season.

While some thought it might have been a case of the All Blacks becoming complacent with the three-match series already won, history shows it was more likely the start of the 15–month decline that would eventually see New Zealand unable to defend their title of world champions at the 1991 tournament in the United Kingdom and Ireland. The all-conquering All Blacks machine had started to stutter and other teams were catching up.

One team among the top tier of rugby nations who had decent grounds to argue that they had not been able to challenge the All Blacks' dominance of 1987–1990 was England. There was no match scheduled between the two countries at all from 1985 right through until the end of 1991. More than six years passed without the two opposing each other. New Zealand was indisputably a better side for a major part of that period, but England had established a solid team by 1990 and were runner-up to Scotland in the Five Nations Championship that year, their highlight a 27–6 trouncing of France in Paris. England went one better the following year in 1991, and won the Grand Slam for the first time since 1980, setting the stage for a highly anticipated showdown with New Zealand in the opening match of the 1991 tournament. England were eventually defeated by the All Blacks in that opening match, and the speculation as to who was the better team during the six-year drought of Test matches between the two was also finally laid to rest.

The 1990 Five Nations champion – Scotland – were another team to unsettle the All Blacks in their post-1987 period of world rugby domination. Scotland came very close to recording their first-ever victory over New Zealand at Eden Park in 1990, but they eventually fell 21–18. The match was largely viewed by the media at the time as another great escape for New Zealand, but moreover it instilled confidence among other nations in the top tier – the All Blacks were no longer a major force and definitely beatable.

'We probably let ourselves down really. We still had the best players in the world at that time, but not the best team,' recalls Sean Fitzpatrick. 'We had come to the end of our tender after we lost to Australia in 1990. We also became a bit arrogant and thought we were a lot better than we really were, and we didn't train as hard.'

Australia was the first to break New Zealand's record run of success, with a rejuvenated team under recalled coach Bob Dwyer. The reappointment of Dwyer after the Alan Jones era was opposed by some pockets of the Australian rugby community, but history shows it was a masterstroke in terms of grooming a squad that would eventually conquer all nations in the wake of an All Blacks-dominated era. After losing a three-Test series narrowly to the touring British and Irish Lions in 1989, Dwyer treated the event as a watershed for the Wallabies and began his quest for youthful change in the playing ranks.

Universally respected in rugby circles for his ability to identify young talent and nurture it to maximum potential, Dwyer went on to introduce some youth that would grow to become four of the finest names to play the game – Jason Little, Tim Horan, Phil Kearns and John Eales. The *Perfect Union*, as Little and Horan were later dubbed through a duel biography published about the parallel lives of the centre pairing, was the first revelation of Dwyer's new legacy.

The Queensland duo literally became the centrepiece of Australian rugby throughout the early 1990s. Horan was a product of Downlands College in Toowoomba, where he was under the guidance of former England coach John Elder while playing in a First XV regarded as one of the finest schoolboy teams Australia has ever seen. The team also had fellow Wallabies Brett Robinson and Brett Johnston, plus Australia rugby league representative Peter Ryan.

Little went to school close by at Toowoomba Grammar and the five were part of a strong rugby contingent from Queensland's famous Darling Downs agricultural region. Horan and Little had played alongside and against each other from schoolboy level, and later became one of the finest international centre pairings rugby has ever seen.

'My first memory of Jason is stealing the ball off him and I scored a try and he started crying, when we were probably only 10 or 11 years old,' Horan said. 'We went to different schools and played on the same team and against each other from time to time. The first team we played together in was a rugby league team made up from the State Championships. We got to know each other pretty well and we were in athletics teams, cricket teams and rugby teams for the next five or six years through our schooling.'

Both made their Test debut for Australia in 1989 at the tender age of 19, with Horan given a baptism of fire by lining up opposite burly veteran centre Joe Stanley when the Wallabies faced the All Blacks in a one-off Bledisloe Cup match in Auckland.

'My first Test match was against New Zealand and I probably didn't feel the aura of the All Blacks as much as I probably should have,' Horan said. 'I played three Test matches before I played for Queensland, so being picked for the Wallabies against the All Blacks so early was just like playing against another rugby side for me. It wasn't until later on that I started to understand the aura of the All Blacks and exactly who they were. I marked Joe Stanley in my first Test match, and I didn't really know who he was … it didn't take long before I did.'

Australia lost the match 24–12, but Horan impressed his opposite number so much that Stanley gave the rookie centre his All Blacks jersey to mark the occasion and insisted Horan keep his own Wallabies jersey too. Hooker Phil Kearns also made his debut in the same game, starting what would become one of rugby's most passionate rivalries when he lined up against All Blacks counterpart Sean Fitzpatrick. Prop Tony Daly also made a solid Test debut at loosehead prop after being plucked from Sydney club rugby. The Australia transformation under Dwyer began in earnest.

Some three months later, Little made his debut against France, and the Horan/Little partnership announced their arrival on the international scene by outplaying Frank Mesnel and the great Philippe Sella, with the Wallabies defeating *Les Bleus* 32–15 in Strasbourg. Australia's puzzle for 1991 was slowly taking shape. Coach Dwyer was forceful in selecting inexperienced players to fill vital gaps in his squad – an approach not necessarily shared by other coaches in Australia at the time.

'Looking back, it was like a Hollywood movie. We were putting a team together and it was like a casting of sorts,' Dwyer recalls. 'We forced the need for youth and freshness in a lot of positions. I remember saying we need a hooker and we plucked Kearnsy from Randwick Second Grade. John Connolly – Queensland coach at the time – said to me, "It's a pity the World Cup is not in 1992 ... Ealesy would be sensational." I said back to him in no uncertain terms that John Eales was sensational now and we needed him in the team. Connolly was right, Eales was going to be much better in 1992, but we were not waiting. He was already a very good player.'

Eales made his Test debut against Wales in 1991, when the Wallabies were victorious to the tune of 63–6 in their first international of the season. The team had taken a whole different shape to that defeated by the Lions less than two years before, and Dwyer's formula was slowly coming together. Along with the inclusion of Eales at lock, the Wallabies had also seasoned a powerful back-row forward named Viliami "Willie" Ofahengaue. The Tongan powerhouse became more popularly known as "Willie-O", adding dynamic running and ruthless defence to a forward unit that slowly built itself up to be one of the most respected packs in world rugby leading up to the 1991 tournament.

After handing out a heavy defeat to Wales, the next opponent for the Wallabies was the reigning Five Nations champion England. With the All Blacks now seemingly on the wane from their post-1987 supremacy, the match against England was quickly built up to be Australia's best litmus test for the impending Rugby World Cup. The visiting English probably wished it had not been billed in such a way because the Wallabies put on a ruthless display that would later have their coach Dwyer describing the match as the best Australian performance he had ever witnessed.

'I had never seen a Wallaby team play such sharp and efficient rugby over 80 minutes,' Dwyer said. 'Everything we did was so precise. Tactically it all just came together so well, and England could do very little to stop it. It was an important win and gave us a good boost ahead of two Tests against the All Blacks before the World Cup.'

After the England rout, Australia went on to beat New Zealand 21–12 in Sydney and all of a sudden the rugby world was talking up the new team to beat. Even the All Blacks considered themselves lucky not to have lost by more in Sydney. Had they not won the return match 6–3 in atrocious Auckland conditions two weeks later, New Zealand's Rugby World Cup squad for 1991 might well have taken a very different shape.

'The Wallabies had clearly caught up to us,' Sean Fitzpatrick reflects. 'Players like Phil Kearns, Tony Daly and Willie-O came into the Aussie team and they were hungrier than us. The writing was on the wall after the loss to Australia in 1990 and it was reinforced again in Sydney a year later, but we were in denial and the win in Auckland probably wasn't such a great thing for our squad in the end.'

New Zealand's dominance on the world stage had certainly waned by 1991, and the considerable distance that had become common-place between the All Blacks and the next best contenders was now obsolete. England was still the worthy champion of Europe, despite the heavy loss to Australia, and they were sure to pose a very different prospect to any opponent on home soil later that year. The English enjoyed an outstanding run of success from 1988 to 1991 prior to the loss against Australia in Sydney, conceding only three defeats from 20 Test matches played. France had also enjoyed a solid build-up to the 1991 tournament, winning seven of eight Tests played. The two northern hemisphere heavyweights appeared to be the only teams likely to challenge the southern hemisphere front-runners – Australia and New Zealand. Four of the Big Five were now genuine title contenders. The stage was set for a more closely-fought contest to claim what had quickly become international rugby's greatest prize.

5

Rugby World Cup 1991: the tournament

RUGBY WORLD CUP 1991 had the advantage of learning from the inaugural tournament and the game developed considerably during that time. The Home Unions had always feared that the staging of a global rugby event would cause an unpreventable shift towards professionalism, and that fear inevitably started becoming a reality during the interim period between the first two Rugby World Cup tournaments. It was perhaps one of the most defining periods for the modern game, with the international focus now clearly shifting from regional tournaments and tours abroad to one ultimate global event every four years. The IRB maintained its tough stance against player payments and the game still remained non-professional at the official level, but training methods and team preparation had taken a turn, with players at the highest level forced to devote more time beyond two training sessions before a Test match.

'The Home Unions warned that creating a Rugby World Cup would push the game towards professionalism. I thought that excuse was a load of rubbish at the time, but they were absolutely right,' Bob Dwyer recalls. 'Suddenly there was this prize every team desperately wanted to win, and in order to win it they had to spend a lot more money and ask a lot more of their players. Inevitably, those players had to sacrifice more work time and they needed to be compensated for it somehow.'

What the 1987 tournament and four-year period beyond it demonstrated was that New Zealand and Australia were a clear cut above the rest in terms of training methods and preparation at the international level. Both countries were well aware that they could not defy the demands of the IRB and grant players any form of payment, but more cleverly thought-out intrinsic methods of compensation ensured a large make-up of their squads could devote more time to training and match preparation. Such methods came through firms, corporations and support networks providing players with employment that granted more flexible hours. Rugby networking became more functional than ever before.

'We had to take measures to stay on the pace with New Zealand and even try to go a step ahead,' Dwyer says. 'We needed our players to go to the gym and build themselves up beyond the training we did. Most of them had families to feed and it was hard to warrant spending money on a gym membership, so we did a deal with a gym and they reduced the membership fees for our players.'

Some astute lateral thinking had Australia and New Zealand quickly advancing their training methods and Test match preparation from 1987 onwards. The two southern hemisphere giants left most countries in their wake in the march to the 1991 tournament, but the method to their quick advancement was not lost on a very shrewd England coach – Geoff Cooke. The former Physical Education lecturer was brought to the helm of English rugby following the 1987 tournament in a period now largely viewed as a vital watershed for the game in its country of origin.

While they were still some considerable distance behind Australia and New Zealand, England slowly formed a group of players that would later become the dominant force in northern hemisphere rugby during the early 1990s. Cooke made some tough decisions early in his tenure, many of which were widely criticised by a large portion of the English media, but ultimately those decisions were what breathed new life into a national squad that had been relatively disappointing at the inaugural tournament.

There were some good signs of improvement when England toured Australia one year later in 1988, but just when the team put in a performance that showed encouraging progress, they would quickly unravel in unceremonious fashion – an unwelcome trait that became synonymous with their rise in the 1990s. England's first of two Tests against the Wallabies in the middle part of 1988 saw a tight game at

Ballymore in Brisbane, where Australia scraped home 22–16, but two weeks later in Sydney England were handed a heavy 28–8 defeat. Following that loss, England went on to Suva in Fiji where they managed to salvage some pride with an unconvincing 25–12 victory. Coach Cooke was far from impressed and made a series of changes that brought a new shape to his side later that year.

It was a classic case of out with the old and in with the new, and Cooke carried out what was perhaps the most controversial decision of his tenure by appointing 22–year-old centre Will Carling as England captain. Carling had only played a handful of Test matches, and was handed the captaincy rather unexpectedly after being openly critical of the leadership of John Orwin during the unsuccessful tour of Australia and Fiji earlier that year. The decision to appoint Carling skipper at such a young age was widely questioned at the time, but that quickly subsided when England avenged their two losses to Australia earlier in 1988 with a four-try 28–19 victory over the Wallabies at Twickenham in November that year. The Carling era dawned and England improved dramatically over the next three years to become the northern hemisphere's strongest contender at Rugby World Cup 1991.

France was always capable of competing with the best teams in the world on any given day, but inconsistency always prevented *Les Bleus* from having sustained periods of success. Such a record was never a good indicator for a tournament that required dependable form over consecutive weeks. Scotland were conceivably a more likely contender than France in the 1991 tournament after their famous Grand Slam triumph in 1990, and so the results would eventually prove as they advanced to the 1991 semi-finals.

Perhaps the most disappointing progress of any northern hemisphere nation between the first two Rugby World Cups was that of Wales. There had been plenty for the Welsh to build on following a strong showing in the inaugural tournament, where they bounced back from a semi-final loss to the All Blacks with a last-minute defeat of Australia in the play-off for third place. But the Triple Crown and shared Five Nations success with France in 1988 was to be their pinnacle, and a rapid fall from grace over the next three years sadly saw one of the world's proudest rugby nations suddenly become the laughing stock. From December 1988 to September 1991, Wales won only three Test matches from 18 played – and two of those victories came against rugby minnows Namibia. It was to become one of the darkest ages in Welsh rugby. Unlike England, who took major measures to improve, Wales rested on their moderate success and paid a major price for doing so.

In contrast, Australia improved remarkably on the world scene under the astute guidance of Bob Dwyer, but the possibility of some key players being tempted to join the professional rugby league ranks posed a constant threat to destabilising the squad. The likes of David Campese and Simon Poidevin were offered large sums to jump codes, while the newly-groomed centre pairing of Tim Horan and Jason Little also became prime targets for rugby league scouts. For the best part of a century the Wallabies had been subjected to the threat of league luring Australia's best rugby talent, and the players took it on themselves to do all they could to keep Horan and Little in the 15–man code. In what is now regarded as a vital event that kept the nucleus of Australia's squad together for the 1991 tournament, senior members of the 1989 Wallabies tour to France subjected Horan and Little to a mock bar-room ceremony where they swore their allegiance to rugby and pledged not to defect to rugby league. It was to become a vital victory for not only Australian rugby, but for the game of rugby itself.

The pool stage

The 16 teams that made up Rugby World Cup 1991 consisted of the eight quarter-finalists from 1987, who were given automatic entry, with the other eight places determined by 33 nations competing in a qualification process. Unlike the inaugural tournament that was by invitation only, the 1991 event gave the lesser rugby nations around the world a chance to qualify. Ultimately it was almost the same complement of teams in 1991 as it had been four years earlier, except for Western Samoa who replaced their Pacific Island neighbours Tonga. The fact that other nations were given a chance to qualify for the big stage was itself considered to be great progress for a fledgling tournament trying to establish recognition as a genuinely global event.

The inaugural tournament had been slated in its post-mortem for being staged between two countries, with critics arguing that the logistics of transporting and managing teams across different countries had a negative impact on the event. But rather than condense the tournament to one nation in 1991, the IRB allowed for 24 pool fixtures to be played across five countries in Europe (albeit a much smaller geographic area) – a decision that was indicative of the new global vision rugby's administrators had to take. There were 19 different venues (eight more than 1987) across the five countries who contested the Five Nations tournament – England, Ireland, Scotland, Wales and France. The final was to be played at Twickenham – the revered home of English rugby that was famously built on an old cabbage patch – with the other host nations sharing the quarter-finals and semi-finals between them.

Rugby World Cup 1991: the pools and order they finished

Pool A	Pool B	Pool C	Pool D
New Zealand	Scotland	Australia	France
England	Ireland	Western Samoa	Canada
Italy	Japan	Wales	Romania
United States	Zimbabwe	Argentina	Fiji

The opening match of 1991 was a highly anticipated showdown between north and south, with England and New Zealand facing off at Twickenham. It was an oddly scheduled Thursday afternoon kick-off, and it came five days after a tournament welcome dinner for all 16 teams at the Royal Lancaster Hotel in London. England had not played New Zealand since June of 1985, and both teams had their own point to prove. For England it was to demonstrate they were a force to be reckoned with among the major tournament contenders, while the All Blacks needed to confirm their near decade-long global superiority of the sport against an opponent they had not played for more than six years. New Zealand eventually won 18–12, but the most interesting feature proved to be how England managed to stay in the match despite an obvious lack of possession. The All Blacks clearly were not the same force that had swept all teams aside four years before, and the opening match proved they were definitely beatable.

When New Zealand defeated the United States by 40 points (46–6) in their second pool match of the 1991 tournament, the perceived vulnerabilities from their match against England were present again as a determined United States commanded respect from the Gloucester crowd. To the untrained eye the All Black machine seemed on track again – running in eight tries, including a memorable hat-trick to fullback Terry Wright – but something still wasn't right. One highlight was the introduction of left wing Va'aiga Tuigamala – who became more commonly known as "Inga the winger". Tuigamala was of Samoan heritage, and an imposing figure lining up in the wing position during that era. His presence brought some much-needed spark and an element of surprise back to the All Blacks, but the same machine that had dominated world rugby for an extended period since 1987 again showed signs of seizing up in their last Pool A match against Italy. Four years earlier New Zealand had thrashed Italy 70–6 in the opening match of the tournament, yet in the corresponding pool match of 1991 they could only scrape a meagre 10-point victory (31–21). Italy had certainly improved a lot during that period, but the All Blacks had diminished considerably and the early signs were there that this tournament would not be theirs.

In contrast, England grew in confidence as the tournament progressed. The loss to New Zealand all but guaranteed that England could finish no higher than second in Pool A, but strong performances in their other two pool matches against an improving Italy (36–6) and United States (37–9) ensured the main host nation would enter the knockout stage with good momentum. On the back of a Five Nations Grand Slam triumph earlier that year, and with an imposing forward pack that included Jeff Probyn, Paul Ackford, Wade Dooley and Dean Richards, England comfortably ensured they would improve on their disappointing performance of 1987.

In Pool B it was Scotland and Ireland who battled it out for the top two places. Scotland were by far the most convincing of the two in their performances against the other countries in the pool – defeating Japan (47–9) and Zimbabwe (51–12). Ireland had enjoyed a similarly comfortable victory over Zimbabwe (55–11), but they were given quite a scare by a determined and flamboyant Japan at Lansdowne Road before finally prevailing (32–16). Previous form usually counts for little when one Home Union meets another, but Ireland was disappointing against Scotland at Murrayfield in the match that decided who would finish top of the pool. Scrum-half Gary Armstrong steered Scotland around the field with tremendous poise. Had it not been for some accurate goal kicking from Ireland fly-half Ralph Keyes, who slotted four penalties and a drop-goal to keep Ireland in the match, the 24–15 score line would have ended much further in favour of Scotland than it finally did. Ireland were still assured second place in Pool B and a home quarter-final, but their opponents would be tournament favourites Australia.

The Wallabies had started the tournament as co-favourites with New Zealand, but patchy form from the All Blacks pushed Australia into the position of favourites for the title as the knockout stage dawned. But the Wallabies also experienced some early tournament jitters, as their opening match against Argentina in Pool C demonstrated. Though Australia remained in control for most of the match, Argentina kept in touch and were only four points adrift in the 60th minute. The Pumas were determined to make amends for a disappointing showing in the 1987 tournament, but some late magic from David Campese and Tim Horan finally put the match beyond Argentina's reach.

'We knew we had a couple of tough pool matches having to face both Argentina and Western Samoa. Both of them provided us with very physical games and we were better for it despite a few casualties along the way,' Dwyer said. 'We thought from late 1990 onwards that if we played to our ability, that if we did certain things well, we could win the tournament. We established a clear process of focusing on what we thought we'd have to achieve in order to win, rather than just simply striving to win.'

Australia faced another stern test in their second Pool C match against Western Samoa before winning 9–3. The Wallabies suffered a big blow 20 minutes into the match when captain and scrum-half Nick Farr-Jones twisted his knee while trying to deliver a pass before being crunched in a heavy tackle. The injury looked so serious that many watching the match doubted Farr-Jones would play any further part in the tournament, but the captain of the Wallabies was a hard man to keep down and with some intense physiotherapy he returned to play a major part in the later stages.

Western Samoa was in many ways the surprise package of the 1991 tournament and the main country to suffer as a result was Wales, who lost 16–13 in front of their home fans at Cardiff Arms Park. That result all but ended Wales's march towards the knockout phase and catapulted Western Samoa into quarter-final contention. Their last hurdle came by way of Argentina, and it was a very rugged affair at Sardis Road in Pontypridd, where referee Jim Fleming from Scotland sent two players off for fighting – Pedro Sporleder from Argentina and Mata'afa Keenan from Western Samoa. The ferocious defence that had quickly become a trademark of the Samoan game was not well received by Argentina, who believed their opponents were tackling illegally. The Pumas were leading 12–9 at one point, but they were eventually overpowered by Western Samoa in convincing fashion (35–12). It was a truly historic moment for the Pacific Island nation as they finished second in Pool C and qualified for a quarter-final showdown with Scotland.

Perhaps the most uneventful and least exciting pool of the tournament was Pool D, where France had the easiest draw of all the major title contenders. In their pool were Canada, Romania and Fiji – hardly stiff opposition for the 1987 finalists. Playing all of their matches on home soil, it seemed a formality that France would finish top of their group, but they were unexpectedly challenged right to the end against Canada in Agen before eventually winning 19–13. Canada had improved a lot between 1987 and 1991, with fullback Mark Wyatt and fly-half Gareth Rees steering their team to a first-ever appearance in the quarter-finals. Along with Wales in Pool C, Fiji also took a big fall from grace four years after they had qualified for the knockout stage in 1987. In 1991 they failed to win a single match and showed very little of the flamboyance that made them one of the most popular teams of the inaugural tournament. The mantle of popularity now sat with their Pacific Island neighbours Western Samoa, who were relishing their moment on the world stage.

The quarter-finals

Unlike 1987 when the quarter-finals took a predictable shape, with the more established rugby nations filling seven of the eight places, the 1991 tournament saw two emerging nations make their mark on the world stage. Western Samoa quite literally made their presence felt from the opening whistle in their Rugby World Cup debut against

Wales, and their march to the quarter-finals became one of the most memorable aspects of the tournament. So too the success of Canada came as quite a surprise to many pundits, and the fact that both these nations progressed to the knockout stage was a great advertisement for Rugby World Cup.

The first quarter-final took place at Murrayfield in Edinburgh, where Scotland hosted a Western Samoa team determined to capture another scalp from the more established rugby nations. Both Wales and Argentina were early casualties in Western Samoa's progress to the quarter-final stage, and such was the confidence among the team that they were not daunted by any prospect. Back in their homeland, a groundswell of support ensured 20,000+ people gathered at the rugby stadium in Apia – the capital city. Neutral fans across the United Kingdom were also feverishly following the progress of Western Samoa, but on this day their memorable run came to an end.

Although Scotland openly admitted prior to the match to being very wary of the unknown quality of their opponents, they seemed a lot better prepared than Wales and Argentina. On the back of an outstanding goal-kicking performance from fullback Gavin Hastings, who landed one penalty goal from almost 10 metres inside his own half, Scotland put in a commanding performance to end the Samoan dream. Flanker John Jeffrey crossed for two tries and right wing Tony Stanger scored another as the home side secured a convincing 28–6 victory. Western Samoa started with the same familiar sting in their defence that had brought them to the quarter-final stage, but an inability to penetrate in attack frustrated them. As the match played out and Scotland forced their way clear, the Samoan defence also subsided and their dream ended. It was an anti-climax of sorts for a team that would leave an indelible mark on the tournament, but the players were given a standing ovation as they walked around Murrayfield to thank their many fans.

Meanwhile, across the English Channel at the Parc des Princes in Paris, a highly anticipated showdown between two European heavy-weights was taking place. In the decade preceding the 1991 tournament, France and England had established an intense rivalry and this match was to be their first-ever contest on the Rugby World Cup stage – one that would seemingly hold the ultimate bragging rights in the ongoing battle for rugby supremacy between the two nations. France had enjoyed a healthy run of success against England for most of the 1980s, but the Geoff Cooke and Will Carling era brought more success for England and they were determined to consolidate their standing as the 1991 Five Nations Grand Slam champions from six months earlier.

The match promised a lot but failed to deliver after France changed their tactics from the instinctive and flamboyant style they were accustomed to, taking England on in the forwards. It was a strange tactic from their coach Daniel Dubroca and one that ultimately played right into the hands of the opposition. With arguably the best pack of forwards at the tournament, England were well placed to deal with France in tight, and they effectively starved *Les Bleus* of possession for extended periods of the match. England captain Will Carling crossed for a well-worked try and Rory Underwood finished another fine backline movement, while fullback Jonathan Webb was on target with the boot – converting one try and kicking three penalty goals. France gave a glimmer of hope when Jean-Baptiste Lafond crossed for a try; and fly-half Thierry Lacroix kept his team in touch with two penalty goals, but it was to be England's afternoon as *Les Bleus* made an undignified exit from the tournament in front of their home crowd.

'We should have played the way we know best, but we changed tactic and this was a very bad thing,' France centre Philippe Sella recalls. 'England had very strong forwards and we did too, but they were not used to playing like this in such a big match.'

The French players were also infuriated by some of refereeing decisions handed down by David Bishop and an incident allegedly occurred when the players were leaving the field, with Dubroca confronting the referee and prop Pascal Ondarts apparently threatening to throw a punch. The matter was denied by those allegedly involved and it was put to rest before becoming a major issue, but suspicions arose when Dubroca resigned as coach soon afterwards. Perhaps the saddest aspect of all though was that legendary fullback Serge Blanco was not given the send-off he so richly deserved. Blanco had played a prominent role in France making the inaugural final in 1987, and it seemed an unfair end to a glorious career, but his Rugby World Cup legacy would be assured by that last-minute try against Australia in the 1987 semi-final.

The third and fourth quarter-finals on the Sunday were not expected to spring any major surprises, with tournament favourites Australia taking on Ireland at Lansdowne Road in Dublin and New Zealand facing Canada in Lille. The two southern hemisphere heavyweights were expected to breeze past their opponents and set up a titanic showdown in the semi-finals, but Ireland did not lie down easily and came close to pulling off one of the biggest upsets in the history of the Rugby World Cup. Australia captain Nick Farr-Jones had returned to the team after apparently recovering from the knee injury he sustained in the pool match against Western Samoa, but he broke down again midway through the first half and fly-half Michael Lynagh was left to steer the ship. When Farr-Jones departed the Wallabies appeared in control after Campese crossed for the first of two tries he scored that afternoon. However, Ireland fly-half Ralph Keyes kicked two penalty goals to bring the scores level (6–6) at the interval, setting the match up for what would be a truly memorable second half.

Australia started the second period stronger, with another try to Campese and the accurate boot of Lynagh positioning the Wallabies for a probable victory. But every time the Wallabies went six points clear, Keyes would bring Ireland back into the match – landing a drop-goal and another penalty goal. Ireland looked to have pulled off an unlikely defeat when flanker Gordon Hamilton crashed over for a try five minutes from the end, but the Wallabies bounced back in injury time to claim one of the most remarkable victories in the history of the game.

The last of the four quarter-finals saw New Zealand advance after dismissing Canada in Lille, but the All Blacks were far from convincing. The first half showed glimpses of the New Zealand dominance that many pundits had expected at the 1991 tournament as they went to the break with an 18-point lead, yet the second period saw Canada outscore their more fancied opponents, and the doubts that had gathered over the All Blacks were reinforced as they stumbled to victory with no apparent urgency and a lack of conviction.

'We played really badly in the quarter-final against Canada,' New Zealand hooker Sean Fitzpatrick recalls. 'I still remember going back into the change room and someone came up to me and said: "Australia has just beaten Ireland in the last minute." I could see the look around the team was almost like "Oh, shit". That was a really defining moment and said a lot about where we were at that stage. Two months earlier, the Wallabies had thumped us in Sydney and the momentum was certainly with them ahead of the semi-final. They had improved a lot, and we hadn't.'

The semi-finals

With the benefit of hindsight, and given the disappointing form of France, victory over England in the opening match of the tournament did not do the All Blacks any favours with their declining form. While England had a loss to build on for their remaining pool games, before testing how much they had improved against France in a quarter-final, New Zealand was left with a false sense of security from victory over the reigning Five Nations champions and what Fitzpatrick admitted was a "softer" path to the semi-finals. The tournament draw is appropriately designed to accommodate those nations that win their pool with an easier run to the semi-finals, but on this occasion it impeded one of the few remaining opportunities the All Blacks had to remedy their dwindling campaign.

The first semi-final between Scotland and England in Edinburgh had historical significance, given that it was a showdown between the same two countries that first contested a rugby Test match back in 1871, but the most memorable aspect was how close the score remained rather than any great display from either side. England coach Geoff Cooke and his assistant Roger Uttley were forthright in their admission before the match that their side only need dominate territory and possession to come out at the right end of the score-board, and that is exactly what the team did. With the forward pack dominating the set pieces at lineout and scrum time through the likes of Paul Ackford and Wade Dooley, England had the steady boot of fly-half Rob Andrew to push the ball to the corners and keep Scotland under pressure. It was a simple and effective formula England mastered in their rise to the top of European rugby in the early 1990s, and one that would serve them well in this semi-final and beyond.

It was a credit to Scotland that they remained in the match despite an obvious lack of possession, and they were partly aided by England fullback Jonathan Webb having an off day with his goal kicking. Webb missed opportunities to put England clear and consolidate their obvious dominance in the territory stakes, while his Scotland counterpart Gavin Hastings slotted the few opportunities he had to keep the home side well in the match. At one point, after nearly an hour of play, Hastings even had an opportunity to kick Scotland into an unlikely 3-point lead going into the final 20 minutes, but he uncharacteristically failed with his attempt from almost in front of the posts. It would prove to be a telling miss from the same player who had played a vital role in Scotland's steady progress to the semi-finals.

From that moment forth England reverted back to their dominant game-plan through the forwards, strangling Scotland of all possession and waiting for that critical moment when a player of quality could deliver the finishing touch. That player on this day was Rob Andrew, who slotted the winning drop-goal for a 9–6 score line that would end Scotland's courageous run and put England into the 1991 Rugby World Cup final at Twickenham.

Their opponent would come from the highly anticipated second semi-final in Dublin between Australia and New Zealand. Test rugby between these two southern hemisphere rugby giants may not date back as far as the England v Scotland rivalry, but the traditions forged since they first faced each other in 1903 are well entrenched through the ongoing trans-Tasman battle to secure the Bledisloe Cup – a trophy widely regarded by rugby populations in both countries as second only to the Rugby World Cup in its significance. New Zealand held the Bledisloe Cup at the time, but form over the previous two seasons and during the earlier part of the tournament had Australia much better placed leading into the semi-final.

The All Blacks needed their full cavalry for this match that fell on a Sunday, but it wasn't to be, following the withdrawal of their star flanker Michael Jones – a devout Christian whose glittering Test career never included any rugby matches played on the day of the Sabbath. The absence of Jones on this day was felt from the opening whistle, as Australia turned on the most dominant first-half performance against New Zealand by any international team for decades. David Campese stole the show early on with a gliding run that saw him take the ball from fly-half near his right wing before angling left across the field, mesmerising the New Zealand backline defence, before sliding over in the left corner untouched after just seven minutes of play.

'They played very well and the game was almost over by half time,' Sean Fitzpatrick recalls. 'I can still see Campo running across in front of the posts. Here I was this old fat hooker trying to catch him, but there were also a number of backs that never laid a hand on him. They played very well and we had nothing to counter it really. It was probably a credit to Australia's defence in the end. They totally dominated early on and shut us out.'

After his earlier heroics, Campese played another key role in Australia's second try scored by Tim Horan, which will undoubtedly remain one of the finest-ever tries scored in Rugby World Cup competition. It all began with a deftly placed chip kick by Michael Lynagh over the top of the New Zealand backline defence. Campese then swooped through to gather the ball, stepping side-to-side to turn the cover defence inside-out before blindly passing a ball over his left shoulder to Tim Horan, who then beat two more cover defenders before running in for the try. The entire stadium at Lansdowne Road erupted in admiration, with a majority of the Irish crowd having now adopted Australia after Ireland lost to the Wallabies in the quarter-final a week before.

'We couldn't believe how well we went in the first 20 minutes,' Australia centre Tim Horan reflects. 'It probably gave us more of a shock than it gave the All Blacks. We came out, and I wouldn't say we didn't expect to win, but we thought the All Blacks would come at us a lot harder. We got really good momentum and Campo was going really well. Many people have said that opening period is the best 20 minutes of rugby they have ever seen. It was great to be a part of it.'

Australia were leading 13–0 after just 20 minutes and New Zealand were given no chance to make inroads into that lead until the second half. The All Blacks threw everything they could at the Wallabies after half time, but the defence of Australia was unyielding, particularly the back row of Willie Ofahengaue, Simon Poidevin and Troy Coker – the latter perhaps not given as much credit in the wash-up as he deserved. New Zealand fly-half Grant Fox slotted two penalty goals in the second half, but Lynagh extended the margin with another penalty goal of his own and the final score was 16–6. For once in their distinguished history, the All Blacks had been totally outplayed and Australia set up a showdown with England for rugby's ultimate prize.

Third place play-off

In 1987 the play-off for third place defied the widespread belief that it was a meaningless and superfluous fixture, with Wales defeating Australia in a close encounter in Rotorua. But four years later that perception was realised when New Zealand lined up against Scotland at Cardiff Arms Park in Wales. Both teams were quite obviously deflated as they took the field, and the sloppy fixture that followed was indicative of two groups of players competing with no great urgency.

The penultimate match of the 1991 tournament also saw the retirement of Scotland flankers John Jeffrey and Finlay Calder – two regular names on the Scotland team sheet from 1984 to 1991, and tremendous servants of the back row art. It seemed a shame the duo would not be given the send-off they deserved, but Jeffrey did have one parting shot in the pre-match rituals. When New Zealand performed the Haka, one of their adopted few – "Inga the winger" Tuigamala, originally from Western Samoa – left the team circle and tried to face-off with Jeffrey and wing Tony Stanger. Jeffrey simply smiled straight back at Tuigamala, adding some spice to the moment, but thankfully nothing unsavoury played out in the match.

Walter Little starred for New Zealand, scoring the try that sealed the match for the All Blacks just a few minutes from the end, while fullback Gavin Hastings topped off an outstanding month with a commanding performance for Scotland. It was a bittersweet end to the tournament for Little, who played against Italy in the pool stage but was then consistently overlooked by the New Zealand selectors for the other fixtures despite some rousing form when given an opportunity. For Hastings it almost seemed as if he was on a mission for redemption from the Scottish fans after missing a vital penalty goal against England in the quarter-final, but thankfully rugby fans are not so fickle in that regard and knew very well that Hastings was one of the main reasons Scotland had made it that far. It would have been easy for Scotland to concede to the All Blacks, but Hastings showed great desperation with several try-saving tackles and a brace of penalty goals that kept the final score respectable for the Scottish, the match finishing 13–6 to New Zealand.

The final

The stage was set at the home of English rugby – Twickenham – for yet another battle royal between the northern hemisphere and southern hemisphere to decide the Rugby World Cup champions for 1991. At lock the Wallabies had a young John Eales, who nervously pondered what lay ahead as he lined up against two of the most streetwise lock forwards in the game at that time – Paul Ackford and Wade Dooley.

'I was a 21-year-old playing in the Rugby World Cup final having to pinch myself at just being there at Twickenham. I was quite anxious knowing what we were about to face and I just looked across the field before kick off and there was our captain Nick Farr-Jones, who just gave me this big smile. It was as if to say: "This is going to be great, this is going to be great fun." That moment alone relaxed me and I was ready to go.'

Australia were the favourite based on their heroic quarter-final comeback that sank Ireland, and a near flawless performance against the All Blacks a week before. But England had made solid progress following the loss to New Zealand in the opening match of the tournament, and was well equipped up front with an experienced pack of forwards capable of dominating their less-travelled Australia counterparts. Why then the host nation deserted their strengths and resorted to different tactics only days out from the match will forever bewilder rugby pundits far and wide.

England had toured Australia three months earlier and played the usual forward-dominated game, for which the Wallabies appeared to have every answer, defeating the visitors comfortably (40–15) at the Sydney Football Stadium. That result still weighed heavily in the mind of England coach Geoff Cooke, who eventually came to a decision with his coaching staff to run the ball at Australia. It would prove to be a costly tactical error, and one England could not recover from by the time they eventually reverted back to the method that had served them so well.

'Campo probably hammed it up a bit too with his hand in the

media ahead of the match, almost daring them to play an open style,' Tim Horan recalls. 'In the first 10 or so minutes when we realised they were playing an open game, I remember looking across at Jason [Little] and we didn't need to say anything but we both knew they were really taking it to us. Will Carling was running the ball all the time, so too was Jeremy Guscott and Rory Underwood. They were all coming at us and I was thinking: "Gee ... how are we going to keep stopping this?".'

But stop it they did. Australia's defence held strong, as it had so well against New Zealand less than one week before, and England became visibly frustrated. Meanwhile one of the few attacking opportunities Australia had from a lineout close to England's line saw the Wallaby forward pack form a driving maul before props Ewen McKenzie and Tony Daly simultaneously dived over for the only try of the match. Daly was awarded the score, and with it Australia had one hand on The Webb Ellis Cup. Fly-half Rob Andrew recounts the disappointment all too well.

'History shows we made a big mistake. We should have stuck with the way we played the previous 18 months. In the course of three days we totally changed the way we planned to play the game, and you cannot expect to succeed in doing that for a Rugby World Cup final. If we'd focused on our normal game from the start, we would have been too strong for Australia. As it turned out we still nearly beat them playing what was in effect an alien game for us. It was a huge disappointment.'

England revised the new tactics at half time and seemingly reverted to the forward-dominated game for the second period, but by that time the Wallabies had their confidence buoyed by a quality defensive effort and the Webb Ellis Cup was on its way to Australia for the next four years.

FIVE MAGIC MEMORIES

New era dawned amid fading All Black dominance

The awarding of the UK broadcast rights for Rugby World Cup 1991 to the commercial television network ITV rather than public broadcaster the BBC, was the precursor to creating a totally new landscape for the marketing and commercial aspects of the tournament. The BBC had been the only rugby broadcaster across the UK for more than three decades, but with ITV offering three times more than the BBC contract in 1987, the 1991 organising committee had little choice but to go with ITV. In 1987 the BBC had screened just 28 hours of the tournament, and they had been slated in the press for not showing the best match – the semi-final between Australia and France. Such an event would not occur in 1991, with ITV committing to 100 hours of coverage, including the live telecast of 24 of the 32 games.

The broadcast rights in France were sold to Canal Plus and TF1 for a similar amount, and a series of agreements in other territories around the world pushed the cumulative television audience projection for the tournament to 2 billion people in 65 countries. Such wide exposure had sponsors queuing up to become part of it, and the event was expected to make a profit of £25 million – a massive improvement on the modest £120,000 profit from 1987. It was clear the face of the game was changing forever.

The opening match of the 1991 tournament brought a global television audience that rugby previously could only have dreamed of, but sadly the game was not worthy of the build-up it had earned. Both teams made plenty of errors and referee Jim Fleming from Scotland blew 27 penalties to ensure there was a distinct lack of continuity. The tension an opening match commands was certainly there, but there was an obvious unwillingness from either side to veer away from a conservative game-plan.

'It probably wasn't a great game for the fans and that was a bit of a shame really after all the build-up it had in the press,' New Zealand hooker Sean Fitzpatrick recalls. 'We had clear instructions on what to do to win and it was never going to be pretty when England tried to play a similar game. I remember there were a lot of scrums [24] and penalties [27], and thankfully a lot of them seemed to go our way.'

The All Blacks eventually prevailed 18–12, and it was their star player from 1987 – flanker Michael Jones – who delivered the only try of the match from a well-worked back row move. In the circumstances, however, England had done remarkably well to be leading at half time and stay in the match given that they were on the wrong end of an unusually large penalty and scrum count. On the surface it was another victory to the All Blacks, yet beneath the result was some indication that New Zealand were nowhere near the force they had been in 1987 and for three years thereafter. The ruthless forward dominance they had shown in every match four years earlier was now a distant memory, and the fear of facing the All Blacks was no longer prevalent in their opponents. The opening match marked the dawn of a new era for rugby's commercial landscape, and despite their victory it also became apparent that New Zealand's dominance was fading. The ensuing tournament would not be a one-horse race. It was there for the taking.

Western Samoa packed a powerful punch

Making their Rugby World Cup debut, Western Samoa brought a physical presence to the 1991 tournament that had rarely been felt before in northern hemisphere rugby. Situated in the Polynesian region of the Pacific Ocean, approximately half way between New Zealand and Hawaii, the country relies on agriculture to employ two- thirds of its entire workforce and that same industry accounts for 90 per cent of its total exports. The country has inhabitants with strong links to the land, and the pride they have for their nation is akin to a lioness protecting her cubs. With a total population of just 180,000 spread across a little less than 3,000 square kilometres, there is not much to it geographically, but any team who lines up against Western Samoa on a rugby pitch certainly knows they will be sorer for it the next day.

The national rugby team is full of powerfully built Polynesian men with warrior instinct and frames tailor-made for contact sports. Such was the recognition Rugby World Cup 1991 brought to the country, that it didn't take long before other football codes caught on. The National Football League (NFL) in the United States now has approximately 40 ethnic Samoans in its ranks, and in the past decade there has been an influx of Samoans on the rather theatrical professional wrestling scene in America – most notably Dwayne "The Rock" Johnson, who has now even starred in many Hollywood action films.

Western Samoa were an unknown quantity coming into the 1991 tournament, and Wales had the unfortunate task of lining up against them first at Cardiff Arms Park. The ferocity of the Samoan tackling put three Welsh players out of the match. Tony Clement, Phil May and Richie Collins were the casualties and their team-mates endured a battering in front of their home fans. What made the loss harder for Wales to bear was a television replay confirming that the winning try to Western Samoa was not in fact a try. But this match was played long before the days of the Television Match Official (TMO), and it was hard for anyone watching to deny that Western Samoa deserved to win. For all the pain it caused Wales, they had done a huge favour to those teams that would later line up against Western Samoa, the next of which was Australia.

'Everyone really stood up to take notice of Western Samoa after they beat Wales, and it was good that we had something to gauge them by,' recalls Wallabies fly-half Michael Lynagh. 'We played them in atrocious weather conditions and it was a big test for our forward pack. There were some really big hits and we lost Nick [Farr-Jones] early on. It took us a while to find our way after that but we eventually kicked three penalties to their one to make it through in the end. We were all pretty sore for a while after that match.'

Western Samoa left a lasting impression on the 1991 tournament after just two games, and their run continued when they comfortably defeated Argentina to qualify for a quarter-final against Scotland. That is where the dream run would finally end. Despite the loss however, rugged prop forward and captain, Peter Fatialofa – a piano remover by day – took great pride in leading his team around Murrayfield to thank their many adoring fans at the ground and around the world. It was a memorable campaign that would command widespread respect from the international sporting community, at the same time bringing a state of sheer delight to a proud rugby nation.

Houdini escape for Australia broke Irish hearts

'Cometh the hour, cometh the man,' Australia coach Bob Dwyer says while describing the actions demonstrated by his vice-captain Michael Lynagh in the dying minutes of the quarter-final against Ireland. 'Noddy', as Lynagh became more affectionately known by his team-mates and fans, was never really noted for being a great leader. He was without doubt one of the most talented and precise goal-kicking fly-halves of his generation, but the mantle of leadership was usually left to scrum-half Nick Farr-Jones – the esteemed captain of Australia at the time. On this occasion, however, Farr-Jones was forced to leave the field early in the match after aggravating a knee injury sustained against Western Samoa earlier in the tournament.

With five minutes remaining and the score 15–12 to Australia, Ireland decided to take a chance and run from a scrum in their own half before putting a kick into the Wallabies' territory. Irish wing Jack Clarke won the foot race to the ball and somehow managed to offload a pass to flanker Gordon Hamilton, who ran a considerable distance before sliding over for the try that brought remarkable scenes of celebration at Lansdowne Road and across the Emerald Isle. Part of the crowd could not be contained, running on to the pitch to congratulate their flanker for what seemed all but certain to be the match-winning score. However, the match was far from over and stand-in Australia captain Lynagh marshalled his troops.

'We came together and I tried to calm everyone down as much as possible, assuring them we still had enough time to win the match. There wasn't much time to think too long about it and that probably helped in the end. I set out what was really just a straightforward plan,' Lynagh recalls. 'We were to go long from the kick-off. Ireland would then kick it out and give us the throw into the lineout. From the lineout we would run the same move that had worked for us earlier in the match and thankfully it all eventually fell into place.'

The winning try did not come straight from that lineout, and Australia was forced to pack down another scrum. The conservative option from there would have been to go for a drop-goal to level the match and take it into extra time, but Lynagh called the same backline move yet again – cut two, loop. This time around, outside centre Jason Little was illegally tackled without the ball but he still managed to maintain possession and deliver a pass to David Campese who was dragged down just short of the line. In the process of falling to the ground Campese popped a pass back inside, which found Lynagh coming through in support. Five minutes earlier Lansdowne Road was in raptures, now it was stunned into silence as Lynagh crashed over in the corner to pull off one of the greatest escapes modern rugby has ever seen. Australia were through to the semi-finals by the barest of margins.

'If Noddy had gone into the game as captain, he probably wouldn't have produced the same leadership the moment demanded of him because he would have thought his way through it,' Dwyer said. 'Very interestingly, the reserves, who were sitting in front of me, turned around and said, "We have enough time, we just have to do it right." That try put into picture the philosophy that the team had developed. If you focus on performance, and doing the small things well, results will follow.'

Farr-Jones and Lynagh steered as Campese reigned supreme

Michael Lynagh certainly made his mark in the quarter-final against Ireland, but the influence of Australia's captain Nick Farr-Jones was one that stretched well beyond the playing surface. While he was restricted from taking part in most of the pool matches and the quarter-final against Ireland, Farr-Jones had played a significant part in the revitalisation of the Wallabies prior to 1991. He had been there four years earlier when Australia lost to France in the semi-final, and his astute thought process was highly valued by the coach Bob Dwyer during the renaissance that followed 1987.

'Nick is one of the great leaders. One of his massive advantages is his capacity to know when to turn the switch on and off,' Dwyer said. 'He also had this ability to recognise what different individuals in the team needed. A couple of blokes might want to go out for a beer, and another bloke might want someone to go to church with him ... Nick equally understood all of those things.'

One of the rookies in the Wallaby ranks at that time, who also praised Farr-Jones' leadership qualities, was centre Tim Horan.

'Nick was, along with Michael Lynagh, one of the most influential people I ever played with. He put a lot of time in off the field. As a captain, he got around to the whole squad and took the younger players under his wing,' Horan said. 'A year or so before the 1991 tournament, he and I would go down to the Dapto dogs at Wollongong on a Thursday night. We chatted about different things and you gain a lot of respect from doing that.'

Before a ball had been kicked at the 1991 tournament, Farr-Jones was faced with an issue that could have derailed Australia's campaign and his steady influence resolved an internal dispute that could have ended a lot worse. Just prior to the Wallabies leaving Australia, David Campese released his book *On A Wing and a Prayer*, in which he was critical of the way Michael Lynagh had played in a match against France in 1990. Campese didn't play in the match, and the Wallabies had won it convincingly, but he accused Lynagh of kicking away too much possession, even going as far as saying he was happy not to be wearing the gold jersey on that day. It was a tactless attack from Campese, and Farr-Jones was left to put out the fire between two of his key players.

'I knew it would be awkward but I insisted the three of us sit down to break bread,' Farr-Jones later wrote in his *Story of the Rugby World Cup* pictorial. 'After 15 minutes of muted chat I realised that while the two would never be the best of buddies, they had at least restored a working relationship.'

Some simple mediation from Farr-Jones prevented what could have been disastrous for the Wallabies. Both Lynagh and Campese played equally vital roles in the ensuing weeks, between them accumulating most of Australia's points – Lynagh as goal-kicker, Campese as try-scorer. His mouth became renowned for such controversy, but Campese's dazzling running mesmerised defences throughout as he went on to be named player of the 1991 tournament. Quite ironically, Lynagh was often the team-mate to deliver the final kick or pass for some of Campese's most memorable touches. Their restored link proved crucial for Australia.

England tactics costly after Wallabies emerged triumphant

Before a ball had been passed in the final between England and Australia, no rugby pundit could deny that the standout player from the 1991 tournament was David Campese. Fans of any sport traditionally don't take kindly to opinionated players who cannot justify their views with solid performances, but as far as the old adage goes, Campese was one who more often than not 'talked the talk and walked the walk'.

'I was only new to the squad at the time, and it was all a big show to me,' recalls John Eales. 'I remember one of the England papers said Will Carling is going to be the first millionaire out of rugby ... then Campo came out the next day and said, "It's too late, I'm already a millionaire out of rugby" after he'd been playing in Italy for so many years.'

Campese always liked his opposition to think he was one step ahead, and he was always one to enjoy playing the mind games. It came as no surprise then that he barbed some sections of the English rugby media ahead of the 1991 final, orchestrating a campaign that seemingly dared England to go against the strength of their forward-dominated game and run the ball at Australia. But Wallabies coach Bob Dwyer remains unconvinced it was a single media crusade that altered England's approach.

'Campo always liked to add his spin before a match, but that theory has grown a lot of legs since the event and I find it hard to believe England would have let that alone influence them. They are the most pragmatic of rugby nations in the world,' Dwyer said. 'It was more likely a combination of events. They played their traditional game against us in Sydney earlier that year and we dished them up, so maybe they thought they would try something different.'

England was without doubt a more experienced team man-for-man, particularly in the forward pack, so it came as a big surprise to the sell-out crowd of 62,500 at Twickenham and millions watching around the world when they ran the ball during the first half, effectively tiring their larger players. Australia defended courageously and they were rewarded with a 9–3 half-time lead. Despite more possession and territory overall, England simply couldn't penetrate the defensive shield set in place by the Wallabies. It was enough for England coach Geoff Cook to alter his approach once more at the break, and the home team seemed to revert to what had served them so well in the past.

'They came out and went back into their comfort zone a bit – a more forward-dominating game – and that probably hurt them in reverse because our forwards had gained confidence by then,' Australia centre Tim Horan recalls. 'England became a bit fearful of the outcome and went back to playing for field position. Our forwards really stood up when that happened in the second half, and that is what really won it for us.'

England was outclassed tactically, which ultimately saw them outplayed physically and mentally. For all the controversy a potentially deliberate knockdown from Campese brought when Rory Underwood looked on his way to scoring a try, the desperate and heroic defence of Australia was perhaps best illustrated by moments like that when an unknown gangly lock forward named John Eales chased down and tackled England fly-half Rob Andrew after he had broken clear. Australia's defence stood strong throughout the second half and they eventually triumphed 12–6 before savouring their special moment in the traditional surrounds of the Twickenham changing rooms.

'It was probably around 9 o'clock at night before we got out of the famous baths and actually left the ground,' recalls Horan. 'It was great boarding the team bus to see friends and family all sharing in the moment. My mum was sitting on Nick Farr-Jones' lap because there weren't enough seats, and the Cup was being passed around to everyone. Not sure if it would ever happen like that anymore ... everything about it [Rugby World Cup] was so raw and new at the time. It was an amazing feeling.'

6

The interim years: 1991–1995

FOR ALL THAT AUSTRALIA'S victory was worth in 1991, there was that nagging sense of incompleteness given that South Africa – one of the strongest teams in world rugby – had again been absent from the tournament. Fortunately for Australia, they had a chance to consolidate their Rugby World Cup triumph and put the icing on the cake with a one-off Test against the Springboks in 1992. South Africa had been restored to the world sporting fold following the release of Nelson Mandela from prison in 1990 and the subsequent disintegration of apartheid. A final hurdle awaited the world champion Wallabies.

In what would prove to be a very famous and historic few weeks for rugby in South Africa during August 1992, the Mandela-led African National Congress (ANC) supported both New Zealand and Australia touring the country for one-off Tests over consecutive weeks based on three conditions. The ANC firstly requested a one-minute silence take place for previous victims of racial violence, secondly that the 'white' national anthem *Die Stem* not be played and thirdly that the old flag (largely seen as symbolic of the apartheid regime) not be flown. Sadly for South Africa, all three conditions of support the ANC set out were intentionally violated for the match against the All Blacks in Johannesburg – as a way of the white regime flexing its muscle. The obvious reaction would have been for the ANC to withdraw its support of the Test against the Wallabies in Cape Town a week later, but quick mediation together with some large concessions made by the selfless Mandela himself ensured the ANC's support would remain for what would be the first Test between Australia and South Africa for more than 20 years. The results were not what the Springboks wanted, however, as they lost both matches to their southern hemisphere rivals.

South Africa had very little contact with the world rugby scene between 1970 and 1992, but they always kept together a good national team to contest matches against touring provincial and international teams that would travel to South Africa despite widespread protests against the apartheid regime. New Zealand toured twice in the 1970s and the Springboks enjoyed 7 victories from 10 matches contested between the two countries during the 1970s and early 1980s. The All Blacks actually won the 1981 series in New Zealand, but South Africa had enjoyed a healthy run of success prior to that.

Following the 1981 series, the two sides did not play again until the 1992 fixture at Ellis Park in Johannesburg. New Zealand narrowly triumphed (27–24) in that match, and in what was the first of four losses from five Tests that year South Africa struggled to find success in their first season back in the international fold.

'It was amazing. I never thought I would tour South Africa as an All Black, and then to go there as the first team back following the end to apartheid and win was just fantastic,' Sean Fitzpatrick recalls. 'I remember arriving at the airport and there was about three or four thousand people there to meet us at one o'clock in the morning. It had been so long since we had been there.'

South Africa were in no way disgraced by a 3-point loss to the All Blacks in their first Test back, and the focus soon turned to Australia travelling one week behind the All Blacks. It was the scalp of the world champion Wallabies that the Springboks wanted more than anything that year.

'When we went to South Africa, every newspaper and every sign was saying, "you are not world champions until you beat us", so that was a massive motivation,' recalls Bob Dwyer. 'Those motivations can sometimes distract you from your real course of action, but we felt like we had a responsibility for the validity of the Rugby World Cup.'

The many fans that flocked to the airport and training venues to meet the All Blacks and the Wallabies were not always pleasant, often holding placards with firm messages summing up their feelings that were perhaps even more negatively amplified by the years of isolation South Africa rugby had endured.

'All the comments when we arrived in South Africa were along the lines of "you are not World Champions until you beat the Springboks" and "Naas will kick your ass" [referring to their great goal-kicking fly-half Naas Botha],' recalls Australia centre Tim Horan. 'It was a big challenge for us. We didn't know what to expect from the Springboks. They had been out of the world fold for the best part of 20 years or so, and to then beat them on their home soil was very special. Things go through your mind like maybe we shouldn't be world champions if we don't beat them, but in the end we beat them well. It was very pleasing to walk out of that country and say: "Ok, now we've beaten everyone in the world".'

Australia scored a 23-point victory (26–3) over the Springboks one week after New Zealand had escaped with a 3-point victory. Suddenly South Africa, back on the world rugby stage for the first time in more than a decade, were on a downward slide early on. Victory over France in Lyon – the first match for the Springboks outside of South Africa for 11 years – brought some solace, but two Test losses after that made 1992 a year that Springbok rugby would rather forget, with just one victory from five Tests.

The following year showed some improvement as they emerged with a 50 per cent win record from seven Tests – three wins, a draw and three losses – against France, Australia and Argentina, but consistency proved hard to attain and there was still some distance to go before the Springboks would be contending with the top tier rugby nations again. The year that fortunes changed for South Africa rugby was 1994, when they toured New Zealand for a three-Test series. The Springboks had not toured New Zealand for 13 years and they were keen to perform well. The first Test of the series was eventually an 8-point victory to the All Blacks, but the Springboks were gallant in defeat and bounced back before narrowly losing the second Test by just four points. The series was gone after that, but Springbok pride was at stake in the third Test and the visitors fought bravely to secure an 18–18 draw in Auckland. It was that performance in the third Test which gave South Africa renewed belief that they were again competitive with the top nations in the world. The Springboks went on from that point to win 15 consecutive Test matches, which included claiming The Webb Ellis Cup in 1995.

The return of South Africa was the final piece of the puzzle for world rugby to prosper in a new era for the game, and the inevitable shift towards professionalism was slowly taking shape. In 1992, the Super Six competition, which included provincial teams from Australia, New Zealand and Fiji, was launched in Oceania. The competition became very popular and in the next year it was expanded to include 10 teams, some of which were from South Africa. From that the Super10 rugby championship was born and the early days of the southern hemisphere rugby alliance between South Africa, New Zealand and Australia Rugby (SANZAR) had begun. Although that southern hemisphere alliance was not officially formed until 1995, when Rupert Murdoch's News Limited announced plans to stage the inaugural Super12 and Tri-Nations tournaments in 1996, the Super10 competition was the precursor to what emerged in the professional era.

The progression towards professionalism in the northern hemisphere was certainly not as rapid as it was in the southern hemisphere, but the way rugby was restructured at club level in England with the formation of the Courage Leagues in 1987 made the game far more competitive. The introduction of tiered leagues, with promotion and relegation, forced clubs to dedicate more time and resources. This in turn placed more demands on players, who were still trying to maintain normal day jobs, and the move towards a more professional structure was inevitable. The IRB remained steadfast in its aim to keep rugby amateur at all levels, despite increasing pressure from many European clubs and the southern hemisphere unions, but the restructuring of the club game across England had already propelled the move towards professionalism. In 1994 the English Premiership expanded further to include a full schedule of home and away matches, and the 1994/95 season was the first to be telecast live on Sky Sports. Henceforth the game of rugby entered a new age across the globe, and the diehard amateur traditionalists were dragged kicking and screaming towards the professional era.

As South Africa slowly found their way after a lengthy absence from world rugby, the emergence of the Big Five as the top tier of rugby nations was becoming even more clearly defined. New

Zealand, Australia and South Africa established themselves early on, while England and France became the only two teams from the northern hemisphere capable of consistently challenging the southern hemisphere heavyweights. Wales showed signs of improvement when they broke through to win the Five Nations Championship in 1994, but they could not be considered part of the top mix without a victory against any major southern hemisphere opponent during 1991 and 1995.

Having secured back-to-back Grand Slams in 1991 and 1992, England were still the dominant force in northern hemisphere rugby during the early part of the 1990s. Had it not been for a handful of inexplicable narrow losses to lesser-rated opposition in 1993 (Ireland and Wales) and 1994 (Ireland), England could have secured an unprecedented five consecutive Grand Slams. But it was those inconsistencies that prevented the Will Carling-led team from reaching the great heights that England would attain under Martin Johnson a decade later.

'England had an outstanding group of players at their disposal from 1990 to 1995, but what that team couldn't do – that Martin Johnson and his team 10 years later did – was to win consistently against any opposition, on any ground, in any country,' Bob Dwyer explains. 'England stumbled too often in the Carling era when they really shouldn't have. One week they would beat France and two weeks later they would lose to a lowly-rated Ireland. Quite often they would be narrow losses, but they were losses nonetheless and that fine line is the difference between a really good team and a great team.'

England secured another Five Nations Grand Slam in 1995, just a few months ahead of the Rugby World Cup tournament in South Africa, and they would again lead the northern hemisphere assault to claim The Webb Ellis Cup that year. France were always a threat, but they too suffered from a lack of winning consistently and history was not kind to *Les Bleus* being recognised as a team that could maintain the steady run of success required to win the Rugby World Cup.

Away from the playing surface during the early 1990s, the IRB made a significant change to rugby's scoring system in an effort to encourage teams to score tries. Critics had for many years argued that the value of a try was not justified given that a penalty goal and a drop-goal were both worth three points. In 1992 the value of a try

was increased from four points to five points, and the change immediately had the desired effect as more tries were scored across all
levels of competition. The most encouraging reflection of this change
came three years later with the large increase of total tries scored at
Rugby World Cup 1995 compared to the 1991 tournament. In 1991
there was a total of 148 tries, and in 1995 that number increased to
187. While the composition of teams in each of the pools was somewhat different, the total number of teams competing in the 1995
tournament was exactly the same as in 1991. From a spectator
perspective, and given the direction the game was now heading, it was
widely regarded as a positive change.

There were some significant changes to the game throughout the
interim period between the 1991 and 1995 tournaments, but none
more so than the reinstatement of South Africa to international rugby
and their subsequent hosting of Rugby World Cup 1995. For more
than two decades the Springboks were left out in the cold as their
government upheld an apartheid regime that isolated their country,
but the early 1990s brought welcome change to South Africa and
world rugby was finally restored to its full compliment. The stage was
set for a truly memorable showpiece to take place in a country determined to shake off its infamously racist tag, and propagate a new
perception to the world as the 'Rainbow Nation' – a term first used
in 1994 by the Anglican Archbishop of Cape Town, Desmond Tutu,
and later carried forth as a symbolic phrase by the ANC and President
Nelson Mandela for Rugby World Cup 1995. In a literal sense the
phrase represented the six rainbow-like colours on the national flag,
but far beyond that it was emblematic of the newly integrated and
multicultural South Africa – united as one.

7

Rugby World Cup 1995: the tournament

THE RUGBY WORLD CUP concept was well and truly entrenched as an institution within the modern game by 1995, but the subsequent onset of professionalism gained momentum at a staggering rate and with it came the threat of a new power struggle to control the future of the game. The greatest fear those early critics of the Rugby World Cup concept had was that the staging of such a tournament would forge an unavoidable path to make rugby a professional sport, and that fear was now a stark reality. The efforts of Sir Nicholas Shehadie and Dick Littlejohn to save rugby by establishing a Rugby World Cup tournament that remained in the control of rugby people were complete, but the game faced a renewed threat as the third tournament dawned in South Africa.

Beyond the control of the IRB, a potential coup of sorts was taking shape in the months ahead of Rugby World Cup 1995. Former Australia player and esteemed businessman Ross Turnbull, together with lawyer Geoff Levy, formed a group of powerful legal folk who devised a grand plan to make rugby a professional code across the globe. Their scheme became known as World Rugby Corporation (WRC) and it had the backing of Australian media mogul Kerry Packer – the same entrepreneur who had transformed cricket in the late 1970s with the introduction of One-Day Internationals. The concept also had the backing of another notable Australian entrepreneur, John Singleton, and the plan was to secretly sign up leading players from the major rugby countries before introducing the concept to the traditional rugby authorities. There are blurred accounts of exactly how many leading players the WRC actually managed to sign, but some countries seemed to be more aware of the concept than others.

'We made a conscious decision not to make a big deal of it with our players in the hope that they would not become distracted,' recalls Australia coach Bob Dwyer. 'But it seemed like all of the other teams knew. England knew because one of the players who joined their squad late because of injury said, "What's going on? All of the boys have told me about this professional thing and they have all signed up," and that is when it started to click with me that WRC had made a lot more progress worldwide than what we had originally thought. South Africa also knew about it and they had all signed. So too had the French. It was a real takeover in the making.'

The proposed plan to 'secretly' sign many leading players unbeknown to the traditional rugby authorities had progressed for the WRC, but that progress did not escape the minds of some leading administrators aligned with the established southern hemisphere unions. The official formation of the SANZAR (South Africa New Zealand Australia Rugby) alliance in 1995 was one of the first major steps to countering the challenges posed by the WRC movement, but it had not been formed as a direct result of that alone. In addition to the threat posed by the WRC, the newly-formed Super League in Australia and Britain was transforming rugby league and the money being promised to prospective players in the rival code was extraordinary. Suddenly rugby was facing a double-barrelled threat: firstly from a select few of its own kind looking to commercialise and profit from what was still a strictly amateur sport; and secondly from the renewed momentum of the century-old menace of rugby league luring rugby's most talented players with lucrative contracts.

Despite widespread concern from most unions about the impending threats to the future of rugby, the IRB was loath to act quickly for fear of generating any negative publicity around the game before the flagship event was scheduled to kick off in South Africa. Something had to be done from the top down, but instead of making any major announcements that could potentially destabilise the game before Rugby World Cup 1995, it was left to the respective unions to counter any immediate threats in the best manner possible before the international governing body would be forced to take the inevitable step of declaring the game professional after the tournament was over.

'I spoke to Bob [Dwyer] at length about the situation before our opening match against South Africa and we decided it was something the team didn't really need to know about at that stage because it would only be a distraction,' recalls Australia's 1995 captain Michael Lynagh. 'But Jason Little and Tim Horan were two major targets for Super League, so we felt we had an obligation to rugby to tell them about what was happening with WRC and the likely move to professionalism. We managed it fairly well in the end, and as it turned out they informed us that Super League had also been targeting Damien Smith and Daniel Herbert – so we decided to tell them too and left it at that.'

The threat posed by Super League was a more pressing concern in Australia because of the strong professional foothold rugby league had in that region, and the sums of money being promised to players were something rugby union could never dream of countering as an amateur sport. The emergence of pay television in Australia around the same time also played a vital part in what eventually unfolded. The Foxtel network owned by Rupert Murdoch, and OptusVision owned by rival media magnate Kerry Packer, became locked in a battle to secure a sports product that would generate monthly subscriptions for their respective pay-TV services. As a result of that Murdoch initiated the Super League concept, throwing rugby league into chaos, and almost tripling players' salaries overnight. The amateur code could not offer its leading players anywhere near enough incentive to counter the lucrative figures being offered by Super League. Thus the game of rugby union at the top level would potentially be vacuumed into non-existence by rugby league in Australia if the move to professionalism did not take place sooner rather than later.

The SANZAR alliance was the first to publicly counter the latest challenges facing international rugby. The Super League concept did pose the greatest threat to rugby in Australia, and to a lesser extent in Britain, but the knock-on effect of that concept directly impacted the onset of professionalism internationally for the amateur code. What happened next was a rather ironic twist, with the SANZAR alliance securing financial backing from Rupert Murdoch's News Corporation (the same media organisation that was backing Super League) to stage two major southern hemisphere rugby tournaments commencing in 1996 – the Super12 and Tri-Nations – in a deal worth US$555 million over 10 years. The agreement, which came on the eve of the Rugby World Cup final in 1995, was a welcome announcement for the future of the game. Inevitably this deal forced the IRB to eventually break the shackles and declare rugby a professional sport, but more importantly it ensured the game would not disintegrate at the hands of a rival code in one of its most competitive regions. The other internal challenge of sorts that was being posed by the WRC movement would in turn also be dealt with after the 1995 tournament, but that threat was also reduced considerably by the SANZAR announcement.

The pool stage

For all the progress the WRC allegedly made behind closed doors ahead of Rugby World Cup 1995 and the threat that Super League also posed, thankfully neither tarnished what would become one of the most significant sporting events of the twentieth century. South Africa had finally emerged from isolation to rejoin the world sporting fold and their beloved Springboks were at last given a chance to compete on rugby's greatest stage.

The 1995 tournament was contested by 16 teams and had the same format as the previous two tournaments. The eight quarter-finalists from 1991 were given automatic qualification, as was the host nation South Africa. The other seven places were contested by a regional qualifying process involving 43 nations around the world. Japan, Argentina, Italy, Romania and Wales somewhat expectedly ended up filling five of those seven places. But from Oceania there was a surprise result as Tonga filled the last position in the draw for that region, meaning Fiji would miss out on the tournament for the first time, and in Africa the Ivory Coast claimed the final qualifying position ahead of Zimbabwe. The United States also missed qualification for the first time after losing out to Argentina for the one position up for grabs in the Americas region.

It was the first time the Rugby World Cup would take place in one country, and the 32 matches were played in nine different stadiums across South Africa. When the tournament was first awarded to South Africa the intention was to use 14 stadiums throughout the country, but those plans had to be revised when facilities at some stadiums were later assessed. There was also still a high security risk in some areas. The Pool A matches were played across three cities – Cape Town, Port Elizabeth and Stellenbosch – while the other three pools each had two venues: Pool B – Durban and East London; Pool C – Johannesburg and Bloemfontein; and Pool D – Pretoria and Rustenburg.

Rugby World Cup 1995: the pools and order they finished

Pool A	Pool B	Pool C	Pool D
South Africa	England	New Zealand	France
Australia	Western Samoa	Ireland	Scotland
Canada	Italy	Wales	Tonga
Romania	Argentina	Japan	Ivory Coast

The opening match of the 1995 tournament between South Africa and reigning world champions Australia in Cape Town promised plenty, and the ceremony preceding the match set the tone for what would be a bright and joyful month for South African sport. Colours were abundant in representation of the Rainbow Nation theme that had gathered so much momentum, and when President Nelson Mandela graced the field the entire stadium stood in applause – black and white united as one in their support of an institution that had been so white-dominated for years. South Africa's slogan for the event was, rather fittingly, 'One team, one nation'.

'It was an unbelievable atmosphere. None of us had experienced anything like that before [because the country had been isolated for so long] and when we ran out on the field you knew all of the emotion around the whole occasion extended beyond the ground and across the whole country,' recalls South Africa's 1995 captain Francois Pienaar.

The emotional charge within the stadium eventually proved to have a positive effect on the home team, while Australia appeared tired after what was later revealed by their coach and many senior players to be over-training in the days leading up to the match. The Wallabies enjoyed a good share of possession as their forwards dominated the lineout, but the Springboks managed to offset that by keeping the upper hand in the territory stakes through the steady boot of fly-half Joel Stransky, who eventually scored 22 of the 27 points the Springboks totalled for the match. For all they lacked, Australia broke through for the opening try to Lynagh after 32 minutes and looked as though they might take a 13–9 lead into half time. But the Springboks bounced back with a beautifully worked try to Pieter Hendricks, who outpaced an ageing David Campese on his way to a memorable score that deservedly gave the home team a 14–13 lead at the break.

The second half was one-way traffic as the Springboks sniffed an opportunity at half time to upset their more fancied opponents before doing everything to capitalise on it. Stransky played a commanding role as his team maintained their dominance in the territory stakes, and his second half contribution of a try, penalty goal and drop-goal effectively put the game beyond Australia's reach. Hooker Phil Kearns crashed over for a try to bring some respectability to the scoreboard for the Wallabies, but victory on this emotional day was for the Springboks, who had defied the odds for a 27–18 triumph, and their reward was a much easier run through the knockout phase of the tournament.

'The flaw in our plan was that South Africa had planned to win the first match and we had planned to win the tournament,' recalls Australia centre Tim Horan, who had to watch from the stands while at the end of a 13-month recovery from a knee injury that threatened to end his career. 'Had we won that match against South Africa we would have been put at a better side of the draw compared to where we ended up, so it was a case of being on the back foot from the start.'

For all that the opening match provided, the other games in Pool A played out with no major surprises. Canada proved to be tougher than expected opposition before losing to both Australia (27–11) and South Africa (20–0), while Romania may have been the lightweights in the pool but they did manage to finish with a relatively respectable losing score (21–8) against the Springboks in Cape Town. On the back of no overly convincing results apart from the opening victory against Australia, some pundits thought South Africa didn't have the imposing dominance required to advance to a final, but in reflection their captain Francois Pienaar says it was all part of the plan that widely respected coach Kitch Christie and team manager Morne du Plesis had devised.

'For the rest of the pool games beyond that opening match we maintained a very simple game plan to dominate the scrums, and just come out of those games with the victory,' Pienaar said. 'We had no intentions of going out there and playing open running rugby; we just wanted to get through with the win and move on.'

It was perhaps the most uninventive method of any Rugby World Cup champions to date, but it proved to be very effective. Meanwhile Australia was still not functioning in the dominant fashion many expected they would after such a solid year leading into the tournament. Not only did Canada test the Wallabies with a physical match in Port Elizabeth, the Rugby World Cup minnows Romania protected their line for a full 28 minutes in Stellenbosch before Australia crossed for their first try. The Wallabies eventually found their way after a clumsy half hour to register a healthy defeat (42–3), but the alarm bells were ringing. The reigning champions were looking less and less like a worthy contender in their pursuit to defend the world title.

Pool B was the most tightly contested of any group in the preliminary stages of the 1995 tournament. England, coming off the back of another Five Nations Grand Slam leading into a Rugby World Cup, eventually topped the standings, but they did so in less than convincing fashion. They conceded two tries and failed to cross the Argentina line in their opening match in Durban, with the boot of fly-half Rob Andrew salvaging the day as he capitalised on ill discipline from the South Americans by slotting six penalty goals and two drop-goals to snatch a narrow (24–18) victory. England had the advantage of being the only team in Pool B to contest all of their matches at one venue in Durban, but they still managed to make hard work of their pool fixtures against opposition they were expected to easily overcome. Their second game was against Italy and, while they managed to cross the line twice and match the *Azzurri* for tries scored, it was again left to the reliable boot of Andrew to kick five penalty goals that would ultimately prove to be the difference between the two sides (27–20).

Western Samoa had another big impact on the world stage in 1995, and their opening Pool B match against a full-strength Italy commanded respect as they secured a comfortable victory (42–18) at the Basil Kenyon Stadium in East London. It was the two wings for the Pacific Island nation – the aptly named George Harder, and Brian Lima, nicknamed 'the chiropractor' for his bone-crunching defence – who wreaked havoc on their opposition, with Harder scoring a memorable hat-trick of tries and Lima crossing for two to compliment his customary strong showing in defence. Western Samoa backed up their victory over Italy with a come-from-behind win over Argentina that was the most exciting match of the pool. The Pumas had been leading 26–13 with only 10 minutes remaining, but Western Samoa rallied back to win the match (32–26) and set up a clash with England that would determine first place in Pool B. Western Samoa had the propensity to play as though their lives depended on it in Rugby World Cup competition, and perhaps it was that reputation which gave England enough incentive to produce their finest performance of the pool stage in their last preliminary match. Without the dependable services of fly-half Rob Andrew, England knew they had to turn the corner and start scoring tries.

'We hadn't played well in our first two pool matches, but we turned that around a little in the game against Western Samoa,' recalls England lock Martin Johnson. 'We tightened things up a lot in the forwards and managed to cross for a few tries, which was relieving after scoring none against Argentina and only two against Italy.'

England eventually defeated Western Samoa comfortably (44–22) to claim first place in Pool B and set up a quarter-final showdown with Australia – a repeat of the Rugby World Cup 1991 final. Western Samoa fought gallantly at the end of the match and put on two memorable late tries to finish with a flurry, but victory was too far from their reach with time running out on the clock and a quarter-final match against South Africa beckoned.

When fans were not watching their own team in action during the 1995 tournament, most eyes of the rugby world became transfixed on Pool C as the New Zealand revelation that was Jonah Lomu entered the game in devastating fashion. The All Blacks already had an intimidating aura that most opposing teams struggled to overcome and now they added something that had never been seen before in international rugby. At six foot five inches (196cm) tall, and weighing in at almost 18 stone (119kg), Lomu would have been considered a large forward at that time, but his mammoth frame lined up on the left wing to terrorise every opposition bar one in Rugby World Cup 1995. World rugby had not witnessed anything like it before, and it came as a surprise to later learn that Lomu was fortunate to make the New Zealand squad.

'Jonah was actually quite lucky to be there. He was sent away to the New Zealand sevens [7-a-side rugby] team because he wasn't up to speed during all of the fitness camps ahead of the tournament,' recalls New Zealand captain Sean Fitzpatrick. 'Laurie Mains [New Zealand coach] told him, "Sorry mate, you're off to play for the New Zealand 7-a-side team, and Eric Rush will play in the final trial". I remember on the Friday afternoon during one of the final practice runs before our last trial, Rushie was running down the left wing and pulled his hamstring. They then put a call out for Jonah to come back and join the team and he played a massive part in the final trial.'

The All Blacks were quick to add Lomu into their mix after a dominating display in that final trial, but with little international experience under his belt much of world was still not aware of the secret weapon New Zealand had within their squad. That was until May 27, 1995 at Ellis Park in Johannesburg, when Ireland was handed the unenviable task of containing Lomu for their opening match in Pool C. The 20-year-old announced his entry on the world stage with a devastating display, scoring two tries and playing a big part in two others as the All Blacks defeated Ireland 43–19. But the proud men in green put up a brave fight and as the tournament unfolded it later became clear how good Ireland's performance was in comparison to most teams that faced New Zealand in 1995.

Wales, to their credit, managed to keep Lomu try-less when they played the All Blacks in Johannesburg four days after Ireland stood tall, but the attention he commanded of the Welsh defence created more opportunities for the skilful selection of players in black jerseys around him to capitalise on, for what was another comfortable New Zealand victory (34–9). After that win, All Blacks coach Laurie Mains rested his top line players against Japan, but their Asian opponents were spared nothing as a second-string New Zealand side racked up a record score (145–17) without the services of their rampaging wing. Centre Mark Ellis starred with a record six tries and fly-half Simon Culhane polished off the emphatic victory with a record personal haul of 45 points, which included one try and 20 conversions.

With New Zealand having well and truly secured first place in Pool C, it was left to Wales and Ireland to battle it out in Johannesburg to determine the runner-up. The match was not a great spectacle but the final score was very close, with Ireland scraping home by just one point (24–23) to secure the second quarter-final berth. Wales rallied well in the latter part of the match, but for the second consecutive time they did not make it to the final eight of the Rugby World Cup. The win meant Ireland was through to the knockout stage, but neither side produced anything that would have given any of the major nations any cause for concern.

In stark contrast, the battle for supremacy in Pool D was a quality showdown between two northern hemisphere nations who had provided the first-ever draw in Rugby World Cup competition back in 1987. Scotland and France gave the inaugural event a much-needed boost when they fought out a thrilling encounter in Christchurch, and the two sides produced another memorable match eight years later at Loftus Versfeld in Pretoria. Just as they had in 1987, in 1995 Scotland enjoyed early ascendancy and took a 13–3 lead to the break. Two further penalty goals to Gavin Hastings after half time ensured Scotland maintained their lead well into the final 10 minutes. But France were far from finished and with the steady boot of Thierry Lacroix, who kicked five penalties from five attempts, they remained in touch. Then came the moment *Les Bleus* broke the hearts of every Scottish fan with a breathtaking counter-attack that covered much of the playing surface before Emile Ntamack scored in the corner. Lacroix converted from the sideline to keep his flawless kicking record for the match intact, and France secured a narrow 22–19 victory that left Scotland to face New Zealand in a quarter-final.

Beyond that single close result, Pool D had taken a predictable shape as Tonga and the tournament newcomers Ivory Coast provided little resistance to France and Scotland. But on the very same day that Scotland and France fought out the most entertaining pool match of Rugby World Cup 1995, a tragic event struck the tournament during the third minute of the Pool D match between Tonga and Ivory Coast in Rustenburg. The unfortunate victim was Ivory Coast wing Max Brito, who was badly injured after an awkward tackle that resulted in many Tonga players falling on top of him. Brito was taken to the intensive care unit of a hospital in Pretoria, where he was operated on to have the fourth and fifth vertebrae in his neck stabilised, but tragically he was left paralysed from the neck down. In an instant, all that was good from the first two weeks paled to insignificance as the rugby world stopped to realise the very real danger a full contact sport brings. Thankfully the Rugby World Cup 1995 organising committee had taken measures to ensure players from all countries were insured for such a tragedy, and to this day the international governing body should be commended in its continued support for Brito and his family.

The quarter-finals

The first quarter-final between France and Ireland took place at King's Park Stadium in front of a meagre crowd of 18,000 – a far cry from the 50,000 capacity that usually fill the stands for an international match in Durban. Perhaps given that Ireland had not beaten France since 1983, most fans thought it was a given that the men in green would yield easily to *Les Bleus*. Both teams were not short of talent, however, and the match promised more than previous encounters between the two, with a semi-final berth up for grabs – but what unfolded was far from being a great advertisement for rugby. In what could only be described as nervous and clumsy tendencies on both sides, the first hour showed very little conviction that either team deserved to go any further in the tournament. France had ample backline talent to spark an attack with the likes of Philippe Sella, Emile Ntamack and Philippe Saint-Andre, and Ireland with Brendan Mullin and Simon Geoghegan were also not short of game-breakers, yet both sides chose forward-dominated tactics that starved their backlines of any ball. When France did decide to use their backs, fly-half Christophe Deylaud often kicked the ball away or botched a drop-goal attempt. And so it was left to the big men up front to battle it out. Ireland tried hard, but the French pack led by Abdel Benazzi ultimately prevailed. Fly-half Thierry Lacroix kicked eight penalty goals, and Saint-Andre and Ntamack crossed for a try each to give *Les Bleus* a comfortable 36–12 victory and a place in the semi-finals one week later.

France's opponent for that semi-final came from what was an eventful quarter-final between host nation South Africa and Western Samoa. The Springboks were treading cautiously after an ugly brawl in their Pool A match against Canada, which ultimately saw two South Africa players – hooker James Dalton and wing Pieter Hendriks – banned from taking any further part in the tournament. But Western Samoa held nothing back and applied their customary fierceness on a Springboks team that had their discipline tested to the full extent. Fullback André Joubert was on the end of a rugged tackle from his opposite number Mike Umaga less than 20 minutes into the match, and perhaps most indicative of the intensity was that South Africa used all four of their replacements for the first time in the tournament. In the end it was a credit to the host nation that they kept their emotions in check amid stiff resistance and provocation from the Pacific Islanders before prevailing comfortably (42–14) to secure a semi-final place.

'We had played Western Samoa on the same ground in a warm-up match before the tournament and we put 60 points on them, so we were fairly comfortable going into that quarter-final,' recalls Springbok captain Francois Pienaar. 'But we really had to be careful with our discipline after the incident against Canada and that was quite a challenge because Western Samoa obviously came at us very hard.'

For all that Western Samoa could muster with their trademark sturdy defence, they could not contain South Africa wing Chester Williams, who scored four tries in what turned out to be his first match of the tournament. Williams was the only black player in South Africa's squad, and his smiling face had become the billboard pin-up for the tournament. Ironically, he had succumbed to a hamstring injury in the warm-up match against Western Samoa and had to be replaced by Pieter Hendriks. But with Hendriks now suspended, there was a vacancy, and Williams was invited to rejoin the squad having recovered from his injury. There had been some criticism as to whether a country should be permitted to replace a suspended player, but very few were willing to press hard on this issue given that it allowed South Africa to reintroduce the player who had been the face of their campaign.

The third quarter-final between England and Australia at Newlands in Cape Town promised the most of all four matches – and it delivered. England skipped to an early lead of 13–3 running into the wind, and looked most promising throughout the opening half, but the boot of fly-half Michael Lynagh kept Australia in touch with a brace of penalty goals before a deftly placed highball to the corner found an airborne Damian Smith, who took the ball above his opposing wing before falling over for a memorable try early in the second half. Australia then seemed to gain some ascendancy and through the boot of Lynagh they managed to go into the lead twice, but his opposite number Rob Andrew held firm with two penalty goals that drew England level on two separate occasions – the second of which locked the scores up at 22–22 with only minutes remaining.

The moment of truth came for England after they were awarded a penalty by New Zealand referee David Bishop. Mike Catt found the touchline and from the resulting lineout well inside Australia's territory, towering lock Martin Bayfield pulled down a crucial lineout ball before his forward pack drove the maul on through Dean Richards. With fly-half Andrew positioned some 20 metres behind the maul, scrum-half Dewi Morris delivered a perfectly placed pass for the England fly-half to strike the killer blow with a 45-metre drop-goal that put reigning champions Australia out of the tournament.

'We probably hadn't progressed as far as we should have,' recalls Australia centre Tim Horan. 'We had a similar game plan to what worked for us in 1991 and England knew what to expect. They were also a bit hungrier than us for victory in that match, and in the end they probably deserved it more than we did.'

The last of the quarter-finals saw Scotland face up to the might of New Zealand at Loftus Versfeld in Pretoria. The euphoria surrounding Jonah Lomu was building further as the tournament progressed and now it was Scotland's turn to try and contain the rampaging wing. It didn't take long for Lomu to strike, as he ran half the length of the field before setting up a try for Walter Little in the fifth minute. Lomu had dismissed Scott Hastings and another would-be tackler twice in his run that resulted in Little's try, and he left Gavin Hastings wanting later in the first half before crossing for his own try. For all the dominance New Zealand showed, however, they only had a 17–9 lead at the break. Gavin Hastings had again kept Scotland in touch with his reliable goal kicking. The second half opened up and it was New Zealand who particularly benefited from playing with more width, as Frank Bunce and Andrew Mehrtens crossed for tries, while Walter Little claimed a second and captain Sean Fitzpatrick crossed for the only try by a forward. Scotland were in no way disgraced, scoring three tries of their own – two to lock Doddie Weir and one to their captain and fullback Gavin Hastings, making his last appearance on the international stage. New Zealand progressed (48–30) to a semi-final against England, but the number of points conceded was very uncharacteristic for the All Blacks.

The semi-finals

With pre-tournament favourites Australia now eliminated from the mix, New Zealand became the bookies' choice for the title on the back of the Jonah Lomu tidal-wave that was now sweeping through the rugby world. The first of the semi-finals was contested between host nation South Africa and France at a soaked King's Park Stadium in Durban. Kick-off was originally scheduled for 3pm, but the rain was so torrential in the usually sun-drenched city that drainage of the ground seemed non-existent and the surface resembled a lake rather than a rugby pitch. The bureau of meteorology advised that the rain was due to stop at 4pm, so the officials made a decision to delay the kick-off, but despite the weather showing some respite there was very little improvement to the playing surface. Referee Derek Bevan from Wales was left to decide whether to proceed, and after long consultation with both captains it was determined the match would kick off 90 minutes after it had been originally scheduled to start.

The match was a predictably scrappy encounter, but a decisive moment came during the first half when Springboks fullback André Joubert swooped on a poor kick from France fly-half Christophe Deylaud that failed to find touch. Joubert, wearing a glove borrowed from the Irish game of hurling to protect a broken bone in his hand from the quarter-final against Western Samoa, scooped up the ball and started an attack that resulted in a crucial try to flanker Ruben Kruger. What made it a particularly vital score was that if the match was abandoned because of the weather, and neither team had scored a try, victory would have been awarded to the team with the best disciplinary record. South Africa would have lost in those circumstances because two of their players had been banned after the brawl against Canada, but the host nation could breathe a temporary sigh of relief because that rule would not be invoked unless France scored a try of their own.

That elusive try never came for France despite many gallant attempts to cross South Africa's line in the second half. Towering lock Abdel Beanazzi came closest to scoring, but he was ruled to have come up short of the try-line by referee Derek Bevan. *Les Bleus* continued to mount pressure on the Springboks and they were positioned well for a pushover try in the final minutes, but South Africa's forward pack withstood the barrage of late threats to hold on for a narrow (19–15) victory.

Some commentators later suggested France were on the receiving end of some very unlucky decisions from referee Bevan, particularly in the final minutes when a penalty try seemed imminent with the Springboks scrum collapsing. Those same tongues were wagging even more when Bevan was presented with a gold watch at the end of the tournament by controversial South Africa rugby president Dr Louis Luyt for being 'the most wonderful referee in the world' – all this coming despite such acclaim usually being reserved for the referee in charge of the final, who was Ed Morrison from England.

The second semi-final between England and New Zealand in Johannesburg didn't have anywhere near the same inclement weather to deal with as the first semi-final, but there was a storm of sorts brewing on the left wing for the All Blacks in the form of none other than Jonah Lomu. The 20-year-old of Tongan heritage had by now drawn attention from around the globe, including the United States where American football scouts were sizing him up as a potential recruit for the National Football League (NFL). Lomu was an overnight success, quickly establishing himself as rugby's first international superstar, and commanding attention for the 15-man code that could have only been dreamed of one month earlier.

New Zealand had lost to England in 1993 at Twickenham on the back of a dominant forward display from the home team. Giving due credit to England for that previous victory, the All Blacks structured a game plan for the 1995 semi-final that would veer away from the forward-dominated contest that England thrived on. From the opening kick-off, the plan began in earnest as Andrew Mehrtens steered the ball to the opposite side of the field where none of England's forwards were placed. The action forced a collision between Will Carling and Tony Underwood, and straight away England was on the back foot. Within 10 minutes of the opening whistle, they were effectively out of the Rugby World Cup. Lomu crossed for his first of four tries in the second minute and from the resulting restart the All Blacks put together a sublime 80-metre team movement that ended with flanker Josh Kronfeld crossing for a memorable try in the same corner where Lomu had crossed just moments before.

'Jonah Lomu was a phenomenon. He was just so huge, so quick and it was great for the fans to watch him destroy teams,' recalls England lock Martin Johnson. 'It wasn't good being on the receiving end though. I remember the first try in 1995 when he ran over Mike Catt and I thought, "It's going to be a long, long day".'

It proved to be a long day indeed for England. Indicative of how shocked they were by the opening period, their usually dependable fly-half Rob Andrew missed a penalty goal and drop-goal attempt that could have given his team some hope against the New Zealand barrage. Instead, his opposite number Mehrtens extended the lead with a penalty goal. Then it was the turn of dynamic back row forward Zinzan Brooke to demonstrate his variety of skills with a successful drop-goal from almost 50 metres out on the angle. Suddenly England was 20–0 down and the pain didn't stop there. Lomu crossed for two more tries before the half-time break and not long after that the All Blacks built up a 35-point lead. To their credit, England brought some respectability to the final score (45–29), with two tries to Carling and another to Rory Underwood, but no one could deny New Zealand their victory. The All Black machine was primed and ready to stake their claim for a second world title, and their new superstar was ready to lead the charge.

Third place play-off

The play-off for the Rugby World Cup bronze medal is constantly criticised and 1995 was no exception, especially after the disappointment that eventuated between New Zealand and Scotland for the penultimate match of the 1991 tournament. In an attempt to bring some meaning to the fixture in 1995, the international governing body decided to award the winner automatic qualification to Rugby World Cup 1999. Previously the qualification process for the following tournament only applied to those teams that failed to make it as far as the quarter-finals, but now all teams that finished outside the top three would be forced to qualify for the 1999 event.

The move was a desperate attempt to give a meaningless fixture some value, but it failed to inspire either side to any great heights. The first half produced nothing except a penalty goal from each side, and the early part of the second period began with the same exchange as the teams moved to 6–6 after 50 minutes of play. France fly-half/centre Thierry Lacroix had an outstanding tournament with the boot, scoring 112 points from six matches – the highest individual tally for any player at Rugby World Cup 1995. His reliable boot gave *Les Bleus* the lead midway through the second half, but the 45,000 fans at Loftus Versfeld became increasingly agitated with the lack of urgency from either side.

'It was very hard to play this game after losing the semi-final against South Africa,' recalls France legend Philippe Sella. 'We had probably best chance ever to win the tournament with this team, after beating New Zealand and many other very good teams, but we lost a very close match to South Africa and it was very hard to play after that.'

The match was in desperate need of some spark and it finally came in the form of Emile Ntamack. The tall French wing took the ball from a Rob Andrew restart and awoke the crowd from its slumber with an impressive run before linking with Laurent Cabannes who made a fine run of his own before delivering the ball to Philippe Saint-Andre. France's captain took delight in running in for the try that put his team clear to set up the victory. *Les Bleus* added another try through Olivier Roumat soon after, and suddenly for England the euphoria of defeating Australia in a quarter-final less than two weeks before was a distant memory as they succumbed to consecutive losses for the first time since 1991. The match was forgettable on most fronts, but for France it was a welcome victory that marked an end to a losing streak against England that extended back to 1988.

The final

South Africa hosted a remarkable tournament in 1995, but sitting behind the colourful Rainbow Nation image being projected to the world were some contentious incidents that later threatened to tarnish the success of the event. South Africa rugby president Dr Louis Luyt deserved applause for his part in the organisation of a fantastic event, but he was also a controversial figure who attracted widespread criticism after the tournament, not only for his embarrassing part in a post-match function after the final, where he claimed South Africa were the first 'real' world champions, but also his antics throughout. Luyt controlled the game with an iron fist both during the apartheid era and immediately after, and his methods of operating were often questioned by the international media.

New Zealand captain Sean Fitzpatrick recalls the words of Luyt when he arrived at Ellis Park for the final: 'Louis Luyt said to me when he arrived there, "Sean, I did everything I could to ensure the Boks would play the All Blacks in the final and now we are here".'

It will never be known exactly what Luyt was referring to when he confidently proclaimed he had done 'everything' to ensure the Boks would play the All Blacks in the final, but the mere suggestion does not sit well alongside the deed of publicly awarding referee Derek Bevan a gold watch after the Welshman controlled South Africa's narrow and widely controversial semi-final victory over France. Bevan later expressed to the *Guardian* in London his surprise and discomfort at the gesture: 'It came out of the blue: I have no idea why he singled me out. It could be misconstrued, and if that is the case, it leaves a bitter taste.'

Another incident that quite literally left a bitter taste on the success of this remarkable event came during the week ahead of the final, when 20 of the 26 players in the New Zealand squad woke up with symptoms of food poisoning just days before the final. Fitzpatrick describes the intimidating atmosphere that surrounded the team hotel leading into the final, with fans stalking the players and parading signs while dishing out plenty of taunting remarks in an attempt to unsettle the All Blacks.

'The fans out the front were all part of it really and we had to just live with that, but we would go down to eat lunch in the hotel and these beautiful ladies would also come up to you and say, "The Bokka are going to kill you",' Fitzpatrick recalls. 'By Thursday we thought we needed a break from it all, so we came home from training and decided to have lunch in this private room. The next morning most of the squad had diarrhoea and vomiting. By the time it came to match day, there were still about five players struggling. Whether it was something that was planned or not we will never know.'

One year after the event, All Blacks coach Laurie Mains revealed he had hired a private investigator who established that a hotel waitress known only as 'Susie' was paid to spike the tea and coffee that the team was drinking. The waitress allegedly used an odourless and tasteless local herb known as 'Indian Trick', which is said to bring on symptoms similar to food poisoning. However, it must also be noted that the allegations by Mains did come just prior to the launch of his autobiography, which doesn't weigh well on the New Zealand side of the argument. All that is known for sure is that 20 New Zealand players were struck down with a mysterious illness. Whether it was the result of a deliberate act the rugby world will perhaps never know, but thankfully the incident did not take too much polish off the unforgettable climax that would unfold.

The setting for the 1995 final at Ellis Park in Johannesburg was not dissimilar to the hotel surrounds the All Blacks had become used to during the week leading up to it.

'When we were arriving at the stadium, there was about 15 guys surrounding the bus in Springboks jerseys and they had these broomsticks and on the end they had Lomu hanging as a rag doll with No11 on the back, and a noose around his neck,' Fitzpatrick recalls. 'It was an unbelievable experience as these fans started rocking the bus as we were driving down this road.'

The 1995 Rugby World Cup final was an intense spectacle between two proud rugby nations who had consistently produced the two best teams in world rugby throughout the twentieth century. But while South Africa was only just reasserting itself as a major rugby power after a period of isolation, New Zealand had adopted a new expansive style of play that was remarkably different to the clinical method they were renowned for.

In 1995 the All Blacks had a lighter and more dynamic forward pack than usual to suit their strategy of moving the ball wide to

Lomu. But when the 1995 final tightened up, the hulking Springboks forward pack was able to gain the ascendancy on their opponents and provide a steady platform upon which South Africa fly-half Joel Stransky could play a match-winning role. Stransky slotted two penalty goals and a drop-goal in the first half, while his opposite number Andrew Mehrtens kicked two penalty goals, giving the Springboks a 9–6 lead at the break. The second half proved to be an even tighter contest than the first, and Mehrtens replied with a drop-goal to bring the scores level midway through the second period. Neither team was giving an inch in the war of attrition up front. With the clock winding down into the final minute of regulation time, Mehrtens attempted another drop-goal that narrowly missed. With scores locked at 9–9, the 1995 tournament became the first Rugby World Cup final decided in injury time.

Mehrtens stepped up in the first period of extra time to give New Zealand a 12–9 lead with a beautifully struck long-range penalty goal, and suddenly the momentum seemed to sway slightly in favour of the All Blacks. They had been by far the most outstanding team of the tournament, and the result would be justified, but then came a twist of fate that would throw the form guide out the window and apply the finishing touch to a truly remarkable four weeks for the newly reformed South Africa. Stransky levelled the scores again with another penalty goal, and as both forward packs trudged exhaustedly around the field waiting for an opportunity to arise, the Springboks fly-half applied the decisive blow with a famous drop-goal from 30 metres out to take the score to 15–12 with seven minutes remaining. It was enough to inspire South Africa to hold on to the lead in the dying minutes before securing a remarkable victory.

'It was just a phenomenal game. We could have won it before full time and New Zealand could have won it before full time and then we went into extra time,' recalls Springboks captain Francois Pienaar. 'Playing at home definitely was an advantage. The crowd support was unreal and gave us that extra edge needed for a close match like that. In the end it was enough to win the Rugby World Cup.'

As the full-time whistle sounded, scenes of ecstatic pandemonium vibrated throughout Ellis Park Stadium and across the entire nation of South Africa. The Springboks had pulled off the unthinkable against their more fancied opponents, who were left in a state of shock by the fact that their opportunity to secure the title had now gone.

And so came the lasting image of President Nelson Mandela dressed in a Springboks number six jersey presenting The Webb Ellis Cup to Francois Pienaar. Not only will it forever be a crowning moment for South Africa sport, but more importantly a symbolic moment for a nation reborn after the tarnish of apartheid. The Springboks, so long an institution emblematic of white supremacy, now had black and white citizens celebrating together for the first time – one team, one nation.

FIVE MAGIC MEMORIES

Opening upset gave Springboks impetus to build campaign

Not only were Australia the reigning Rugby World Cup champions leading into the opening match against South Africa, they were also unbeaten for more than 12 months prior to the tournament and therefore clear favourites to defend the title. But the home advantage proved vital as the Springboks leaped into their first Rugby World Cup campaign with the backing of an entire population of 43 million for the first time.

South Africa were clearly inspired by the colourful opening ceremony and fanatical support that reverberated throughout Newlands Stadium in Cape Town as President Nelson Mandela opened the event. The Springboks showed their intentions early with menacing defensive pressure on the Wallabies. The occasion eventually appeared to overawe their more fancied opponents, with Australia fly-half and captain Michael Lynagh not his usual steadying influence and young scrum-half George Gregan consistently under pressure from his opposite number Joost van der Westhuizen and the hulking Springbok forward pack.

South Africa fly-half Joel Stransky, who was a third-choice selection only a few months before the tournament and considered lucky to be a part of the final squad, became an instant feature of the strategy employed by the Springboks. As the Wallabies became increasingly unsettled, Stransky controlled the game with an impeccable kicking display to lead the host nation to an unlikely upset.

'We targeted that game for a while and knew we had to have a great start for our campaign to be successful,' recalls Stransky. 'I was lucky to score a lot of the points, but those opportunities were created by guys like Joost and the forwards, particularly our back row led by Francois Pienaar. Ruben Kruger had a great game too, and Francois was completely inspirational as our leader. He worked particularly well with Kitch Christie [coach] and Morne du Plesis [manager]. They seemed to always have a plan together and everything was always 100 per cent well organised from start to finish.'

The winner of the opening match was ultimately granted a run to the final that would not include overcoming the All Blacks and the loser was left to contemplate a quarter-final against England and, if they survived that, a semi-final against New Zealand. Australia was left with the more challenging path and one that would ultimately prove too difficult for a squad that later admitted to being over-trained and carrying too many injured players into the tournament.

'We were in South Africa for what was about 10 days before the opening game, and we were training for long periods of time,' recalls Australia's 1995 captain Michael Lynagh. 'I've always thought you should train for an hour and make it really slick as opposed to training for three hours, and we were training for long periods day after day. We were also carrying a few injured players – Tim Horan, David Wilson and Rod McCall – and in hindsight that really wasn't a great way to go into the tournament.'

Horan was a spectator that day as he continued his recovery from a lengthy rehabilitation for a knee injury that had sidelined him for more than a year.

'I had only just made the squad because I was carrying a knee injury, and I remember watching from the stands in Cape Town. After we had beaten the Springboks so well there only a couple of years before that, it was hard to take watching on as a spectator. You could see the joy on all of the Springbok players, and our guys were really disappointed knowing that things would be a lot tougher after that.'

South Africa coach Kitch Christie was adamant that his team prevail in the opening match so they could take the 'high road' to the final. His command was granted and the Springboks had the impetus to build their first-ever quest for rugby's ultimate prize.

Quarter-final revenge for England after four years of waiting

From the moment Australia lost the opening match to South Africa, a quarter-final clash with England was inevitable. In what was a highly anticipated rematch of the 1991 final, there was no dominance displayed by either side in their earlier pool matches to suggest who should be the rightful favourite, although the Wallabies were given that status and still remained favourites for the title on the back of their impressive year prior to the tournament. Form usually means little when these two sides meet, and so it was in Cape Town on June 11, 1995.

There were nine surviving members of Australia's team that had triumphed in the final at Twickenham four years earlier, and six England players were still carrying unpleasant recollections of that day. England had to wait a long time before the opportunity came for revenge, with no match contested between the two countries since the 1991 final, but the painful memories were still fresh enough to inspire a memorable triumph.

In what was a see-sawing affair that had England in a prime position early on as they enjoyed a 10-point cushion, Australia would not lie down and through the dependable right boot of fly-half Michael Lynagh they remained in touch. Lynagh had produced mixed form during the pool stages, but his kicking radar returned at the right time to keep the Wallabies in the quarter-final. Early in the second period, he produced a pinpoint highball to the left corner where Damien Smith performed some fine acrobatics before scoring a try that brought the scores level. From that point, Lynagh and his opposite number Rob Andrew went blow-for-blow with penalty goals. Then in the dying minutes when the match seemed destined for extra time it was Andrew who gave his team the final say with a 45-metre drop-goal that ended Australia's campaign while exacting some revenge for the loss England endured in the 1991 final.

'We were euphoric in the dressing room afterwards, and it was a fantastic night,' Rob Andrew told BBC Radio after the triumph. 'In some ways it felt like we had won the World Cup. We were so disappointed in 1991, and for those of us who played in that final I guess it was some kind of revenge.'

England celebrated long and hard after that quarter-final triumph and Australia was left to pick up the pieces of a failed campaign. John Eales, who had played an outstanding match for Australia, was reduced to tears in the dressing room as the Wallabies pondered what went wrong.

'Had we beaten England we probably wouldn't have gone any further anyway and probably didn't really deserve to, but it was hard to take for a lot of us after being at the top of the game since 1991,' recalls Lynagh.

As though the quarter-final loss wasn't enough for the Wallabies to endure, many of the team members say it was the plane trip home that brought the most painful memory of all. Their return flight from Johannesburg to Sydney had a stopover in Perth, and while the players exited the passenger lounge they were forced to watch a large group of Australia supporters dressed in green and gold setting off to South Africa with no team to support. It was an agonising experience for all players involved. Australia's pain was England's gain, as the mother country gained revenge after four long years of waiting.

Springbok courage came to the fore amid semi-final deluge

The city of Durban in the South African province of Natal is usually a sun-drenched coastal setting that rarely experiences any rain in winter, but the skies opened up like never before when South Africa lined up against France for the first semi-final in 1995. The match would most likely have been abandoned had it not been a Rugby World Cup tournament, but postponing the fixture was an option that officials and tournament organisers were not willing to take given the many logistical issues it would have created with transport and security.

In what was an ugly reminder of South Africa's past, a group of black women were seen sweeping excess water from the field in a desperate effort to improve the playing surface after kick-off was delayed. Thankfully some white men soon assisted the women to prevent what would have been a public relations nightmare for tournament organisers.

Kick-off eventually took place some 90 minutes later than scheduled after referee Derek Bevan consulted the team captains, who were both very keen for the match to proceed. South Africa played the smartest strategy during the early stages and eventually broke through for a crucial try to Ruben Kruger after a tremendous kick-return from fullback André Joubert. The try gave the Springboks a half-time lead, but France remained in touch with their opponents through the ever-reliable boot of Thierry Lacroix.

Then through the dominant presence of their back row forwards – Abdel Benazzi, Laurent Cabannes and Marc Cecillon – France threw everything at South Africa in the second half in search of a try. Emile Ntamack crossed the line for what seemed a score, but he was called back for a knock-on; Benazzi looked to have crossed for the match-winner near full time, but he was judged to have come up just short of the line. The Springboks were then forced to endure four reset scrums five metres out from their line as France went for the pushover try, but South Africa's forward pack stood tall for a memorable victory (19–15) and a place in the Rugby World Cup final.

'They really pushed us and I actually thought Benazzi scored, but when everyone became untangled his arm was between the try-line and the ball and it was marginal,' recalls 1995 Springboks captain Francois Pienaar. 'We were very lucky. He could have scored and we probably wouldn't have had enough time to hit back. There was three minutes left on the clock, but in the end our scrum held firm and we won.'

Later Pienaar described in his autobiography *Rainbow Warrior* how Springboks lock Kobus Wiese had taken hold of his tight-head prop and life-long friend Balie Swart just before South Africa's last heroic defence of their line and shouted: 'You can go forward, you can go up, you can go down and you can go under … but you are not coming back!'

The actions of Wiese epitomised the courage that the Springboks showed amid a barrage of French attacks in the Durban deluge. Some critics later suggested *Les Bleus* were unfortunate not to be awarded a penalty try in the dying minutes, with South Africa thought to be deliberately collapsing the scrum, but few can deny the Springboks showed outstanding courage to protect their line on the flooded King's Park surface. The defensive platform successfully endured its sternest test of the tournament, and it seemed that destiny had chosen South Africa for a memorable finale in Johannesburg.

All Blacks altered traditional tactics to unleash superstar

New Zealand rugby endured one of its least successful periods of the modern era in 1994, and their form leading into the 1995 tournament was patchy for a team that had consistently produced outstanding results. France won a series on New Zealand soil for the first time in 1994 and despite a narrow series victory over the Springboks the All Blacks also lost the Bledisloe Cup to Australia. Unbeknown to many however, including some New Zealand players and fans, they had an international superstar sitting within their wings who would transform the spectacle of rugby like never before.

'I always remember Jonah Lomu when he first played in a 1995 All Black trial,' recalls New Zealand back row legend Zinzan Brooke. 'I was playing open-side flanker against him that day and no one knew about him. They were all saying "You've got to watch out for this guy. He's six foot five inches, and he can run 100m real fast". We thought it was just another one of those stories, but I found out pretty quickly in that match that he was no ordinary winger when he ran onto an inside ball from Andrew Mehrtens. I went to hit him and he just flicked me off with such ease.'

Rugby World Cup 1995 became the stage upon which 20-year-old Lomu would be unleashed to the international sporting world. So vital was this new player to New Zealand's tactics that their previously tight and clinical structure was displaced by an expansive style that used the width of the field to best effect. This game plan was carried out in an attempt to deliver Lomu the ball with as much space as possible, so he could then use his size and speed to devastating consequence on the opposition.

'There has never been a player like Jonah Lomu before 1995 and there has never been a player like Jonah Lomu since 1995,' says former Australia coach Bob Dwyer. 'No player has ever been able to dominate defences like him. He even very quickly became a recognised figure in the United States during that tournament, which is just unheard of given the insularity of that country and its sports.'

On the back of the Lomu tornado, New Zealand forged a devastating path throughout the preliminary stages of the 1995 tournament before carrying their same game-plan into the knockout stage. It was in the semi-final against England that Lomu was at his devastating best, scoring four tries and setting up two others, as the All Blacks put the game beyond doubt after just 20 minutes. For all the warning they had of New Zealand's tactics to spread the ball wide to their try-scoring machine, England were desperately unprepared for the semi-final onslaught. Like so many teams before them, England was steam-rollered into submission by Lomu as the All Blacks marched into the final.

Lomu had become an international superstar within a matter of weeks, and in a period when rugby in South Africa was enjoying a new groundswell of support from the black population, the game now had an international superstar of Tongan origin commanding worldwide attention. The Lomu phenomenon teamed with the on-field success of the host nation provided the perfect script for the 1995 tournament to unfold. The ideal finale now beckoned for South Africa, but a man mountain and a classy team of All Blacks around him still stood firmly between the Springboks and Rugby World Cup glory.

Swarming Springboks startled All Blacks in historic finale

South Africa's victory over France in the drenched Durban semi-final was built on a profound defensive effort, and the Springboks team management eventually tailored another defensive game-plan for the final against New Zealand despite early consideration of a different approach.

'We changed on the initial strategy where we wanted to play open and running rugby and speed the pace up to the extent that it would almost become frenetic. It just didn't work within the team, so we had to sit back down on the Wednesday and reconsider it,' recalls Francois Pienaar. 'The game plan we had been training for on the Monday and Tuesday was just not comfortable for all the players. So then we started to strategise on defence and how to contain Lomu as well as containing all of their other very good players. By the Thursday we were training in a way we were comfortable with, and in a way we thought we could win the match.'

South Africa's defensive strategy for the final was dependant on a near perfect performance from their forward pack, particularly the back row, and scrum-half Joost van der Westhuizen more or less played as an extra loose forward. There had been concerns that van der Westhuizen might have played his last match of the tournament after coming off during the semi-final against France with a trapped nerve in his ribs, but the courageous scrum-half recovered in time to play a vital role in the tournament decider.

'It was an absolute delight to play outside Joost,' recalls South Africa fly-half Joel Stransky. 'He always delivered perfect ball and he had that special ability to beat people one-on-one, but most importantly he was a strong defender. He made a couple of great tackles on Jonah Lomu in the final.'

The tactics employed by South Africa proved a success as they swarmed

Lomu in defence before going on to outmuscle the All Blacks up front in the forwards.

'We played the right game around Jonah for the entire tournament and it was probably our downfall in the final,' recalls Sean Fitzpatrick. 'If any team was going to stop us it was the Boks. We had a vision that we were going to be the fittest and fastest team in world rugby and the game we played just hadn't been seen before. In doing that though, we sacrificed some physical aspects and the Boks managed to outmuscle us in the final. Mark Andrews and the big guys in the pack really took it to us and they swarmed Jonah.'

No tries were scored, but the match was still a gripping spectacle as two rugby heavyweights fought out a bruising encounter. Stransky had the final say with a drop-goal in extra time, but it was the lasting impression of President Nelson Mandela, dressed in a Springboks number six jersey, presenting The Webb Ellis Cup to Francois Pienaar that will forever be the imprint of Rugby World Cup 1995 on world history.

'It was very special. I've been very blessed in my life,' says Pienaar. 'I never thought that Nelson Mandela would be wearing a Springbok jersey, and I never thought he would have my number on the back. It was the first time the Springboks were supported by 43 million people right across South Africa and getting the cup from Mandela was the ultimate. He is a guy with incredible humility and he has done phenomenal work in bringing our country together. In my opinion, it was the whole catalyst for bringing the entire nation together for the first time in support of one team.'

8

The interim years: 1995–1999

HAD THERE BEEN A tournament script to follow it could not have played out much better for Rugby World Cup 1995. South Africa returned from international isolation to host one of the most poignant and colourful sporting celebrations of the twentieth century. While the scars left by the apartheid regime were still very deep among those who suffered most, the healing process was given an immense boost by the events that unfolded throughout the Rainbow Nation in 1995. Not only had the impression of a reunified country been successfully projected to the outside world, but South Africa claimed the title and the lasting impression will forever be that of President Nelson Mandela presenting Francois Pienaar with the trophy. Those two key figures went on to develop a strong friendship that would become a symbolic pillar of the new South Africa, with Mandela later becoming the godfather to one of Pienaar's sons.

It was a long trip home for defeated finalists New Zealand. They had put in a courageous fight until the end, but the famous feats of record-winning margins and Jonah Lomu terrorising opposition defences all paled to insignificance without the one piece of extra luggage they wanted to bring home from South Africa. The All Blacks did salvage some pride less than one month after the 1995 tournament, however, when they defeated Australia in a two-Test series for the Bledisloe Cup. New Zealand had lost the trans-Tasman trophy in 1994, but they prevailed in both matches of 1995 to start rebuilding what had become a dwindling trophy cabinet. Those two matches also held extra significance as the last two international rugby Tests ever played in the amateur era.

Rugby had reached a major crossroads prior to Rugby World Cup 1995. While the game remained non-professional throughout the tournament, there were still major threats to the future of the sport as it desperately tried to uphold its amateur roots. Bold agendas to control the future of the game – such as the WRC backed by Australian media magnate Kerry Packer – were still progressing in the background as rugby's flagship event unfolded. The 1995 tournament further demonstrated the commercial value the game could generate, and the entrepreneurial vultures were circling overhead once again.

The SANZAR alliance announced the formation of the inaugural Super12 and Tri-Nations tournaments on the eve of the 1995 final, which had in effect already set the game towards professionalism, and the international governing body was faced with little choice but to declare it officially two months later. The late Vernon Pugh, who was chairman of the IRB Amateurism Committee at the time, announced to the world on August 26, 1995: 'Subsequent to the repeal of the amateur regulations, rugby will become an open game. There will be no prohibition on payment or the prohibition of any other material benefit to any person involved in the game.'

Thereafter the game was changed forever. For better or for worse will always be a contentious issue between rugby purists and those who have embraced the modern professional game, but most importantly of all it was guaranteed a viable future within the professional sporting landscape of its largest market and historical backbone – England, Scotland, Wales and Ireland – the Home Unions.

The decision to make the game professional effectively nullified the threat posed by the WRC movement, which suddenly found itself isolated through a lack of affiliation with the established rugby governing bodies around the world. Players who had aligned themselves with the WRC began to lose faith in the movement, and South Africa's governing body even threatened to ban players who did not pledge their allegiance to the establishment. Thereafter the WRC initiative was doomed.

The Super League war playing out in Australia was one of the most pressing immediate concerns that pushed the international governing body to turn professional earlier than it might otherwise have done.

'Super League genuinely threatened the future of rugby in Australia,' says former Wallabies coach Bob Dwyer. 'Australia really needed to do something to protect its playing stocks. The best players were like sitting ducks waiting for league to pluck them out and throw big money in front of them. When Super League came in, it was going to be open slather on rugby players.'

Two such players who appealed to rugby league from the moment they broke on to the international scene were Tim Horan and Jason Little. There had been other Australia (mainly backline) players targeted, such as Daniel Herbert and Damien Smith, but the battle to sign the Queensland centre pairing was one that became an interesting tug-of-war between the two rival codes. Australian rugby authorities knew they had to act fast to keep Horan and company in the game, and as it turned out the WRC threat combined with that of Super League effectively brought forward the move to professionalism.

'It all happened very quickly after the 1995 tournament. There was no real order to it all except for when WRC came in just before Rugby World Cup 1995 and unsettled the status quo,' recalls Horan. 'It would be interesting to know how long it would have taken for professional rugby to come along if the WRC hadn't turned up. The WRC probably bought it forward by about 10 years or so. There was no way I thought rugby would go professional while I was playing, and that was why I was about to sign with rugby league for the last four or five years of my career.'

Horan and Little eventually signed with Queensland Reds for the inaugural Super12 in 1996, as did Daniel Herbert and Damien Smith, and Australian rugby won a vital off-field battle to demonstrate to other players in their code that rugby league was no longer the only option for those seeking financial reward. In many ways it was an important milestone for the sport of rugby, which had suffered at the hands of rugby league fleecing its finest talent for the best part of a century. But while the battle was won to secure the big names, rugby then had to convince the purists.

'There was definitely a lot of teething problems and one of the biggest pressures I felt was from some of the rugby public saying, "Why is it going professional? The game will never be the same",' Horan said. 'But it only took a few matches of that first Super12 competition in 1996 for people to realise that so much better rugby was going to be produced because players were being paid and could spend a lot more time training. The quality of rugby improved really quickly and that was very pleasing because there were a lot of knockers out there early on.'

While most of the momentum for the game eventually adopting professionalism had come from the southern hemisphere with the initiation of SANZAR and the Super12 and Tri-Nations tournaments, the Five Nations committee in the northern hemisphere made similar inroads during the European summer of 1995 through the inauguration of the Heineken Cup. This new international competition served as a club championship involving the best teams from the major rugby-playing nations across Europe, and suddenly the game was offering top club players very attractive salaries on the back of strong currencies throughout the region. The temptation proved too hard to resist for some, with two of South Africa's Rugby World Cup heroes – Francois Pienaar and Joel Stransky – signing for English clubs Saracens and Leicester respectively within 18 months of the Springboks' 1995 triumph. Pienaar's decision attracted criticism throughout South Africa, with many believing he was deserting the national side, but the former captain had been controversially dropped by new coach Andre Markgraaff in 1996 and forging his way back into the side after that seemed highly unlikely given that he was almost 30 years old at the time.

On the surface it seemed little could go wrong with money entering the game at such a rapid rate across the world. However, unbeknown to many at the time, there was an immense problem developing throughout Europe (particularly within England) as rich clubs backed by wealthy businessmen gained increasing control over the best players in the game. Ironically, the Five Nations committee (made up of the national governing bodies from the Home Unions and France, who developed the Heineken Cup initiative) started suffering from the first symptoms of the Club v Country dispute through growing publicity of the club game. The situation quickly developed to become a major problem for northern hemisphere rugby in the professional era.

'Many of the older heads within the administration of the Home Unions expended all of their energy trying to block professionalism, and then when it did come along they took too long to harness it and eventually that created a massive problem,' says Michael Lynagh, who played with Saracens in London from 1996 to 1998. 'Rather than taking the line of knowing professionalism was inevitable and developing a structure, they spent their time trying to beat it. England put a moratorium on it, saying they would think about it for a year, and in the meantime the club owners started to control the players.'

Players quickly became torn between remaining loyal to their club and those who paid their wages, and the honour of representing their country. Unfortunately money now held the power, and international rugby in the northern hemisphere would eventually suffer greatly as a result. Heated disputes between club and country continue to simmer throughout Europe. Administrators within the international governing body now face the ongoing task of remedying the dismal situation created by their predecessors among the Home Unions, who failed to establish a proper structure during the formative years of professionalism. The ongoing saga has effectively given more weight to the argument for those purists who opposed the onset of professionalism, but very few who have played at the highest level across both eras feel that the game is not better for breaking the shackles of amateurism.

'When we went professional I loved it because you could actually try and do it properly, without trying to fit training and playing in Test matches around work,' recalls former England captain Martin Johnson. 'I can clearly remember our prop forward Darren Garforth at Leicester coming in off the building site to a big club game just after 2 o'clock in the afternoon before a 3 o'clock game. [Professionalism] made sure all of that ended and we were able to concentrate on rugby alone. The game was better for it.'

On the playing surface the standard of rugby improved across both hemispheres at a rapid rate. The Super12 introduced a brand new dimension to rugby across South Africa, Australia and New Zealand as bigger, stronger, fitter and faster players brought rugby of a Test-match standard to the provincial arena. New Zealand were leading the way immediately after Rugby World Cup 1995, as Auckland Blues dominated the Super12 and the All Blacks controlled the Tri-Nations.

'New Zealand in 1996 was the best team I ever played against,' says former Australia captain John Eales. 'They built up a formidable side after the 1995 tournament and it was hard to find any weaknesses to target when you were playing against them.'

The All Blacks were a step ahead of most teams during the formative years of the professional era, losing only once to the Springboks in 22 Tests they played during 1996 and 1997. Their counterparts from Australia and South Africa were forced to lift their standards quickly in order to be competitive in the Tri-Nations tournament. The pace of the southern hemisphere game increased dramatically as a result, and the perceived gap in standards between the two hemispheres became more apparent through international results with no single nation from the northern hemisphere recording a victory against Australia, New Zealand or South Africa during 1996 or 1997. The schism largely resulted from a lack of professional ethos at international level in the northern hemisphere, and the problem was compounded by the Club v Country row that engulfed rugby within the Home Nations. But it was not all doom and gloom for the northern hemisphere during those years, with the British and Irish Lions recording a series triumph in South Africa during 1997, while England managed to draw with both Australia and New Zealand at the end of that same year. The latter of those two draws at Twickenham marked a major turning point for England, and the northern hemisphere, as they slowly began to close the gap that had developed between the two hemispheres.

'New Zealand, Australia and South Africa were a long way ahead of us in terms of the way they played, but we did a little bit to close the gap during the autumn internationals of 1997,' recalls former England captain Lawrence Dallaglio. 'The last game against New Zealand was obviously a major highlight for everyone. New Zealand had been all-conquering on their tour and had already beaten us at Old Trafford so there were not a lot of expectations on England, but we played a great first half and almost recorded what would have been a big upset. We missed too many tackles in the second half to go on and win the game, but it was perhaps a sign of things to come.'

Throughout 1998 a power shift came in the southern hemisphere as the domination of New Zealand ended abruptly following the retirement of some key players – Sean Fitzpatrick, Zinzan Brooke and France Bunce. The All Blacks had easily won the first two Tri-Nations in 1996 and 1997, but they failed to win a single match in the 1998 tournament as the team entered a rebuilding phase. Meanwhile South Africa became the dominant rugby nation in the world, maintaining a record unbeaten run of 17 consecutive Test matches throughout 1997 and 1998. The team to finally end the Springboks' outstanding run of success was England in December of 1998, with a memorable 13–7 victory at Twickenham. England's triumph came at a vital time for northern hemisphere rugby when it seemed the southern hemisphere heavyweights were again skipping clear in the world pecking order.

The interim period between Rugby World Cup 1995 and the 1999 tournament was the most significant four-year period for the modern game. Further threats to the future of rugby were averted by the announcement of professionalism, and playing standards improved rapidly ahead of the fourth Rugby World Cup to be hosted by Wales and contested throughout the United Kingdom, Ireland and France. There was widespread expectation that the southern hemisphere nations would again dominate the tournament, but the ever exciting and unpredictable French ensured the northern hemisphere would not be disgraced.

9

Rugby World Cup 1999: the tournament

RUGBY ENDURED A TUMULTUOUS period immediately after the third tournament ended in South Africa, and the winds of change swept through at a rapid rate. The onset of professionalism was largely forced on to the international governing body by the increasing threat of the WRC hijacking significant forces in the game and creating an event that would have effectively superseded the Rugby World Cup. But while the WRC had powerful corporate backing and a strong collective business influence in the major rugby markets, there was a significant flaw to the concept in relation to growing the game in the developing rugby nations. The WRC vision was to make the game bigger and better for the major rugby nations, and the lesser rugby countries were left out in the cold. The WRC also seemed to be catering for elite players only within those major rugby countries and the grassroots looked likely to suffer. It would then only be a matter of time before the talented crop of players within the WRC ranks would dwindle as a result of foundation clubs and provincial level organisations not being able to produce the same quality players. In many ways the WRC was a supermodel of sorts, but its catwalk would eventually deteriorate to the point where no one could walk on it.

What the IRB and other conventional rugby governing bodies around the world did offer that the WRC lacked, was familiar and traditional foundations. There was also a hint of arrogance within the

WRC movement that it did not have to work with the established bodies early on because the established bodies would eventually have to work with it – a costly stance for the WRC, which seemed to be flexing muscle it did not yet have. But what the WRC, together with Super League, did have the power to do, was force the international governing body to declare the game open to professionalism sooner than many had anticipated. The double-barrelled threat had the potential to destroy rugby as a major sport and a move into the professional era seemed the only possible saviour.

The IRB had been housed in the rather modest surrounds of Bristol in England up until 1996, but the move to professionalism brought with it a new full-time administration with a headquarters based in Dublin, Ireland. The international governing body was forced to adapt quickly to the new professional landscape and the quadrennial Rugby World Cup tournament became the breadwinner to feed the administration coffers. The threats posed by the WRC and Super League eventually subsided and by the time the 1999 tournament came in Wales, the IRB had established a firmer hold of the game internationally at the administrative level.

Not since the Empire Games (as the Commonwealth Games were once known) in 1958 had Wales hosted a major international sporting event. The decision to give the event to Wales was officially announced in 1994, after they defeated a combined bid from Australia and Japan when the tournament was put out to tender for the very first time, but some commentators suggest it was established well before then. When England was awarded the 1991 tournament, the late Keith Rowlands – one of the serving committee members from Wales at the time and the first ever paid secretary of the IRB – suggested that when the event next returned to Europe it should be hosted by Wales. Sure enough it was, and the esteemed Rowlands came out of retirement to lead the organisation of the 1999 tournament.

The pool stage

Only 12 years had passed since rugby first staged its international showpiece in 1987, but almost a century worth of transformation to the game had occurred in a little more than a decade. The number of teams participating in the tournament increased from 16 to 20 for the first time in 1999 and only four countries were granted automatic qualification. In an attempt to bring more meaning to the third place play-off that preceded the final in 1995, it was decided that only the top three teams would be guaranteed a place in 1999, together with the country hosting the event. That meant that 1995 world champions South Africa, runners-up New Zealand, third-placed France and host nation Wales did not need to partake in the qualification process that involved a record 65 countries from five continents vying for the remaining 16 places in the draw.

The qualification process yielded three teams that would make their Rugby World Cup debut in 1999 – Uruguay, Spain and Namibia – while the United States and Fiji rejoined the fold after the disappointment of missing out in 1995. The 20 participating teams were split across five pools, with 41 matches to be played over 37 days. Only nine of those matches would be played within the host country Wales, while the other 32 were contested across England (nine), Scotland (eight), France (eight) and Ireland (seven). The new format was such that only the winning team from each pool was guaranteed a place in the quarter-finals, while the runners-up in each pool and the best third-placed team overall would play off for the last three quarter-final places.

Rugby World Cup 1999: the pools and order they finished

Pool A	Pool B	Pool C	Pool D	Pool E
South Africa	New Zealand	France	Wales	Australia
Scotland	England	Fiji	Argentina	Ireland
Uruguay	Tonga	Canada	Samoa	Romania
Spain	Italy	Namibia	Japan	USA

The opening ceremony in 1999 had a typically Welsh theme headed by some of the country's finest entertainers – Shirley Bassey, best known internationally for singing the theme songs to three James Bond films during the 1960s and 70s – and a varied series of acts ranging from contemporary opera with Bryn Terfel through to the popular 1990s band Catatonia brandishing their No. 1 UK hit 'International Velvet' with a chorus declaring 'Every day when I wake up, I thank the Lord I'm Welsh'. Some critics suggested the opening ceremony was too blatantly Welsh, but a host nation for any major international sports event is granted the opportunity to showcase its own culture and home-grown entertainers while welcoming the world. Wales simply did what most other host nations had done in the past, yet some pockets of the media from neighbouring rival countries couldn't resist criticising the spectacle.

The ceremony had a relatively low budget, despite being the first time a Rugby World Cup was being staged in the professional era, but the venue was quite spectacular. Wales had won the right to host the 1999 tournament on the back of a tender that promised to demolish the old Cardiff Arms Park and build the new state-of-the-art £126 million Millennium Stadium. There had been many setbacks during construction and at one stage it looked highly unlikely to be ready for the tournament. Thankfully the stadium was completed just in time for a few warm-up matches prior to the opening match on October 1, 1999. Complete with a retractable roof, it was the largest stadium in the United Kingdom at the time of its construction. The Welsh Rugby Board had endured many restless nights, but the country was finally ready to host the rugby world.

Unfortunately the match that followed the opening ceremony, between Wales and Argentina, did very little to light up the occasion. The host nation had enjoyed renewed success under their new coach Graham Henry from New Zealand. Henry was hailed as the 'Great Redeemer', with Wales winning nine from 12 coming into the tournament, including victories over England, France and South Africa, and the home crowd now had reason to expect their team would not only win the opening match, but win it comfortably. Wales did eventually prevail on the back of a try each to Colin Charvis and Mark Taylor, together with a solid goal-kicking performance from fly-half Neil Jenkins, but it was far from easy as Argentina fly-half Gonzalo Quesada – who was eventually the top scorer in the tournament with 102 points – kept his team in the contest with six penalty goals before the Pumas lost by five points (23–18).

The opening match was the first of two very close Pool D contests for Wales as they battled to live up to the expectations of a hopeful yet demanding rugby public. The host nation faced Japan eight days after their match against Argentina and enjoyed a comfortable victory (64–15) that relieved some of the early pressure placed on the team, but waiting in the wings was a dangerous opponent who had inflicted an embarrassing loss on Wales eight years earlier. Samoa established itself as a surprise packet by defeating Wales at Cardiff Arms Park during the 1991 tournament and those ghosts came back to haunt the new Millennium Stadium as the Pacific Islanders scored five tries to three to pull off another remarkable upset (38–31). Samoa had also enjoyed an easy victory over Japan (43–9) in their first pool match, but after losing to Argentina (32–16) in their second pool match they came up against Wales needing a victory to advance to the knockout stage.

With two former All Blacks in their ranks – Va'aiga 'Inga' Tuigamala and Stephen Bachop – and a group of old heads who had enjoyed their 1991 success against Wales, Samoa brought their trademark brutal physicality to the general play but their scrum suffered at the hands of Wales and conceded two penalty tries. The response thereafter was for Samoa to run the ball and they did so with tremendous effect to turn the score around and record a victory that would leave Pool D deadlocked between three after Argentina defeated Japan (33–12) as expected. Despite progressing as the pool winner courtesy of a better for-and-against, Wales coach Graham Henry was hoping his team would learn something from the loss.

'Frankly, I hope they don't get over the loss in a hurry. I want them to remember how bad it feels and gain new resolve,' Henry said. 'You develop as a team by absorbing the lessons of defeat rather than pretending it never happened. Losing can often give you a much sharper mental edge and you only need to look at the Samoans for proof of that. Being beaten by Argentina wounded them, and they came out against us desperate to atone.'

The first match from Pool A involved two newcomers to the Rugby World Cup stage – Spain and Uruguay. While the major rugby powerhouses had rapidly embraced professionalism for three years ahead of the 1999 tournament, these two minnows were still very much amateur, but it did not take away from the passion showed by both teams at Netherdale in Galashiels – a town in the Scottish Borders. The passion was of a different kind though, and did not merely stem from a will to win. These two teams were just happy to be a part of the greatest rugby show on earth, and they savoured every moment in front of a modest crowd of 3,800. Uruguay emerged the victor (27–15), with their charismatic 40-year-old captain Diego Ormachea scoring the first try of the match before leading the way throughout. This day was one for the purists of the rugby code as two international teams of the older kind gave their all on the playing surface before celebrating together after the match.

As Spain and Uruguay toasted their first fixture in Rugby World Cup competition, the two main contenders from Pool A – Scotland and South Africa – were preparing for battle at Murrayfield in Edinburgh. The stage was set for a great encounter between two of the stronger teams in world rugby, yet there was a disappointing crowd of only 57,000 at Murrayfield – some 10,000 short of capacity. At half time the match was there for the taking for either side, with only three points separating the teams, but some uncharacteristic errors from Gregor Townsend proved costly for Scotland in the final result. Townsend had a disappointing kicking game, with two kick-returns from Springboks fullback Percy Montgomery resulting in tries to South Africa. Just when it looked like the Scotland fly-half might redeem himself, after kicking a drop-goal and setting up Alan Tait for a try to keep Scotland in with a chance, South Africa centre Deon Kayser intercepted a Townsend pass before running half the length of the field to score. The Springboks eventually prevailed (46–29), but Scotland had put in a fine performance.

That result effectively handed South Africa top billing in Pool A, as they went on to easily defeat Spain (47–3) and Uruguay (39–3). The victories were indeed comfortable for the Springboks, and allowed the team to gather some much-needed momentum before the knock-out stage, but some commentators suggested that their lack of ability to really put a large score on the lesser nations was a sign the defending champions simply were not as strong as the likes of other major nations – such as New Zealand and England – who were scoring more than 100 points against similar opposition from the lower tier of the world rugby rankings. Scotland produced comparable winning margins against Uruguay (43–12) and Spain (48–0) to comfortably finish runner-up in Pool A, and a quarter-final play-off match now beckoned.

The opening match in Pool B saw England take on Italy at Twickenham. Having beaten the *Azzurri* by only eight points in a Rugby World Cup qualifier one year earlier, England were keen to stamp their mark on the 1999 tournament early and they did so with a crushing eight tries to one victory. A 20-year-old by the name of Jonny Wilkinson played a starring role for England, scoring a record 32 points to guide his team to a comfortable 67–7 victory. England were a team building well under the astute guidance of their coach Clive Woodward, who brought a sense of competitiveness to his squad that gave them an ability to put sizable scores on the lesser teams while no longer fearing the top nations in the game.

'When Clive came in 1997, the first thing he said to all of us was that we should be good enough to be taking on the best in the world,' recalls Martin Johnson. 'It was a big statement for English rugby at that time and it took us a while to get there, but we created an environment where we eventually had the belief in our side that we could go out and beat the best.'

England's dominant display against Italy in their opening match of the 1999 tournament was a bold statement, but the truest measure of their improvement would come against New Zealand at Twickenham one week later. England had suffered two heavy defeats to the All Blacks in New Zealand during 1998, but Woodward had formed a much stronger team this time around. The first half was a tense struggle, with All Blacks openside flanker Josh Kronfeld in the thick of it at the breakdown and having a tremendous game.

'We had a plan to try and play away from their strengths and we considered Kronfeld a major threat,' Johnson said. 'We went out to try and minimise the impact he would have on the game, but he was a real nuisance and we just couldn't get the better of him.'

New Zealand eventually skipped clear to a 16–3 lead not long after half time and looked to be stamping their authority, but to England's credit and the delight of the Twickenham crowd they came back and levelled the scores at 16–16 after a converted try to centre Phil de Glanville and two penalty goals to Jonny Wilkinson. Then came the moment so many England fans feared when New Zealand fly-half Andrew Mehrtens sent a long ball out to Jonah Lomu lurking on the left wing in open space – just how he likes it. Four would-be tacklers tried, and four would-be tacklers were cast aside. It was a classic case of déjà vu as a rampaging Lomu, who tore England to shreds with four tries in the Cape Town semi-final of 1995, ran half the length of the field to slam the ball down for a try that broke the deadlock. It was a huge psychological blow to England and when New Zealand scrum-half Byron Kelleher crossed for another try soon after, it was clear there was no coming back for the home side this time. The All Blacks held on for what seemed a comfortable victory on the score-board (30–16), but England stood tall and showed tremendous courage to fight back when most teams would have folded.

Victory over England all but ensured New Zealand would win Pool B and automatically qualify for the knockout stage. That outcome was confirmed when the All Blacks thrashed Italy (101–3) in their final pool match at Huddersfield. Coach John Hart made 11 changes to the team that defeated England six days earlier, but it was the back three of Lomu, Jeff Wilson and Glen Osborne who scored seven tries between them as New Zealand amassed 14 tries against a solitary penalty goal from Italy fly-half Diego Dominguez. It turned out to be a very disappointing tournament for the *Azzurri*, as they also went down to Tonga by three points (28–25) at Welford Road in Leicester, where fullback Sateki Tuipulotu steered the Pacific Islanders to a memorable victory with a 20-point haul that included the winning drop-goal from almost 50 metres out during injury time. But it was England who had the final say in Pool B with an emphatic (101–10) victory over Tonga, overcoming the disappointment of losing to the All Blacks in convincing fashion by crossing for 13 tries to one at Twickenham.

Pool C was contested throughout France in Toulouse, Bordeaux and Béziers. While it was undoubtedly the national team – *Les Bleus* – that commanded most attention from the local population, the flair shown by Fiji soon made them a second favourite among French fans. Generally recognised as seven-a-side specialists in more recent years, Fiji still holds the traditional 15-man game in high regard and they were incredibly disappointed after failing to qualify for the 1995 tour-nament. Their opening match in 1999 was seen as a time for redemption as they came up against Namibia. In front of a crowd of more than 10,000 in Béziers, Fiji ran in nine tries to register their first victory (67–18) in Rugby World Cup competition since 1987, when they captured the hearts of many at the inaugural tournament after defying the distraction of a military coup in their homeland to reach the quarter-finals.

The second match in Pool C saw France take on Canada at the Stade de la Méditerranée in Béziers. There was mounting pressure on the home team to put in a commendable performance after a 12-month period that rated among their worst in recent history. France had gone from winning back-to-back Five Nations Grand Slams in 1997 and 1998 to just three victories from 10 Tests leading into Rugby World Cup 1999. The team were desperate to make amends, and so it showed in their opening match as Canada troubled *Les Bleus* through the steady influence of their captain and fly-half Gareth Rees. Canada had every right to think they were posing a threat when trailing by just eight points at half time, but they lost their talisman Rees to injury early in the second period and with that their hopes of an upset diminished. Much to their credit Canada came back to within one point, but France eventually held on for a relatively narrow victory (33–20).

The following weekend *Les Bleus* faced Namibia in Bordeaux – a match that was seen as an opportunity for the home side to produce a solid showing and instil some much-needed confidence in the side. France were expected to put a hefty score on their lowly opponents, so it came as quite a shock when the scores were level during the first half. Namibia provided stiff opposition, but they were eventually worn down and the home side prevailed unconvincingly (47–13) to secure a place in the knockout stage.

Canada needed to secure victory against Fiji the following day if they were to continue past the pool stage in the 1999 tournament, and they made an encouraging start to be comfortably leading throughout the first half hour. Then a sudden turnaround came with Fiji lighting up the match after two tries to centre Viliame Satala. The Bordeaux crowd had further warmed to the free-flowing playing style of the Pacific Islanders after being deprived by their own, and on the back of some very vocal support Fiji went on to control the match in the second half and hold on for a 38–22 victory that would secure their place in the knockout round.

The local support Fiji had enjoyed in their earlier pool matches was obviously not present when they faced France in Toulouse on the final day of the pool stage. The French fans were growing increasingly frustrated with the apparent disharmony within their national squad and a lack of cohesion on the field, but it was trying times like these when the Gallic spirit would band together stronger than ever. Fiji did not lie down easily and were leading the match by six points after 70 minutes of play. *Les Bleus* had tried at times to create opportunities out wide but it was eventually left to the men up front to complete the job. As France pressured the Fiji line for much of the final 10 minutes, with a number of scrums needing to be reset, referee Paddy O'Brien finally awarded a penalty try that proved decisive in the final outcome. A penalty goal soon after to Christophe Lamaison gave France a four-point lead and wing Christophe Dominici scored a try in injury time to produce a final score line (28–19) that flattered the home side.

The Pool E fixtures in 1999 were contested throughout the Republic of Ireland and Northern Ireland. Ireland was to enjoy the home advantage against Australia, Romania and the United States, and so it would prove a valuable asset in their opening pool match against the United States. On the back of a vocal crowd, the ever-present and mobile hooker Keith Wood scored four tries as Ireland enjoyed a comprehensive victory (53–8) much to the delight of the Lansdowne Road faithful. Players had scored four tries in Rugby World Cup competition before, but for a front row forward to do so was an astounding statistic that ensured Wood left an indelible mark on the tournament.

It was another mismatch the following day when Australia opened their account against Romania at Ravenhill Stadium in Belfast, where Northern Ireland hosted their first Rugby World Cup match since 1991 when Japan defeated Zimbabwe at the same venue. It was by no means the most exciting fixture the Belfast crowd could have hoped for, but a male and female from the crowd certainly added to the spectacle late in the proceedings when they decided to bare all and cartwheel their naked bodies to the centre surface. Prior to that No. 8 Toutai Kefu had crossed for a hat-trick of tries to commence his great contribution to the tournament, and the Wallabies eventually scored nine unanswered tries to earn a comfortable 57–9 victory that gave coach Rod Macqueen and his team the steady start they were after.

'We enjoyed a fairly low-key build-up ahead of the 1999 tournament just outside Dublin and we were very well prepared,' recalls Australia captain John Eales. 'The first match against Romania was great to have before facing Ireland, because it gave us a good chance to work on combinations but at the same time not give too much away.'

Australia's next match against Ireland was billed as a major show-down in Pool E for no apparent reason other than their being the two teams who fought out the famous 1991 quarter-final at Lansdowne Road eight years earlier. The stadium was full of life as fans from both sides sang to inspire their teams, but it was the Irish song that started to fade first after centre Tim Horan carved through the midfield to score a try under the posts before playing a big part in setting up Australia's other try to wing Ben Tune. A meagre penalty goal from David Humphreys was all Ireland could muster, and with Matt Burke finding his kicking range after a rusty start, the Wallabies went on to win comfortably (23–3). One particular moment that stood out was when Australia No. 8 Toutai Kefu retaliated with a flurry of punches to Ireland flanker Trevor Brennan. It earned Kefu a two-week suspension from the tournament, while Brennan was given 10 days for his part in provoking the incident.

Victory over Ireland all but assured Australia a direct path to the quarter-finals for securing first place in Pool E, and when a second-string Wallabies team defeated the United States (59–19) in Limerick that result was confirmed. Ireland bounced back with victory over Romania (44–14) to secure second place in the pool, but like all runners-up from the other pools they had to overcome an extra qual-ifying match before sealing their place in the quarter-final round – a challenge that would prove one too many.

The quarter-final qualifiers

Samoa was the team to benefit most from the five-pool qualifying structure of the 1999 tournament after they finished third in Pool D, yet their coach Bryan Williams was still openly critical of the fact his team had to potentially play three Test matches in a little more than one week. Their opponents were Scotland and the venue was Murrayfield – a repeat of the 1991 quarter-final, only this time it was in front of a dismal crowd of a little more than 15,000. One of the less appealing factors of the game turning professional meant that ticket prices increased. It did not seem to bother most other countries that staged matches in 1999, because ticket sales well and truly exceeded 1995 sales, but Scottish rugby fans made a collective statement by not attending matches in 1999 and poor crowd figures resulted across the region.

Back on the playing surface the 1999 scenario had a very similar feel to eight years earlier, with Samoa causing a stir after defeating Wales during the pool stage and with their trademark physical approach they had become a team that many opponents were increasingly wary of. Just as in 1991 however, Scotland it seemed was not fazed by the Samoa threat. From the opening whistle they fulfilled tactics targeting the set pieces at scrum and lineout time. It paid dividends early on when Scotland were awarded a penalty try when Irish referee David McHugh lost his patience after there had been a scrum for every one of the first 10 minutes played. Scotland did not concede the lead at any stage, at one point enjoying a 21-point advantage, but Samoa did well to come back late in the match and ensure it was not an embarrassing final score (35–20).

While it could be argued that the five-pool structure had been the fairest outcome for those in Pool D, England was a team that perhaps did not deserve to be tasked with another game. They had been outstanding in Pool B, amassing 184 points despite a loss to New Zealand, and now they had to face Fiji to earn a place in the quarter-finals. Coach Clive Woodward already had an eye on the following weekend, resting a number of first-string players. It seemed a risky strategy against an unpredictable opponent, but England eventually prevailed (45–24) despite some promising attacks from Fiji's outside backs. While the score often indicated that England was in a secure position throughout, their injury toll was far less comforting. Woodward eventually used all seven replacements – Joe Worsley, Dan Luger and Austin Healey all came off at half time, while Matt Perry and Jonny Wilkinson were later substituted in what seemed like a precautionary measure, but a controversial change at fly-half was imminent with Woodward replacing Wilkinson with Paul Grayson for the quarter-final.

The last of the quarter-final qualifiers saw Ireland take on Argentina at the Stade Félix Bollaert in Lens, France. The match promised little as a spectacle with Ireland far from impressive during the pool stage, and Argentina having scored just three tries up to that point. Both teams employed tactics that revolved around their respective fly-halves – David Humphreys for Ireland and Gonzalo Quesada for Argentina – kicking penalty goals and looking for territorial advantage rather than running with the ball in hand. Ireland maintained the lead for most of the match, then in the final five minutes Argentina wing Diego Albanese woke the small Lens crowd from its slumber and crossed for the match-winning try. The result gave the Pumas their first-ever appearance in the Rugby World Cup quarter-finals, while Ireland was left to ponder their worst-ever performance of failing to reach the final eight for the first time.

The quarter-finals

The new Millennium Stadium in Cardiff hosted the first quarter-final, with Wales taking on Australia, and plenty of pre-match hype centred not so much on the fixture itself, but on whether the roof of the stadium would be open or closed. It was left to the tournament organisers to decide, so it came as no surprise that the host nation decided to leave the roof open to the elements and not allow the Wallabies any advantage of having a dry surface. As expected the conditions were wet, and the relatively new surface did not hold up well under foot. Sensing that the Wallabies were out of their comfort zone, the Welsh crowd were vocal from the stands in an effort to lift the home side. Australia crossed for a try to scrum-half George Gregan in the sixth minute and Matt Burke converted before adding a penalty goal late in the first half. But Wales showed tremendous heart and were trailing by just one point (10–9) at the break thanks to the radar boot of their fly-half Neil Jenkins, who kicked three penalty goals to keep his team in the contest.

The second period saw Wales throw everything they possibly could at Australia in attack, but the wall of gold defence stood firm as it had done and would do for the entire tournament. The home side eventually began to tire and Australia broke through with a try to wing Ben Tune off a perfectly weighted grubber kick from fly-half Stephen Larkham. That score deflated Wales and when Australia's forward pack asserted their dominance in the closing stages it was left to their usually humble captain John Eales to have the final say in a scrum that packed down deep in Wales territory. The Quinnell brothers – Craig and Scott – were the heavyweights within a large Welsh pack and they prided themselves on being part of a strong forward unit. So when Australia put the squeeze on Wales in a scrum late in the match, it came as no surprise that one of the brothers confidently yelled out: 'Where do you think you are going boyos?' Then came the reply from Eales: 'To Twickenham son . . . we're going to ****ing Twickenham!' George Gregan scored his second try soon after that and the Wallabies were indeed on their way to Twickenham as the first team to qualify for the 1999 semi-finals after a 24–9 victory.

'I remember talking to the team before the quarter-final against Wales and emphasising how if we lost that game we were out of the tournament,' recalls Tim Horan. 'I spoke about some experiences of 1991 and the quarter-final in Ireland when I don't think the team realised that, and also the disappointment of 1995 against England. I wanted to make sure the team had it locked into their heads that when we play Wales if we lose we are gone.'

The decision to leave the stadium roof open drew a lot of criticism from Australia, who preferred to recycle the ball fast and play an expansive game. Together with coach Macqueen, Horan was scathing in his assessment of the decision and used a metaphor that would be remembered long after the event.

'If you have the roof you should use it,' Horan said. 'It's a bit like having a Ferrari in the garage, but then going out to catch a bus. The weather spoiled the game when there was a great atmosphere and a great occasion.'

The second quarter-final took place at the Stade de France in Paris, where England lined up against South Africa. The Springboks had been gathering momentum at the right end of their campaign, but England were also finding good rhythm after scoring more points than any other team during the pool stage. The match was typified by a monumental clash of two strong forward packs, and it was clear that something special would be required to eventually split the teams when they went to the break with South Africa narrowly in front (16–12). In the second period an unlikely hero stood up to produce *that* special something. Springbok fly-half Jannie de Beer had been a fourth-choice player six months prior to the tournament, but he quickly became South Africa's hero and England's worst nightmare. Under the directive of coach Nick Mallet, who was convinced the game had become a dogfight with limited opportunities to score, centre Pieter Muller was used to drive the ball forward through the England midfield and draw in defenders, which effectively created enough space for de Beer to apply the five-punch combination. In a faultless kicking display, the 28-year-old from Free State province kicked a world record five drop-goals to break English hearts and send South Africa into the semi-finals. It was a paranormal performance that even de Beer struggled to explain.

'Some of the things which happened out there were supernatural. God gave us this victory. I am just happy to be part of his game plan,' de Beer said in the post-match press conference. 'Sometimes things happen in a way that you just don't have an answer for them. I personally feel God had a hand in this. I believe in my heart that this victory was not just about me as a player. I thank the Lord for the talent he gave me and I thank the forwards for the ball they gave me.'

Just as Argentina legend Diego Maradona had ended England's run with the infamous 'Hand of God' goal during a quarter-final at the football World Cup in 1986, England's national rugby team suffered a similar fate but this time it was courtesy of what was soon dubbed the 'Foot of God' by the British press. England captain Martin Johnson rates the loss as his worst rugby experience. Four years earlier Johnson was part of team that would fall victim to a freak of nature in the form of a rampaging Jonah Lomu in Cape Town, and that ugly feeling of helplessness was present once again.

The third quarter-final between France and Argentina at Lansdowne Road in Dublin attracted the least attention of all four, with neither side expected to progress past the semi-final and regarded by many as fortunate to be gifted an easier path than most other teams. France were recovering from one of their leanest periods in the modern game, while Argentina were in uncharted waters making their first ever quarter-final appearance. Few pundits were expecting a great spectacle, but like a classic French red wine pulled from the cellar after years of maturing, *Les Bleus* finally gave the rugby world a small sample of their finest with a solid opening period against Argentina. Confidence again filled the back line as they spread the ball freely before skipping to a 24-point lead, but the Pumas would not give in and came back to trail by just seven points (27–20) at half time. The second period saw the game tighten up and it was left to the goal kickers – Christophe Lamaison for France and Gonzalo Quesada for Argentina – to try and settle the score. Lamaison added one while Quesada added another two and only four points (30–26) split the teams with 15 minutes remaining. Then the extra qualifying match the Pumas had endured four days earlier started taking its toll, and *Les Bleus* seized their opportunity with two tries in the last 10 minutes to secure a victory (47–26) that would mark the resurrection of their campaign and sound a warning sign for prospective opponents.

'The danger of this French team is they can wake up in the morning, feel good, and produce something special,' New Zealand coach John Hart commented after France's victory. 'They looked as if they had lost confidence but they found their way back against Argentina. You have to be wary of them. If they get it right they're extremely dangerous.'

First the All Blacks had to overcome Scotland in the last of the four quarter-finals at Murrayfield on a wet Edinburgh evening. It was the second consecutive time the two teams were meeting in the Rugby World Cup quarter-finals, and the All Blacks were again expected to win comfortably, but Scotland did not lie down easily. New Zealand made a frenetic start to the match and put 17 unanswered points on Scotland in a short period, but complacency then seemed to stall the All Black machine as the home side outscored their more fancied opponents by 10 points in the second half. The final result was a victory for New Zealand (30–18), but the narrow margin drew criticism from many sections of the rugby media. Former Australia legend David Campese could not hold himself back from a damning assessment at the time in *The Australian*: 'The hallmark of great All Black teams down through the years has been the ruthless manner in which they destroy their opposition ... I know they put 100 points on Italy in the pool games, which is no mean feat. But Scotland were there for the taking at Murrayfield and the Kiwis let them wriggle free and escape what should have been a slaughter.'

Chinks were appearing in the All Blacks' armour, but many others believed it was just a case of rustiness resulting from New Zealand's mystifying tactic of having a relaxation period in the French Riviera after the pool stage of the tournament. Unbeknown to most, the infamous Rugby World Cup curse on the Land of the Long White Cloud was taking shape again and a revitalised France was ready to pounce.

The semi-finals

There had been very few matches during the 1999 group stage and quarter-finals that fell within the memorable category, and it is fair to say that for the most part the first tournament of the professional era was by no means setting the rugby world alight. But the lacklustre first four weeks were soon put to distant memory after the semi-final weekend at Twickenham. It took just two matches, so very different in the style they were played, yet each equally captivating as the other, to ensure that Rugby World Cup 1999 would go down as having produced what some still describe as one of the finest weekends of rugby the tournament has ever seen.

The first semi-final was an all southern hemisphere affair between defending champions South Africa and the 1991 champions Australia. Many pundits had expected these two heavyweights to lock horns at this stage of the tournament and it turned out to be a colossal showdown to decide the first team through to the final. The Springboks were full of confidence after defeating England on the back of a solid showing from their forward pack and Australia was now wary of the drop-goal threat posed by the so-called 'Foot of God' – South Africa fly-half Jannie de Beer.

'We were very aware of him as a threat, but the important thing for us was to ensure we didn't focus too much on him and allow some other player an opportunity,' recalls Australia captain John Eales. 'It's very hard to contain drop-goals. You can't concentrate too much on that. You need to just focus more on the other aspects of the game that lead to that player being put in a position to kick a drop-goal.'

Australia did exactly that and played the game as much as possible in South Africa territory. Fly-half Stephen Larkham, not renowned for being strong in the general kicking department, played a more conventional style at first receiver to contain the Springboks in their own half. However, for all the well-rehearsed tactics Australia deployed with near perfect precision, South Africa was gallant in defence and remained in touch on the scoreboard as both goal kickers – Matt Burke for the Wallabies and de Beer for the Springboks – went blow for blow throughout regulation time. Man of the Match Tim Horan was the closest any player went to scoring a try, and when he went off after 75 minutes it became increasingly clear that the goal-kickers would determine the end result. By the 79th minute it looked as though Australia would hold on for victory as they held a six-point lead (21–15) on the back of seven penalty goals from Burke, but de Beer stepped up to slot another and bring his side within reach again. The Springboks continued to mount pressure from the resulting restart and de Beer was presented with an opportunity to equalise when Australia replacement Owen Finegan was penalised for not allowing Andre Venter to release the ball. It was not an easy kick, with de Beer lining up some 45 metres out and near the sideline, but there was never any doubt as the ball went sailing through the centre of the uprights before referee Bevan blew full time. The scores were deadlocked (21–21) and two 10-minute periods of extra time would eventually determine who would be going through to the tournament decider.

After a short break the teams recommenced their war of attrition in extra time and it was clear the directive from both camps was to maintain possession and control discipline to the point of not conceding any kickable penalties. At such a time it seemed South Africa would have the advantage with drop-goal specialist de Beer in their ranks, but an ironic twist of fate came the way of the Springboks as Australia fly-half Larkham slotted a drop-goal from 45 metres out as the rain continued to fall. It was far from sweetly timed and looked an awkward strike, but it sailed straight through the goalposts and gave Australia a match-winning lead they would not surrender.

'There had been so much made of how we would contain Jannie de Beer and the ironic thing was that a drop-goal eventually decided the contest, but thankfully it was ours at the end of the day,' recalls Eales, who also made an outstanding contribution with a towering presence in the lineout – none more important than the three he secured in the final minutes of extra time with South Africa camped on Australia's line.

Burke kicked another penalty goal to take his overall tally to eight for the match and deliver the Wallabies a six-point victory (27–21), yet it was Larkham's single drop-goal that will remain etched in tournament history as the lasting memory of a monumental contest between two courageous teams. Defending champions South Africa had done their nation proud considering where they were six months earlier, but it was Australia who would live to fight another day and progress to their second Rugby World Cup final.

Most fans were excused for thinking the second semi-final at Twickenham had very little chance of living up to the match on the previous day, and it certainly seemed that way as New Zealand controlled most of the first half against France through the steady and reliable boot of Andrew Mehrtens. The All Blacks fly-half kicked four penalty goals and when Jonah Lomu crossed for two trademark tries either side of the break it looked as though it could be an embarrassing day for *Les Bleus*, but it turned out to be quite the opposite. The All Blacks were enjoying what seemed a commanding lead of 14 points (24–10) seven minutes into the second half. Then, like a swift gust of wind across the English Channel, the French spirit suddenly infiltrated Twickenham with a paralysing effect on New Zealand. In a period of 27 minutes, France scored 33 unanswered points and the All Blacks were left dumbfounded. Christophe Lamaison was one of only a few to stand tall for *Les Bleus* in the early exchanges when New Zealand dominated, and it was the man French fans call 'Titou' who sparked their revival with two drop-goals and two penalty goals in quick succession for his team to trail by just two points. The tremendous poise shown by Lamaison soon inspired his team-mates to try to spread the ball with confidence as only France know how and they did so with devastating consequences for the All Blacks. First it was scrum-half Fabien Galthie who chip-kicked for wing Christophe Dominici to come flying through and gather the ball for the try, then it was 'Titou' again who struck for *Les Bleus* with a cross-field kick that found centre Richard Dourthe perfectly placed for the score.

New Zealand did all they could to try and play their way back into the match, but nothing worked. Six minutes from time, with the All Blacks desperate to score, a pass went to ground and Lamaison was there to toe the loose ball through. The ever-present flanker Olivier Magne was chasing it down, as Jeff Wilson and his two team-mates came across in cover defence. The ball was kicked ahead again and then Philippe Bernat-Salles glided past Magne and Wilson before sliding on the ball under the posts to seal a remarkable victory. It was heartbreak once again for the All Blacks, but even a former legend from their own ranks could not help but be swept up in the pandemonium that gripped Twickenham as he watched many of his former team-mates endure the heartache of knowing their chance had gone for another four years.

'France always had that ability to flip a game on its head, and everything they tried in that second half worked. It was tough to watch [as a former All Black], but it's just great to see France play that way,' said Zinzan Brooke. 'I was actually sitting beside Bernat-Salles' father when he scored their final try underneath Jeff Wilson and he just gave me a big hug and he said, "That's my son" and he pulled out his wallet and showed me a picture of his son.'

Wilson scored a try near full time to bring some mild respectability to the scoreboard, but it was too little too late. New Zealand were gone and France were through to their second Rugby World Cup final. A roaming television commentator later asked France captain Raphael Ibanez how his team managed to turn the game around so quickly. Lost for words, Ibanez replied rather simply with a beaming smile: 'Errm ... we are French.'

Third place play-off

Four days after their devastating loss to France, New Zealand faced South Africa in the third place play-off at Millennium Stadium. The two finalists from four years earlier had been part of one of the most memorable weekends in Rugby World Cup history, but now they were subjected to something quite the opposite. It was clear from the outset that neither side was enthusiastic about the fixture. Defence from both teams was impressive but they failed to find cohesion in attack and it resulted in a disjointed game that yielded an appalling 33 handling errors.

Andrew Mehrtens was the sole contributor for New Zealand, kicking six penalty goals, while Percy Montgomery became the drop-goal exponent for South Africa in the absence of Jannie de Beer, who was replaced by Henry Honiball in the Springbok line-up. Montgomery kicked two drop-goals while Honiball added three penalty goals and converted the only try of the match to wing Breyton Paulse. Playing in his first match of the tournament, Paulse provided the only highlight with a kick and chase before doing well to ground the ball after avoiding the attempted tackle by Christian Cullen.

The two strongest rugby nations of the twentieth century have fought out many brilliant encounters, but this was one of their less impressive duels. South Africa eventually emerged the winner (22–18) and many people associated with the All Blacks were soon in the firing line after what was their eighth defeat from 18 Tests. Coach John Hart became the first to fall in what seemed a classic case of jumping before he was pushed, resigning one day after losing to the Springboks, and skipper Taine Randell became another casualty later on. New Zealand had come to the tournament as favourites, but their preparation had not been ideal and their form was reflective of a team carrying the added burden of a fear of failure. It also seemed they had still not reformed properly after the loss of key personnel such as Sean Fitzpatrick, Zinzan Brooke and Frank Bunce at the end of the 1997 season.

'The All Blacks had a huge fear of failure in 1999 and they had a terrible run in,' says Fitzpatrick. 'In 1997, a lot of us retired and 1998 was a shocker where they lost five games in a row. We should have realised then that it was time to cut our losses and make some tough decisions, but we stuck with the same guys and when the pressure came on against France in 1999 we just fell over.'

Suffice to say that 1999 is not a year any All Blacks fan remembers fondly.

The final

As far as finals go the 1999 tournament decider was a let-down as a spectacle in comparison to the previous weekend, and it was not helped by a playing surface that more resembled the torn-up battle-fields of Normandy rather than a rugby venue. France gave everything in the opening exchanges, but the solid wall of defence from Australia was ever-present again. The Wallabies had conceded just one try in the entire tournament – scored by Juan Grobler from the United States in a pool match – and such was the wrath of their highly regarded defensive coach John Muggleton for that single blemish that not one player in the team dared shirk his responsibility in the tackling stakes for the most important clash of all.

The score was all locked up (6–6) after almost 20 minutes, and France had actually taken the lead on two separate occasions, but there was a sense that Australia still had something in reserve as *Les*

Bleus exhausted their options for little reward before growing increasingly frustrated. Macqueen had devised a game plan around tiring the French back row early on, and trapping them at the breakdown to ensure they could not spark any major counter-attacks. That part was successfully fulfilled in the first half hour. The second part was to maintain discipline at all times and not retaliate to any foul play but instead report it to South Africa referee Andre Watson. France had allegedly carried out tactics of eye-gouging and groping testicles in their semi-final upset win over New Zealand, and Macqueen repeatedly warned his team not to fall victim to the same in the final. Just as Australia had expected, France started their unsettling tactics soon before the half-time break and skipper John Eales immediately brought it to the attention of referee Watson. Two penalties resulted and Matt Burke landed two further penalty goals to extend Australia's lead to six points (12–6) at the break.

The second period began in much the same way as the first ended, and France continued with their attempts to unsettle Australia behind the cover of rucks and mauls. Prop Richard Harry and his front-row partner Michael Foley were allegedly subjected to eye-gouging, as was scrum-half George Gregan, and when Eales received some extra focal treatment of his own the Wallabies captain went as far as threatening to take his players off the field unless the foul play was dealt with in a stricter manner. Part two of the Macqueen game plan effectively reached its pinnacle with that threat and referee Watson did well to control the circumstances. Australia enforcer Toutai Kefu was not convinced it was enough though, and laid a solid blow on flanker Olivier Magne just to let the Frenchman know he would not be taking a backward step. Eventually it was lock Fabien Pelous who received a yellow card, but so too did Eales after it appeared that Watson had received enough refereeing advice. With a player less on either side it would seem that space might open up, but the game continued in the same way with Burke and Christophe Lamaison exchanging penalty goals.

Then it was the turn of fresh legs for Australia and the injection of back row forward Owen Finegan after one hour proved decisive for the Wallabies. Finegan played a linking role out wide for the first try of the match after 67 minutes, with wing Ben Tune bulldozing his way over Xavier Garbajosa in the right corner, and then with the game all but sealed the rampaging back row replacement received a deft inside pass off George Gregan from a lineout before powering over for the try that gave Australia an insurmountable lead. Burke added another late penalty and the final score of 35–12 may have resembled an easy victory, but Australia knew well that they had only come in command during the last 20 minutes and the closing moments were theirs to savour.

'There is no easy way to win a final, but the great thing about that final was for that few minutes at the end when we knew we couldn't be beaten,' recalls John Eales. 'You just don't get that opportunity much in a big match. The 1991 final was frantic until the end, and the 1999 semi-final against South Africa was much the same, but for that final we were really able to enjoy those last few minutes and look around and soak it up.'

When the full-time whistle finally sounded, Australia began celebrating their second Rugby World Cup victory – the first country to ever achieve that feat, and at that time the only country to ever win the title on foreign soil. More than three-quarters of the crowd remained as the players made their way around for a victory lap with 'Land Down Under' – the No. 1 hit from Australian band Men at Work – blasting through the stadium. The Wallabies had set out on their pursuit to 'Bring back Bill' and the coveted trophy boarded the return plane for another four-year stint Down Under.

FIVE MAGIC MEMORIES

Host nation emerges top of the mix amid fiery Pool D deadlock

Pool D – featuring Argentina, Samoa and the host nation Wales – was intriguing not only for how close the contest was between three of the four teams battling for top billing, but also for the verbal fires that simmered beyond the playing surface. The concept of a match commissioner citing a player post-match for illegal play, with the use of television cameras, was still relatively new to the Rugby World Cup. It had been present at the 1995 tournament and avoided major scrutiny, but the same could not be said for 1999 when it received widespread criticism. The negative response largely stemmed from an inconsistency with the number of cameras covering different matches, and as the tournament rolled on other vagaries emerged.

The incident that commanded most interest in the opening match between Wales and Argentina came when Pumas prop Roberto Grau received a yellow card for being at the centre of a fracas with Welsh flanker Colin Charvis. Both were later suspended – Grau for three weeks and Charvis for two weeks – by the match citing commissioner. The citing and punishment seemed acceptable at the time, but after a similar incident went unpunished when Japan played Samoa in the other Pool D match during the opening weekend it didn't sit well with Wales. Samoa prop Brendan Reidy was cited for punching and he escaped unpunished for an act no less serious than that of Charvis.

Such were the inconsistencies that there were nine different camera angles to call on when Charvis and Grau were cited in the opening match, whereas other venues were lucky to have three or four different angles. Wales coach Graham Henry became increasingly critical of the process, and the issue was escalated when Wales played Japan in Cardiff. The match was played in good spirits, but when wing Gareth Thomas scored a try for Wales in the 75th minute he promptly lifted his red jersey to reveal a white shirt adorned with a 'Free Colin Charvis' insignia. Rugby World Cup officials were not impressed. It was against tournament rules for any team to display political messages or advertising, and this message had been directed straight at the officials themselves. There may well have been more serious consequences for Thomas had Wales not been the host nation behind the incident, but those in charge were also keen to bury the issue from major scrutiny in the public eye and chose to let it slide.

While Wales progressed with an easy victory over Japan (64–15) to make it two wins from two matches, Argentina produced a brilliant second period to turn a 13-point half-time deficit into a 16-point victory (32–16) over Samoa. Those two results effectively gave Wales some breathing space ahead of their final pool match against Samoa, but they also triggered complacency. The Samoa match was always going to be a memorable one for fly-half Neil Jenkins, who went on to pass the all-time points-scoring record of Michael Lynagh, but that would be all the host nation would have to cheer at full time as Samoa inflicted another upset on Wales to leave Pool D deadlocked between three.

Wales, Samoa and Argentina all finished with two victories, but the host nation was declared winner of the pool courtesy of having the best for-and-against record. Much to the delight of their players and fans, and despite the loss to Samoa, Wales had still fulfilled the best qualifying path available to them. Argentina and Samoa also lived to fight another day, but they would have to do so via an extra match in the newly formed quarter-final qualifying round. Pool D produced an intriguing battle of three at the 1999 tournament and it was one of few major highlights in an otherwise dull preliminary stage.

Horan star rises from sickbed before Larkham drop-goal genius

On match day morning ahead of the semi-final against South Africa, Australia woke to the news that star centre Tim Horan was still suffering from a bad stomach virus that had kept him awake and vomiting all night. But the stocky centre known for his resilience was given until the very last minute to decide if he would take his place in the side later that day. Skipper John Eales spoke with Horan at breakfast that morning and they shared fond memories of Australian international cricketer Dean Jones, who had defied similar circumstances by scoring an unbeaten double century that saved his team from certain defeat against India in the famous tied Test of 1986 in Madras. It didn't take long after that conversation for Horan to commit, and Australia would be thankful he did.

Buoyed by the return of No. 8 Toutai Kefu, who was back from the two-week suspension he served after delivering a flurry of punches to Ireland flanker Trevor Brennan in the pool rounds, the Wallabies found much-needed parity up front against a hulking Springbok forward pack. Kefu reformed a hard-hitting defensive combination with blindside flanker Matt Cockbain, while openside flanker David Wilson proved menacing for the Springboks with his speed to the breakdown. Kefu also brought back an important dimension to the Wallabies in attack with his ability to carry the ball over the advantage line, allowing the backline room to move and creating space for the ever-present Tim Horan to slice through the Springbok midfield. Horan was lucky to be playing, but there was no trace of any sickness as he produced a Man of the Match performance. The Australia centre was the only player from either side who ever looked like scoring a try, only to be tackled at the last minute by a desperate South Africa defence. Such was the speed and intensity of the match, Australia were tired with their support play and therefore unable to capitalise on Horan splitting the defence.

With the two teams deadlocked (21–21) after regulation time, it was clear that something special was required for a winner to prevail in the scheduled period of extra time. While most would have been excused for thinking drop-goal specialist Jannie de Beer would be the man to break the stalemate, it was his Australia counterpart Stephen Larkham who dealt the killer blow with an awkward-looking 45-metre drop-goal – his first in any form of senior rugby – as the rain continued to drizzle at Twickenham.

'I was on the sideline at the time because I had been replaced after being sick the night before,' recalls Horan. 'I was on the bench and had my boots off. When we saw him shape up, we thought he was going to kick possession away, and we all sort of went: "Oh no!" But sure enough he went for the drop-goal and it didn't look like a good strike, but it probably had about 10 metres left on it after sailing through the posts. It was an amazing kick.'

What made it even more remarkable was that Larkham had internal bleeding in his right knee at the time and his leg was barely stable thanks to a strained medial ligament that would threaten his taking part in the final. But the fly-half who team-mates like to call 'Bernie' – named after the corpse character from the Hollywood comedy *Weekend at Bernie's* – had made it back from four operations during the season preceding the 1999 tournament and unlike his nick-namesake from the film he would not lie down easily. Larkham and Horan left an indelible mark on the tournament during the semi-final against South Africa, and miraculously they both defied further injury limitations to line up in the title decider one week later.

Jonah Lomu: final snapshot of a Rugby World Cup icon

There was always a sense among the wider rugby public that the revelation of Jonah Tali Lomu at the 1995 tournament in South Africa was something quite exceptional, and as the game quickly embraced professionalism it became even clearer that few players would ever have as big an impact on the world stage. Lomu had such a presence in 1995 that New Zealand created their entire game plan around moving the ball to their left wing as often as possible, and as quickly as possible, to maximise the space their 120kg giant had to move, and it worked with devastating consequences against most opposition. Ultimately his presence also forced South Africa to change their tactics for the 1995 final.

'In 1995 we were all sitting around one week before the final watching New Zealand's earlier games in the tournament and wondering how we were going to play against this bloke,' recalls 1995 Springboks fly-half Joel Stransky. 'To prove just how significant an influence he was, we changed our entire game plan to counter his presence and thankfully it worked.'

The Springboks swarmed Lomu in defence during the 1995 tournament decider and the tactics worked. From that point it would seem that most defences now knew how to contain the rampaging Lomu, but the New Zealand giant of Tongan heritage thrived on the Rugby World Cup stage again some four years later in 1999.

'There has only been one player to have as big an impact on the Rugby World Cup as Jonah Lomu did in 1995 and that was Jonah Lomu four years later,' recalls France legend Philippe Sella. 'When he scored against England that try [in the Pool B match at Twickenham] he ran 50 metres and no player could tackle him. Then against France for the semi-final, there were eight French players who try to tackle him and they all fail. That is very unique in the Rugby World Cup.'

Despite his size Lomu could run 100 metres in 10.89 seconds and few teams in world rugby could contain him. The game adopted professionalism at a rapid rate from 1996 and players were given more time and money to build up their own physiques, yet it was still the towering presence of Lomu who instilled the greatest fear in every opponent and kept the crowds coming. Rugby had its own international superstar, but in 1996 Lomu was diagnosed with a rare kidney disorder that would limit his time in the game and ultimately ensure that his appearance for New Zealand in the 1999 semi-final against France would be his last in the Rugby World Cup. The kidney disorder was known as nephritic syndrome and Lomu would eventually succumb to needing dialysis treatment three times a week. Some of the side-effects of the dialysis meant that he experienced chronic nerve damage to his feet and legs, and doctors warned him that if a kidney transplant was not performed as soon as possible he could spend the rest of his life in a wheelchair.

Lomu had been reluctant to have the transplant because it would ultimately end his rugby career, but it finally took place and the new kidney was positioned in an area that gave him another shot at playing for his beloved All Blacks. No one could ever doubt Lomu's determination, as he tried everything possible to resurrect his international career following the transplant in July of 2004, but sadly rugby's greatest stage has seen the last of this phenomenal player. His record as the top Rugby World Cup try-scorer (15) may well be surpassed one day, but it's hard to envisage any player having the same impact across just two tournaments.

All Blacks stunned by France semi-final revival

New Zealand were expected to account for France easily in the second semi-final at Twickenham to set up a 1999 tournament decider with Australia, but predictions are bold when *Les Bleus* are involved and so it would prove on this occasion. The All Blacks dominated the first 45 minutes to be leading 24–10 after two explosive tries to Jonah Lomu either side of half time, and they looked to be in a position whereby one more score would have probably put the game beyond France's reach, yet within a period of less than 10 minutes the course of the game changed dramatically. *Les Blues* had been pressuring the New Zealand line for an extended period with no reward, so their fly-half Christophe Lamaison decided to capitalise with two quick drop-goals. The drop-goal had already played a major part in the tournament, and for the injection of confidence it gave France, these two vital scores from Lamaison proved equally important as those in other matches.

Lamaison added a brace of penalty goals in quick succession together with the drop-goals and all of a sudden France were only two points adrift. New Zealand were clearly stunned as their opponents grew in confidence. France's first two tries came from deftly placed kicks and they soon skipped to a 12-point lead. The All Blacks merely had to shift the ball to Lomu to revive their own cause, but their game-breaker saw limited ball as the self-assurance of France also crippled New Zealand's confidence in attack. When a backline movement broke down with the All Blacks mounting a desperate assault inside the French quarter, France pounced with the killer blow as the ball was toed ahead twice before Philippe Bernat-Salles slid under Jeff Wilson for the match-winning score. It was a victory that not only defied expectations but also the trend for how the game was being played and won across the world at the time.

David Campese – one of rugby's finest advocates of enterprising play – aptly captured the victory in *The Australian*: 'For so long we have been treated to the power games of the southern hemisphere heavyweights – New Zealand, South Africa and Australia. Everyone has been talking about the lack of physical size in the northern hemisphere as the reason for their being behind the eight ball. Wrong. France have shown with that walloping of the All Blacks that there is more to this game than brawn.'

It later emerged that France had the inspiration of two of their 1998 football World Cup winners Marcel Desailly and Didier Deschamps visiting the team before the match against New Zealand. The country was growing increasingly aware of the possibility they could secure an historic world title double, and it was these premature thoughts that worried some former French legends ahead of the final hurdle to claim the title.

'Sometimes when we play one or two good games, or one great game, inside we have a lot of satisfaction. This was the same for the 1999 team that beat New Zealand as it was for the team in 1987 after beating Australia [in the semi-final],' says Philippe Sella. 'But to be consistent enough to win a World Cup, we need to be afraid for each game and stay focussed … we need to have something very tense inside the stomach for every game.'

France as a nation had awoken to the success of their national rugby team and the same media that poured scorn on their team in the early part of the tournament was now applying the pressure of expecting a world title. Their performance against the All Blacks was truly remarkable and will remain part of tournament folklore for years to come, but the final hurdle beyond that victory would prove to be one too many for *Les Bleus*.

Wallabies revisit tactics before ending *Les Bleus* sensation

The French players were buoyed by the fact their entire country had finally awoken to the success of the national team after the semi-final victory over New Zealand. Support flowed in from far and wide with France's bishops, who were gathering in the sacred town of Lourdes – a world famous spiritual area in the rugby heartland of the country's south-west, renowned for producing miracles – among many organisations to announce their support. Australia started the final as favourites to win their second Rugby World Cup title, but there was rising optimism among some pockets of the rugby community who believed France might be able to defy the odds again and produce yet another upset. The Wallabies were very wary of their opponents and the team management was forced to rethink their preparation after expecting to meet New Zealand in the final.

'We certainly felt New Zealand was the likely opponent in the final. We had a lot of different video tapes and planned moves, but we didn't get too far ahead of ourselves,' recalls Tim Horan.

Australia quickly adjusted their focus to France and coach Rod Macqueen ordered his video analysts to gather as much footage as possible. Macqueen was a supreme advocate of knowing your enemy before going into battle and there was no way Australia would make it to the final and leave a single stone unturned. In stark contrast, France was feeding off spontaneity and the hope that they could reproduce another superhuman performance as they did against New Zealand. This time it wasn't to be, however, and not even the blessing of their bishops gathering in Lourdes with 800 young priests and deacons could wake the rugby gods for another *Les Bleus* miracle.

Inspired by former Australia prop and commentator Chris 'Buddha' Handy, who presented the jerseys before the final, the Wallabies were given a passionate reminder of how proud their country was and how equally honoured they should feel to be wearing Wallaby gold that day. At the end of the presentation, 'Buddha' presented skipper John Eales with a bottle of 1991 Grange Hermitage – one of Australia's finest wines – and explained how that year had been a vintage year for the Wallabies after their first Rugby World Cup success. It was a stirring introduction for all and 'Buddha' beamed with confidence before letting his audience know he looked forward to sharing the bottle with the team later.

'Go nude!' became a commonly used phrase throughout the squad during Australia's 1999 campaign, referring to how the team would strive for a clean sheet from every match and not concede any tries. The Macqueen game plan was built on having impenetrable defence, and so it would prove again as France failed to break through Australia in the final. Victory was for the Wallabies on this day and after returning from their lap of honour, 'Buddha' rejoined the team to share a drop of the Grange along with plenty of other celebratory drinks while the players savoured their final moments together before fulfilling post-match duties.

'There was four of us – myself, Joe Roff, Jason Little and Daniel Herbert – still sitting in the baths smoking cigars while everyone was waiting on the bus,' recalls Horan. 'We didn't want to leave because we knew that once we left that dressing room that was it.'

The team celebrations reluctantly ended at the stadium, but Australians rejoiced for days throughout Cardiff and around the world after their Wallabies captured a second Rugby World Cup title. The 1999 pursuit was complete and Australia would hold the crown as rugby continued its rapid global growth into the next millennium.

10

The interim years: 1999–2003

THE FIRST RUGBY World Cup of the professional era heralded yet another new beginning for the sport in what had been an eventful 14-year period from when the international governing body first voted in 1985 to stage a worldwide tournament. As with most major international events, the administrators faced an increasing number of challenges that came with expansion, but for rugby there were an extra few obstacles associated with the transformation from being a strictly amateur code to one that needed to rapidly embrace professionalism at the top level yet still maintain a solid connection with its grassroots community. While players at the highest level could now become dedicated sports professionals, most rugby clubs around the world still had to operate under an amateur structure and it was this situation that had many critics of the Rugby World Cup still very vocal in their stance against the event. The number of tournament detractors had certainly dwindled throughout the 1990s, but some traditionalists still argued that most rugby clubs faced an uncertain future as they tried to sustain their existence in a sport that was becoming increasingly top-heavy as a commercial entity.

Tournament critics argued that the Rugby World Cup had created an unsustainable future for its grassroots, but the accusation was perhaps a little premature given the sport was receiving most of its newfound income at the top level and it still needed time to be digested to the lower ranks. Unlike the growth of the event, which was occurring at an unprecedented rate, it would take much longer for the new funds generated at the top level to filter down to club level – an ongoing process that is still taking shape within the major rugby countries let alone those who are still trying to implement professionalism at the top level. With such extraordinary growth also comes some demanding public expectations, and both the tournament organisers and rugby administrators became increasingly aware of this following the 1999 tournament.

'If anything has occurred which has left a fairly strong impression on us it is the fact we've grown up so quickly as a tournament that both the public, and viewer, and other's expectations have become so high,' the late Vernon Pugh (IRB Chairman) told reporters on the eve of the 1999 final. 'Expectations on us are not just to run the tournament now, but to ensure that we have a big social impact, a broad commercial impact.'

Match attendance figures had increased by 37 per cent from 1.1 million spectators in 1995 to 1.75 million spectators in 1999, and with that also came an 11 per cent increase in the cumulative worldwide television audience figures from 2.67 billion viewers in 1995 to 3 billion viewers in 1999. It was all positive growth for rugby in the wake of those challenges posed by the WRC and Super League during the formative years of professionalism. For the game's administrators, however, perhaps the most comforting of all statistics from the 1999 tournament was that the disparity of how professionalism was advancing in both hemispheres was less apparent after England performed admirably in the pool rounds before an unlucky exit against South Africa in the quarter-finals while France unexpectedly advanced to the final.

While the southern hemisphere heavyweights continued leading the way beyond the 1999 tournament, the likes of England under coach Clive Woodward were quickly learning from their rivals how to best operate in the professional rugby environment. Australia coach Rod Macqueen was widely acclaimed for his part in the Wallabies succeeding at Rugby World Cup 1999, and the structure he developed in the years before and after that triumph became the coaching model that many would strive for.

'What Rod Macqueen did for Australian rugby was quite amazing. When we won in 1999 we had basically the same pool of players as when we were struggling in 1996–97,' recalls former Australia captain John Eales. 'Rod created a structure that turned that all around, and a fairly average team became a very good team in the space of less than two years. He also had a great vision for how the game could be played and how to win a Rugby World Cup.'

More than just a great vision for how the game could be played and some lateral thinking to create a structure for his coaching methods to thrive in, Macqueen brought an unprecedented amount of research to pre-match preparation. The Wallabies coach revealed in his auto-biography *One Step Ahead* that his team more often than not had a checklist of up to 60 points they would assess against every opponent. He also realised that his rugby coaching mind alone was not enough and the use of specialist coaches was paramount for his team to succeed.

'Rod was probably a few years before his time and the first person to really use a business model on an international rugby team,' says former Australia centre Tim Horan. 'He knew all of the aspects of the game that he needed to, and all of the people around him like Tim Lane, Jeff Miller, John Muggleton and the other specific coaches knew their own area really well. He had good ideas as a coach as well, but he was a great rugby manager. He heralded a new age in coaching and you probably realised that the most when we were at Camp Wallaby and there were other coaches there taking notes on what we were doing. Not copying moves, but copying our coaching structure and how it was all put together. It wasn't rocket science, but he picked up a good business model, brought it to the sporting arena, then put really good people around him and it worked.'

One of those from the northern hemisphere to assess the Macqueen coaching structure was England coach Clive Woodward. The former international centre is credited for having an astute rugby brain in his own right, but he had no qualms about swallowing some pride to learn how a successful rival was operating. England had advanced their game at an impressive rate under Woodward since he came to the helm in 1997, and they were becoming more competitive with the top nations in the world, yet the England coach knew his team needed to gain that extra edge not only to compete with the best but also to beat the best. Woodward's efforts to apply some lateral thinking to his own management structure would eventually reap rewards in the latter part of the interim years between 1999 and 2003, but first it was the reigning world champions Australia who would continue to dominate the world stage under Macqueen and bask in the glory of winning successive Tri-Nations titles in 2000 and 2001, while also claiming their first ever series victory over the British and Irish Lions in 2001.

The 2001 series against the Lions was in many ways the final frontier for Macqueen and in the end an appropriate means for his successful tenure to conclude. The Wallabies had been disappointing in the opening Test against the Lions, losing 29–13 in Brisbane, but they bounced back in Melbourne one week later to turn the series around with a resounding 35–14 victory. Almost as though he sensed his world champion team was descending from their peak, Macqueen came out with the shock announcement that he would stand down after the third and deciding Test in Sydney regardless of the result. Macqueen had been expected to retire after the Tri-Nations later that year, but an apparent change of heart during the week leading into the second Test made him believe it was time for his successor Eddie Jones to take the helm after the Lions series.

'I believe it's time for a fresh approach for the team and now seems the appropriate time,' Macqueen told a packed press conference after victory in the second Test. 'We've planned for Eddie Jones to come in and he's been involved with the side since day one this year. He's done an excellent job and he's ready to go on from here. From my perspective … when I reflect over my career, I've enjoyed every moment – I've got no regrets. I'm pleased to be making this decision after a win and not after a loss.'

On the surface it seemed like Macqueen simply felt he had reached the end of his coaching term earlier than expected. However, whether it was done so consciously or not, one of the most successful rugby coaches of the modern era was playing the final trump card of his outstanding tenure. The Wallabies were not playing as solidly as they had been in 1999 and 2000, and a little extra incentive to perform well for their outgoing coach in the deciding Test against the Lions provided a welcomed boost for a team on the wane. Australia went on to win a thrilling match in Sydney (29–23) and seal their first series victory over the Lions. Macqueen had conquered all, and a new era dawned for the Wallabies under their next coach Eddie Jones.

Victory over the Lions brought the Wallabies an extra crown – the

Tom Richards Cup – to an already well-occupied trophy cabinet, and they reconfirmed their status as world champions later that year by defending both the Bledisloe Cup and Tri-Nations in dramatic circumstances to provide the perfect farewell for another one of their finest – dual Rugby World Cup winner and captain John Eales. South Africa had troubled Australia in 2001, defeating the Wallabies 20–15 in Pretoria and drawing 14–14 in Perth, but Australia made up some ground in the overall Tri-Nations standings with a memorable victory (23–15) over the All Blacks in Dunedin. The stage was then set for a thrilling decider between Australia and New Zealand in Sydney, with the winner securing both the Bledisloe Cup and Tri-Nations trophies. The All Blacks looked to be on their way to victory in the closing minutes until a storming run from Australia No. 8 Toutai Kefu, who beat numerous tackles on his way to scoring a try that would hand the Wallabies back-to-back Tri-Nations titles and their fourth consecutive Bledisloe Cup series. It had been a deserving end for Eales, who had been a great servant to Australian rugby and the international game. Many fans thought it might have been too premature to call an end on his distinguished career, but Eales has no regrets.

'It was an easy decision for me to retire. I had just had enough of playing and I wanted to do other things. The training didn't interest me any more and I just wanted to go and do other things in life,' Eales said. 'I definitely wanted to keep playing after the 1999 World Cup and didn't even contemplate retirement at that stage because I really wanted to play in the British Lions series. The last time they came to Australia was two years before I first played Test rugby, and I knew it was a one and only opportunity. The Tri-Nations was another one that I wanted to do. We hadn't won that and we managed to do so in 2000 and 2001.'

And so the post-1999 Australian fairytale ended with a fitting farewell to one of their finest legends at the end of 2001. Two other key veterans of the squad – Tim Horan and David Wilson – had also retired the year before and the departure of Eales signalled the start of a major rebuilding period for the Wallabies under Eddie Jones. New Zealand reclaimed the Tri-Nations trophy in 2002, and the Bledisloe Cup finally returned to their shores in 2003 after a record five-year stay in Australia. South Africa remained solid against Australia, but they couldn't trouble New Zealand and the balance of power shifted in the southern hemisphere as the All Blacks resumed their dominance.

Meanwhile, in the northern hemisphere, England were clearly establishing themselves as the leading force in Europe under their reinvigorated coach Clive Woodward. While France had produced an outstanding Six Nations campaign to secure the Grand Slam in 2002, the following year would signal total world domination for Woodward and his men. Fresh from claiming their first Six Nations Grand Slam since 1995, England set out in 2003 to do what none of their predecessors had done before by defeating Australia and New Zealand away from home over consecutive weeks. First there came a hard-fought and narrow victory (15–13) over the All Blacks in Wellington, before a forward-dominating performance against Australia in Melbourne one week later yielded an historic double. Woodward had finally created the dominant structure he longed for with English rugby.

'I don't like it when anyone says it was a business approach because it's rugby, it's about passion, it's about going out there and giving it your all,' says Martin Johnson. 'It's not a business strategy; it's a game of rugby.'

It is indeed just a game of rugby after all, but in the new era of professionalism there are constantly evolving coaching methods required to bring out the best a rugby nation has to offer. Macqueen quickly discovered and applied those methods in the fledgling stages of professionalism ahead of 1999, and Woodward took it to another level during the cycle that preceded Rugby World Cup 2003. England established a formidable home record at 'Fortress Twickenham' – winning 22 consecutive home matches between 1999 and 2003. On the back of a successful tour to Australasia in 2003, just months before the main event, England was primed to lead the most success-ful northern hemisphere assault that Rugby World Cup had ever experienced.

11

Rugby World Cup 2003: the tournament

THE FIFTH RUGBY World Cup turned out to be a vibrant and spectacular event in Australia three years after that country played host to the largest world sport audience of all via the Olympic Games. Sydney was host to the world once again. The 2003 tournament had originally been awarded as a co-hosted event between Australia and New Zealand, with Australia acting as the main host and New Zealand as the sub-host, but it was eventually awarded solely to Australia in controversial circumstances. One of the pre-tournament requirements for the Rugby World Cup is for the host nations to provide clean stadiums, which are free of all advertising and with corporate boxes relinquished by those sponsors and/or companies who normally hold them. However, one major difference between the clean stadium requirements for the 2003 tournament and the event in Wales four years earlier was that the international governing body requested 100 per cent of the corporate boxes to be available compared to just 50 per cent in 1999.

In many ways it was yet another adjustment that rugby needed to make at the top level as the Rugby World Cup became a bigger commercial entity. While it seems the host nations in 2003 were dealt with unfairly compared to previous hosts, it was a necessary change for the growth of the tournament and plenty of warning had been given by the tournament organising committee. Some commentators suggested there were problems with the co-hosting arrangement between Australia and New Zealand as far back as July 2001, and the clean stadium debacle was the so-called final straw in an already doomed partnership. But a closer investigation reveals it was much more of an issue between the New Zealand Rugby Union (NZRU) and the international governing body, rather than a dispute between the co-hosts – as it was later perceived by many.

According to a detailed article on the clean stadium fiasco by Paul Panckhurst in the New Zealand business magazine *Unlimited* in June 2002, the NZRU lost the co-hosting rights 'through a mixture of apathy, incompetence and childish behaviour'. The apathy part came from the top level in terms of its lack of urgency to deal with ensuring the stadiums were clean. As far back as May 1999, the then NZRU chief executive David Moffett reportedly spoke of how important the issue of securing clean stadiums was for New Zealand to co-host the event, yet those administrators who succeeded Moffett – chairman Murray McCaw and chief executive David Rutherford – failed to carry forward that same sense of urgency and the problem was shelved until it was all too late. With the deadline for New Zealand to give the guarantee of clean stadiums fast approaching in early March of 2002, some of the corporate box holders at Eden Park and the other main stadiums were contacted for the first time with a request to relinquish their rights to those boxes. Most were very accommodating but some were not so obliging and there was clearly no time to negotiate the issue at a domestic level. Meanwhile, Australia had guaranteed 100 per cent clean stadiums months before and under the shrewd leadership of John O'Neill the Australian Rugby Union (ARU) devised a viable plan to take sole hosting rights of the event if New Zealand could not fulfil their part of the agreement.

On March 8, 2002, the IRB and Rugby World Cup Limited decided to strip New Zealand of its co-hosting status and award the entire event to Australia. The NZRU had one final chance to reverse the decision at a special meeting of the IRB Council more than one month later on April 18, but the vitriol conveyed in the media by McCaw and Rutherford together with personal attacks on key stakeholders saw New Zealand's chances of reversing the decision all but fade away. At one stage McCaw directed a remark at the IRB Chairman Vernon Pugh he would later regret: 'I'm not prepared to say it's an abuse of power, but it does open up the question ... you can't have someone who's a town planning QC running a global sport, let alone trying to run what is commonly referred to as the third or fourth biggest sporting event in the world.'

One day after New Zealand lost their co-hosting rights, the sports minister Trevor Mallard also weighed in with unsavoury comments directed at Pugh by saying on Radio Sport that he would like to insert a bottle of Heineken (Rugby World Cup sponsor and event beer supplier to all stadiums) in an uncomfortable place for both Pugh and ARU administrator John O'Neill. The comments were beamed throughout the rugby world and New Zealand was left in an untenable position ahead of the final meeting that would decide their fate. Not surprisingly the IRB Council voted overwhelmingly against New Zealand playing any part in hosting the event. Hence the combined incompetence and resulting childish behaviour of leading administrators at the NZRU denied the country a chance to play co-host, and retired judge Sir Thomas Eichelbaum was asked to conduct a full inquiry. The findings of Sir Thomas were best summed up in the *New Zealand Herald* on July 24, 2002:

'Personal attacks by the heads of the New Zealand Rugby Football Union on International Rugby Board chief Vernon Pugh were "inexcusable", says retired judge Sir Thomas Eichelbaum. His investigation into New Zealand's handling of the 2003 rugby World Cup debacle was unequivocal in condemning chief executive officer David Rutherford and chairman Murray McCaw for their outbursts. Both men quit as the report was made public to compensate for New Zealand's loss of hosting rights to world rugby's lucrative showpiece. Sir Thomas said: "With justification, Mr Pugh, Rugby World Cup Limited directors and IRB councillors regarded them as offensive and hurtful".'

Sir Thomas was also very keen to point out that Mr Pugh had in fact done a lot to help New Zealand in the co-hosting arrangement rather than prevent their inclusion:

'Mr Pugh had helped NZRU in three significant respects in particular. He fended off ARU attempts to take over the New Zealand semi final, effected the financial settlement which rescued NZRU when faced with a loss and was instrumental in New Zealand salvaging something in its bid.' [Independent Rugby World Cup Inquiry: Report of The Reviewer (Sir Thomas Eichelbaum), section 12.7]

Pugh had been the unfair target of criticism from NZRU officials, yet his unquestioned commitment to the administration of the game would be highlighted in years to come. Sadly the IRB chairman died abruptly from cancer on April 24, 2003, aged 57, before the fifth Rugby World Cup would take place in Australia some six months later, but his legacy continues to be played out on rugby's greatest stage and beyond. The leading QC who gave up the opportunity to become a High Court judge to lead rugby into the professional era will be forever remembered as one of the most influential administrators the game has ever seen.

The pool stage

While the co-hosting dramas played out on the administrative front, the 2003 qualifying process was in full swing as 81 countries took part in a series of regional events that would determine the 12 remaining places at the Rugby World Cup in Australia. The eight quarter-finalists from the 1999 tournament – Australia, France, South Africa, New Zealand, Argentina, Scotland, England and Wales – were all guaranteed qualification. The only new team welcomed to the fold in 2003 was Georgia, who made it to the finals as the fourth and final qualifier from Europe – a position previously held by Spain in 1999. The former Soviet state, located on the juncture of Eastern Europe and Western Asia, is a developing rugby nation to say the least. It is widely reported that they only had one scrum machine in the entire country and just a few professional players running around in France. They did not have the same infrastructure to compete with most other nations at the 2003 tournament, but the *Lelos* – a nickname developed from an indigenous Georgian sport that has many similarities to rugby – brought plenty of passion and pride that the Australian population quickly warmed to.

The cumulative stadium capacity for Australia in 2003 was less than it had been for Wales in 1999, but ticket sales still hit a record high of more than 1.8 million – an increase of approximately 83,000 overall. More significantly, following the fall-out of the co-hosting arrangement with New Zealand, the ARU was able to schedule games in regions less familiar with rugby and they did so with tremendous success. Most notably it was Adelaide in South Australia, and Launceston in Tasmania, where Test match rugby had never been played before, which benefited most. Both venues experienced sell-out crowds for lowly fixtures that might not have drawn such interest in the major rugby regions. Perth in Western Australia, another city outside the rugby stronghold states of Queensland and New South Wales, also had a good share of the action as it hosted five games from the pool featuring England and South Africa.

In addition to the major stadiums in the metropolitan areas of the traditional rugby states within Australia, there were also some more regional areas that hosted memorable matches. Townsville in tropical North Queensland was given a taste and so too were Gosford and Wollongong in New South Wales. Rugby World Cup 2003 captured an entire nation still riding the success of hosting the Olympic Games three years before. The tournament again consisted of 20 teams, but the five-pool format from 1999 was cast aside in favour of four pools of five teams.

Rugby World Cup 2003: The pools and order they finished

Pool A	Pool B	Pool C	Pool D
Australia	France	England	New Zealand
Ireland	Scotland	South Africa	Wales
Argentina	Fiji	Samoa	Italy
Romania	United States	Uruguay	Canada
Namibia	Japan	Georgia	Tonga

The Opening Ceremony at Rugby World Cup 2003 was remarkably different to that of 1999. The Australian organising committee opted for a more even spread of entertainment that included some music acts but more of a cultural focus with Australian Aboriginal dance prominent among numerous performances involving children. Former Australia captain and dual Rugby World Cup winner John Eales played a part and so too did a fortunate young boy named James Patrick from the under-13 team at St Joseph's College in Sydney. Patrick lined up an impossible 80-metre place kick during the Opening Ceremony and, with the aid of some special effects, kicked the goal much to the delight of the sell-out crowd. But the main highlight came when a large group of children, holding cards of different colours, formed the shape of a giant rugby player before fulfilling a sequence that had the player run the length of the field ahead of scoring a try in the corner to a rousing applause. Then it was time for the main act.

Host nation Australia was tasked with facing Argentina in the opening match of the tournament, and it proved to be a closer encounter than most pundits predicted. The two teams were in Pool A along with Ireland and it was widely dubbed the 'Pool of Death' for 2003, with only the top two teams able to qualify for the knockout stage. The Wallabies showed touches of class but they were far from convincing, aided by some poor execution from the Pumas. Argentina hooker Mario Ledesma was guilty of seven crooked lineout throws that resulted in Australia being handed possession, and fly-half Felipe Contepomi managed to slot just one goal from five attempts while the top points scorer from Rugby World Cup 1999 – Gonzalo Quesada – sat unused on the bench. Australia had only a nine-point cushion well into the final 10 minutes of play, but a late try to Joe Roff sealed the victory (24–8). The biggest blow for the Wallabies came after the match when it was confirmed that lock David Giffin would be side-lined for two matches after taking a kick-off in the second half and landing awkwardly on his shoulder.

Ireland opened their account against a spirited Romania side in Gosford the following day. Throngs of Irish supporters made their way north of Sydney to the Central Coast of New South Wales, but a large portion of the local community were supporting Romania and it made for some entertaining banter among the crowd. It took Ireland 20 minutes to score their first try as the Romania forwards put in a gallant effort to unsettle their more fancied opponents. At one stage the Romania pack stole a tight-head scrum and despite trailing 26–0 at half time they came back at the Irish early in the second half. However some brilliant running from fullback Girvan Dempsey saw Ireland score two quick tries that thwarted the Romanian challenge before the men in green eventually prevailed 45–17. One of the more humorous highlights of the match came when Ireland hooker and captain Keith Wood took a pass from scrum-half Peter Stringer more than 30 metres out from the Romania line before winding up his front row legs to add yet another try to his impressive international tally. The sight of a front row forward scoring a try always brings a smile, and Wood was given due recognition from the Gosford crowd.

Argentina played Namibia three days later at the same venue and the Pumas won comfortably (67–14) to put their campaign back on track after the loss to Australia. Centre Martin Gaitin starred for the

Pumas with three tries, and their forward pack dominated to force two penalty tries while No. 8 Pablo Bouza also scored a double.

The second weekend in Pool A saw Australia notch up a record score against Romania (90–8) in Brisbane. The Wallabies set off to an explosive start when Elton Flatley scored the fastest try in Rugby World Cup history after just 13 seconds of play, but a series of handling errors (14 in total) gave some cause for concern. Perhaps the least flattering statistic of all for Australia though was the crowd, with the stadium almost 4,000 short of capacity as only 48,778 spectators attended. According to organisers most of the vacant seats had apparently been paid for and just not used. However, some critics suggested ticket prices for the match were too high and fans simply were not prepared to pay such a high price to watch their team destroy lowly-ranked opposition.

Record scores continued to mount across Pool A as Ireland defeated Namibia (64–7) in the pouring rain at Aussie Stadium in Sydney, and Argentina notched up another healthy victory at that same venue against Romania (50–3) – with the Pumas pack dominating again for two pushover tries and Martin Gaitin enjoying another fine performance in the midfield. Australia recorded a cricket score (142–0) against a Namibia side that missed 81 tackles at the Adelaide Oval, where fullback Chris Latham starred with five tries and Mat Rogers had an individual haul of 42 points.

Romania and Namibia were both on the receiving end of some heavy defeats at the 2003 tournament, but a positive memory both teams took home was playing a part in the historic match at Launceston in Tasmania. The island state off the south-east corner of the Australian mainland had never hosted a rugby Test match, and it proved to be a memorable occasion as the local community and more than 15,000 people attending the match were encouraged to adopt either one of the teams based on whether they were born in an odd year or an even year. It was a great marketing ploy and brought widespread interest to a fixture that might have otherwise failed to lure a crowd half that size.

Without doubt the two most captivating matches in Pool A came over the final two weekends of the preliminary rounds when Ireland faced Argentina at the Adelaide Oval before backing up one week later to face Australia in Melbourne. In Adelaide it was Argentina playing to stay alive in the tournament. Four years earlier the Pumas had defeated Ireland in a quarter-final qualifier and the men in green were out to atone for that blemish from 1999. It was a close encounter, with only one point deciding the final outcome, but Ireland triumphed this time around (16–15) to keep their 2003 dream alive. Skipper Keith Wood fronted the media after the match and appeared a touch frustrated yet clearly relieved with the victory.

'We played poorly for periods of the game,' Wood said. 'There was obviously a lot of pressure and we seemed to freeze somewhat out there. But there was the weight of expectation that has been building the last four years. The shackles are now off.'

The victory over Argentina sealed a quarter-final place for Ireland, but they were not content with second place in Pool A and would go on to mount a stern challenge against Australia. On a cool night in Melbourne after the famous Victoria Derby Day during the annual Spring Racing Carnival, frocked up fans made their way to the Telstra Dome for what turned out to be another thriller. After the joy of being on the winning end of a one-point triumph over Argentina one week earlier, Ireland were less fortunate this time as Australia escaped with the narrowest of victories (17–16) despite a solid start that saw them leading by eight points after 17 minutes. Brian O'Driscoll scored an outstanding try for Ireland, and they were in a position to steal the match when David Humphreys lined up a long-range drop-goal in the closing minutes, but the shot failed to hit its mark and Australia held on to win the pool. Wallabies captain George Gregan took his team in a huddle for a long time at the end of the match and when faced by the media he rather aptly commented: '. . . we weren't at our best, but we survived.'

Pool B was undoubtedly the most entertaining of all four pools during the preliminary stages of Rugby World Cup 2003. With the enthusiasm and adventure of Japan and Fiji, combined with the class of France and dogged style of Scotland, it was always likely to produce some entertaining matches. The first ended with a lopsided result as France defeated Fiji (61–18) in front of sell-out crowd in Brisbane, but the final score was not reflective of the promising signs shown by Fiji early on. Only in the final 20 minutes of the match did France stamp their authority to produce what was described by some as their best-ever performance in a pool match. *Les Bleus* were clinical in attack as fly-half Frederic Michalak guided the backline with assurance, and they absorbed pressure in defence while maintaining discipline. It was a stark contrast to French teams past, who were often let down by ill discipline when under pressure and not renowned for consistency. For Fiji it was their exciting wing Rupeni Caucaunibuca who demonstrated his outstanding scoring capabilities with a 70-metre try that left a series of French defenders scratching their heads. 'Caucau', as he is more widely known, was a crowd favourite, but his temperament proved a lot less impressive than his running after he was eventually banned for two weeks after punching France flanker Olivier Magne.

The following day saw Japan take on Scotland in Townsville, where the local population quickly warmed to the Asian champions. The Cherry Blossoms played three of their four pool games in the tropical North Queensland city and despite not taking a single victory away from the tournament they captured the hearts of many with some brave and entertaining play led by their exciting wing Daisuke Ohata. Japan were trailing Scotland by just four points with 15 minutes remaining before eventually losing (32–11), and against Fiji they trailed by just three points at half time before tiring in the second period to lose 41–13. A similar scenario eventuated against France, where Japan were just one point behind during the second half. However, as was the case in their previous matches, the Cherry Blossoms wilted in the latter stages and were eventually defeated 51–29. Japan's best chance of a victory was when they lined up against the United States in Gosford, but the move some 2500km south from the familiar surrounds of Townsville did them no favours as they were overcome (39–26) by a determined United States team that was delighted to end the longest losing streak in Rugby World Cup history – stretching 10 matches back to 1987.

The United States had been equally courageous as Japan throughout the pool rounds and they were very unlucky not to pull off a victory over Fiji in Brisbane, where fly-half Mike Hercus was presented with a decisive conversion attempt from the sideline after Kort Schubert scored in injury time. Unfortunately for the United States, Hercus missed the kick and was left shattered, but his teammates rushed to console their star player, and coach Tom Billups also came to the defence of his fly-half: 'It's a 15-man game and it's not Mike's job to win the game at the death.'

France had been clinical in their opening match against Fiji, but *Les*

Bleus lost their way slightly against Japan and the lapse in form coincidently came when they lost their popular mascot 'Doimede'. The live rooster – borrowed from a chicken farm at Capalaba in Brisbane's east – was happy to be returned to female company following a two-week period travelling with the team. Concerned flanker Patrick Tabacco, who has a farming background, told his team-mates the rooster looked stressed and was 'missing his hens', so the team decided to let the mascot return to his fowl yard. Perhaps it had a greater affect on the team than first thought as France produced a shaky performance against an enthusiastic Japan side, but they bounced back with a convincing victory over Scotland (51–9) in Sydney. *Les Bleus* then followed up that success with a comfortable victory (41–14) over the United States in their final match of the preliminary stage in Wollongong to claim top place in Pool B, and Scotland scraped through for second place after a last-gasp victory over Fiji in Sydney.

Perth in Western Australia played host to the opening five matches in Pool C – an intriguing group that featured two heavyweights in the form of England and South Africa, plus crowd favourites Samoa, South American qualifiers Uruguay, and Rugby World Cup debutants Georgia. The opening match saw South Africa take on Uruguay in a game where the Springboks were rarely tested on their way to enjoying a comfortable victory (72–6). It was a similar lopsided story at the same venue the following day, but England had to defy some strong early resistance from tournament newcomers Georgia. The revered might of 'Dad's Army', as England had been tagged by the local media for their aging team, was subdued a number of times when reaching for their trump card rolling maul, and the scrum did not have the same ferocity as usual. Georgia came out firing early on and even drew level after 10 minutes, but England soon found their rhythm to hand Georgia a heavy defeat (84–6).

Samoa also opened their campaign with a comprehensive victory (60–13) over Uruguay, but the match that generated most interest early in Pool C came on the second weekend when England lined up against South Africa. It was crucial for the fact the winner would effectively claim top place in the group, while the loser would most likely be tasked with the unenviable path of facing New Zealand in the quarter-finals. It was an intense showdown from the opening whistle and it was clear early on that the goal kickers would play a vital role in determining the final result. While South Africa fly-half Louis Koen misfired with four attempts in the first half, his opposite number Jonny Wilkinson kicked England to an early lead that they would never surrender despite increasing pressure from the Springboks in the set pieces. Wilkinson eventually produced a flaw-less kicking display that included four penalty goals, two drop-goals and a conversion from the only try of the match to centre Will Greenwood, which came off a charge-down from Lewis Moody. Koen managed two penalty goals in reply and England overcame the first major hurdle of their campaign with an emphatic victory (25–6).

Most fans could be forgiven for thinking that match would be the only major showdown in Pool C, but there was a proud Samoa team that would go very close to pulling off the biggest upset in Rugby World Cup history one week later. The Pacific Islanders had been quietly going about their business and followed up their impressive showing against Uruguay with another comfortable victory over Georgia (46–9) in the last match played in Perth before the group made its way to the east coast of Australia for the second half of the preliminary stage.

First it was Georgia who sent a few shockwaves through a second-string South Africa team at Aussie Stadium in Sydney before the Springboks eventually prevailed (46–19), but on the following night in Melbourne it was England – the number one ranked team in the world – trailing by 10 points early on against a very spirited and underrated Samoa side. When Jonny Wilkinson missed some early shots at goal and Samoa took a 16–13 lead to the break, an upset seemed very possible, but England eventually played their way back into the match and overcame the Pacific Islanders in the closing stages to escape with what seemed a comfortable victory (35–22) – but one of the tournament favourites were given an almighty scare much earlier than they had expected in their campaign.

Samoa had caught England off-guard and South Africa were not going to be fooled the following week. Unfortunately when the Pacific Islanders faced the Springboks they could not muster the same exuberance that saw them send shockwaves through the England camp, and they were defeated convincingly (60–10) in Brisbane. However, one memorable moment for Samoa fans came when 'The Chiropractor' – Brian Lima – pulled off a trademark bone-jarring tackle on Springboks fly-half Derick Hougaard.

'It's definitely the hardest tackle I've taken in my life, but I'm still breathing and that's a good sign,' Hougaard quipped after the match.

Uruguay and Georgia fought out an entertaining duel to avoid the Pool A wooden spoon at Aussie Stadium in Sydney, where there were emotional scenes in front of a near capacity crowd as the South Americans secured their first Rugby World Cup victory. But their joy was short-lived and the final say in Pool C was for England, who recovered from the shock against Samoa to trounce Uruguay (111–13) and put their campaign back on track. The most impressive aspect of the 17 tries scored by England against Uruguay was the great boost they gave to the Nick Duncombe Memorial Fund, with Zurich pledging to donate £10 for every point scored by England at the tournament. Duncombe, a promising young scrum-half who was likely to be part of the England squad, tragically lost his life in February 2003 to a mysterious blood infection while holidaying with friends in Spain.

Pool D opened in the same lopsided fashion as most others, with tournament heavyweights New Zealand opening their campaign with a comprehensive victory over Italy (70–7), but the win came at a major price for the All Blacks after they lost their outside centre Tana Umaga to a knee injury in the 26th minute – an injury that would see him take no further part in the tournament. New Zealand has struggled to find a dominant player to fill the No. 13 jersey for much of the Rugby World Cup era, and just when they seemed to have one it was cruelly taken away. While the All Blacks looked to have easily overcome the loss of Umaga against Italy, his absence from the backline became more apparent against stronger opposition later on.

Despite having lost to Italy earlier that year and being handed the dreaded wooden spoon from the 2003 Six Nations, Wales was the team widely tipped to progress as runner-up in Pool D behind the All Blacks. However, they didn't have it all their own way as both Tonga and Italy provided stern challenges for the Red Dragons in Canberra. First Wales had to overcome a spirited first-half challenge from Canada in Melbourne before eventually prevailing (41–10) as the Canucks began to tire in the second period. Then their campaign moved to Canberra where Tonga provided the stiff physical resistance teams come to expect, but the Pacific Islanders were unable to convert the opportunities they had to win the match and Wales would maintain their unbeaten start with a narrow victory (27–20) that effectively ended Tonga's chances of a quarter-final berth. The shootout for second place in the pool then came down to the clash between Wales and Italy. The *Azzurri* had the mental edge following a victory over Wales in the Six Nations earlier that year, but their form at the tournament had been questionable. It was not a match for spectators to savour – a war of attrition between two teams scrapping for a single ticket to the knockout phase. Wales won the day (27–15) and secured their place in the quarter-finals, and Italy were left to ponder yet another campaign that would end after the preliminary rounds. Their coach – former All Blacks legend John Kirwan – was convinced his side needed to be in front at half time to have their best chance of defeating Wales. Lost opportunities cost them, but the Italy coach was determined to maintain a positive outlook for his team.

'We made errors mid-way through the first half when we needed to turn it into points. We had 40 minutes [in the second half] to win and we knew after half time the fatigue would get to us,' Kirwan said. 'We had a couple of opportunities and when you're talking Test match rugby and the difference between going to the quarter-finals or not, we're talking about inches. We missed a couple of tries by inches.'

While Italy secured third place with two wins and two losses, it was left to Canada and Tonga to battle it out to avoid the wooden spoon in Pool D. The Canucks could not match their best-ever performance at a Rugby World Cup – a quarter-final appearance in 1991 – but they could walk away with pride intact from victory over Tonga and they did exactly that (24–7) to give their veteran captain Al Charron the farewell he richly deserved. The towering 37-year-old forward would struggle to remember much from the match after he was knocked out cold from a sickening head-clash early on, but his team-mates ensured that both their campaign and their captain's career would end on a high.

New Zealand continued on their destructive path through Pool D, casting aside Canada (68–6) in Melbourne before dishing out another heavy defeat to Tonga (91–7) in their third pool match in Brisbane. However, while the All Blacks continued to flex their strongest muscle by attacking with width and using the superior speed and skill of their backline to devastating effect, there were some early glimpses that if a team held on to possession and denied New Zealand turnover ball, some chinks started appearing in the All Black armour. This weakness became even more apparent in the final game of the group stage when a second-string Wales team gave New Zealand the fright of their lives in Sydney. The bookies gave Wales a 40-point start after their coach Steve Hansen named an under-strength side with a view to preserving his top players for a looming quarter-final clash with England, but the second tier group gave everything asked of them and more before almost pulling off the unthinkable. Wales were leading for a majority of the match and looked poised for victory with less than 10 minutes remaining, but New Zealand eventually found their feet in the final minutes to overcome a gallant challenge by the Red Dragons (53–37).

New Zealand scored a record 42 tries during the pool stage, which was 12 more than the cumulative total of all four other teams in Pool D, yet for all of the attacking prowess shown there was a weakness exposed by Wales in Sydney and the flaw was not lost on other major contenders set to face the All Blacks later in the tournament.

The quarter-finals

After a successful pool stage that went close to spanning the entire landmass of Australia, the quarter-finals were held in Melbourne and Brisbane. The first took place at the Telstra Dome in Melbourne, where two southern hemisphere heavyweights – New Zealand and South Africa – squared off for a place in the final four. The Springboks had easily cast aside every opponent in their pool but they endured an agonising loss to England, while the All Blacks had been sensational in their march to the knockout phase, only to have shown some vulnerability in a 50-minute period against Wales one week before. New Zealand were tipped to win, but there were a few nagging statistics that the Springbok fans were quick to remind their All Black counterparts of. New Zealand had never defeated South Africa in Rugby World Cup competition, and even more significantly the All Blacks had never crossed for a try against the Springboks in Rugby World Cup competition.

New Zealand started the match like a team desperate to atone for past failures, denying South Africa possession for the opening 10 minutes on the back of a dominating scrum and lineout. The Springboks were feeling the pressure early on, and the solid platform provided by the All Blacks forward pack allowed Carlos Spencer to weave his magic at fly-half. Spencer made the break that created New Zealand's first try and the boot of Leon MacDonald ensured they would enjoy a 13–6 lead at the break. To their credit, South Africa rallied well with minimal possession and trailed by just seven points until the 59th minute when All Blacks hooker Keven Mealamu ran 25 metres to score a try that would extend New Zealand's lead to 12 points. MacDonald added another penalty soon after, and when Spencer cheekily passed through his legs after a turnover forced by flanker Rueben Thorne, Joe Rokocoko was presented with an easy run to the line that would seal an historic victory (29–9).

The second quarter-final in Brisbane saw host nation Australia line up against Scotland. It was tipped to be a mismatch after Scotland scraped into the knockout stage with a narrow victory over Fiji, while Australia were coming in after withstanding a stern challenge from Ireland. The Wallabies enjoyed most of the possession during the opening half, but a series of backline blunders saw them waste a number of opportunities. The scores were locked at 9–9 as the teams went to the break, with Chris Paterson landing a drop-goal from near halfway and converting the two penalty goal opportunities Scotland were given. To the delight of the frustrated Brisbane crowd, Australia finally crossed for their first try five minutes into the second half as outside centre Stirling Mortlock clutched on to a long ball from Elton Flatley before crossing with a swan-dive under the posts. Mortlock's score gave the Wallabies extra confidence and finally the passes began to hit their mark. Lote Tuqiri was in devastating form for Australia and his efforts were rewarded when he did all the groundwork for George Gregan to grubber through and score the second try of the night. When No. 8 David Lyons crossed from the back of a scrum five minutes later, Australia were home, but Scotland were given one last chance to shine with a try to replacement hooker Rob Russell. It was a sluggish start, but the Wallabies gained some confidence from a second half when passes started to stick and they were through to the final four on the back of 33–16 victory.

The third quarter-final promised to be a close encounter between France and Ireland in Melbourne, but the men in green were left wanting against a classy French outfit looking more like a title contender as the tournament unfolded. Some enterprising play from a lineout deep in Irish territory led to an outstanding team try to Olivier

Magne within the first five minutes to give *Les Bleus* the lead, and it was a lead they never looked likely to surrender. The first score seemed to give France more confidence, and with total dominance in the scrum and lineout they had the complete foundation to put the game beyond Ireland's reach. Christophe Dominici finished a breathtaking counter-attack from inside France's quarter, and when No. 8 Imanol Harinordoquy dived over just before the break, Ireland went into half time trailing 27–0. The pain continued straight after the interval as Frederic Michalak kicked another penalty goal to stretch France's lead, and when prop Jean-Jacques Crenca scored a try soon after it was quickly becoming embarrassing for Ireland as France led 37–0 with more than half an hour remaining.

'The French scrum was incredibly powerful, they completely outmuscled us and we were completely punch-drunk after 30 minutes,' Ireland coach Eddie O'Sullivan said after the match. 'They strangled us to death for the best part of 60 minutes. The French have always had flair and power, but this French team is different. They have a clarity of thought that makes them very menacing.'

France appeared to be in a zone where they could do no wrong and Ireland were forced to defend for extended periods. Eventually *Les Bleus* showed some respite with their dominance when hooker Raphael Ibanez received a yellow card for killing the ball, and Ireland fought gallantly in the closing 20 minutes to bring some respectability back to the final score. Brian O'Driscoll scored two tries and his centre partner Kevin Maggs also crossed for an impressive try, but it was all too late and France triumphed comfortably (43–21) to move through to the final four. The match was a sad end to a distinguished career for Ireland captain Keith Wood, who retired after the 2003 tournament. A lasting emotional memory for many fans was when Wood embraced his French counterpart Fabien Galthie as the players shook hands after the match. Galthie would also retire after the tournament, but the French captain lived to fight another day, while Wood reluctantly pulled the curtain down on a famous career.

'The heart is willing, the head is willing, but the body's had enough,' Wood said after the match. 'It's very disappointing ... we just didn't play in the first half. We can hold our heads up, we tried really hard in the second half, we tried our damnedest ... it just didn't come off. I've had a lot of great times. I think this World Cup and this group of players was very special. It is very sad that it ends on a downer.'

The last of the quarter-finals took place in Brisbane where two old foes – England and Wales – lined up for yet another battle royal. Earlier results from that year were pointing to the 2003 Six Nations Grand Slam champions England as the likely victor over the Six Nations wooden spoon holders, but form so often counts for little when these two nations meet in rugby and so it would prove again in Brisbane. England were humbled in the first half and trailing 10–3 when Wales backed up a sensational team try to fly-half Stephen Jones with another to Colin Charvis in the 35th minute.

England were on the ropes at half time, and their coach Clive Woodward called on the steadying influence of veteran utility Mike Catt to calm his side. It proved to be a masterstroke. Catt consistently pushed the ball into the opposition half throughout the second period and Jonny Wilkinson fulfilled England's comeback with five consecutive penalty goals. Wales lost their discipline – giving away 17 penalties – and Wilkinson pounced on every goal-kicking opportunity he was presented with in the second half before Jason Robinson sliced through the midfield to set up a try for Will Greenwood and seal England's return. Wales had been poised to pull off a remarkable upset after scoring three tries to one, but ill discipline cost them dearly and England regrouped to claim a 28–17 victory.

Woodward's men had shown impressive resolve to return from the dead twice within three weeks – firstly against Samoa and then Wales – but some senior players within England's ranks felt there were aspects that simply had to change for the remaining two weeks, particularly the long training sessions in the Australian heat that seemed to be draining their energy reserves. In an article for *The Times* two years to the day after the Rugby World Cup 2003 final, chief sports reporter Owen Slot described how four senior players – Lawrence Dallaglio, Jason Leonard, Mike Catt and Paul Grayson – went out for a beer and before long they were debating into the early hours about the issue of overtraining. At the end of it they were determined to air their views at the team meeting the next day, and it was Dallaglio who finally took a stand.

'The next day in the team meeting, Clive had his say, the coaches had their say and eventually Clive asked: 'Has anyone got anything else?' The other boys were shaking their heads going: 'No, it's not the time.' I thought: 'I've got to say something.' So I did. I said: 'We've got to do things more sensibly. Why are we training in the middle of the day when we're playing at night?' The coaches had been quite critical saying that we had been walking during the game. I said that was hardly surprising, having two and a half hour training sessions in 80-degree heat in Brisbane. I remember getting pretty animated and pretty emotional.'

Clive Woodward and his management team were effectively forced by a senior playing group to reassess their training strategy, and to his credit the England mentor listened rather than dictating terms. It was a crucial change to the England structure for the final two weeks and one that would prove to serve them very well in the end.

The semi-finals

The first of the 2003 semi-finals saw Australia take on tournament favourites New Zealand on a humid Saturday night in Sydney. The host nation had made it to the final four on the back of some unconvincing performances against Ireland and Scotland, while New Zealand had shown some vulnerability against Wales in their final pool match, but a quarter-final trouncing of South Africa seemed to quash most doubts surrounding the All Blacks. New Zealand were expected to win, and rightly deserved to be favourites after totally dominating the 2003 Tri-Nations and Bledisloe Cup, but Australia always had belief in their strategy for the semi-final and some astute tactics from coach Eddie Jones saw them unsettle the All Blacks from the opening whistle.

When the Wallabies first received the ball in their own quarter, to the amazement of many they did not go for the clearing kick but instead ran from deep inside their own territory. Jones and his combatants had clearly planned to play out the match with ball in hand and deny the potent New Zealand back three any chance to counter-attack from a kick return. Jones devised a strategy built on maintaining possession for extended periods, penetrating the gain line with good go-forward in attack, and in defence closing down space early to deny the New Zealand backline a chance to mount any attack. It was a strategy that required supreme fitness to be executed effectively, and the Wallabies timed their conditioning to perfection in preparation for a draining showdown with their rivals.

'Against New Zealand, you've got to hit the line hard. That's what our forwards did and the result was good ball,' Jones said. 'We also felt within their backline we could expose certain individuals if we executed well. But we had to get the go-forward first. Playing with width doesn't just come from throwing the ball wide, it comes from going forward. We wanted to keep the ball in hand and attack them.'

Australia's forwards provided the solid platform and go-forward the Jones master-plan required and the All Blacks were left reeling in search of a plan B that simply wasn't in their armoury. When Stirling Mortlock intercepted a Carlos Spencer cut-out pass within the first 10 minutes before running untouched to score under the posts, the Wallabies had made a perfect start. Mortlock was also at the forefront of a sub-plot to target perceived weaknesses in his opposite number Leon MacDonald, who was a fullback playing at outside centre after the injury to Tana Umaga, and his penetration through the midfield proved invaluable. The All Blacks were clearly in trouble, but a try late in the first half gave them something positive to take from an opening period totally domi-nated by Australia. New Zealand desperately needed to counter Australia's strategy with something from their coach John Mitchell during the break, but it never came. The Wallabies maintained their composure and continued to strangle the All Blacks into submission in the second half. Flankers Phil Waugh and George Smith were given a mission to stop New Zealand's two main ball carriers – Jerry Collins and Keven Mealamu – and they did so effectively. Elton Flatley sealed New Zealand's demise with three further penalty goals in the second half to give Australia an historic upset (22–10). New Zealand was a nation shattered, and players past and present were left scratching their heads for answers. Former captain Sean Fitzpatrick tells of a scathing phone call he received from fellow legend Colin Meads after a newspa-per column backfired.

'Jim Tucker from *The Courier Mail* in Brisbane called me and asked if I could select an ANZAC [combined Australia and New Zealand] team. I said to him I'd probably have no player from Australia except George Gregan and it was all over the back pages after that,' Fitzpatrick said. 'Then Colin Meads called me up after the All Blacks lost and said "Don't you ever f***ing do that again! You gave them the team talk". But to this day I still believe New Zealand had a better team man-for-man. They just totally misfired on the day.'

The second semi-final was played in contrasting conditions to the first as the temperature dropped 15°C and the skies opened up over Sydney for two stormy hours before the match commenced between France and England. The weather was a cruel blow for *Les Bleus*, who had set the quarter-finals alight against Ireland by playing an expansive game they promised to bring to the semi-finals. England were rightly favourites and quietly enjoying their opponent's anguish at the weather, convinced they could deal with any conditions to overcome France on the day, but knowing full well a rain-soaked surface would give their forward pack a distinct advantage.

On the back of a revised match preparation following an uprising from Dallaglio and a group of senior players after the quarter-final victory over Wales, England came into the match having spent less time on the training paddock and looked much more fresh from the outset. The match was evenly balanced for most of the first half, with Wilkinson claiming two drop-goals and a brace of penalty goals while flanker Serge Betson crossed for what would turn out to be France's only score of the night. England enjoyed a lead of 12–7 at the interval, but their dominance in the forwards was more telling than the scoreboard indicated. The match continued in the same vein after the break and key players for France became increasingly frustrated. The dynamic back row of Betson, Olivier Magne and Imanol Harinordoquy were given no space to roam as the English forward pack kept the ball in close quarters and forced the trio to defend. Fly-half Frederic Michalak was also misfiring in all departments and when Betson received a yellow card for a late tackle on Wilkinson, France's chances of victory diminished quickly. Wilkinson then quite literally put in the boot with a flawless 24-point kicking display in challenging conditions to give England a comfortable victory (24–7).

'We based our whole World Cup campaign on playing on hard grounds with a dry ball and there is no question that we were handi-capped by the rain,' France coach Bernard Laporte said after the match. 'But we are not going to use that as an excuse. The conditions were the same for both sides, and at this level of competition you have to be able to adapt. England were more efficient, more intelligent, they adapted better.'

Among England's squad there were some courageous performances and a memorable milestone for veteran prop Jason Leonard, who claimed a world record 112th international Test cap after he came on as a blood-bin replacement early in the match and a genuine replacement late in the second half. The second semi-final was also an emotional occasion for France captain Fabien Galthie, who played his last Test match after an outstanding career that included playing in four Rugby World Cups.

Third place play-off

New Zealand and France were left shattered after demoralising losses in their respective semi-finals, but both teams were forced to pick up the pieces and square off for one final 80-minute duel to determine who could rightly claim third place and walk away with the Rugby World Cup 2003 bronze medal. The All Blacks were lining up in the third place play-off for a second consecutive tournament, and after narrowly losing to the Springboks at Cardiff in 1999 they were determined to finish one better in 2003.

To the delight of more than 60,000 fans that turned out to watch, both teams played an expansive style and seven tries were scored as New Zealand's forward pack provided a solid foundation upon which Carlos Spencer confidently orchestrated a rampaging All Blacks attack. However, despite New Zealand's perceived dominance for much of the match, only one point split the teams (14–13) early in the second half. But two tries to New Zealand within 10 minutes finally saw them consolidate on the dominance they were enjoying up front, and two further scores soon after ensured the All Blacks would finish the tournament on a high with a comfortable victory (40–13).

'We had no choice but to move on from what was a shattering event [against Australia in the semi-final],' New Zealand captain Rueben Thorne said. 'We got some good tries and showed we wanted to play with the ball. It's been a long, hard year, and it's been draining physically and emotionally. We didn't get what we wanted here, and we were pretty heartbroken about that, but the guys have all grown and I think the tournament has been great for rugby.'

It was a bitter-sweet feeling for the New Zealand team as they walked around Telstra Stadium to thank the fans who had turned out. They had scored a tournament record 52 tries in total, and were undoubtedly the dominant attacking force in world rugby for a sustained period leading into the tournament, but it mattered little without the one prize that meant the most. As a diehard rugby nation that comes to expect nothing less than victory from their usually all-conquering All Blacks, being denied The Webb Ellis Cup for another four years was a hard pill to swallow for their population. Inevitably heads would roll. Within weeks their coach John Mitchell was sacked and Reuben Thorne stripped of the captaincy soon after.

Mitchell was in many ways the unlucky fall guy after his tactics failed in one game that mattered more than any other.

The final

After 43 entertaining days, 20 teams came down to two. The host nation had overcome a clumsy start to the tournament with a memorable semi-final defeat of the All Blacks, while England – the number one team in the world – had been tested throughout and forced to readjust their approach in the closing weeks of what would lead to their finest two hours in a period of dominance that had lasted the best part of two years. It was no surprise that Clive Woodward's men would start the match as favourites, but it was Australia who struck first with a perfectly placed cross-kick from Stephen Larkham finding Lote Tuqiri on the left wing surging above his opposite number Jason Robinson before diving over for the first try.

England were stunned early on, but the measure of a champion side is how well they respond to pressure and it didn't take long for Martin Johnson and his forward pack to gain early ascendancy up front before Jonny Wilkinson kicked three penalty goals over a 20-minute period to give England the upper hand. Later in the first half Robinson atoned for the early Tuqiri try with one of his own to give England a nine-point cushion (14–5) at half time. The lead would have been more had it not been for Ben Kay having the ball knocked from his possession by a desperate tackle from Australia flanker Phil Waugh when the England lock seemed certain to score.

Australia coach Eddie Jones made a tactical change after the break, bringing on reserve locks David Giffin and Matt Cockbain in a bid to remedy a lineout that was buckling under pressure once again. The change worked wonders and Australia was able to gain much-needed parity in the set pieces, and the dominant England scrum soon found itself on the end of some mystifying penalties from South Africa referee Andre Watson. The infringements gave Elton Flatley a chance to kick Australia back into the match, and he did so with tremendous courage under pressure. In a half where neither side was granted any space to move through gallant defence, Flatley calmly slotted three penalty goals to bring the scores level after 80 minutes of regular time. England still seemed in control, but the Wallabies showed outstanding discipline not to grant Wilkinson any further opportunities to extend England's lead. To the surprise of many, England failed to score a single point in the second half and the match would go to extra time with the scores locked at 14–14.

'We made so many silly errors and we didn't score a point in the second half,' Martin Johnson recalled of a frustrating period for England. 'It was unlike us because once we've got ahead, if we'd got into position, Jonny would have kicked us three, six, nine points to win us the game.'

Wilkinson kicked a penalty goal two minutes into the first period of extra time to give England an early lead and it seemed they would extend it at any point, but Flatley again drew the scores level for Australia in the 99th minute and it was clear something special would be required to split the teams. Rather fittingly it came one minute later through Jonny Wilkinson – the player who had guided England with his radar boot throughout their campaign. Matt Dawson became entangled at the breakdown after making a great dash forward. Martin Johnson then gave it one more carry in an effort to free up his scrum-half for the pass to Wilkinson and so it played out to perfection as the England fly-half received the pass before kicking the drop- goal that would seal an historic victory. Wilkinson had missed three earlier attempts and replacement centre Mike Catt had another charged down, but this one struck from Wilkinson's less-favoured right boot went sailing through the goal posts to grant England a well-deserved victory.

'We came very close to blowing it. Every decision seemed to go against them, and yet they still won, and that is the sign of a champion team,' England coach Clive Woodward beamed after the match. 'They are a great bunch of players with a great captain, and I am just very proud and privileged to be in charge of them.'

England became the first northern hemisphere team to win the Rugby World Cup, and the country would rejoice far and wide after their first major international sporting triumph since the 1966 Football World Cup. Letters of congratulation flowed from some of the most unexpected areas.

'Rarely have I seen a match of such commitment and intensity,' the French President Jacques Chirac wrote to British Prime Minister Tony Blair. 'This deserved victory is also a victory for Europe.'

No one could deny England. Woodward and his so-called 'Dad's Army' defied their critics and were finally on top of the rugby world.

FIVE MAGIC MEMORIES

Samoa scare left England shell-shocked

Every Rugby World Cup produces surprises, and Samoa is a proud rugby nation with a national team that so often yields performances to capture the imagination of all fans and breathe life into a tournament. Wales had been on the receiving end of Samoan ambushes in both 1991 and 1999, and while they did not upset any major rugby powers in 2003, Samoa gave eventual champions England an almighty scare at Telstra Dome in Melbourne. Ironically the Pacific Islanders had been denied some of their finest playing talent because English clubs threatened to tear up playing contracts if their contracted Samoan players chose to go to the tournament instead of fulfilling their club commitments. The infamous Club v Country row had stooped to a new low, but Samoa still assembled a competitive squad and England were forced to work hard for their victory.

England had made seven changes to the team that defeated South Africa in Perth one week before, and the new combination was clearly struggling against an enthusiastic Samoa team determined to make their mark. Fly-half Earl Va'a opened the scoring with a penalty goal for Samoa in the second minute, and in the sixth minute captain Semo Sititi scored one of the tries of the tournament after 11 phases of possession that travelled through 40 pairs of Samoan hands. It was the first try England had conceded at the tournament and suddenly they were 10–0 down inside 10 minutes against a team gathering more confidence as the match progressed.

Va'a was once signed by Newcastle as cover for Jonny Wilkinson in the English premiership, but it was the Samoan enjoying the upper hand in the fly-half duel as Wilkinson uncharacteristically missed some early shots at goal in the first half and Samoa took a 16–13 lead to the break. An upset seemed very possible, and England coach Clive Woodward was forced to ring in the changes at half time and bring back some of his heavy artillery. Hooker Steve Thompson and prop Phil Vickery replaced Mark Regan and Julian White, while in the back row Lewis Moody came on for Joe Worsley. The changes brought immediate stability to England's forward pack and improved discipline eventually saw them grind their way back into the match with a try to Neil Back from a rolling maul before a penalty try also came their way when referee Jonathan Kaplan grew impatient with

Samoa collapsing a scrum. Wilkinson found his kicking radar again and two late tries to Iain Balshaw and Phil Vickery gave England a flattering final score line (35–22) after being on the receiving end of the sternest test they had received for years, according to skipper Martin Johnson.

'Samoa asked us questions that we have not been asked for a long, long time. We had to dig ourselves out of a hole. We were 10–0 down and hadn't touched the ball. We made too many mistakes and need to look at ourselves as players,' Johnson said. 'That was just not good enough. Full credit to Samoa, they could have beaten us. We're not going to win anything if we play like that.'

The Samoa scare gave England a quick reality check midway through the tournament. They were the number one team in the world, but they were far from invincible.

Scotland the brave denies Fiji despite 'Caucau' domination

Scotland has a proud Rugby World Cup history as one of only five nations to have made the quarter-finals or better at every tournament, and when drawn in Pool B for 2003 along with France and Fiji they were always gong to face a tough challenge to keep that record intact. France was rightfully the favourite to claim first place in the pool and they lived up to that rating with comprehensive victories over all opponents throughout the preliminary stage, but it was the battle for second place that was always going to be the most intriguing aspect of Pool B. It was largely deemed to be a contest between Scotland and Fiji to see who would gain the second quarter-final place, but some courageous performances from Japan and the United States kept fans guessing until the end.

The United States almost pulled off a remarkable upset over Fiji, with their fly-half Mike Hercus tasked with a conversion from the sideline after full time to steal an unlikely victory, but it wasn't to be. Fiji lived to fight another day in the challenge for a quarter-final place, and both they and Scotland fell heavily to France before clumsily making their way past the other Pool B opponents. Then it came to the ultimate showdown in the final match of the pool, with fired-up Scotland squaring off against flamboyant Fiji in front of a sell-out crowd at Aussie Stadium in Sydney.

The battle for second place had come down to the final match of the pool and both teams turned on a captivating encounter. Returning from a two-match suspension for punching in Fiji's heated opening clash with France, Rupeni Caucaunibuca totally bamboozled the Scotland defence to score two scintillating tries and give his side a 14–6 lead at half time. But the second half saw Scotland claw their way back through the boot of Chris Paterson before taking the lead in the 65th minute. It was Fiji's turn to come back entering the final 10 minutes, with Nicky Little kicking two goals to push the game back in favour of the Pacific Islanders. Then with only three minutes remaining, Scotland secured a lineout just metres from the Fijian line before veteran prop Tom Smith crashed over for a try that brought the scores level. Scotland's celebrations had already begun because a draw was enough to see them claim second place, but the ever-reliant Paterson kicked the winning conversion to ensure Scotland scraped through to the knockout stage on the back of a victory.

'That was very close,' Scotland captain Bryan Redpath said after the match. 'That man Caucau just killed us. They were exceptional. He is one of the best wingers out there, no question.'

Unfortunately 'Caucau' had only appeared in two matches, but the explosive Fiji wing scored three tries and left an indelible mark on both despite his team coming out on the wrong end of the scoreboard. Not since the rampaging efforts of the great Jonah Lomu in 1995 and 1999 had the Rugby World Cup witnessed a wing that could turn a match so quickly with one single touch. However, the final say in Pool B was not from a fine-finishing wing but rather a workhorse prop by the name of Tom Smith who ensured Scotland the brave kept their proud quarter-final record intact.

Red Dragons breathe fire against heavyweight contenders

Wales came into Rugby World Cup 2003 with little to show except a Six Nations wooden spoon, and not even the most optimistic fan had cause to believe the Red Dragons could do anything more than challenge Italy for second place in Pool D behind New Zealand. But as Wales slowly progressed through their pool matches with victories over Canada, Tonga and Italy to secure their place in the knockout stage, they were gradually building towards two significant clashes which would demonstrate to the rugby world that they were back and ready to test the major contenders. The first signs of the Welsh resurgence came in the final pool match of the tournament at Telstra Stadium in Sydney, where a second-string team lined up against the might of the All Blacks before providing one of the most captivating matches of the tournament.

The floodgates were poised to open as New Zealand led 28–10 inside the first half hour, but a sudden loss of concentration from the All Blacks in defence saw Wales rack up 24 unanswered points. New Zealand's willingness to spread the ball wide on all occasions is reliant on near-perfect handling and when mistakes crept into the All Black attack it allowed Wales to feed off the scraps and play their way right back into the game. With just over 20 minutes remaining Wales were leading 37–33 and well in sight of pulling off the biggest upset of the tournament, but the All Blacks regained their composure and three late tries gave them a flattering score line (53–37) for what was an almighty scare for one of the tournament favourites. Wales unveiled a new star in exciting scrum-half turned wing Shane Williams and New Zealand coach John Mitchell was quick to admit his team were caught out by him.

'I've never seen him before, but he has pretty good footwork,' Mitchell quipped during the post-match conference.

Wales coach Steve Hansen – also a New Zealander – was impressed by the performance of his second-string side, but quick to give a realistic perspective on the outcome.

'The performance was good but at the end of the day we lost,' Hansen said. 'We're trying to get consistent performances that will allow us to win games against the best sides in the world. I've been harping on for a long time that we need to play our best against one of the top teams when they're playing well to assess where we are. The All Blacks played very well and so did we. So we've closed the gap a little bit.'

One week later Wales were at it again, this time against arch rivals England. The Red Dragons scored arguably the finest try of the tournament through fly-half Stephen Jones. With England on the attack centre Mike Tindall attempted to angle a kick across field to open space, but the ball found speedy Welsh wing Shane Williams who jinked his way past Ben Kay before running half the length of the field and offloading to scrum-half Gareth Cooper. Cooper then linked up with Gareth Thomas flying through and Williams emerged for one final touch again before juggling the ball and delivering the final pass for Jones to score the try. It was a sensational movement that ignited the entire crowd. Wales did not prevail against their old enemy, but they won plenty of respect for both of their performances against tournament heavyweights New Zealand and England.

Shrewd Australia awoke All Black curse in tense semi-final

The great Rugby World Cup enigma of the all-conquering All Blacks not having won the title since the inaugural tournament in 1987 was quickly dubbed by many opposing fans as the All Black curse. The New Zealand team of 2003 were determined to put those demons to rest, but it was not to be once again as they succumbed to a very committed and tactically superior Australia. The Wallabies had not been convincing in their lead-up games, but on the night that mattered they carried out a master-plan with near perfect precision, choking New Zealand of possession and running them ragged in the first half. The All Blacks were forced to make 68 more tackles than Australia in the opening period, and the energy reserves were no longer there in the final 20 minutes when they needed to throw all they had at the Wallabies.

Some key moments proved vital in the final outcome, not just Stirling Mortlock's intercept try, but also the less publicised incidents like George Smith's late tackle on New Zealand scrum-half Justin Marshall. Smith was penalised at the time, but the damage was done as Marshall suffered rib cartilage damage that nullified his contribution and saw him replaced early in the second half.

'That try in the first 10 minutes could well have been a try the other way, but Mortlock grabbed the intercept and that swung it all in Australia's favour,' says All Blacks legend Sean Fitzpatrick. 'And when that warhorse Smith late-tackled Marshall, he was never the same after that, but that is what it's all about really. New Zealand just didn't fire.'

It was not all joy for every Australia player though, as prop Ben Darwin experienced a horrifying scare after losing feeling from the neck down when a scrum collapsed early in the second half. Darwin had a prolapsed disc pressing against his spinal cord, and had it not been for some quick-thinking from his opposing prop Kees Meeuws, Darwin might well have spent the rest of his life in a wheelchair.

'I heard a crack and immediately called out "neck, neck, neck" and to his credit Kees Meeuws stopped pushing which was fortunate because I lost feeling in my body and he could have really crashed me into the ground,' Darwin said in a statement issued by team management. 'When I was on the ground I had no feeling from my neck down for about two minutes. It was terrifying, but the medical staff did a great job of getting me into the right position and then I felt pins and needles in my arms and legs, which was a great relief. In the ambulance on the way to hospital, the staff were nice enough to put the game on the radio so I could hear what was going on.'

Needless to say Darwin played no further part in the tournament and sadly he was forced to retire from rugby prematurely following the advice of doctors. The promising tight-head lost his livelihood, but he was simply thankful to still be alive and able to walk from his hospital bed later the following week. New Zealand had no such life-threatening casualties but it was total heartbreak across their nation. Their Rugby World Cup curse struck once more and they would have to endure another agonising four-year wait before they could stake another claim for rugby's greatest prize.

Veterans staved off fatigue factor and Jonny sealed the deal

As Australia and England changed ends in the 2003 final to begin two 10-minute periods of extra time, many local pundits in the media section were tipping the ageing England team to tire in the closing stages. But those same doubters were not aware of the transformation that had occurred within the England camp during the final few weeks of their campaign. It was in this testing period that the uprising from senior players after the Wales match would bear its finest reward. 'Dad's Army' had one major general in Clive Woodward, but his policy was such that none of his troops were ever afraid to air their views. Lawrence Dallaglio was the first to raise the issue of overtraining and how it was affecting the team's performance, and after an outstanding showing against France in the semi-final many other senior players echoed their support.

'We got our way [with less training ahead of the semi-final] against France, and then played our best game of the tournament,' prop Jason Leonard later told *The Times*. 'After that they wanted us out there flogging it in training again. We said: 'Haven't you learned anything?' And we got our way again. Fair play, Clive did listen. And I think that's why, in the final, we survived extra time as well as we did.'

England had enough chances to put the game beyond Australia's reach in regulation time, but brave defence from the Wallabies together with an unwavering boot from goal-kicker Elton Flatley in the second half ensured England would have to work for their victory. To his credit Flatley overcame three missed opportunities at goal in the first half to kick Australia back into the final and force extra time. The Wallabies made 43 more tackles throughout the match – a telling statistic when talking 100 minutes of rugby – and the extra energy reserves England had later in the match thanks to the lighter preparation throughout the week was perhaps the most vital factor of all.

And so fitting it was that the finest player in the world at the time – Jonny Wilkinson – had the final say at a truly remarkable tournament. Despite an off period of 30 minutes early in the match against Samoa, Wilkinson proved across the course of six weeks to be the most valuable player at the tournament. His unswerving boot saw off the early challenge of South Africa in the pool stages, and Wales were given their share in the quarter-final, but it was against France in the semi-final that England's kicking maestro reigned supreme to totally snuff out any challenge from *Les Bleus*. Wilkinson didn't quite have it all his own way one week later in the final, missing three drop-goal attempts throughout the match, but the one that mattered most in the 99th minute found its mark to put England on top of the rugby world.

'It's indescribable. It's something we've wanted, we've worked for so long both individually and as a team,' Wilkinson said after the match. 'The work goes back four or five years. We've said we wanted to win every single game. We've put ourselves under that pressure and we knew it was going to be hard. We have had a hard year ... and now we are here, and we feel like hopefully we deserve this.'

England did deserve their victory after sustained dominance for two years leading into 2003, and Rugby World Cup as a tournament is better for finally having a northern hemisphere team triumph.

12

The interim years: 2003–2007

FOR SO LONG Rugby World Cup had been criticised by many rugby purists as an exhibition for southern hemisphere dominance on the world stage, but England's triumph in Australia subdued that theory as they cast aside every major opponent over a two-year period prior to winning Rugby World Cup 2003. It was in effect also a victory for northern hemisphere rugby, but this moment was one for England to savour and the team was given a memorable home-coming as more than 10,000 fans gathered at Heathrow airport to welcome the squad back to home soil. Celebrations continued throughout the country for months but the highlight for many was the victory parade through the streets of London on December 8. Police estimated that 750,000 people attended the parade, where two red open-top buses aptly named 'Sweet Chariot' carried the victorious squad through the streets of central London while multiple renditions of English rugby's adopted anthem 'Swing Low, Sweet Chariot' reverberated throughout the capital.

'We're overwhelmed. It matters so much to get this support and being on this bus now is one of the greatest moments of my life,' drop-goal hero Jonny Wilkinson told the BBC. 'It's great to be able to pay back the fans that travelled half way around the world as well as those who stayed at home. We owe everyone a massive amount.'

The parade came to an end at Trafalgar Square, where skipper Martin Johnson thanked the masses before the squad moved on to afternoon tea with the Queen at Buckingham Palace. Princess Anne, Prince William, Prince Philip and Prince Edward also joined the royal celebrations, and after a quick photo with the Queen and her corgis the squad made their way to 10 Downing Street for a reception with Prime Minister Tony Blair and a selection of political figures including the Conservative Party leader Michael Howard, Liberal Democrat leader Charles Kennedy and Sports Minister Richard Caborn. It was a day of celebration like no other Britain has even seen and the squad received further acclaim in the New Year's Honours List for 2004, with coach Clive Woodward receiving a knighthood while team captain Martin Johnson received a CBE – a Commander in the Order of the British Empire, the third rank below the top two ranks of knighthood. Most other team members received an MBE – the fifth 'member' rank of the Order.

Back to the playing surface and it was business as usual for Martin Johnson and a number of other team members immediately after tasting Rugby World Cup glory, as they lined up for their club sides in the English Premiership.

'After winning the Rugby World Cup in 2003 we were back in the club on Wednesday, back training Thursday, and played the Saturday game,' recalls Johnson. 'It was a pride thing. I didn't want my club to go down [and suffer relegation to a lower division]. We had to come back and try and start winning, and get things going. To be honest, someone would have to have told me not to play.'

The decision by Johnson and many of his England team-mates to compete so soon after their 2003 triumph was a welcome boost for Premiership rugby as gate takings increased with fans taking a renewed interest in the domestic competition given the prospect of seeing England's Rugby World Cup heroes in action. But while the Premiership played out over the northern hemisphere winter and the England celebrations continued for many months after, the 2004 Six Nations tournament was fast approaching and England would face their first major test on the international stage as the reigning world champions. Their first two matches of the 2004 tournament were easy victories against Italy (50–9) and Scotland (35–13), but England's third match against Ireland was the first real challenge to their world champion tenure and 'Fortress Twickenham' was humbled for the first time in 22 matches stretching back to 1999 as a determined Ireland defeated England 19–13.

Unlike previous Rugby World Cup champions, who all went on to reach their playing peak after their respective triumphs, the victorious

England team of 2003 had dominated the international stage for an extended period leading into Rugby World Cup 2003 – but that success would be the final reward for an ageing squad that seemingly had little choice but to enter a rebuilding phase. England owned the tag of world champions for another four years ahead of Rugby World Cup 2007, but a transfer of power was clearly evident in European rugby as France went on to claim the Six Nations Grand Slam in 2004 while Ireland secured the Triple Crown after victories over England, Scotland and Wales. Both France and Ireland had formed impressive squads in the wake of Rugby World Cup 2003, but neither could maintain that consistency in 2005 and a surprise winner emerged as Wales claimed their first Six Nations title since 1994 and first Grand Slam since 1978. The Red Dragons had shown signs of being a team on the rise at Rugby World Cup 2003, almost pulling off a remarkable upset over the All Blacks before a commendable performance against eventual champions England in the quarter-finals. Under the guidance of new coach Mike Ruddock from March 2004, Wales continued to build and some much-needed pride was restored to a proud rugby nation longing for a return to its glory days of the 1970s.

Following the surprise Grand Slam triumph of Wales in the 2005 Six Nations, a selection of the finest players from the Home Unions of England, Ireland, Scotland and Wales embarked on a British & Irish Lions Tour of New Zealand under the guidance of Sir Clive Woodward. The squad of 44 players and 26 management staff was the largest of its kind ever assembled, and Woodward was widely criticised after announcing a list of players that consisted of 20 from England, 11 from Ireland, 10 from Wales and three from Scotland. Many critics found it hard to accept England having such a high representation despite performing poorly in the 2004 and 2005 Six Nations, and Woodward came under even more fire when the squad returned home after being whitewashed 3–0 in the series against the All Blacks while also losing a match to the New Zealand Maori.

The tour generated widespread interest across the rugby world, but unfortunately many of the lasting memories are of controversial moments such as the infamous spear tackle by Tana Umaga and Keven Mealamu on Brian O'Driscoll in the second minute of the first Test, which resulted in the Lions captain playing no further part in the tour. Neither Mealamu nor Umaga were cited for the indiscretion after the citing committee reviewed the match video, and tensions between the Home Unions and New Zealand started to simmer further when amateur footage later emerged in October 2005 clearly showing that the tackle was illegal and dangerous play. There was also the issue of all-New Zealand refereeing panels officiating on all non-Test matches throughout the tour, which never rubbed well with the Home Unions, and what was built up as classic showdown between two of the greatest powerhouses of world rugby sadly degenerated into a tour embroiled with controversy.

The course of events was unfortunate for New Zealand, who clearly looked the more dominant side and well on their way back to the top of the world rugby rankings after the disappointment of losing to Australia in the semi-finals of Rugby World Cup 2003. The All Blacks called on the highly regarded former Auckland coach Graham Henry to lead their next generation beyond 2003 after he had returned to his native country following some coaching abroad, which included extended time at the helm of Wales when they enjoyed one of their most successful periods of the modern era ahead of Rugby World Cup 1999. Henry established a coaching and selection panel widely dubbed the 'dream team' – with himself as defence coach, Steve Hansen as forwards coach, Wayne Smith as attack coach and Sir Brian Lochore as a selector. The All Blacks were soon restored as the number one team in the world after claiming a second Grand Slam on their tour of the United Kingdom and Ireland in 2005, followed by successive Tri-Nations championships in 2005, 2006 and 2007.

After advancing to the Rugby World Cup 2003 final Australia enjoyed another relatively successful year in 2004, winning nine of the 12 Tests they played, but the Wallabies experienced a rapid decline after July 2005, losing eight of the nine Tests they played during the second half of that year. The fast demise resulted in the sacking of coach Eddie Jones, and Australia was forced to re-group quickly ahead of Rugby World Cup 2007. Former coach Rod Macqueen and a series of advisors were involved in a swift selection process to determine the next head coach and it was Queensland veteran John 'Knuckles' Connolly who was eventually announced as the new mentor for the Wallabies on a short-term contract specifically targeting success at the 2007 tournament. Connolly is credited for the resurrection of Bath in the English Premiership during the 2003–04 season, and with further experience coaching Stade Français in the country where the next Rugby World Cup would be played his credentials fitted the criteria well. Connolly's tenure began positively with two comfortable victories over England, and a little more than 12 months later the Wallabies became the first team to defeat New Zealand in 2007 when they claimed an important victory over their trans-Tasman rivals in Melbourne. 'Knuckles' had piloted a remarkable turnaround for Australia and they were well placed for another attempt to claim The Webb Ellis Cup.

Ironically, world champions England also suffered an appalling run on the international stage around the same time as Australia and their coach Andy Robinson was eventually dismissed and replaced by Brian Ashton. Ashton had succeeded Connolly as the head coach at Bath in 2005 and now he was tasked with an equally challenging role of reversing a national team's fortunes in a very short timeframe. Both Ashton and Connolly performed their tasks admirably and Rugby World Cup 2007 would see their two worlds collide in a memorable quarter-final showdown.

Perhaps the most colourful story of all from the southern hemisphere during the interim period of 2003 to 2007 was the emergence of the forgotten nation Argentina. The Pumas have maintained an isolated existence on the international scene, largely as a result of the country still playing under an amateur structure domestically, and the national team not being involved in any major competition such as the Six Nations or Tri-Nations. But with a majority of their top-level players now playing professionally in France and Ireland, Argentina have formed a squad capable of beating any team in world rugby, as England found out at Twickenham in the latter part of 2006. The Pumas' success over England on that day provided the impetus for their squad to go on and flourish on the world stage and the energy they would eventually bring to the 2007 tournament captured the imagination of all rugby fans.

South Africa also enjoyed some success during the interim years, winning the closest Tri-Nations series ever contested when all three teams finished with two victories in 2004. The Springboks claimed one more bonus point than Australia and it was enough to secure their second Tri-Nations title. But while South Africa continued to uphold an impressive record on home soil, their success abroad was limited and some critics within South African rugby questioned whether the Super14 and Tri-Nations series was fair to South Africa teams that were required to travel for more extended periods compared to their Australia and New Zealand counterparts. It was a valid point, but to his credit Springboks coach Jake White devised a strategy rather than battle the system. The sudden dominance of South Africa teams in the 2007 Super14 gave the Springboks renewed confidence in their ability to compete on the road and White nurtured that belief while resting a majority of his key players from the second (away) leg of the 2007 Tri-Nations. The decision to send a second-string squad received a barrage of criticism from Australia and New Zealand, but it was the Springboks coach who would enjoy the last laugh at the end of Rugby World Cup 2007.

13

Rugby World Cup 2007: the tournament

FOLLOWING THE DEMISE of England as a significant force in world rugby, and with no apparent heir in the northern hemisphere fold to consistently challenge the dominant southern hemisphere nations, some observers noted a change of tack at the breakdown as a major cause for concern. Throughout their reign at the top of world rugby for two years prior to claiming the 2003 title, England had prided themselves on being a dominant force at the tackle area. But as the likes of battle-hardened forwards such as Martin Johnson, Neil Back and Richard Hill retired from the international scene, there was a distinct lack of competitiveness in that area and it coincided with England's rapid slide in the international rankings. Former captain Martin Johnson was one key figure perplexed by the increasing lack of competition among forwards at the breakdown when England were at their lowest point after an abysmal 2006 season that saw them lose seven of the 11 Tests they played that year.

'We've gone away in the UK from competing at breakdowns and it's a major problem for when we come up against the likes of South Africa, New Zealand and Australia,' Johnson said. 'I used to play at a club where we'd get vilified: "Oh, Leicester slow the ball down at the breakdown," yeah, too right we do because that's the game, you have to compete at breakdowns and if we stop doing that we will not be as competitive at the top level of international competition.'

Three months out from Rugby World Cup 2007, England toured South Africa and this apparent flaw became blatantly obvious as they were exposed at the breakdown and well beaten in two Tests against the Springboks. Coach Brian Ashton and his management team quickly had to devise a plan to restore what had been such a crucial pillar to England's previous success. More credible performances followed against France during their Rugby World Cup warm-up matches, but they were still finishing on the wrong end of the scoreboard. Most of the other main contenders were much better placed leading into the 2007 tournament and England had to quickly remedy core areas of their game to ensure they would not become an international embarrassment. On the second weekend of the tournament they suffered total humiliation at the hands of South Africa again, but a form reversal like no other would ensure their defence of the world crown was admirable.

The pool stage

The number of teams and format for the 2007 tournament was exactly the same as 2003, with 20 countries split into four pools of five for a preliminary round-robin stage. The top two from each pool then advanced to the knockout quarter-finals stage, but one slight variation in 2007 was that the third placed country in each pool would earn automatic qualification for Rugby World Cup 2011 in New Zealand. Previously only the quarter-finalists from past tournaments were granted automatic entry to the next tournament, but this new measure was taken in an effort to give more incentive to the smaller nations competing at the tournament.

With the eight quarter-finalists from 2003 granted automatic entry to 2007, there was a total of 86 teams that took part in regional qualifying competitions to determine the other 12 places across the four pools. Of the 20 teams to make it to Rugby World Cup 2007, Portugal was the only new country to join the fold after defeating Uruguay 24–23 on aggregate in a thrilling home-and-away qualification showdown. They were the only wholly amateur team competing at the tournament, but the energy they brought to every game was warmly welcomed by the French crowds.

Of the 48 matches played over 44 days, France hosted a total of 42 across 10 cities while Cardiff hosted four matches and Edinburgh the other two. Ireland was originally scheduled to host some fixtures, but with the reconstruction of Lansdowne Road coinciding with the event they decided to forfeit their games and the matches were reallocated to French cities. A record number of people attended the 2007 tournament (2.27 million), and by the time it drew to a close at the Stade de France on October 20 it was widely being dubbed the greatest Rugby World Cup ever – not only in a commercial capacity but also for the sheer excitement generated by multiple upsets in key matches and the extraordinary improvement of the smaller nations.

Rugby World Cup 2007: The pools and order they finished

Pool A	Pool B	Pool C	Pool D
South Africa	Australia	New Zealand	Argentina
England	Fiji	Scotland	France
Tonga	Wales	Italy	Ireland
Samoa	Japan	Romania	Georgia
USA	Canada	Portugal	Namibia

Paris turned on a balmy early autumn evening for the Opening Ceremony of Rugby World Cup 2007, and a capacity crowd at the Stade de France was treated to a vibrant and colourful spectacle highlighted by percussion, dancing and appearances from some of the greatest legends of the game. The performance started with a number of percussionists assembled around the field with bright red oil drums, beating out powerful rhythms as multi-coloured dance troupes joined the celebration. The tricolours of the host nation's flag were dominant and a group of air force jets flying over the stadium with a smoke trail of blue, white and red received a rapturous cheer from the French crowd.

New Zealand legend and tournament icon Jonah Lomu was part of an elite group of former players including Gareth Edwards from Wales, dual Rugby World Cup winner John Eales from Australia and the great Hugo Porta from Argentina, who all played a part in representing the competing nations at the tournament. The greatest cheer of all, though, came when former France captain Jean-Pierre Rives entered the arena, but when the group of legends were all given the task of throwing a ball into a mock lineout it was Rives who failed to find his mark while Argentina's Porta performed it with ease – an omen perhaps for what was about to play out in the opening match between France and Argentina. The ceremony reached its climax as the dancers formed what was described as 'the world's biggest scrum', and from the centre of that scrum emerged a giant replica of The Webb Ellis Cup. The entire performance lasted only 30 minutes and set a lively tone for the main act to follow.

For the third consecutive tournament, Argentina lined up in the opening match against the host nation and it was clear from the early exchanges that the Pumas were ready to spoil the French party. Under the astute leadership of Agustin Pichot at scrum-half behind a marauding forward pack, Argentina stunned France with ferocious defence that rarely saw *Les Bleus* penetrate the advantage line. The match also unveiled the raw talent and super boot of Juan Martin Hernandez on the international stage. Playing at fly-half, Hernandez orchestrated a strong territorial advantage for Argentina with his general kicking and tested the French defence with a series of high balls that more often than not yielded the Pumas a positive result. Hernandez also attempted a series of drop-goals, and while none were successful it kept the French defence thinking and in turn created more opportunities to run the ball. The only try of the match was scored by Argentina fullback Ignacio Corleto, from an intercepted pass when France was mounting a promising counter-attack, and it took some gallant French defence to deny them more. Felipe Contepomi kicked four penalty goals in a Man of the Match performance to give the Pumas an 8-point lead at half time, and that lead was enough to see Argentina pull off a remarkable upset (17–12) despite a more spirited effort from France in the second half.

'Maybe we got lulled into a false sense of security by the results of the friendlies,' France captain Raphael Ibanez said after the match. 'The weight of the whole event obviously got to us and we didn't see it coming. That's why I am angry against myself because generally I do see things coming.'

Few people saw the surprise result coming in the opening match and it set the tone for an eventful tournament to unfold in the ensuing weeks. France's opening loss also indirectly applied extra pressure on Ireland in Pool D – fittingly tagged the 'pool of death' with France, Argentina and Ireland all vying for only two quarter-final places.

France legend Philippe Sella played a key part in his team qualifying for the inaugural Rugby World Cup final in 1987.

New Zealand captain David Kirk is presented with The Webb Ellis Cup after victory over France in the 1987 final.

All Blacks flanker Michael Jones charges forward against Wales during Rugby World Cup 1991. Jones, who was named Player of the Tournament in 1987, is widely regarded as one of the finest back row forwards ever to play the game.

Australia wing David Campese stretches the Ireland defence during the famous 1991 quarter-final at Lansdowne Road. Campese scored two tries in a match that saw the Wallabies escape with a one-point victory after a well-worked try to fly-half and stand-in captain Michael Lynagh in injury time.

England lock Wade Dooley leaps high in a free-for-all lineout during the Rugby World Cup 1991 final. Before lifting was permitted in the lineout, the locks and other taller forwards had to jump as best they could without assistance from team-mates.

England captain Will Carling takes the ball forward as Australia lock John Eales prepares to make the tackle during the Rugby World Cup 1991 final. England changed their tactics by running the ball at Australia in the final, and it ultimately cost them the title.

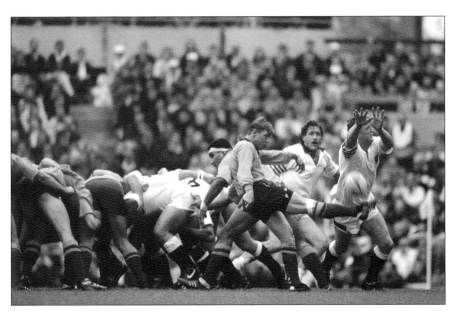

Australia captain Nick Farr-Jones with a successful clearing kick from the base of a scrum in the 1991 final, despite an attempted charge-down from England flanker Mickey Skinner. Farr-Jones was a crucial steadying force for the Wallabies.

Australia players celebrate as referee Derek Bevan from Wales awards a try to prop Tony Daly in the 1991 final against England at Twickenham. The Wallabies scored the only try of the match off a rolling maul from a lineout near the England line.

Australia players – Troy Coker (top), Simon Poidevin (middle left), Phil Kearns (middle right) and Michael Lynagh – relax with The Webb Ellis Cup and a celebratory beer in the famous baths at Twickenham after victory over England in the 1991 final.

The 'Rainbow Nation' in full colour as the Rugby World Cup went to South Africa in 1995. After the release of Nelson Mandela from prison in 1990 and the subsequent disintegration of apartheid, South Africa was welcomed back to the sporting world and they made 1995 an event to savour.

New Zealand wing Jonah Lomu on the rampage against England in the 1995 semi-final at Newlands in Cape Town, South Africa. Lomu scored four tries in the match and was later named Player of the Tournament. His impact on the world stage was phenomenal.

France scrum-half Guy Accoceberry passes the ball clear during the 22–19 victory over Scotland in 1995.

Wales flanker Hemi Taylor scores during the 1995 Pool C match against Ireland. Ireland eventually won 24–23.

South Africa wing Chester Williams crosses for one of his four tries during the Rugby World Cup 1995 quarter-final against Western Samoa at Ellis Park, Johannesburg. The Springboks prevailed 42–14 to set up a semi-final against France.

One low, one high ... South Africa used swarming tactics on Jonah Lomu to good effect in the 1995 final against New Zealand. Lomu had a devastating impact on the tournament but the Springboks gave him no room to move in the final.

South Africa fans spared nothing in their thoughts for how Jonah Lomu should be contained in the final. All Blacks captain Sean Fitzpatrick remembers this same group of fans shaking the team bus as it arrived before the 1995 final.

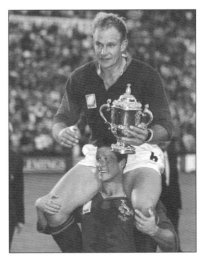

South Africa captain Francois Pienaar celebrates victory on the shoulders of Hennie le Roux after the 1995 final.

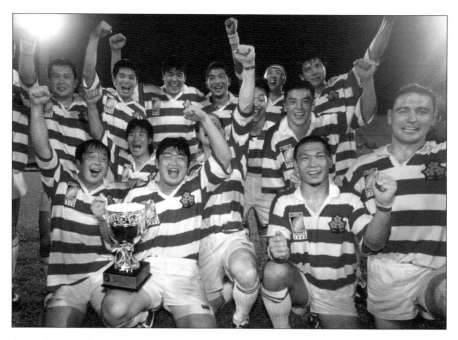

Japan forward Takeomi Ito holds the Asia Rugby Championship trophy and celebrates with team-mates after beating Hong Kong at Singapore National Stadium. Japan won the final 47–7 to qualify for Rugby World Cup 1999 in Wales.

Former South Africa captain Francois Pienaar and Welsh rugby legend Gareth Edwards walk out between a line of flags representing all participating countries during the Rugby World Cup 1999 Opening Ceremony at the Millennium Stadium in Cardiff, Wales.

England No. 8 Lawrence Dallaglio claims a lineout against Italy in their Pool B clash in 1999. England won the match 67–7.

One of Scotland's finest – legendary full-back Gavin Hastings on the fly during Rugby World Cup 1999.

Samoa is renowned as one of the most physical of all nations to play against in the Rugby World Cup. Pictured here is Argentina prop Mauricio Reggiardo, knocked out cold, after being on the receiving end of some stern Samoan defence. Argentina held their nerve to win 32–16.

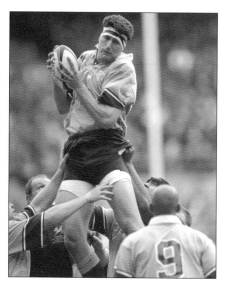

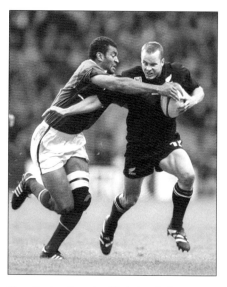

Australia captain John Eales secured three vital lineouts in the dying minutes of the 1999 semi-final victory over South Africa.

New Zealand centre Christian Cullen is wrapped up by Emile Ntamack in the famous 1999 semi-final won by France.

Australia players Jason Little and Tim Horan hold The Webb Ellis Cup aloft during the victory lap at the Millennium Stadium in Cardiff after the Wallabies defeated France 35–12 in the 1999 final. Horan was later named Player of the Tournament for his outstanding contribution to Australia's triumph.

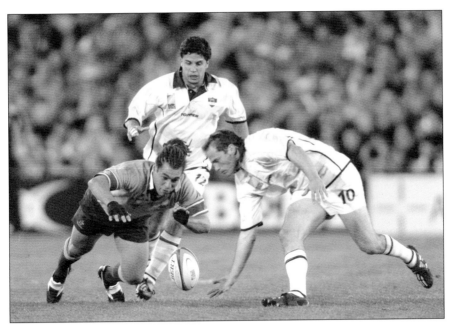

Argentina fly-half Felipe Contepomi calmly scoops up a loose ball before Australia flanker George Smith can pounce during the opening match of Rugby World Cup 2003 in Sydney. The Wallabies had to overcome some strong resistance from the Pumas before prevailing 24–8.

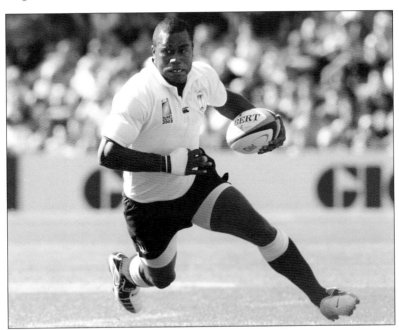

Fiji flyer Rupeni Caucaunibuca starts a counter-attack against Scotland during the thrilling Rugby World Cup 2003 Pool B clash at Aussie Stadium in Sydney. Caucaunibuca scored two scintillating tries to almost inspire Fiji to an improbable upset, but Scotland eventually fought back to win 22–20.

A rare sight as George Gregan misses a tackle. Ireland captain Keith Wood puts a heavy fend on the Australia scrum-half during the 2003 Pool A match in Melbourne. The Wallabies escaped with a one-point victory to win the pool and set up a quarter-final with Scotland, while Ireland was left to face France.

Thousands of England fans travelled Down Under with great humour and enthusiasm for Rugby World Cup 2003.

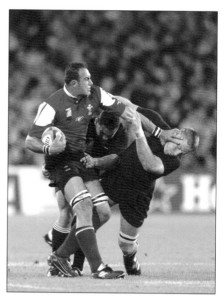

Wales forward Chris Wyatt fends off New Zealand lock Brad Thorn in the 2003 pool match that gave the All Blacks a big scare ahead of the knockout stage.

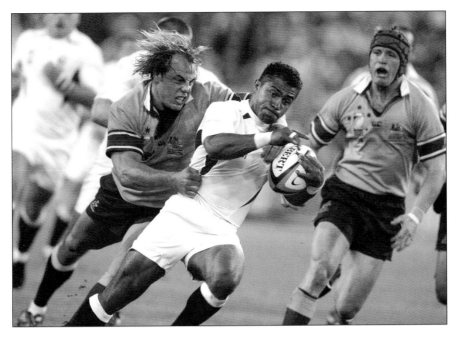

Australia flanker Phil Waugh tries to contain England wing Jason Robinson during the Rugby World Cup 2003 final in Sydney. After being under a highball that saw his opposite wing Lote Tuqiri score an early try, Robinson retaliated with his own memorable score for England later in the first half.

Fly-half Jonny Wilkinson kicks the winner for England in extra time during the 2003 final. Australia flanker Phil Waugh tried in vain to charge it down as Wilkinson kicked the winning drop-goal off his less-favoured right boot to seal a 20–17 victory. Ironically, he had missed three earlier opportunities with his favoured left.

South Africa 20-year-old Francois Steyn was called on to replace the injured Jean de Villiers at inside centre during the 2007 tournament and he performed brilliantly.

Argentina emerged as a major international force at Rugby World Cup 2007 and their star fly-half Juan Martin Hernandez was a key figure in their outstanding campaign.

Fiji celebrates victory over Wales in the final Pool B match of Rugby World Cup 2007. The win secured Fiji a place in the quarter-finals – their first appearance in the knockout stage since the inaugural tournament in 1987. Wales were left shattered as their campaign came to an abrupt end.

All photographs supplied by Action Images Limited

France reserve fly-half Frederic Michalak makes the break that leads to a match-winning try for *Les Bleus* in a thrilling 2007 quarter-final against New Zealand in Cardiff. Trailing the All Blacks 13–3 at half time, France clawed their way back in the second half before claiming another historic upset.

Bearded France forward Sebastien Chabal thanks his cult following after *Les Bleus* defeated the All Blacks in Cardiff.

Scrum-half Andy Gomarsall was a key figure in England's resurrection for the knockout stage of 2007.

Prince Harry and Prince William show contrasting emotions after England's 'no try' to wing Mark Cueto in the 2007 final.

South Africa president Thabo Mbeki celebrates with the Springboks after their victory over England in the 2007 final.

Springbok celebrations: South Africa captain John Smit holds The Webb Ellis Cup aloft as his team-mates savour their new world champion status after defeating England (15–6) in the 2007 final at the Stade de France in Paris. South Africa became only the second country to win the title twice.

That pressure showed when the men in green struggled across the line against a spirited challenge from tournament minnows Namibia. Ireland looked to be cruising to victory when they were leading 27–3 midway through the second half, but two quick tries to Namibia rattled their more fancied opponents. After being on the end of an attacking barrage throughout the final 20 minutes, Ireland were happy to hear the final whistle as they recorded an unconvincing victory (32–17) to start their 2007 campaign.

'That was our worst performance for a long time,' Ireland coach Eddie O'Sullivan said after the match. 'We were very, very poor and I can't remember when we last made so many unforced errors.'

The Ireland coach didn't have to wait long to see an equally abominable performance when his team lined up against Georgia one week later. Ireland were desperate to atone for their relatively poor showing against Namibia, but they faced some stern defence and were left trailing 10–7 late in the second period after Georgia wing Giorgi Shkinin intercepted a long pass from Peter Stringer before racing 70 metres to score. Ireland were clearly rattled and when flanker David Wallace received a yellow card it seemed that Georgia were on the verge of pulling off what would have been the biggest upset in Rugby World Cup history, but a late score to fullback Girvan Dempsey saw Ireland escape with a narrow victory (14–10) to save the Emerald Isle from international humiliation.

'I wish I could explain why we're not firing on all cylinders at the moment,' O'Sullivan said after the Georgia escape. 'We've certainly trained hard and been assiduous in all our preparations. I know that it's frustrating for the supporters, but it's equally frustrating for the players. We just haven't clicked yet.'

The sad story for Ireland was that they never clicked at Rugby World Cup 2007, and without gaining a valuable bonus point against Georgia their path to qualifying for the knockout stage became increasingly difficult. First they had to face a resurgent France, who recovered from their opening loss to Argentina with a crushing defeat of Namibia (87–10) in Toulouse. There were signs of some improvement as Ireland successfully defended their try-line for the first hour of the match, but ill discipline saw Jean-Baptiste Elissalde capitalise with five penalty goals to ensure *Les Bleus* remained in control. Vincent Clerc eventually broke through for the first try of the match in the 59th minute, and when Irish lock Paul O'Connell was sent to the sin bin following repeated offside infringements in the lineout, France dealt the killer blow with Clerc's second try sealing a comfortable victory (25–3).

Ireland's hopes of progressing to the knockout stage were hanging by a thread after the loss to France and in their final pool match against Argentina they required a bonus point victory by scoring four tries. It was a tough ask for a team struggling to find the form that secured them successive Six Nations Triple Crowns in 2006 and 2007, but Ireland were desperate to atone for a disappointing campaign with victory of any kind against a team with whom they had established a long Rugby World Cup rivalry. Argentina knocked Ireland out of the 1999 tournament, but Ireland then ended the Pumas' campaign in 2003 with a thrilling 1-point victory at Adelaide Oval. That trend would suggest that 2007 was Argentina's turn and so it would prove, despite a much-improved effort from Ireland. In a tense first half it looked as though the Irish might have gained the upper hand when Brian O'Driscoll broke through the midfield to give his team the lead, but the Pumas struck back when fly-half Juan Martin Hernandez kicked the second of three drop-goals before a try to wing Horacio Agulla gave them an 8-point lead at half time. Felipe Contepomi added another penalty goal soon after the break, but Ireland fullback Geordan Murphy finished off a magnificent backline move to put his team in touch again. It didn't last for long though, as Contepomi landed another two penalty goals before Hernandez sealed the victory (30–15) with his third drop-goal of the afternoon. The result ended Ireland's campaign and secured top place in Pool D for Argentina – their best ever performance in the pool stage. France claimed second place but with that came the unenviable task of facing New Zealand in the quarter-finals. Well ... unenviable most would think.

Unlike the 2003 tournament where the pool stage was widely criticised for lopsided results, Rugby World Cup 2007 produced the most exciting preliminary stage in the history of the tournament. The other group to spring some surprising and close results was Pool A, featuring defending champions England along with title contenders South Africa, Samoa, Tonga and the United States. The opening weekend saw England struggle past the United States (28–10) in Lens and frustration within the ranks of the reigning title holders was typified by their captain Phil Vickery, who inconceivably tripped an opposing player and went on to receive a two-match suspension. England started the tournament on the back foot with a training injury to fly-half Jonny Wilkinson, and their opening performance was indicative of an unsettled team struggling to find any rhythm.

In contrast, South Africa started their campaign in convincing style against Samoa at the Parc des Princes in Paris. The Pacific Islanders have traditionally proved to be strong opposition at Rugby World Cup level and they showed some early signs of troubling the Springboks, only to be let down by a dysfunctional lineout that gifted possession to a potent South Africa backline. Springboks wing Bryan Habana scored four tries and Percy Montgomery had a personal haul of 29 points as South Africa went on to secure a comfortable victory (59–7). Samoa were typically bruising with their defence, led by No. 8 Henry Tuilagi, but their most notable achievement on the day was when Brian Lima came on as a replacement. The 35-year-old veteran – known as 'the Chiropractor' for his brutal tackling – became the first player ever to appear in five Rugby World Cup tournaments, but in an unfortunate twist Lima was forced to leave the field groggy after one of his attempted tackles resulted in a head clash. The final result turned out to be one Samoa would rather forget, but Springboks coach Jake White was quick to point out that the score was not reflective of how much Samoa tested his team.

'It was tough. It didn't go as we expected. It was a really physical performance from Samoa and they were tough competition,' White said. 'At one stage, when it was 14–7, I was worried ... full credit to Samoa.'

As the battered and bruised recovered from that clash, the United States were tasked with lining up against Tonga in Montpellier four days after they gave strong resistance to England. The Eagles had been instilled as favourites after their impressive showing against the reigning world champions, but Tonga were first to score through their rampaging No. 8 Finau Maka, who revealed to a stunned media pack in the build-up to the match that he likes to bang his head against a wall for motivation before taking to the field. The United States were trailing by 10 points at half time, but they clawed their way back to within three with a try to lock Louis Stanfil in the 67th minute. It set the match up for a thrilling finish and exciting wing Takudzwa Ngwenya threatened to steal it for the United States, but the final say was for Tonga substitute Viliami Vaki who brushed off four defenders to score the try that sealed victory (25–15).

The early clashes in Pool A had provided some entertaining rugby, but it was the looming clash between England and South Africa that had captured the most attention throughout the rugby world. It was the first time two former Rugby World Cup champions would meet in the pool stage, and the fixture was played at the ground where the same two teams contested the 1999 quarter-final when Jannie 'Foot of God' de Beer sank England with a world record five drop-goals. On that day, a very good England team were overwhelmed by the freakish feats of one individual and in 2007 they suffered a similar fate as South Africa scrum-half Fourie du Preez orchestrated a totally dominant team display that saw the Springboks humiliate England to the tune of 36–0. With captain Phil Vickery suspended and fly-half Jonny Wilkinson and his back-up Olly Barkley also both on the sidelines with injury, Martin Corry was left to lead a makeshift line-up.

'What happened is we gifted them pretty much 20 points, and they didn't have to work particularly hard for those 20 points, which is disappointing. Then after that we were playing catch-up, which was very difficult against one of the best sides in the world,' Corry said. 'Both sides realised they would have to fight for every score, [but] South Africa didn't for their first three scores, which is the most disappointing thing.'

The Springboks were ruthless in both defence and attack, with du Preez controlling the match through magnificent tactical kicking, and his running from the base of the ruck had England guessing all night. In front of what turned out to be the largest crowd of the 2007 tournament (80,430), England were kept scoreless for the first time ever in a Rugby World Cup fixture and the result all but ensured South Africa would advance to the knockout stage as the winner of Pool A.

Two days after England were humiliated by South Africa, a fiery Pacific Island showdown between Samoa and Tonga produced a gripping spectacle at the Stade de la Mosson in Montpellier. Samoa were enjoying a run of nine successive victories against Tonga and most pundits favoured them to carry that into double figures, but Tonga showed tremendous courage to hold on for victory (19–15) after playing most of the final 10 minutes with just 13 players. Brutal defence was the order of the day from both sides, and referee Jonathan Kaplan warned a number of players for dangerous play before losing patience with Tonga blindside flanker Hale T Pole and handing out a red card in the 73rd minute. Kaplan then pulled out a yellow card minutes later to dismiss replacement prop Muliufi Salanoa, and Tonga were forced to defend for their lives as Samoa desperately tried to steal the match in the closing stages.

'I said to the boys before the game: "Today you either die or come back to the changing room with nothing",' Tonga captain Nili Latu said. 'I said, "Let's prepare to go out there and die today to win" and that's how much it meant to us, to lose our life.'

A converted try to inside centre Epeli Taione in the 59th minute proved decisive for Tonga, and the proud Pacific Island nation celebrated for days after their national team claimed successive Rugby World Cup victories for the first time to set up an unprecedented tilt at claiming a place in the quarter-finals.

Tonga's two final pool matches were against South Africa and England, and while it seemed that an under-performing England would be the most likely target for an upset, it was a second string Springboks team that received the fright of their lives when Tonga almost pulled off the unthinkable at the Stade Felix-Bollaert in Lens. With the Springboks defending a 5-point lead in the closing stages, Tonga fly-half Pierre Hola chip-kicked behind South Africa's defence for his right wing to run through and claim a last-minute try that would have brought the scores level with a kick to come, but the ball bounced into touch and the Springboks breathed a collective sigh of relief after holding on for a narrow victory (30–25).

That victory for South Africa secured them first place in Pool A, and the tight tussle for second came down to the match between England and Tonga at the Parc des Princes in Paris. The reigning world champions put their campaign back on track with an impressive victory over Samoa (44–22) after Jonny Wilkinson rejoined the team to add some much-needed stability at fly-half. Wilkinson was vital to England's survival and so it would prove again as he kept them calm in trying circumstances against a spirited Tonga team. The Pacific Islanders took an early lead when outside centre Sukanaivalu

Hufanga broke through three tackles to score under the posts in the 18th minute, but England clawed their way back through the steadying influence of Wilkinson, who kicked two drop-goals and caught Tonga out with a perfectly placed cross-field kick for Paul Sackey to score in the corner when Tonga were expecting him to kick at goal. It was a brave move, but it had the desired result and gave England confidence to spread the ball wide and score three further tries to secure victory (36–20) and a place in the quarter-finals.

South Africa and England's opponents in the quarter-finals were to come from Pool B – featuring Australia, Wales, Fiji, Canada and Japan. The opening match in the pool saw Australia put Japan to the sword with a dominant second-half performance at the Stade Gerland in Lyon. The Wallabies took a while to find their feet before leading 23–3 at half time, but the second period was one-way traffic as they piled on 68 unanswered points to record an emphatic victory (91–3). Blindside flanker Rocky Elsom scored the fastest hat-trick by a forward in Rugby World Cup history when he crossed for his third try in the opening minute of the second half. The floodgates then opened and Australia went on to score a total of 13 tries for a promising start to their 2007 campaign.

Wales faced Canada at the Stade de la Beaujoire in Nantes for their opening match of the 2007 tournament and the Red Dragons were given an early scare as a spirited Canucks side claimed two first-half tries to be leading 12–9 at the break. Canada were courageous throughout, but they started to tire after 50 minutes and Wales scored four tries in quick succession to open up a 25-point lead they would not surrender before going on to secure a comfortable victory (42–17). The Red Dragons were given a stern test in the opening period, and Canada coach Ric Suggitt gave the first of many animated responses in the post-match media conference when a journalist acknowledged the commendable first half effort from his team.

'We can compete against the top teams in the world and Wales is one of those teams. We're not shy about what we want to achieve and we'll keep backing ourselves no matter what all the critics say about the segregation of rugby. They can stuff themselves,' Suggitt said. 'Part of the segregation is that we keep being called "two-tier" and they should stop calling us "two-tier" countries. We're all playing for the same trophy and as long as they keep labelling us like that then people keep looking at us like that, and that's not what we should be about. We do deserve to be here.'

Much of the focus in Pool B then turned to the highly anticipated clash between Wales and Australia in Cardiff the following weekend, but prior to that match Fiji opened their 2007 campaign with a thrilling midweek victory (35–31) over Japan in Toulouse. Backing up four days after being comprehensively defeated by Australia, Japan tested Fiji right until the end but their tired legs were unable to muster enough energy to overhaul the energetic Pacific Islanders. Two tries to flanker Akapusi Qera proved vital for Fiji as they secured an all-important bonus point victory after scoring four tries.

The stage was then set in Cardiff for Wales to host Australia in a vital clash for determining top place in Pool B. The Wallabies received an early blow as veteran fly-half Stephen Larkham failed to shake off a nagging knee injury. At first it seemed the 33-year-old would only miss one match, but minor surgery the following week resulted in an infection that sadly meant he would eventually play no further part in the tournament. Larkham's place in the team was taken by 21-year-old rookie Berrick Barnes. The late change to the starting line-up resulted in a desperate search to find a smaller No. 10 jersey to fit the shorter frame of Barnes, with team management frantically arranging for a smaller No. 10 to be shipped from the team base in France. After a flight across from France and a special courier from Cardiff airport, the jersey just made the 1.20pm deadline ahead of the 2pm kick-off.

Barnes had made a try-scoring Test debut one week earlier after coming on for Australia against Japan in the second half of their opening match, but Wales was sure to pose a tougher challenge for the charismatic rookie, who was also – as the youngest member of the squad – tasked with looking after the team mascot – 'Joey' the stuffed Wallaby. There were no signs of early nerves from Barnes though, as he set up an early try for Matt Giteau before calmly slotting a drop-goal to give Australia an early 10–0 lead. Two further tries to Stirling Mortlock and Chris Latham soon followed and a penalty goal from Mortlock gave the visitors a 25–3 lead at half time, but Wales staged a brave comeback in the second half with tries to Jonathan Thomas and Shane Williams. James Hook also took over the goal-kicking duties from Stephen Jones to kick two penalties and suddenly Wales were in touch with Australia, but Chris Latham then received a fortuitous bounce off one of his towering high balls before running in his second try to give Australia a bonus-point victory (32–20) and maximum points from their first two matches of the tournament.

'We were happy enough with the first half and lost our concentration in the second half. It was only our second game in three months, but we got the five points and we'll now get ready for Fiji,' Australia coach John Connelly said. 'We fluffed three or four try-scoring opportunities. We gave Wales a chance to get back in at 25–3. At half-time we took our foot off the pedal and a number of penalties went against us.'

Australia went on to defeat both Fiji (55–12) and Canada (37–6) to secure first place in Pool B. Japan and Canada fought out a thrilling midweek draw (12–12) in Bordeaux, which was only the second deadlocked pool match in Rugby World Cup history after France and Scotland in 1987. However, it was the battle for second place in Pool B between Wales and Fiji that provided one of the most entertaining matches of the tournament. Fiji stunned the Red Dragons with three tries over 10 minutes in the first half and it was déjà vu for Wales in the west of France as they trailed 25–3 at the break – the same half-time score they faced one week earlier against Australia.

If Wales gained anything from their loss to the Wallabies it was the belief that they could fight their way back into a match, and they did exactly that again in the second half against Fiji. After losing flanker Akapusi Qera to the sin-bin just before the break, Fiji struggled with only 14 players against a revitalised Wales early in the second period. Both Shane Williams and Gareth Thomas crossed for tries when Qera was off the field, bringing the Red Dragons back into contention, and when wing Mark Jones scored, suddenly Wales had taken the lead. Two penalty goals to fly-half Nicky Little saw Fiji regain it, but when flanker Martyn Williams intercepted a stray pass it was Wales who took a 3-point lead again with only six minutes remaining. Just when it seemed that score would be enough to see the Red Dragons through to the knockout stage, Fiji came back again through a try to prop Graham Dewes that needed to be confirmed by the television match official. It was a gripping encounter and not a single person in the stadium was prepared to say there would not be another score, but the try to Dewes was enough to secure Fiji a historic victory (38–34) and their first appearance in the quarter-finals since the inaugural tournament in 1987. Wales were left shattered after their campaign ended before the knockout stage for the first time since 1995, and for the third time in Rugby World Cup history. It was a particularly sad result for their captain Gareth Thomas, who received a commemorative cap for making his 100th Test appearance.

'I'd give the cap back just for a win today. It is a bit hollow now we're going home tomorrow,' Thomas said. 'We gave them too much ball, we gave them too much space and we made stupid errors on their line. Our goal was to make it at least to the quarter-finals, so this [campaign] is a failure and we are very disappointed.'

Wales were left to pick up the pieces of a disappointing campaign and the fallout began immediately with coach Gareth Jenkins meeting Welsh Rugby Union group chief executive Roger Lewis and chairman David Pickering at the team base in France before announcing his immediate resignation. One day after that, former skipper Martyn Williams also announced his retirement from international rugby after 76 Tests for the Red Dragons. Wales were set to enter yet another rebuilding phase for their elite rugby programme, while Fiji and Australia lived to fight another day.

Pool C at Rugby World Cup 2007 did not produce the most captivating contests compared to other groups in the tournament, but with title favourites New Zealand in the fold there was always a fair amount of interest generated despite every All Blacks pool match resulting in a lopsided affair. The first team to suffer at the hands of New Zealand was Italy on a balmy Saturday afternoon at the Stade Velodrome in Marseille. The All Blacks took only two minutes to register their first try to skipper Richie McCaw, and the floodgates opened thereafter as they ran in 10 more tries to secure a comfortable victory (76–14). Doug Howlett scored a hat-trick to draw level with Christian Cullen as the highest try-scorer (46) in All Blacks history, and perhaps the only blemish for New Zealand was when prop Carl Hayman received a yellow card early in the second half for punching.

Realistically, Italy never expected to win the match or even come close, but it was important for the *Azzurri* to show some fight to ensure their confidence was not dented for the all-important clashes that lay ahead to determine second place in Pool C. Their main rival for that second place and a berth in the knockout round was Scotland, who started their campaign against tournament newcomers

Portugal with what was eventually a comfortable victory (56–10), but the Scots didn't have it all their own way. Portugal started the game strongly with ferocious defence that left a number of Scottish players battered and bruised. Prop Allan Jacobsen was taken to hospital after suffering a calf injury, while outside centre Marcus Di Rollo received a knock to his temple. So impressive was Portugal's effort in the first hour that their captain and No. 8 Vasco Uva was awarded Man of the Match despite being on the losing team. The biggest cheer of the day came when Portugal wing Pedro Carvalho scored his country's first ever Rugby World Cup try in the 28th minute, but for many on the losing side it was simply an experience to savour on rugby's ultimate stage.

'I was crying during the anthem today. I've never seen so many people in front of me,' Portugal reserve hooker João Correia said after the match. 'When I see the Haka – I can't imagine what that will be like. It's a dream of a lifetime.'

Correia had less than a week to wait before his team would face the mighty All Blacks, and despite knowing they would be on the receiving end of a hiding to nothing it was a moment to savour for a group of amateurs from football-crazy Portugal as they lined up against the number one team in the world. Just as they did against Scotland, Portugal started the match with great vigour and defended their line with brutal defence. The class of New Zealand didn't take long to break through however, with Joe Rokocoko scoring twice in the first 15 minutes. Unbeknown to many at the time, Portugal had something to celebrate with fly-half Gonçalo Malheiro kicking the first drop-goal of the tournament. It was also one that would stay in the history books for at least another four more years after it ended the longest wait in Rugby World Cup history for a drop-goal. Amazingly it took until the 14th match of the tournament for the first drop-goal to come in 2007, which was five more matches than the previous slowest, kicked by Gregor Townsend for Scotland in 1999 after nine matches. An obscure statistic perhaps, but one Portugal could hang their hat on despite eventually suffering a record defeat (108–13) to the All Blacks in Lyon.

Scotland returned to the familiar surrounds of Murrayfield in Edinburgh for their second clash of the tournament against Romania, and local fans were happy to see the end of a long dry spell when legislation banning the sale of alcohol at the ground was relaxed after more than two decades. Finally the Scottish faithful could enjoy a beer while watching their team play, but the decision did not come lightly and included a strict quota on the number of drinks a person could buy, together with a message from Scotland captain Jason White about responsible drinking played out on the big screen. Thankfully no major issues were reported and the Scottish fans enjoyed a relaxed atmosphere as their team went on to comfortably defeat Romania (42–0) and draw level with New Zealand in the pool standings after gaining maximum points from their first two matches. Openside flanker Allister Hogg starred for the home side with a hat-trick of tries, and fullback Rory Lamont chimed in with an impressive double, while goal-kicking maestro Chris Paterson kept his 100 per cent record intact by slotting every conversion.

Scotland's next game was against the All Blacks and despite not openly conceding defeat, their coach Frank Hadden selected a second-string team as an obvious ploy to rest his main players for the looming second place shoot-out against Italy less than a week later. Hadden was widely criticised for his selection and when questioned by reporters ahead of the match he rather humorously claimed: 'It's pretty simple beating the All Blacks, in my opinion. If we do what we have been practising better than they do what they have been practising, we will win the game.'

A fair assessment in theory perhaps, but in 25 matches between the two countries since 1905 the best result Scotland has ever managed against the All Blacks is two draws – one in 1964 and the other in 1983. It was a bold suggestion to think a second-string team including two debutants in the forwards – prop Alasdair Dickinson and flanker John Barclay – could reverse that trend, but Hadden was certainly right in one assessment when he said they would do their country proud. New Zealand were expected to put a solid score on Scotland, but the All Blacks failed to capitalise on their dominance, with 20 handling errors throughout the match. New Zealand went on to win the match comfortably (40–0), but chinks started appearing in the All Black armour against the same opposition and at the same venue they did back in 1999 one week before an unexpected exit against France. Any other team would have been savouring a 40-point victory over Scotland, but many New Zealand pundits were scathing in their assessment of the All Blacks performance.

'The New Zealand camp will be concerned at the moment and the New Zealand public will be too. The execution is just not there in attack,' said All Blacks legend Zinzan Brooke. 'The intent is certainly there, as displayed in the Haka before the match, but now is the time to deliver on the big stage. The New Zealand public want the Cup and nothing less. It's time to start catching the ball, stop poking tongues out with too much energy in the Haka, and put more grunt into the match itself.'

The All Blacks claimed top place in Pool C with the win over Scotland and they finished off the pool stage with an emphatic victory (85–8) over Romania in Toulouse, but the nerves were undoubtedly still prevalent in the New Zealand camp as they were left to ponder a looming quarter-final against their Rugby World Cup nemesis France in Cardiff.

As expected, the battle for second place in Pool C came down to the clash between Italy and Scotland in St-Etienne, and in wet conditions at the Stade Geoffroy-Guichard it was goal-kicking ace Chris Paterson who secured Scotland a narrow victory (18–16) and an all-important place in the quarter-finals. Paterson again maintained his perfect tournament kicking record with six penalty goals from six attempts, and Scotland also kept their proud record intact of having made the quarter-final stage of every Rugby World Cup tournament. Italy had arguably been the better team after enjoying more possession and scoring the only try of the match through their veteran scrum-half and captain Alessandro Troncon, but a final opportunity for the *Azzurri* to snatch a late victory was lost when David Bortolussi narrowly missed a penalty goal attempt in a closing stages. So close for Italy in their pursuit to reach the knockout stage, yet so far away again and it was a sad farewell for one of their greatest servants as Troncon made his last appearance.

The quarter-finals

The first 2007 quarter-final was a rematch of the 2003 final as defending champions England lined up against Australia in Marseille. The Wallabies had swept all before them in Pool B, claiming maximum points and never really being tested apart from the second half against Wales in Cardiff, while England had been humiliated by South Africa two weeks earlier before limping into the quarter-final stage with victories over Samoa and Tonga. Expectations of an Australia victory were widespread, but from the opening kick-off it was clear that England were not going to be swept aside easily as their forwards showed ruthless effectiveness at the breakdown and in the set pieces.

Despite having significantly less possession and limited periods in England territory during the first half hour, Stirling Mortlock was presented with three penalty goal opportunities but he was only successful with one. England fly-half Jonny Wilkinson also missed some opportunities, however as always he seemed to kick the ones that mattered most to give his team a 6–3 lead after 26 minutes. That score woke Australia's forwards from their slumber as they gained parity at the breakdown for a short period before some sustained attacking phases resulted in the only try of the match to Lote Tuqiri – a welcome score for the Fijian-born wing who was in the midst of a try-scoring drought. Mortlock converted from out wide to give Australia a 10–6 lead, which they managed to maintain through half time and right up until the 60th minute when Wilkinson slotted his fourth penalty goal to put England back into the lead at 12–10. As time ticked by Australia became desperate and mistakes crept in as they started to feel the match slipping away. Mortlock was given one last opportunity to steal it for the Wallabies with a penalty goal in the final five minutes, but the shot was waved away and England held on for an astonishing victory to bring Australia's promising campaign to an abrupt end.

'Personally, obviously goal-kicking-wise, I'm very disappointed. I should've kicked them,' a shattered Mortlock told a packed press conference after the match. 'It's an extremely quiet, dull change room at the moment. They're extremely disappointed with the way we played today. But credit goes to England with their [performance at the] breakdown. We didn't get any rhythm.'

Before the rugby world had a chance to fully digest England's upset victory over Australia in Marseille, the focus turned to Cardiff for an intriguing showdown between an all-conquering New Zealand and the tournament hosts France. Since their loss in the opening match to Argentina, *Les Bleus* had resurrected their campaign with convincing victories over Namibia, Ireland and Georgia, but they were still not expected to provide major resistance to an All Black machine growing in confidence and still strong favourites to win the tournament. The first half went the way that many predicted as New Zealand skipped to a 13–3 lead and they looked in complete control, but France were far from done. Just as they did in the 1999 semi-final, *Les Bleus* turned the match around with a series of attacking raids that eventually saw All Blacks centre Luke McAlister receive a yellow card from referee Wayne Barnes after blocking his opposite number Yannick Jauzion from chasing a chip-kick that was a possible try-scoring opportunity. Fly-half Lionel Beauxis also kicked the resulting penalty goal to reduce New Zealand's lead to seven, and when flanker Thierry Dusautoir crossed for a try less than 10 minutes later suddenly the scores were level at 13–13. McAlister then returned from the sin-bin, but the All Blacks were dealt another blow as their star fly-half Dan Carter limped from the field before being replaced by Nick Evans. New Zealand actually responded well to the changes, and when No. 8 Rodney So'oialo powered over for a try in the 63rd minute it seemed the All Black machine was back in motion. But this match was set for another twist after replacement fly-half Frederic Michalak was injected into the fray for the closing stages. Two minutes after coming on Michalak made the vital break that led to a try to Jauzion in the 69th minute before Jean-Baptiste Elissalde converted to put France in front at 20–18 – a lead they would not concede while going on to claim another monumental upset over the All Blacks.

'In the first half, we got forced into playing aerial ping-pong. We didn't play our set-pieces,' All Blacks captain Richie McCaw said. 'At half time we came in and said to keep pressure on and we didn't do that. Then we had a guy in the [sin-]bin and France lifted, and we can't afford to let them do that. If I knew the answers we would have sorted it out. We will be thinking about it for a long time.'

The shock defeat by France meant the 2007 All Blacks were the worst performing New Zealand team in Rugby World Cup history after all previous sides had at least made the semi-finals or better. New Zealand always takes failure at the Rugby World Cup hard, and the country even experienced a change of government after the 1999 mishap against France, but it didn't stop some loyal fans gathering at

Christchurch airport to greet part of the squad as they returned home. One group had a sign that said: 'All Blacks, We Are Loyal – We KNOW you're the BEST TEAM IN THE WORLD!' It was flattering support for a team expecting to arrive home and be vilified by fans and media, but on the inside each and every New Zealand player felt the agony of knowing another chance had slipped by and they faced a four-year wait before they would have another chance to redeem themselves.

The third quarter-final saw South Africa take on Fiji in Marseille. Following the unexpected exit of the All Blacks, the Springboks were quickly elevated to favourites to win the tournament and they looked to be cruising past Fiji as they held a 20–6 lead early in the second half. Fiji then lost centre Seru Rabeni to the sin-bin in the 52nd minute and the match looked to be slipping away. But just as their Pacific Island neighbours Tonga did to South Africa in the pool stage, Fiji came back hard and fast with two converted tries in the space of two minutes to bring the scores level with 20 minutes remaining. Percy Montgomery then kicked a penalty goal to give the stunned Springboks some breathing space, but Fiji came back again and looked certain to score a try in the corner to lock Ifereimi Rawaqa, until J.P. Pietersen pulled off a try-saving tackle that denied his much larger opponent from grounding the ball.

'I just closed my eyes and tried to hit as hard as possible. I guess I was lucky that he was carrying the ball in the wrong hand,' Pietersen said.

It was a vital moment and while Fiji continued to attack, the efforts of Pietersen appeared to lift South Africa in the closing stages as their forwards tightened the game up and choked Fiji of the turnover possession they had been feeding off so well. When flanker Juan Smith crossed for a try in the 70th minute, the Springboks regained command and a late try to fly-half Butch James made it a flattering final score-line (37–20) for South Africa. Springboks coach Jake White was obviously delighted with his team and attributed their victory to some outstanding leadership from his captain John Smit.

'The captaincy today was outstanding. John [Smit] was outstanding,' White said. 'The last 20 minutes was the best Test rugby we've played in the past six months. He [Smit] spoke in the huddle to his players and said: "Look, there's still 20 minutes to go and remember the look in the Aussies' and Kiwis' eyes yesterday." I think that those were very special words said at the right time.'

South Africa were through to the final four and their opponent in the semi-finals would come from the fourth and last quarter-final of the weekend between Argentina and Scotland at the Stade de France in Paris. France had expected their own team to be lining up in this fixture, but Argentina spoiled those plans after claiming top place in Pool D. Scotland were quietly confident of progressing through to their first semi-final since 1991 and they came very close after a spirited second half performance almost saw them overcome the Pumas in the dying stages. After trailing 13–6 at the break, Scotland maintained a clever game-plan that looked to tire Argentina's forwards after an hour of play before replacement scrum-half Chris Cusiter dived over to bring them within three points of the Pumas. But Scotland then appeared to release the pressure they had been applying so well, instead holding out in hope of penalty goal opportunities to come their way for Chris Paterson to work his magic, but those opportunities never came. Argentina defended bravely and in the end it was a Juan Martin Hernandez drop-goal that gave the Pumas enough breathing space to hold on for an historic victory.

The semi-finals

The first semi-final of Rugby World Cup 2007 was an unexpected clash between arch rivals France and England at the Stade de France in Paris. The home side started as favourites on the back of their shock upset over New Zealand and a dominant home record that had not seen England win in Paris for seven years. *Les Bleus* lined up with the same team as that which defeated the All Blacks and many pundits were surprised to see flanker Serge Betson in the side after he was knocked out cold against the All Blacks. Betson provided the English-speaking media with a comical moment when asked ahead of the match how serious the head knock was before replying in English: 'We did a brain scan on Wednesday and there was nothing there.'

England started the match in explosive style with a fortuitous try to wing Josh Lewsey in the opening two minutes. It came after scrum-half Andy Gomarsall weighted a kick perfectly into the corner before France fullback Damien Traille slipped and the ball bounced up perfectly for Lewsey to charge over for the opening score. Jonny Wilkinson was unable to convert from near the sideline, but England skipped to an early 5–0 lead before the real arm-wrestle began.

France recovered well from the opening try and their territorial advantage over the course of the first period was rewarded with two penalty goals to fly-half Lionel Beauxis to give *Les Bleus* a narrow 6–5 lead at the break. Beauxis then extended that with a penalty goal in the 44th minute, but Wilkinson returned fire three minutes later with one of his own to bring his side within a point once more. The England fly-half was not enjoying his tournament with the boot, and had been very critical of the balls being used, but as always he seemed to find his radar when it mattered most and in the 75th minute he slotted a penalty goal that saw England reclaim the lead for the first time since the 18th minute. As the pressure increased, France started to force the ball and errors crept into their play before Wilkinson applied the finishing touch with a drop-goal from over 40 metres out on the angle. Against all odds England held on for their second memorable upset in the space of two weeks, and the humiliating loss to South Africa was a distant memory as the defending champions advanced to their second consecutive final.

'When you put a new team together, as we have, in the context of a rugby or soccer season, we are only six or seven games into the season and you need five to bed down,' England coach Brian Ashton told the media the following day. 'In that regard the South Africa match came at the right time as it was a kick up the backside and showed we needed to get our act together. That was the defining moment of the tournament for me. Since then we've won four games on the bounce and we'll hopefully make it five next week.'

Ironically England's opponent for the final was shaping up to be South Africa, but first the Springboks had to overcome an energetic Argentina team determined to add to their record run and spring another surprise for the 2007 tournament. The Pumas started the match with their usual spark, but this time that enthusiasm was perhaps their undoing as forced passes failed to find their mark and South Africa capitalised to push on to a 24–6 lead by half time. It seemed that Argentina's memorable run was about to come to an abrupt and undignified end, but the Pumas came out in the second period and fought bravely to come back into the match after a dubious try to centre Manuel Contepomi in the 45th minute. Argentina continued to apply pressure in attack throughout the second half, but the Springboks defence stood firm and the ever-reliant Percy Montgomery slotted two penalty goals in the 71st and 75th minutes to put the result beyond doubt. Bryan Habana then crossed for his second try of the night one minute later – a score that also saw him move to the top of the overall try-scorers list and equal Jonah Lomu's record for the most tries (8) scored by a player at a single Rugby World Cup. Montgomery converted the Habana try for a personal haul of 17 points to seal a comfortable victory (37–13) for South Africa. The stage was set for their second showdown with England in the space of four weeks, but this time the winner would be crowned champions of the world.

Third place play-off

So often this fixture is criticised for being a match with little meaning, but from the opening kick-off between France and Argentina at the Parc des Princes it was clear that both sides had come to play. Desperate to atone for their semi-final loss to England, the host nation started better, but Argentina's defence stood firm amidst a barrage of French pressure. *Les Bleus* controlled the game early on and struck the first blow with a penalty goal to Jean-Baptiste Ellisalde, but Felipe Contepomi cancelled that out with one of his own to bring the scores level after 21 minutes. France had enjoyed all the possession and territory over the course of the first half hour and should have been well in front, but when Contepomi crossed for a try in the 28th minute the Pumas were ignited into an attacking frenzy before suddenly leaping to a 17–3 lead.

Frustrations from both sides losing their semi-finals came to the fore and some fiery exchanges resulted, with France captain Raphael Ibanez receiving a yellow card just before half time for dangerous rucking of an opponent. Argentina also lost Rimas Alvarez Kairelis at the same time, as New Zealand referee Paul Honiss – who became the world's most capped referee (45 Tests) in the match – tried to keep a lid on what had quickly developed into an emotional encounter. The Pumas were first to strike in the second half with a try to Federico Martin Aramburu, and that was soon followed by an impressive length-of-the-field score to fullback Ignacio Corleto after Argentina forced a mistake from France. *Les Bleus* finally broke through for their first try of the match in the 70th minute to Clement Poitrenaud, but it was too little too late for the home side as they suffered their worst ever defeat to Argentina (34–10). Heads were down for France, but tears of joy were flowing for the Pumas as they finished their impressive campaign with victory in the bronze medal play-off.

'I am feeling such great happiness, this whole week was going to be really difficult for us but the players equipped themselves well. Today they played an incredible game; from a technical point of view every aspect was spot on,' Argentina coach Marcelo Loffreda said in beaming admiration of his troops. 'I am so proud, grateful, to all of them for the eight years we have spent together and especially with the captain [Agustin Pichot] who has allowed me to spend a spectacular time with him.'

The final

After 44 days that yielded some of the most compelling action the Rugby World Cup stage has ever seen, South Africa and England lined up to contest a final that few had ever considered after the pool stages. While the odds were clearly stacked in favour of a South Africa victory, there was renewed belief in the England camp and a sense that if they could be close to the Springboks in the closing stages they had a proven match-winner in Jonny Wilkinson who could complete the fairytale again.

The match began in the tense manner expected for a tournament decider, and England held their own in most areas except the lineout, where South Africa locks Victor Matfield and Bakkies Botha turned on a dominant performance to consistently claim their own ball with ease while stealing possession off England's throw on numerous occasions. Percy Montgomery secured first points for the Springboks through a penalty goal in the 7th minute after Mathew Tait slipped over deep in England territory before being swarmed by South Africa defenders and penalised for not releasing the ball. Wilkinson evened the score up with his first penalty goal of the night in the 13th minute, but it was South Africa who maintained their composure the best with fewer errors in the opening half while Montgomery kicked two further penalty goals to ensure a 9–3 lead at the break.

The second half started brilliantly for England as Tait broke through some flimsy midfield defence from South Africa, only to be dragged down by Matfield just short of the line. England needed quick ball and when it finally came to the left Mark Cueto crossed for what seemed a try in the corner, only to be denied by the television match official after long deliberation showed his left foot shaved the sideline before he grounded the ball. England fans were not happy, but Wilkinson kicked a penalty goal to bring the score back to 9–6 and ensure his team didn't walk away with nothing from the movement. Unfortunately for England their lineout woes continued, losing seven of their own throws as Matfield and Botha continued to dominate that area for South Africa. England suffered another cruel blow in the 48th minute when fullback Jason Robinson was forced to leave the field with a shoulder injury, and Montgomery gave the Springboks a 6-point lead once again when he slotted a penalty goal three minutes later. England battled bravely with a reshuffled backline, and their coach Brian Ashton brought on fresh legs in the hope of finding some extra spark, but Francois Steyn kicked South Africa's fifth penalty goal from 46 metres out in the 60th minute to give the Springboks a 15–6 lead – a lead they would not surrender before holding on to claim their second Rugby World Cup title.

England dominated territory and possession, but a dysfunctional lineout together with 10 handling errors was too much for them to overcome against a polished Springboks side that executed their game-plan very effectively with fewer errors and more composure. As referee Alain Rolland blew the whistle to indicate full time, South Africa's players leaped for joy as they became only the second nation to win the Rugby World Cup twice. After the presentations were made, the Springboks victory celebrations rekindled fond memories of 1995, when a divided nation became united as one through the common language of sport. This time, however, it was Nelson Mandela's successor Thabo Mbeki who savoured the moment with the national side.

'This is much bigger than South Africa rugby,' Springboks coach Jake White said after celebrations subsided. 'To see our state president on the shoulders of one of the players, with the William Webb Ellis Trophy in his hands, there's no bigger statement in our country than that. What we need as a nation is to understand how big this is ... there's a lot we can draw from this little cup.'

FIVE MAGIC MEMORIES

Argentina produced early shock in thrilling 'pool of death'

On the back of a vibrant opening ceremony that set the tone for the opening match of Rugby World Cup 2007, the French party was cut short by a determined Argentina team ready to make a statement in world rugby. With no professional domestic playing structure in place within their country, Argentina has long been in the cold since the game turned professional in 1996. But with a solid nucleus of top players now enjoying successful professional careers throughout Europe, the Pumas have formed a national side capable of beating any team in world rugby.

Prior to the 2007 tournament Argentina had enjoyed an impressive run of success, including their first ever victory over England at Twickenham in 2006 and back-to-back success against Triple Crown champions Ireland, however few people knew how well the team would stack up in the pressure of a Rugby World Cup environment. The Pumas were determined to make a big impact early on: not only to make a statement to the rugby world but also to garner the vital support of many passionate sports fans in their home country who usually only have eyes for the round ball code.

'If we start on the right foot, the people will follow the team,' Argentina captain Agustin Pichot said ahead of the opening match against France. 'But if we start losing, they will prefer to watch any football match, even one from the 4th Division.'

The Pumas faced a tough road ahead at Rugby World Cup 2007 after being drawn alongside both France and Ireland in Pool D – the so-called 'pool of death' – but the dream start Pichot and his team-mates longed for soon became a reality as they pulled off a major upset in the opening match to defeat the host nation. That victory over France had the desired result as Argentina embraced their national rugby team while they powered to first place in Pool D before going on to reach the semi-finals for the first time. It was there that the dream run finally ended against the eventual world champions South Africa, but their parting shot came with another emphatic victory over France in the bronze (third place) final.

'I have been playing in the national team for several years and it's hard to find a group with such well-defined goals,' Pichot declared proudly after victory over France in the bronze final. 'After '99 there were huge changes. It was at that point we began creating a team. It's a process, a long one, but a historic process. We all need to enjoy these lovely moments of success. We have played together so well, there have been positives and negatives, but we face everything as a family.'

The 'family' from Argentina were in unprecedented territory. The feats of the Pumas captured the imagination of the rugby world and the usually soccer-mad nation from South America quickly embraced the success of their rugby team to the point that the most popular match on their domestic soccer calendar between River Plate and Boca Juniors had the kick-off time rescheduled to ensure there was no clash with the live coverage of their quarter-final against Scotland. *Los Pumas* were savouring a new existence.

Fiji and Tonga emerged from the shadows

Rugby World Cup 2007 will long be remembered as the tournament when the smaller nations stood up to be counted on the world stage, and it could not have come at a better time as administrators mooted the possibility of the next tournament being reduced to 16 teams in an effort to avoid lopsided score lines during the early stages. While Georgia captured the hearts of many rugby fans, and almost pulled off the biggest upset in tournament history before narrowly losing to Ireland (14–10) in Bordeaux, it was the collective improvement of the Pacific Island nations of Tonga and Fiji that was a welcome surprise. Samoa has often enjoyed the most success of the Pacific Island teams in the Rugby World Cup, but the 2007 tournament saw Fiji and Tonga emerge from their shadow as two of the most improved nations in world rugby.

Following the move to professionalism, these smaller countries were left without adequate training programmes and infrastructure to effectively prepare their national teams for competition against the top nations in the world. So often the likes of Fiji, Samoa and Tonga were competitive with the bigger rugby nations for the first 50 minutes of a match, only to fall away in the latter stages when the superior fitness of their opponents would prevail, but 2007 more often than not saw the Pacific Island teams remain competitive for the entire match.

'We used to just lift coconuts and banana trees, now we've got dieticians, weights, everything,' Samoa forwards coach Peter Fatialofa said about the improving state of Pacific Island rugby. 'The players look after their bodies now. Once we go fully professional, once we get a big sponsor, we'll have 15 Michael Joneses, so look out!'

In the case of Tonga, they even gained a reputation as the comeback kings after almost pulling off a stunning upset victory over eventual world champions South Africa. Less than two years before Rugby World Cup 2007, Tonga was in a diabolical state financially and their future in the international game looked very grim, but the proud nation has picked up the pieces and victory over Samoa in their Pool A clash in Montpellier ended a 7-year losing streak to their Pacific Island neighbours. The win also propelled Tonga to their best tournament campaign ever, and their powerful back row that included inspirational captain Nili Latu, Finau Maka and Hale T Pole will long be remembered by many opponents for their brutal defence and enterprising play.

Fiji completed the Pacific Island improvement with a memorable victory over Wales to seal their first appearance in the quarter-finals since the inaugural tournament in 1987. For so long a dominant force in the 7-a-side version of the game, Fiji also enjoyed a successful campaign that brought tremendous joy to their homeland.

'In one of the boy's villages, they have to carry the one TV to the top of the mountain just to get reception so they can watch the games,' said Fiji captain Mosese Raulini in reference to the undying support from the most dedicated fans in their country. 'The hardcore fans are the ones we really play for.'

So raw and genuine – a part of the tournament landscape that simply must be preserved.

Two southern giants crumbled in quarter-final thrillers

While the excitement of a thrilling final weekend to the pool stage had only just settled, Rugby World Cup 2007 was about to enter another gripping period as the first weekend of the knockout stage yielded the closest quarter-finals in tournament history. The total of all four winning margins from the 2007 quarter-finals was just 27 points – 21 points less than the previous smallest aggregate set in 1991. The first two quarter-finals featured a double showdown between the northern hemisphere and southern hemisphere as England lined up against Australia in Marseille, while France faced the might of New Zealand in Cardiff. It was expected to be a southern whitewash, but yet another twist in the 2007 tale was about to take place.

Like many of their fans, perhaps the Wallabies were guilty of looking too far beyond the match they were involved in, as England dominated every forward exchange with ease in the opening stages. Two years earlier at Twickenham, England's front row destroyed Australia and it was déjà vu for the Wallabies as Andrew Sheridan, Mark Regan and Phil Vickery led a marauding pack that was ruthless at the breakdown and immovable in the scrum. When it seemed Australia might gain some ascendancy over the oldest starting XV in tournament history (at an average age of 31 years, 358 days), England's forwards lifted again to overpower the Wallabies up front before holding on for a narrow victory (12–10) to seal their place in the final four.

Sadly Australia's loss also meant that the international rugby world had seen the last of former Wallabies captain and scrum-half George Gregan – the most capped player (136) in Test history. Gregan and his long-time partner in the halves Stephen Larkham (102 Test caps), who was likely to return from a knee injury for the semi-final if Australia made it, were given an unceremonious ending to their distinguished careers after playing a record 79 Tests together. A teary Larkham described how he could not contain his emotions after walking on to the field and seeing his shattered team-mates before noticing Gregan and realising it was all over.

'It's not the fairytale ending but life's like that,' Larkham said. 'I'm very disappointed for the guys. It was quite emotional, the fact that I won't be playing for Australia again.'

While England's triumph came as a surprise, nothing could top what unfolded six hours later in Cardiff where France rekindled memories of their classic 1999 semi-final triumph over New Zealand with another come-from-behind victory to topple the mighty All Blacks once again. In the week leading into the match, France captain Raphael Ibanez was asked at a press conference how his team planned to contain the All Blacks. Ibanez thought for a moment before replying: 'We know they're very confident but you can knock their machine out of synch [if you] throw some sand into the gearbox. When that happens their beliefs can turn into doubts.'

Perhaps France filled their pockets with sand at half time in Cardiff, because the team that came out for the second period was totally rejuvenated while New Zealand inexplicably lost focus. Within the space of 10 hours two southern hemisphere giants were gone from the 2007 tournament.

England resurrection brings out best of bulldog spirit

In what much of the British media was describing as one of the most impressive form reversals of any sporting team in modern times, England picked up the pieces from their 36–0 humiliation at the hands of South Africa and were lining up against the same opposition 36 days later with an opportunity to become the first ever team to successfully defend the world title. It had been a long and bumpy ride for England coach Brian Ashton and his men, but with renewed confidence in the knockout stage they were a team with belief after looking so rudderless in the early weeks of the pool stage.

Following the shattering loss to South Africa in Paris on the second weekend of the tournament, England were tasked with finding a quick remedy to prevent their campaign from spiralling to the lowest depths by becoming the first defending champions not to qualify for the knockout stage. A crisis meeting was called the following morning and players describe a room full of tension and frustration. Not only had England been denied through injury two of their most important players in fly-half Jonny Wilkinson and his backup Olly Barkley for the match against South Africa, but there was also an apparent lack of conviction from the coaching staff as to who they should select for the No. 10 jersey with no third-choice specialist fly-half in the squad. Eventually rugby league convert Andy Farrell was selected in the position but when pressed one day before the match as to why he came to that decision, Ashton became flustered and declared that veteran Mike Catt would play at No. 10 and Farrell at No. 12.

It was this indecision that apparently frustrated many in the England squad, who considered it to be a major contributor to the diabolical performance against South Africa. But just as Clive Woodward had done in 2003, Ashton encouraged an open forum for players to vent their thoughts and it was Mike Catt who confronted the head coach for his lack of tactical preparation. What followed thereafter was a clearer direction for the key players who managed the game, and the squad also gladly welcomed back Jonny Wilkinson at fly-half for their first do-or-die match against Samoa to remain in contention for the quarter-finals.

It was far from perfect but England put in more cohesive performances against Samoa and Tonga to scrape into the knockout stage. However, it was in the quarter-final against Australia that the best of bulldog spirit came to the fore as their marauding forward pack ground the Wallabies down to secure a place in the final four. One week later a stirring speech from Phil Vickery on the eve of the semi-final against France gave the squad even more bite, and within 24 hours they had advanced to a second consecutive Rugby World Cup final against all odds.

'Sometimes in sport things don't make sense,' Vickery grinned after England's semi-final victory. 'Even the predictions couldn't get it right. Today the underdog managed to rise up. It's a fantastic result for the team and our supporters.'

Few pundits could make sense of England's comeback from the doldrums, and while they did not go on and complete the fairytale, the 2007 squad will long be remembered for fulfilling one of the greatest resurrections of modern day sport.

'Rainbow nation' beams again as Springboks reign supreme

South Africa started the 2007 final as clear favourites largely on the back of their 36–0 slaughter of England during the pool stage, but their superior preparation was also evident in the gradual momentum the Springboks made throughout their campaign. While their second-string side was given an almighty scare against Tonga, and Fiji provided stiff opposition in the quarter-finals, it was South Africa's comprehensive victory over Argentina in the semi-finals that made it clear England would require something special to deny the Springboks their second Rugby World Cup crown.

The odds were stacked against the defending champions, but they had conceded fewer points than any other team during the 2007 knockout stages and history showed that four of the five previous Rugby World Cup winners had been in that same position before going on to win the tournament – the only exception being Australia in 1991. However, with England's impressive defensive record also came a lack of firepower in attack, with the 2007 team having the lowest points-scoring average of any finalist in history. Clearly England needed to force a tight battle fought in close quarters near the strength of their forward pack, and they could not afford to let South Africa have a good start.

England began that task well, but when the lineout failed on their first throw the towering presence of Victor Matfield, Bakkies Botha and Juan Smith for the Springboks became increasingly obvious – and their strength continued as the match wore on. South Africa conceded two penalty goals in the first half, but beyond that they produced outstanding discipline to deny Jonny Wilkinson any opportunities to keep England in the match with his goal-kicking. The England fly-half then became frustrated and he was forced to take high-risk options that came to nothing.

As South Africa's players leaped for joy after holding on for a 15–6 victory, one of their oldest servants – prop Os du Randt – could only just raise his arms after playing himself to a standstill. The Springboks giant nicknamed the 'Ox', who had also triumphed in the victorious South Africa side of 1995, had become the fourth in an elite group of players to claim two Rugby World Cup titles – joining John Eales, Tim Horan and Jason Little.

'I don't remember the first one, it's too long ago but I'm still enjoying this one,' du Randt said after the final. 'All the guys put the hard work in and it's just great to be out here.'

South Africa captain John Smit struggled for words in the post-match media conference as he tried to express the joy he and his team felt.

'I'm sitting here and trying not to cry. It's a feeling you can't put into words,' Smit said. 'It's a reward for four years of dedication and hard work. England gave us a good run. But we responded well to their technical kicking.'

Some 12 years after claiming their first Rugby World Cup title, South Africa was on top of the world once more. In 1995 it was the image of Nelson Mandela wearing a Springboks No. 6 jersey while presenting the Cup to Francois Pienaar that left a lasting impression on world sport, and in 2007 it was Mandela's successor Thabo Mbeki celebrating on the shoulders of the winning players while holding The Webb Ellis Cup that infused another iconic sporting memory for South Africa on the world stage. The 'Rainbow Nation' was in full colour once again.

14

Rugby World Cup all-time records

THERE HAVE BEEN six Rugby World Cup tournaments since the inaugural event in 1987, and throughout that period there have been some remarkable team and individual records set on rugby's ultimate stage. From the overall scoring dominance of New Zealand to the individual brilliance of tournament icon Jonah Lomu and drop-goal genius Jannie de Beer, Rugby World Cup has produced an array of talent throughout both the amateur and professional eras. While the following statistics represent some of the most important records achieved, it must be noted that the reigning world champions South Africa only rejoined the international rugby community in 1992. Therefore the Springboks have only competed in four tournaments and their lack of presence within some of these team statistics is largely a result of that.

Team records

Rugby World Cup champions and runners-up					
Year	Champion	Score	Runner-up	Venue	Crowd
1987	New Zealand	29–9	France	Eden Park, Auckland	48,350
1991	Australia	12–6	England	Twickenham, London	60,208
1995	South Africa	15–12	New Zealand	Ellis Park, Johannesburg	63,000
1999	Australia	35–12	France	Millennium Stadium, Cardiff	72,500
2003	England	20–17	Australia	Telstra Stadium, Sydney	82,957
2007	South Africa	15–6	England	Stade de France, Paris	80,430

Most points scored overall	
1711	New Zealand (36 matches)
1212	Australia (34 matches)
1195	France (36 matches)
1097	England (35 matches)
899	Ireland (29 matches)

Most points during the pool stage	
309	New Zealand (2007)
282	New Zealand (2003)
273	Australia (2003)
255	England (2003)
222	New Zealand (1995)

Most points conceded in the pool stage	
310	Namibia (2003)
258	Uruguay (2003)
252	Japan (1995)
212	Namibia (2007)
210	Japan (2007)

Most tries in a single tournament	
52	New Zealand (2007)
46	New Zealand (2003)
43	New Zealand (1987)
43	Australia (2003)
41	New Zealand (1995)

Most tries overall	
232	New Zealand (36 matches)
153	Australia (34 matches)
142	France (36 matches)
111	England (35 matches)
109	Scotland (29 matches)

Most tries in a match	
22	Australia v Namibia in 2003
21	New Zealand v Japan in 1995
17	England v Uruguay in 2003
16	New Zealand v Portugal in 2007
14	New Zealand v Italy in 1999

Biggest winning margin	
142	Australia v Namibia (142–0) in 2003 at Adelaide
128	New Zealand v Japan (145–17) in 1995 at Bloemfontein
98	New Zealand v Italy (101–3) in 1999 at Huddersfield
98	England v Uruguay (111–13) in 2003 at Brisbane
95	New Zealand v Portugal (108–13) in 2007 at Lyon

Individual records

Most points overall	
249	Jonny Wilkinson (England)
227	Gavin Hastings (Scotland)
195	Michael Lynagh (Australia)
170	Grant Fox (New Zealand)
163	Andrew Mehrtens (New Zealand)

Most points in a tournament	
126	Grant Fox (New Zealand) in 1995
113	Jonny Wilkinson (England) in 2003
112	Thierry Lacroix (France) in 1995
105	Percy Montgomery (South Africa) in 2007
104	Gavin Hastings (Scotland) in 1995

Most points in a match	
45	Simon Culhane for New Zealand v Japan in 1995
44	Gavin Hastings for Scotland v Ivory Coast in 1995
42	Mat Rogers for Australia v Namibia in 2003
36	Tony Brown for New Zealand v Italy in 1999
36	Paul Grayson for England v Tonga in 1999

Most matches played	
22	Jason Leonard (England)
20	George Gregan (Australia)
19	Mike Catt (England)
18	Martin Johnson (England)
18	Brian Lima (Samoa)

Most points in a final	
25	Matt Burke (AUS v FRA–1999)
17	Grant Fox (NZL v FRA–1987)
15	Joel Stransky (RSA v NZL–1995)
15	Jonny Wilkinson (ENG v AUS–2003)
12	Percy Montgomery (RSA v ENG–2007)

Most tries overall	
15	Jonah Lomu (New Zealand)
13	Doug Howlett (New Zealand)
11	Joe Rokocoko (New Zealand)
11	Rory Underwood (England)
10	David Campese (Australia)
10	Brian Lima (Samoa)
10	Chris Latham (Australia)

Most tries in a tournament	
8	Jonah Lomu (New Zealand) in 1999
8	Bryan Habana (South Africa) in 2007
7	Jonah Lomu (New Zealand) in 1995
7	Marc Ellis (New Zealand) in 1995
7	Doug Howlett (New Zealand) in 2003
7	Mils Muliaina (New Zealand) in 2003
7	Drew Mitchell (Australia) in 2007

Most tries in a match	
6	Marc Ellis for New Zealand v Japan in 1995
5	Chris Latham for Australia v Namibia in 2003
5	Josh Lewsey for England v Uruguay in 2003
4	Ieuan Evans for Wales v Canada in 1987
4	Craig Green for New Zealand v Fiji in 1987
4	John Gallagher for New Zealand v Fiji in 1987
4	Brian Robinson for Ireland v Zimbabwe in 1991
4	Gavin Hastings for Scotland v Ivory Coast in 1995
4	Chester Williams for South Africa v Samoa in 1995
4	Jonah Lomu for New Zealand v England in 1995
4	Keith Wood for Ireland v USA in 1999
4	Mils Muliaina for New Zealand v Canada in 2003
4	Bryan Habana for South Africa v Samoa in 2007

Most drop-goals overall	
13	Jonny Wilkinson (England)
6	Jannie de Beer (South Africa)
5	Rob Andrew (England)
4	Juan Martin Hernandez (Argentina)

Most drop-goals in a tournament	
8	Jonny Wilkinson (England) in 2003
6	Jannie de Beer (South Africa) in 1999
5	Jonny Wilkinson (England) in 2007
4	Juan Martin Hernandez (Argentina) in 2007
3	Jonathan Davies (Wales) in 1987
3	Joel Stransky (South Africa) in 1995
3	Rob Andrew (England) in 1995
3	Andrew Mehrtens (New Zealand) in 1995

Most drop-goals in a match	
5	Jannie de Beer (South Africa) v England in 1995
3	Jonny Wilkinson (England) v France in 2003
3	Juan Martin Hernandez (Argentina) v Ireland in 2007
2	Jonny Wilkinson (England) v Samoa in 2007
2	Jonny Wilkinson (England) v Tonga in 2007
2	Jonny Wilkinson (England) v South Africa in 2003
2	Tomasi Rabaka (Fiji) v Romania in 1991
2	Percy Montgomery (South Africa) v New Zealand in 1999
2	Christophe Lamaison (France) v New Zealand in 1999
2	Rob Andrew (England) v Argentina in 1995
2	Jonathan Davies (Wales) v Ireland in 1987
2	Joel Stransky (South Africa) v New Zealand 1995
2	Lisandro Arbizu (Argentina) v Australia in 1991

Youngest players to appear in a final	
20 years and 43 days	Jonah Lomu (New Zealand) v South Africa in 1995
20 years and 159 days	Francois Steyn (South Africa) v England in 2007
21 years and 54 days	Matt Giteau (Australia) v England in 2003
21 years and 243 days	Jeff Wilson (New Zealand) v South Africa in 1995
21 years and 256 days	Mathew Tait (England) v South Africa in 2007

Oldest players to appear in a final	
36 years and 33 days	Mike Catt (England) v South Africa in 2007
35 years and 265 days	Mark Regan (England) v South Africa in 2007
35 years and 100 days	Jason Leonard (England) v Australia in 2003
35 years and 42 days	Os du Randt (South Africa) v England in 2007

Players capped for more than one country	
Graeme Bachop	New Zealand in 1991 & 1995; Japan in 1999
France Bunce	Western Samoa in 1991; New Zealand in 1995
Adrian Garvey	Zimbabwe in 1991; South Africa in 1999
Jamie Joseph	New Zealand in 1995; Japan in 1999
Dylan Mika	Western Samoa in 1995; New Zealand in 1999
Matt Pini	Australia in 1995; Italy in 1999
Ilie Tabua	Australia in 1995; Fiji in 1999
Va'aiga Tuigamala	New Zealand in 1991; Samoa in 1999

Rugby World Cup 1987

Tournament Statistics

Pool Stage – Final Standings

Pool 1							
Team	**Wins**	**Draws**	**Losses**	**For**	**Against**	**Tries**	**Points**
Australia	3	0	0	108	41	18	6
England	2	0	1	100	32	15	4
USA	1	0	2	39	99	5	2
Japan	0	0	3	48	123	7	0

- Australia and England advanced to the quarter-finals.

Pool 2							
Team	**Wins**	**Draws**	**Losses**	**For**	**Against**	**Tries**	**Points**
Wales	3	0	0	82	31	13	6
Ireland	2	0	1	84	41	11	4
Canada	1	0	2	65	90	8	2
Tonga	0	0	3	29	98	3	0

- Wales and Ireland advanced to the quarter-finals.

Pool 3							
Team	**Wins**	**Draws**	**Losses**	**For**	**Against**	**Tries**	**Points**
New Zealand	3	0	0	190	34	30	6
Fiji	1	0	2	56	101	6	2
Italy	1	0	2	40	110	5	2
Argentina	1	0	2	49	90	4	2

- New Zealand and Fiji advanced to the quarter-finals. Fiji qualified ahead of Italy and Argentina as a result of scoring more tries.

Pool 4							
Team	**Wins**	**Draws**	**Losses**	**For**	**Against**	**Tries**	**Points**
France	2	1	0	145	44	25	5
Scotland	2	1	0	135	69	22	5
Romania	1	0	2	61	130	6	2
Zimbabwe	0	0	3	53	151	5	0

- France and Scotland advanced to the quarter-finals. France advanced as highest qualifier of the two after scoring more tries than Scotland.

Pool Stage – Results Snapshot

Pool 1		
Australia	19–6	England
USA	21–18	Japan
England	60–7	Japan
Australia	47–12	USA
England	34–6	USA
Australia	42–23	Japan

Pool 2		
Canada	37–4	Tonga
Wales	13–6	Ireland
Wales	29–16	Tonga
Ireland	46–19	Canada
Ireland	32–9	Tonga
Wales	40–9	Canada

Pool 3		
New Zealand	70–6	Italy
Fiji	28–9	Argentina
New Zealand	74–13	Fiji
Argentina	25–16	Italy
Italy	18–15	Fiji
New Zealand	46–15	Argentina

Pool 4		
Romania	21–20	Zimbabwe
France	20–20	Scotland
France	55–12	Romania
Scotland	60–21	Zimbabwe
Scotland	55–28	Romania
France	70–12	Zimbabwe

Rugby World Cup 1987: The Finals

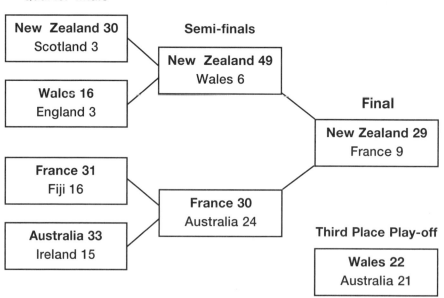

Quarter-finals

New Zealand 30
Scotland 3

Wales 16
England 3

France 31
Fiji 16

Australia 33
Ireland 15

Semi-finals

New Zealand 49
Wales 6

France 30
Australia 24

Final

New Zealand 29
France 9

Third Place Play-off

Wales 22
Australia 21

Detailed Results

Pool 1 — Australia 19–6 England

Date: May 23, 1987.
Venue: Concord Oval, Sydney.
Referee: Keith Lawrence (New Zealand).

Australia	Position	England
Andy McIntyre	*Prop*	Gary Pearce
Tom Lawton	*Hooker*	Brian Moore
Topo Rodriguez	*Prop*	Paul Rendall
Bill Campbell	*Lock*	Wade Dooley
Steve Cutler	*Lock*	Nigel Redman
Troy Coker	*Flanker*	Gary Rees
Simon Poidevin	*Flanker*	Peter Winterbottom
Steve Tuynman	*Number 8*	Dean Richards
Nick Farr-Jones	*Scrum-half*	Richard Harding
Michael Lynagh	*Fly-half*	Peter Williams
David Campese	*Right Wing*	Mike Harrison (c)
Brett Papworth	*Centre*	Jamie Salmon
Andrew Slack (c)	*Centre*	Kevin Simms
Peter Grigg	*Left Wing*	Rory Underwood
Roger Gould	*Fullback*	Marcus Rose
Steve James	*Reserve 1*	Jon Webb

Score: Australia 19 (D. Campese, S. Poidevin tries; M. Lynagh con, 3 pen) defeated England 6 (M. Harrison try; J. Webb con).

Pool 1 — USA 21–18 Japan

Date: May 24, 1987.
Venue: Ballymore, Brisbane.
Referee: Guy Maurette (France).

USA	Position	Japan
Rick Bailey	*Prop*	K. Horaguchi
John Everett	*Hooker*	Tsuyoshi Fujita
Fred Paoli	*Prop*	H. Yasumi
Ed Burlingham (c)	*Lock*	Toshiyuki Hayashi (c)
Kevin Swords	*Lock*	Atsushi Oyagi
Gary Lambert	*Flanker*	Sinali-Tui Latu
Blane Warhurst	*Flanker*	Katsufumi Miyamoto
Brian Vizard	*Number 8*	Michihito Chida
Mike Saunders	*Scrum-half*	H. Ikuta
Joe Clarkson	*Fly-half*	Seiji Hirao
Gary Hein	*Right Wing*	S. Onuki
Roy Helu	*Centre*	Eiji Kutsuki
Kevin Higgins	*Centre*	K. Yoshinaga
Mike Purcell	*Left Wing*	N. Taumoefolau
Ray Nelson	*Fullback*	S. Mukai
N/A	*Reserves*	N/A

Score: USA 21 (G. Lambert, R. Nelson, M. Purcell tries; R. Nelson 3 con, pen) defeated Japan 18 (N. Taumoefolau 2, K. Yoshinaga tries; E. Kutsuki pen, K. Yoshinaga pen).

Pool 1	**England 60–7 Japan**	

Date: May 30, 1987.
Venue: Concord Oval, Sydney.
Referee: René Hourquet (France).

England	Position	Japan
Gareth Chilcott	*Prop*	K. Horaguchi
Brian Moore	*Hooker*	Tsuyoshi Fujita
Paul Rendall	*Prop*	T. Kimura
Steve Bainbridge	*Lock*	S. Kurihara
Nigel Redman	*Lock*	Atsushi Oyagi
Gary Rees	*Flanker*	Toshiyuki Hayashi (c)
Peter Winterbottom	*Flanker*	Katsufumi Miyamoto
Dean Richards	*Number 8*	Michihito Chida
Richard Harding	*Scrum-half*	M. Hagimoto
Peter Williams	*Fly-half*	Seiji Hirao
Mike Harrison (c)	*Right Wing*	S. Onuki
Jamie Salmon	*Centre*	Eiji Kutsuki
Kevin Simms	*Centre*	Katsuhiro Matsuo
Rory Underwood	*Left Wing*	N. Taumoefolau
Jon Webb	*Fullback*	S. Mukai
Rob Andrew	*Reserve 1*	N/A
Fran Clough	*Reserve 2*	N/A

Score: England 60 (M. Harrison 3, R. Underwood 2, N. Redman, G. Rees, D. Richards, J. Salmon, K. Simms tries; J. Webb 7 con, 2 pen) defeated Japan 7 (K. Miyamoto try, K. Matsuo pen).

Pool 1	**Australia 47–12 USA**	

Date: May 31, 1987.
Venue: Ballymore, Brisbane.
Referee: Brian Anderson (New Zealand).

Australia	Position	USA
Cameron Lillicrap	*Prop*	Butch Horwath
Tom Lawton	*Hooker*	Pat Johnson
Andy McIntyre	*Prop*	Fred Paoli (c)
Bill Campbell	*Lock*	Bill Shiflet
Troy Coker	*Lock*	Kevin Swords
Jeff Miller	*Flanker*	Stephen Finkel
Steve Tuynman	*Flanker*	Tony Ridnell
David Codey	*Number 8*	Brian Vizard
Brian Smith	*Scrum-half*	Dave Dickson
Michael Lynagh	*Fly-half*	Dave Horton
David Campese	*Right Wing*	Gary Hein
Brett Papworth	*Centre*	Roy Helu
Andrew Slack (c)	*Centre*	Tom Vinick
Matthew P. Burke	*Left Wing*	Kevin Higgins
Andrew Leeds	*Fullback*	Ray Nelson
N/A	*Reserve 1*	Gary Lambert
N/A	*Reserve 2*	Mike Saunders

Score: Australia 47 (A. Leeds 2, D. Campese, D. Codey, B. Papworth, A. Slack, B. Smith tries; pen try; M. Lynagh 6 con, pen) defeated USA 12 (R. Nelson try, con, pen; D. Horton drop-goal).

Pool 1 — England 34–6 USA

Date: June 3, 1987.
Venue: Concord Oval, Sydney.
Referee: Kerry Fitzgerald (Australia).

England	Position	USA
Gareth Chilcott	Prop	Rick Bailey
Graham Dawe	Hooker	John Everett
Gary Pearce	Prop	Neal Brendel
Steve Bainbridge	Lock	Ed Burlingham (c)
Wade Dooley	Lock	Bob Causey
Gary Rees	Flanker	Stephen Finkel
Peter Winterbottom	Flanker	Gary Lambert
Dean Richards	Number 8	Brian Vizard
Richard Hill	Scrum-half	Mike Saunders
Rob Andrew	Fly-half	Joe Clarkson
Mark Bailey	Right Wing	Gary Hein
Fran Clough	Centre	Kevin Higgins
Jamie Salmon	Centre	Tom Vinick
Mike Harrison (c)	Left Wing	Mike Purcell
Jon Webb	Fullback	Ray Nelson
N/A	Reserves	N/A

Score: England 34 (P. Winterbottom 2, W. Dooley, M. Harrison tries; J. Webb 3 con, 4 pen) defeated USA 6 (M. Purcell try; R. Nelson 1 con).

Pool 1 — Australia 42–23 Japan

Date: June 3, 1987.
Venue: Concord Oval, Sydney.
Referee: Jim Fleming (Scotland).

Australia	Position	Japan
Mark Hartill	Prop	Magaharu Aizawa
Mark McBain	Hooker	Tsuyoshi Fujita
Topo Rodriguez	Prop	T. Kimura
Steve Cutler	Lock	Toshiyuki Hayashi (c)
Ross Reynolds	Lock	Yoshihiko Sakuraba
Simon Poidevin (c)	Flanker	Y. Kawasi
Steve Tuynman	Flanker	Katsufumi Miyamoto
David Codey	Number 8	Sinali-Tui Latu
Brian Smith	Scrum-half	H. Ikuta
Michael Lynagh	Fly-half	Seiji Hirao
Matthew P. Burke	Right Wing	M. Okidoi
Michael Cook	Centre	Eiji Kutsuki
Andrew Slack	Centre	K. Yoshinaga
Peter Grigg	Left Wing	N. Taumoefolau
David Campese	Fullback	S. Mukai
Bill Campbell	Reserve 1	N/A
Brett Papworth	Reserve 2	N/A

Score: Australia 42 (M.P. Burke 2, A. Slack 2, D. Campese, P. Grigg, M. Hartill, S. Tuynman tries; M. Lynagh 5 con) defeated Japan 23 (E. Kutsuki 2, T. Fujita tries; M. Okidoi con, 2 pen, 1 drop-goal).

Pool 2 — Canada 37–4 Tonga

Date: May 24, 1987.
Venue: McLean Park, Napier.
Referee: Clive Norling (Wales).

Canada	Position	Tonga
Eddie Evans	Prop	Soakai Motu'apuaka
Mark Cardinal	Hooker	'Amone Fungavaka
Bill Handson	Prop	Hakatoa Tupou
Hans de Goede (c)	Lock	Kasi Fine
Ron Vanden Brink	Lock	Poluaiele Tuihalamaka
R. Frame	Flanker	Taipaleti Tu'uta Kakato
Roy Radu	Flanker	Fakahau Valu (c)
John Robertson	Number 8	Kinisiliti Fotu
Ian Stuart	Scrum-half	Talai Fifita
Gareth Rees	Fly-half	'Alamoni Liava'a
Pat Palmer	Right Wing	Soane 'Asi
Spence McTavish	Centre	T. Fukakitekei'aho
P. Vaesen	Centre	Samiu Mohi
Tom Woods	Left Wing	Kutusi Fielea
Mark Wyatt	Fullback	Tali Eta'aki
Glen Ennis	Reserve 1	Sione Tahaafe
N/A	Reserve 2	Leaeki Vaipulu

Score: Canada 37 (P. Palmer 2, P. Vaesen 2, R. Frame, I. Stuart tries, pen try; G. Rees con, pen, M. Wyatt 2 con) defeated Tonga 4 (F. Valu try).

Pool 2 — Ireland 6–13 Wales

Date: May 25, 1987.
Venue: Athletic Park, Wellington.
Referee: Kerry Fitzgerald (Australia).

Ireland	Position	Wales
Des Fitzgerald	Prop	Stuart Evans
Terry Kingston	Hooker	Kevin Phillips
Phil Orr	Prop	Jeff Whitefoot
Willie Anderson	Lock	Dick Moriarty (c)
Donal Lenihan (c)	Lock	Bob Norster
Philip Matthews	Flanker	Richie Collins
Derek McGrath	Flanker	Paul Moriarty
Brian Spillane	Number 8	Gareth Roberts
Michael Bradley	Scrum-half	Robert Jones
Paul Dean	Fly-half	Jonathan Davies
Keith Crossan	Right Wing	Ieuan Evans
Michael Kiernan	Centre	John Devereux
Brendan Mullin	Centre	Mark Ring
Trevor Ringland	Left Wing	Adrian Hadley
Hugo MacNeill	Fullback	Paul Thorburn
N/A	Reserves	N/A

Score: Wales 13 (M. Ring try; J. Davies 2 drop-goals, P. Thorburn pen) defeated Ireland 6 (M. Kiernan 2 pen).

Pool 2 — Wales 29–16 Tonga

Date: May 29, 1987.
Venue: Showgrounds Oval, Palmerston North.
Referee: David Bishop (New Zealand).

Wales	Position	Tonga
Anthony Buchanan	Prop	Viliami Lutua
Kevin Phillips	Hooker	'Amone Fungavaka
Stuart Evans	Prop	Hakatoa Tupou
Dick Moriarty (c)	Lock	Kasi Fine
Huw Richards	Lock	Mofuike Tu'ungafasi
Phil Davies	Flanker	Taipaleti Tu'uta Kakato
Paul Moriarty	Flanker	Fakahau Valu (c)
Gareth Roberts	Number 8	Maliu Filise
Robert Jones	Scrum-half	Talai Fifita
Malcolm Dacey	Fly-half	'Aasaeli Amone
Adrian Hadley	Right Wing	Kutusi Fielea
Kevin Hopkins	Centre	T. Fukakitekei'aho
Mark Ring	Centre	Samiu Mohi
Glen Webbe	Left Wing	Manu Vunipola
Paul Thorburn	Fullback	Tali Eta'aki
Steve Blackmore	Reserve 1	'Alamoni Liava'a
Jonathan Davies	Reserve 2	Latu Va'ene

Score: Wales 29 (G. Webbe 3, A. Hadley tries; J. Davies drop-goal, P. Thorburn 2 con, 2 pen) defeated Tonga 16 (K. Fielea, T. Fifita tries; A. Amone pen, A. Liava'a con, pen).

Pool 2 — Canada 19–46 Ireland

Date: May 30, 1987.
Venue: Carisbrook Stadium, Dunedin.
Referee: Fred Howard (England).

Canada	Position	Ireland
Eddie Evans	Prop	Des Fitzgerald
Mark Cardinal	Hooker	John McDonald
Bill Handson	Prop	Phil Orr
Hans de Goede (c)	Lock	Willie Anderson
Ro Hindson	Lock	Donal Lenihan (c)
R. Frame	Flanker	Paul Collins
Roy Radu	Flanker	Derek McGrath
Glen Ennis	Number 8	Brian Spillane
Ian Stuart	Scrum-half	Michael Bradley
Gareth Rees	Fly-half	Tony Ward
Pat Palmer	Right Wing	Keith Crossan
John Lecky	Centre	Michael Kiernan
Spence McTavish	Centre	Brendan Mullin
Tom Woods	Left Wing	Trevor Ringland
Mark Wyatt	Fullback	Hugo MacNeill
N/A	Reserve 1	Terry Kingston

Score: Ireland 46 (K. Crossan 2, M. Bradley, H. MacNeill, T. Ringland, B. Spillane tries; M. Kiernan 5 con, 2 pen, drop-goal, A. Ward drop-goal) defeated Canada 19 (M. Cardinal try; G. Rees 3 pen, drop-goal, M. Wyatt pen).

Pool 2 — Ireland 32–9 Tonga

Date: June 3, 1987.
Venue: Ballymore, Brisbane.
Referee: Guy Maurette (France).

Ireland	Position	Tonga
J. Langbroek	Prop	Viliami Lutua
Terry Kingston	Hooker	'Amone Fungavaka
J.J. McCoy	Prop	Hakatoa Tupou
Willie Anderson	Lock	Kasi Fine
Donal Lenihan (c)	Lock	Mofuike Tu'ungafasi
Neil Francis	Flanker	Taipaleti Tu'uta Kakato
Philip Matthews	Flanker	Fakahau Valu (c)
Derek McGrath	Number 8	Maliu Filise
Michael Bradley	Scrum-half	Talai Fifita
Tony Ward	Fly-half	'Aasaeli Amone
Keith Crossan	Right Wing	Kutusi Fielea
David Irwin	Centre	'Alamoni Liava'a
Brendan Mullin	Centre	Samiu Mohi
Trevor Ringland	Left Wing	T. Fukakitekei'aho
Hugo MacNeill	Fullback	Tali Eta'aki
N/A	Reserves	N/A

Score: Ireland 32 (B. Mullin 3, H. MacNeill 2 tries; A. Ward 3 con, 2 pen) defeated Tonga 9 (A. Amone 3 pen).

Pool 2 — Canada 9–40 Wales

Date: June 3, 1987.
Venue: Homestead Stadium, Invercargill.
Referee: David Bishop (New Zealand).

Canada	Position	Wales
Bill Handson	Prop	Steven Blackmore
Karl Svoboda	Hooker	Allan Phillips
Randy McKellar	Prop	Jeff Whitefoot
Hans de Goede (c)	Lock	Bob Norster
Ro Hindson	Lock	Steve Sutton
Bruce Breen	Flanker	Phil Davies
R. Frame	Flanker	Paul Moriarty
Glen Ennis	Number 8	Gareth Roberts
Ian Stuart	Scrum-half	Ray Giles
Gareth Rees	Fly-half	Jonathan Davies (c)
Steve Gray	Right Wing	Ieuan Evans
John Lecky	Centre	Bleddyn Bowen
Tom Woods	Centre	John Devereux
Pat Palmer	Left Wing	Adrian Hadley
Mark Wyatt	Fullback	Paul Thorburn
Dave Tucker	Reserve 1	Kevin Hopkins
N/A	Reserve 2	Dick Moriarty

Score: Wales 40 (I. Evans 4, B. Bowen, J. Deveruex, A. Hadley, A. Phillips tries; P. Thorburn 4 con) defeated Canada 9 (G. Rees 3 pen).

Pool 3

New Zealand 70–6 Italy

Date: May 22, 1987.
Venue: Eden Park, Auckland.
Referee: Bob Fordham (Australia).

New Zealand	Position	Italy
Richard Loe	*Prop*	Tito Lupini
Sean Fitzpatrick	*Hooker*	Giorgio Morelli
Steven McDowell	*Prop*	Guido Rossi
Murray Pierce	*Lock*	Franco Berni
Gary Whetton	*Lock*	Mauro Gardin
Michael Jones	*Flanker*	Piergianni Farina
Alan Whetton	*Flanker*	Marzio Innocenti (c)
Buck Shelford	*Number 8*	Giuseppe Artuso
David Kirk (c)	*Scrum-half*	Fulvio Lorigiola
Grant Fox	*Fly-half*	Rodolfo Ambrosio
Craig Green	*Right Wing*	Marcello Cuttitta
Joe Stanley	*Centre*	Oscar Collodo
Warwick Taylor	*Centre*	Fabio Gaetaniello
John Kirwan	*Left Wing*	Massimo Mascioletti
John Gallagher	*Fullback*	Serafino Ghizzoni
N/A	*Reserves*	N/A

Score: New Zealand 70 (C. Green 2, D. Kirk 2, J. Kirwan 2, M. Jones, S. McDowell,
J. Stanley, W. Taylor, A. Whetton tries, pen try; G. Fox 8 con,
2 pen) defeated Italy 6 (O. Collodo pen, drop-goal).

Pool 3

Fiji 28–9 Argentina

Date: May 24, 1987.
Venue: Rugby Park, Hamilton.
Referee: Jim Fleming (Scotland).

Fiji	Position	Argentina
Sairusi Naituku	*Prop*	Luis Molina
Salacieli Naivilawasa	*Hooker*	Diego Cash
Rusiate Namoro	*Prop*	Fernando Morel
Koli Rakoroi (c)	*Lock*	Eliseo Branca
Laitia Savai	*Lock*	Gustavo Milano
Tekeli Gale	*Flanker*	Jose Mostany
Manasa Qoro	*Flanker*	Gabriel Travaglini
John Sanday	*Number 8*	Jorge Allen
Pauliasi Tabulutu	*Scrum-half*	Fabio Gomez
E. Rokowailoa	*Fly-half*	Hugo Porta (c)
Kaveniki Nalaga	*Right Wing*	Marcelo Campo
Tomasi Cama	*Centre*	Diego Cuesta Silva
E. Naituku	*Centre*	Fabian Turnes
Serupepeli Tuvula	*Left Wing*	Juan Lanza
Severo Koroduadua	*Fullback*	Sebastien Salvat
Paolo Nawalu	*Reserve 1*	Alejandro Schiavio
Samu Vunivalu	*Reserve 2*	N/A

Score: Fiji 28 (T. Gale, K. Nalaga, K. Rakoroi, I. Savai tries; S. Koroduadua 2 con, 2 pen;
E. Rokowailoa con) defeated Argentina 9 (G. Travaglini try; H. Porta con, pen).

Pool 3 — New Zealand 74–13 Fiji

Date: May 27, 1987.
Venue: Lancaster Park, Christchurch.
Referee: Derek Bevan (Wales).

New Zealand	Position	Fiji
John Drake	Prop	Mosese Taga
Sean Fitzpatrick	Hooker	Epeli Rakai
Steven McDowell	Prop	Peni Volavola
Albert Anderson	Lock	J. Cama
Gary Whetton	Lock	Laitia Savai
Michael Jones	Flanker	Lilvai Kididromo
Alan Whetton	Flanker	Samu Vunivalu
Buck Shelford	Number 8	Koli Rakoroi (c)
David Kirk (c)	Scrum-half	Paolo Nawalu
Grant Fox	Fly-half	E. Rokowailoa
Craig Green	Right Wing	Tomasi Cama
Joe Stanley	Centre	Jone Kubu
Warwick Taylor	Centre	Sirilo Lovokure
John Kirwan	Left Wing	Serupepeli Tuvula
John Gallagher	Fullback	Severo Koroduadua
N/A	Reserves	N/A

Score: New Zealand 74 (J. Gallagher 4, C. Green 4, D. Kirk, J. Kirwan, A. Whetton tries, pen try; G. Fox 10 con, 2 pen) defeated Fiji 13 (J. Cama try; S. Koroduadua 3 pen).

Pool 3 — Argentina 25–16 Italy

Date: May 28, 1987.
Venue: Lancaster Park, Christchurch.
Referee: Roger Quittenton (England).

Argentina	Position	Italy
Serafin Denigra	Prop	Tito Lupini
Diego Cash	Hooker	Antonio Galeazzo
Luis Molina	Prop	Guido Rossi
Eliseo Branca	Lock	Antonio Colella
Sergio Carrosio	Lock	Mauro Gardin
Alejandro Schiavio	Flanker	Marzio Innocenti (c)
Gabriel Travaglini	Flanker	Mario Pavin
Jorge Allen	Number 8	Gianni Zanon
Martin Yanguela	Scrum-half	Fulvio Lorigiola
Hugo Porta (c)	Fly-half	Oscar Collodo
Juan Lanza	Right Wing	Marcello Cuttitta
Diego Cuesta Silva	Centre	Stefano Barba
Rafael Madero	Centre	Fabio Gaetaniello
Pedro Lanza	Left Wing	Massimo Mascioletti
Sebastien Salvat	Fullback	Daniele Tebaldi
Fabio Gomez	Reserve 1	N/A

Score: Argentina 25 (F. Gomez, J. Lanza tries; H. Porta con, 5 pen) defeated Italy 16 (M. Cuttitta, M. Innocenti tries; O. Collodo con, 2 pen).

Pool 3 — Fiji 15–18 Italy

Date: May 31, 1987.
Venue: Carisbrook Stadium, Dunedin.
Referee: Keith Lawrence (New Zealand).

Fiji	Position	Italy
Sairusi Naituku	Prop	Giancarlo Cucchiella
Salacieli Naivilawasa	Hooker	Stefano Romagnoli
Peni Volavola	Prop	Tito Lupini
W. Nadolo	Lock	Antonio Colella
Laitia Savai	Lock	Mauro Gardin
John Sanday	Flanker	Raffaele Dolfato
Manasa Qoro	Flanker	Marzio Innocenti (c)
Koli Rakoroi (c)	Number 8	Piergianni Farina
Paulo Nawalu	Scrum-half	Alessandro Ghini
E. Rokowailoa	Fly-half	Oscar Collodo
Tomasi Cama	Right Wing	Marcello Cuttitta
T. Mitchell	Centre	Stefano Barba
Kaiava Salusalu	Centre	Fabio Gaetaniello
Serupepeli Tuvula	Left Wing	Massimo Mascioletti
Severo Koroduadua	Fullback	Daniele Tebaldi
Jone Kubu	Reserve 1	N/A
E. Naituku	Reserve 2	N/A

Score: Italy 18 (M. Cuttitta, G. Cucchiella, M. Mascioletti tries; O. Collodo pen, drop-goal) defeated Fiji 15 (S. Naivilawasa try; S. Koroduadua con, 2 pen, M. Qoro drop-goal).

Pool 3 — New Zealand 46–15 Argentina

Date: June 1, 1987.
Venue: Athletic Park, Wellington.
Referee: Roger Quittenton (England).

New Zealand	Position	Argentina
John Drake	Prop	Serafin Denigra
Sean Fitzpatrick	Hooker	Diego Cash
Richard Loe	Prop	Luis Molina
Murray Pierce	Lock	Eliseo Branca
Gary Whetton	Lock	Sergio Carrosio
Zinzan Brooke	Flanker	Jorge Allen
Alan Whetton	Flanker	Gabriel Travaglini
Andy Earl	Number 8	Alejandro Schiavio
David Kirk (c)	Scrum-half	Fabio Gomez
Grant Fox	Fly-half	Hugo Porta (c)
John Kirwan	Right Wing	Marcelo Campo
Bernie McCahill	Centre	Rafael Madero
Joe Stanley	Centre	Fabian Turnes
Terry Wright	Left Wing	Juan Lanza
Kieran Crowley	Fullback	Guillermo Angaut
N/A	Reserve 1	Pedro Lanza
N/A	Reserve 2	Jose Mostany

Score: New Zealand 46 (Z. Brooke, K. Crowley, A. Earl, D. Kirk, J. Stanley, A. Whetton tries; G. Fox 2 con, 6 pen) defeated Argentina 15 (J. Lanza try; H. Porta con, 3 pen).

Pool 4 — Romania 21–20 Zimbabwe

Date: May 23, 1987.
Venue: Eden Park, Auckland.
Referee: Stephen Hilditch (Ireland).

Romania	Position	Zimbabwe
Ion Bucan	*Prop*	George Elcom
E. Grigore	*Hooker*	Lance Bray
Gheorghe Leonte	*Prop*	Andy Tucker
Stefan Constantin	*Lock*	Michael Martin
Laurentiu Constantin	*Lock*	Tom Sawyer
Haralambie Dumitras	*Flanker*	Dirk Buitendag
Florica Murariu	*Flanker*	Rod Gray
Christian Raducanu	*Number 8*	Mark Neill
Mircea Paraschiv (c)	*Scrum-half*	Malcolm Jellicoe (c)
Dumitru Alexandru	*Fly-half*	Craig Brown
V. David	*Right Wing*	Eric Barrett
Adrian Lungu	*Centre*	Campbell Graham
Stefan Tofan	*Centre*	Richard Tsimba
Alexandru Marin	*Left Wing*	Peter Kaulback
M. Toader	*Fullback*	Andy Ferreira
L. Hodorca	*Reserve 1*	Errol Bradenkamp
Vasile Ion	*Reserve 2*	Andre Buitendag

Score: Romania 21 (L. Hodorca, M. Paraschiv, M. Toader tries; D. Alexandru 3 pens) defeated Zimbabwe 20 (R. Tsimba 2, M. Neill tries; A. Ferreira 2 pens).

Pool 4 — France 20–20 Scotland

Date: May 23, 1987.
Venue: Lancaster Park, Christchurch.
Referee: Fred Howard (England).

France	Position	Scotland
J.-P. Garuet-Lempirou	*Prop*	Iain Milne
Daniel Dubroca (c)	*Hooker*	Colin Deans (c)
Pascal Ondarts	*Prop*	David Sole
Jean Condom	*Lock*	Alan Tomes
Alain Lorieux	*Lock*	Derek White
Eric Champ	*Flanker*	Finlay Calder
Dominique Erbani	*Flanker*	John Jeffrey
Laurent Rodriguez	*Number 8*	Iain Paxton
Pierre Berbizier	*Scrum-half*	Roy Laidlaw
Franck Mesnel	*Fly-half*	John Rutherford
Patrick Esteve	*Right Wing*	Matthew Duncan
Denis Charvet	*Centre*	Keith Robertson
Philippe Sella	*Centre*	Douglas Wyllie
Patrice Lagisquet	*Left Wing*	Iwan Tukalo
Serge Blanco	*Fullback*	Gavin Hastings
N/A	*Reserve 1*	Alan Tait

Score: France 20 (P. Berbizier, S. Blanco, P. Sella tries; S. Blanco con, 2 pen) drew with Scotland 20 (M. Duncan, D. White tries; G. Hastings 4 pen).

Pool 4 — France 55–12 Romania

Date: May 28, 1987.
Venue: Athletic Park, Wellington.
Referee: Bob Fordham (Australia).

France	Position	Romania
Louis Armary	Prop	F. Opris
Philippe Dintrans (c)	Hooker	V. Ilca
J.-P. Garuet-Lempirou	Prop	V. Pascu
Jean Condom	Lock	Laurentiu Constantin
Francis Haget	Lock	N. Veres
Alain Carminati	Flanker	Gheorghie Dumitru
Eric Champ	Flanker	E. Necula
Dominique Erbani	Number 8	Christian Raducanu
Pierre Berbizier	Scrum-half	Mircea Paraschiv (c)
Guy Laporte	Fly-half	R. Bezuscu
Marc Andrieu	Right Wing	Adrian Lungu
Denis Charvet	Centre	V. David
Philippe Sella	Centre	Stefan Tofan
Patrice Lagisquet	Left Wing	M. Toader
Serge Blanco	Fullback	Vasille Ion
Didier Camberabero	Reserve 1	E. Grigore

Score: France 55 (D. Charvet 2, P. Lagisquet 2, M. Andrieu, D. Camberabero, D. Erbani, G. Laporte, P. Sella tries; G. Laporte 8 con, 1 pen) defeated Romania 12 (R. Bezuscu 4 pen).

Pool 4 — Scotland 60–21 Zimbabwe

Date: May 30, 1987.
Venue: Athletic Park, Wellington.
Referee: David Burnett (Ireland).

Scotland	Position	Zimbabwe
Iain Milne	Prop	Alex Nicholls
Colin Deans (c)	Hooker	Lance Bray
David Sole	Prop	Andy Tucker
Alan Tomes	Lock	Michael Martin
J. Campbell-Lamerton	Lock	Tom Sawyer
Finlay Calder	Flanker	Dirk Buitendag
John Jeffrey	Flanker	Rod Gray
Iain Paxton	Number 8	Mark Neill
Greig Oliver	Scrum-half	Malcolm Jellicoe (c)
Douglas Wyllie	Fly-half	Marthinus Grobler
Matthew Duncan	Right Wing	Eric Barrett
Keith Robertson	Centre	Andre Buitendag
Alan Tait	Centre	Campbell Graham
Iwan Tukalo	Left Wing	Shawn Graham
Gavin Hastings	Fullback	Andy Ferreira
N/A	Reserves	N/A

Score: Scotland 60 (M. Duncan 2, I. Paxton 2, A. Tait 2, I. Tukalo 2, G. Hastings, J. Jeffrey, G. Oliver tries; G. Hastings 8 con) defeated Zimbabwe 21 (D. Buitendag try; M. Grobler con, 5 pen).

Pool 4   Scotland 55–28 Romania

Date: June 2, 1987.
Venue: Carisbrook Stadium, Dunedin.
Referee: Stephen Hilditch (Ireland).

Scotland	Position	Romania
Norrie Rowan	*Prop*	Ion Bucan
Colin Deans (c)	*Hooker*	E. Grigore
David Sole	*Prop*	Gheorghe Leonte
Alan Tomes	*Lock*	Stefan Constantin
Derek White	*Lock*	Laurentiu Constantin
Finlay Calder	*Flanker*	Haralambie Dumitras
John Jeffrey	*Flanker*	Florica Murariu
Iain Paxton	*Number 8*	Christian Raducanu
Roy Laidlaw	*Scrum-half*	Mircea Paraschiv (c)
Douglas Wyllie	*Fly-half*	Dumitru Alexandru
Matthew Duncan	*Right Wing*	A. Pilotschi
Scott Hastings	*Centre*	Adrian Lungu
Alan Tait	*Centre*	Stefan Tofan
Iwan Tukalo	*Left Wing*	M. Toader
Gavin Hastings	*Fullback*	Vasile Ion
J. Campbell-Lamerton	*Reserve 1*	Gheorghie Dumitru
Richard Cramb	*Reserve 2*	N/A

Score: Scotland 55 (J. Jeffrey 3, G. Hastings 2, A. Tait 2, M. Duncan, I. Tukalo tries; G. Hastings 8 con, pen) defeated Romania 28 (F. Murariu 2, M. Toader tries; D. Alexandru con, 3 pen, V. Ion con, pen).

Pool 4   France 70–12 Zimbabwe

Date: June 2, 1987.
Venue: Eden Park, Auckland.
Referee: Derek Bevan (Wales).

France	Position	Zimbabwe
Pascal Ondarts	*Prop*	George Elcome
Daniel Dubroca (c)	*Hooker*	Lance Bray
Jean-Lewis Tolot	*Prop*	Andy Tucker
Jean Condom	*Lock*	Michael Martin
Alain Lorieux	*Lock*	Tom Sawyer
Alain Carminati	*Flanker*	Dirk Buitendag
Jean-Luc Joinel	*Flanker*	Rod Gray
Laurent Rodriguez	*Number 8*	Mark Neill
Rodolphe Modin	*Scrum-half*	Malcolm Jellicoe (c)
Franck Mesnel	*Fly-half*	Marthinus Grobler
Marc Andrieu	*Right Wing*	Eric Barrett
Eric Bonneval	*Centre*	Campbell Graham
Denis Charvet	*Centre*	Richard Tsimba
Patrick Esteve	*Left Wing*	Peter Kaulback
Didier Camberabero	*Fullback*	Andy Ferreira
Guy Laporte	*Reserve 1*	Neville Kloppers
Philippe Sella	*Reserve 2*	Alex Nicholls

Score: France 70 (D. Camberabero 3, R. Modin 3, D. Charvet 2, L. Rodriguez 2, D. Dubroca, P. Esteve, G. Laporte tries; D. Camberabero 9 con) defeated Zimbabwe 12 (P. Kaulback try; M. Grobler con, 2 pen).

Quarter-final — New Zealand 30–3 Scotland

Date: June 6, 1987.
Venue: Lancaster Park, Christchurch.
Referee: David Burnett (Ireland).

New Zealand	Position	Scotland
John Drake	*Prop*	Iain Milne
Sean Fitzpatrick	*Hooker*	Colin Deans (c)
Steven McDowell	*Prop*	David Sole
Murray Pierce	*Lock*	Alan Tomes
Gary Whetton	*Lock*	Derek White
Michael Jones	*Flanker*	Finlay Calder
Alan Whetton	*Flanker*	Derek Turnbull
Buck Shelford	*Number 8*	Iain Paxton
David Kirk (c)	*Scrum-half*	Roy Laidlaw
Grant Fox	*Fly-half*	Douglas Wyllie
Craig Green	*Right Wing*	Matthew Duncan
Joe Stanley	*Centre*	Keith Robertson
Warwick Taylor	*Centre*	Alan Tait
John Kirwan	*Left Wing*	Iwan Tukalo
John Gallagher	*Fullback*	Gavin Hastings
Bernie McCahill	*Reserve 1*	N/A

Score: New Zealand 30 (J. Gallagher, A Whetton tries; G. Fox 2 con, 6 pen) defeated Scotland 3 (G. Hastings pen).

Quarter-final — France 31–16 Fiji

Date: June 7, 1987.
Venue: Eden Park, Auckland.
Referee: Clive Norling (Wales).

France	Position	Fiji
J.-P. Garuet-Lempirou	*Prop*	Sairusi Naituku
Daniel Dubroca (c)	*Hooker*	Epeli Rakai
Pascal Ondarts	*Prop*	Rusiati Namoro
Francis Haget	*Lock*	Koli Rakoroi (c)
Alain Lorieux	*Lock*	Laitia Savai
Eric Champ	*Flanker*	Salacieli Naivilawasa
Dominique Erbani	*Flanker*	Manasa Qoro
Laurent Rodriguez	*Number 8*	Lilvai Kididromo
Pierre Berbizier	*Scrum-half*	Paolo Nawalu
Guy Laporte	*Fly-half*	Severo Koroduadua
Denis Charvet	*Right Wing*	J. Damu
Franck Mesnel	*Centre*	Tomasi Cama
Philippe Sella	*Centre*	Kaiava Salusalu
Patrice Lagisquet	*Left Wing*	T. Mitchell
Serge Blanco	*Fullback*	Jone Kubu
Didier Camberabero	*Reserve 1*	W. Nadolo
N/A	*Reserve 2*	Samu Vunivalu

Score: France 31 (L. Rodriguez 2, P. Lagisquet, A. Lorieux tries; G. Laporte 3 con, 2 pen, drop-goal) defeated Fiji 16 (J. Damu, M. Qoro tries; S. Koroduadua con, 2 pen).

Quarter-final Australia 33–15 Ireland

Date: June 7, 1987.
Venue: Concord Oval, Sydney.
Referee: Brian Anderson (New Zealand).

Australia	Position	Ireland
Cameron Lillicrap	*Prop*	Des Fitzgerald
Tom Lawton	*Hooker*	Terry Kingston
Andy McIntyre	*Prop*	Phil Orr
Bill Campbell	*Lock*	Willie Anderson
Steve Cutler	*Lock*	Donal Lenihan (c)
Jeff Miller	*Flanker*	Philip Matthews
Simon Poidevin	*Flanker*	Derek McGrath
Steve Tuynman	*Number 8*	Neil Francis
Nick Farr-Jones	*Scrum-half*	Michael Bradley
Michael Lynagh	*Fly-half*	Paul Dean
Matthew P. Burke	*Right Wing*	Keith Crossan
Brett Papworth	*Centre*	Michael Kiernan
Andrew Slack (c)	*Centre*	Brendan Mullin
Peter Grigg	*Left Wing*	Trevor Ringland
David Campese	*Fullback*	Hugo MacNeill
Brian Smith	*Reserve 1*	David Irwin
N/A	*Reserve 2*	Brian Spillane

Score: Australia 33 (M.P. Burke 2, A, McIntyre, B. Smith tries; M. Lynagh 4 con, 3 pen) defeated Ireland 15 (M. Kiernan, H. MacNeill tries; M. Kiernan 2 con, pen).

Quarter-final England 3–16 Wales

Date: June 8, 1987.
Venue: Ballymore, Brisbane.
Referee: René Hourquet (France).

England	Position	Wales
Gary Pearce	*Prop*	Anthony Buchanan
Brian Moore	*Hooker*	Allan Phillips
Paul Rendall	*Prop*	Dai Young
Wade Dooley	*Lock*	Dick Moriarty (c)
Nigel Redman	*Lock*	Bob Norster
Gary Rees	*Flanker*	Richie Collins
Peter Winterbottom	*Flanker*	Gareth Roberts
Dean Richards	*Number 8*	Paul Moriarty
Richard Harding	*Scrum-half*	Robert Jones
Peter Williams	*Fly-half*	Jonathan Davies
Mike Harrison (c)	*Right Wing*	Ieuan Evans
Jamie Salmon	*Centre*	Bleddyn Bowen
Kevin Simms	*Centre*	John Devereaux
Rory Underwood	*Left Wing*	Adrian Hadley
Jon Webb	*Fullback*	Paul Thorburn
Gareth Chilcott	*Reserve 1*	Huw Richards

Score: Wales 16 (J. Devereaux, R. Jones, G. Roberts tries; P Thorburn 2 con) defeated England 3 (J. Webb pen).

Semi-final Australia 24–30 France

Date: June 13, 1987.
Venue: Concord Oval, Sydney.
Referee: Brian Anderson (New Zealand).

Australia	Position	France
Cameron Lillicrap	*Prop*	J.-P. Garuet-Lempirou
Tom Lawton	*Hooker*	Daniel Dubroca (c)
Andy McIntyre	*Prop*	Pascal Ondarts
Bill Campbell	*Lock*	Jean Condom
Steve Cutler	*Lock*	Alain Lorieux
Jeff Miller	*Flanker*	Eric Champ
Simon Poidevin	*Flanker*	Dominique Erbani
Troy Coker	*Number 8*	Laurent Rodriguez
Nick Farr-Jones	*Scrum-half*	Pierre Berbizier
Michael Lynagh	*Fly-half*	Franck Mesnel
Matthew P. Burke	*Right Wing*	Didier Camberabero
Brett Papworth	*Centre*	Denis Charvet
Andrew Slack (c)	*Centre*	Philippe Sella
Peter Grigg	*Left Wing*	Patrice Lagisquet
David Campese	*Fullback*	Serge Blanco
David Codey	*Reserve 1*	N/A
Anthony Herbert	*Reserve 2*	N/A

Score: France 30 (S. Blanco, P. Lagisquet, A. Lorieux, P. Sella tries; D. Camberabero 4 con, 2 pen) defeated Australia 24 (D. Campese, D. Codey tries; M. Lynagh 2 con, 3 pen, drop-goal).

Semi-final Wales 6–49 New Zealand

Date: June 14, 1987.
Venue: Ballymore, Brisbane.
Referee: Kerry Fitzgerald (Australia).

Wales	Position	New Zealand
Anthony Buchanan	*Prop*	John Drake
Kevin Phillips	*Hooker*	Sean Fitzpatrick
Dai Young	*Prop*	Steven McDowell
Dick Moriarty (c)	*Lock*	Murray Pierce
Huw Richards	*Lock*	Gary Whetton
Richie Collins	*Flanker*	Mark Brooke-Cowden
Phil Davies	*Flanker*	Alan Whetton
Paul Moriarty	*Number 8*	Buck Shelford
Robert Jones	*Scrum-half*	David Kirk (c)
Jonathan Davies	*Fly-half*	Grant Fox
Ieuan Evans	*Right Wing*	Craig Green
Bleddyn Bowen	*Centre*	Joe Stanley
John Devereaux	*Centre*	Warwick Taylor
Adrian Hadley	*Left Wing*	John Kirwan
Paul Thorburn	*Fullback*	John Gallagher
Steve Sutton	*Reserve 1*	Bernie McCahill

Score: New Zealand 49 (J. Kirwan 2, B. Shelford 2, M. Brooke-Cowden, J. Drake, J. Stanley, A. Whetton tries; G. Fox 7 con, pen) defeated Wales 6 (J. Devereux try; P. Thorburn con).

3rd Place Play-off   Australia 21–22 Wales

Date: June 18, 1987.
Venue: Rotorua International Stadium.
Referee: Fred Howard (England).

Australia	Position	Wales
Cameron Lillicrap	*Prop*	Steven Blackmore
Tom Lawton	*Hooker*	Allan Phillips
Andy McIntyre	*Prop*	Anthony Buchanan
Troy Coker	*Lock*	Dick Moriarty (c)
Steve Cutler	*Lock*	Steve Sutton
David Codey	*Flanker*	Gareth Roberts
Simon Poidevin	*Flanker*	Richard Webster
Steve Tuynman	*Number 8*	Paul Moriarty
Brian Smith	*Scrum-half*	Robert Jones
Michael Lynagh	*Fly-half*	Jonathan Davies
David Campese	*Right Wing*	Ieuan Evans
Matthew P. Burke	*Centre*	John Devereaux
Andrew Slack (c)	*Centre*	Mark Ring
Peter Grigg	*Left Wing*	Adrian Hadley
Andrew Leeds	*Fullback*	Paul Thorburn
Nick Farr-Jones	*Reserve 1*	N/A
Topo Rodriguez	*Reserve 2*	N/A

Score: Wales 22 (A. Hadley, P. Moriarty, G. Roberts tries; P. Thorburn 2 con, 2 pen) defeated Australia 21 (M.P. Burke, P. Grigg tries; M. Lynagh 2 con, 2 pen, drop-goal).

The Final   New Zealand 29–9 France

Date: June 20, 1987.
Venue: Eden Park, Auckland.
Referee: Kerry Fitzgerald (Australia).

New Zealand	Position	France
John Drake	*Prop*	J.-P. Garuet-Lempirou
Sean Fitzpatrick	*Hooker*	Daniel Dubroca (c)
Steven McDowell	*Prop*	Pascal Ondarts
Murray Pierce	*Lock*	Jean Condom
Gary Whetton	*Lock*	Alain Lorieux
Michael Jones	*Flanker*	Eric Champ
Alan Whetton	*Flanker*	Dominique Erbani
Buck Shelford	*Number 8*	Laurent Rodriguez
David Kirk (c)	*Scrum-half*	Pierre Berbizier
Grant Fox	*Fly-half*	Franck Mesnel
Craig Green	*Right Wing*	Didier Camberabero
Joe Stanley	*Centre*	Denis Charvet
Warwick Taylor	*Centre*	Philippe Sella
John Kirwan	*Left Wing*	Patrice Lagisquet
John Gallagher	*Fullback*	Serge Blanco
N/A	*Reserves*	N/A

Score: New Zealand 29 (M. Jones, D. Kirk, J. Kirwan tries; G. Fox con, 4 pen, drop-goal) defeated France 9 (P. Berbizier try; D. Camberabero con, pen).

Rugby World Cup 1991

Tournament Statistics

Pool Stage – Final Standings

Pool A							
Team	Wins	Draws	Losses	For	Against	Tries	Points
New Zealand	3	0	0	95	39	13	9
England	2	0	1	85	33	9	7
Italy	1	0	2	57	76	7	5
USA	0	0	3	24	113	2	3

- New Zealand and England advanced to the quarter-finals.

Pool B							
Team	Wins	Draws	Losses	For	Against	Tries	Points
Scotland	3	0	0	122	36	17	9
Ireland	2	0	1	102	51	12	7
Japan	1	0	2	77	87	13	5
Zimbabwe	0	0	3	31	158	6	3

- Scotland and Ireland advanced to the quarter-finals.

Pool C							
Team	Wins	Draws	Losses	For	Against	Tries	Points
Australia	3	0	0	79	25	11	9
W. Samoa	2	0	1	54	34	8	7
Wales	1	0	2	32	61	3	5
Argentina	0	0	3	38	83	4	3

- Australia and Western Samoa advanced to the quarter-finals.

Pool D							
Team	Wins	Draws	Losses	For	Against	Tries	Points
France	3	0	0	82	25	12	9
Canada	2	0	1	45	33	4	7
Romania	1	0	2	31	64	5	5
Fiji	0	0	3	27	63	1	3

- France and Canada advanced to the quarter-finals.

Pool Stage – Results Snapshot

Pool A		
New Zealand	18–12	England
Italy	30–9	USA
New Zealand	46–6	USA
England	36–6	Italy
England	37–9	USA
New Zealand	31–21	Italy

Pool B		
Scotland	47–9	Japan
Ireland	55–11	Zimbabwe
Ireland	32–16	Japan
Scotland	51–12	Zimbabwe
Scotland	24–15	Ireland
Japan	52–8	Zimbabwe

Pool C		
Australia	32–19	Argentina
W. Samoa	16–13	Wales
Australia	9–3	W. Samoa
Wales	16–7	Argentina
Australia	38–3	Wales
W. Samoa	35–12	Argentina

Pool D		
France	30–3	Romania
Canada	13–3	Fiji
France	33–9	Fiji
Canada	19–11	Romania
Romania	17–15	Fiji
France	19–13	Canada

Rugby World Cup 1991: The Finals

Quarter-finals

Scotland 28
Western Samoa 6

Semi-finals

England 19
France 10

England 9
Scotland 6

Final

Australia 12
England 6

Australia 19
Ireland 18

Australia 16
New Zealand 6

New Zealand 29
Canada 13

Third Place Play-off

New Zealand 13
Scotland 6

Detailed Results

Pool A   England 12–18 New Zealand

Date: October 3, 1991.
Venue: Twickenham, London.
Referee: Jim Fleming (Scotland).

England	Position	New Zealand
Jason Leonard	*Prop*	Richard Loe
Brian Moore	*Hooker*	Sean Fitzpatrick
Jeff Probyn	*Prop*	Steve McDowell
Paul Ackford	*Lock*	Ian Jones
Wade Dooley	*Lock*	Gary Whetton (c)
Mike Teague	*Flanker*	Michael Jones
Peter Winterbottom	*Flanker*	Alan Whetton
Dean Richards	*Number 8*	Zinzan Brooke
Richard Hill	*Scrum-half*	Graeme Bachop
Rob Andrew	*Fly-half*	Grant Fox
Chris Oti	*Right Wing*	John Kirwan
Will Carling (c)	*Centre*	Craig Innes
Jeremy Guscott	*Centre*	Bernie McCahill
Rory Underwood	*Left Wing*	John Timu
Jon Webb	*Fullback*	Terry Wright
N/A	*Reserve 1*	Andy Earl

Score: New Zealand 18 (M. Jones try; G. Fox con, 4 pen) defeated England 12 (J. Webb 3 pen, R. Andrew drop-goal).

Pool A   Italy 30–9 USA

Date: October 5, 1991.
Venue: Cross Green, Otley.
Referee: Owen Doyle (Ireland).

Italy	Position	USA
Massimo Cuttitta	*Prop*	Chris Lippert
Giancarlo Pivetta	*Hooker*	Tony Flay
Franco Properzi-Curti	*Prop*	Fred Paoli
Giambattista Croci	*Lock*	*Bill Leversee*
Roberto Favaro	*Lock*	Kevin Swords
Carlo Checchinato	*Flanker*	Rob Farley
Roberto Saetti	*Flanker*	Brian Vizard (c)
Gianni Zanon (c)	*Number 8*	Tony Ridnell
Ivan Francescato	*Scrum-half*	Barry Daily
Diego Dominguez	*Fly-half*	Mike de Jong
Marcello Cuttitta	*Right Wing*	Gary Hein
Stefano Barba	*Centre*	Kevin Higgins
Fabio Gaetaniello	*Centre*	Mark Williams
Paolo Vaccari	*Left Wing*	Eric Whitaker
Luigi Troiani	*Fullback*	Ray Nelson
N/A	*Reserve 1*	Shawn Lipman

Score: Italy 30 (S. Barba, I. Francescato, F. Gaetaniello, P. Vaccari tries; D. Dominguez 4 con, 2 pen) defeated USA 9 (K. Swords try; M. Williams con, pen).

Pool A — New Zealand 46–6 USA

Date: October 8, 1991.
Venue: Kingsholm, Gloucester.
Referee: Efrahim Sklar (Argentina).

New Zealand	Position	USA
Steven McDowell	*Prop*	Chris Lippert
Sean Fitzpatrick	*Hooker*	Pat Johnson
Graham Purvis	*Prop*	Norm Mottram
Ian Jones	*Lock*	Kevin Swords (c)
Gary Whetton (c)	*Lock*	Chuck Tunnacliffe
Michael Jones	*Flanker*	Shawn Lipman
Alan Whetton	*Flanker*	Mark Sawicki
Andy Earl	*Number 8*	Tony Ridnell
Graeme Bachop	*Scrum-half*	Mark Pidcock
Jon Preston	*Fly-half*	Chris O'Brien
John Timu	*Right Wing*	Gary Hein
Craig Innes	*Centre*	Joe Burke
Bernie McCahill	*Centre*	Mark Williams
Va'aiga Tuigamala	*Left Wing*	Eric Whitaker
Terry Wright	*Fullback*	Paul Sheehy
N/A	*Reserve 1*	Lance Manga

Score: New Zealand 46 (T. Wright 3, A. Earl, C. Innes, G. Purvis, J. Timu, V. Tuigamala tries; J. Preston 4 con, 2 pen) defeated USA 6 (M. Williams 2 pen).

Pool A — England 36–6 Italy

Date: October 8, 1991.
Venue: Twickenham, London.
Referee: Brian Anderson (New Zealand).

England	Position	Italy
Jason Leonard	*Prop*	Massimo Cuttitta
Brian Moore	*Hooker*	Giancarlo Pivetta
Jeff Probyn	*Prop*	Franco Properzi-Curti
Paul Ackford	*Lock*	Giambattista Croci
Nigel Redman	*Lock*	Roberto Favaro
Mike Teague	*Flanker*	Massimo Giovanelli
Peter Winterbottom	*Flanker*	Roberto Saetti
Dean Richards	*Number 8*	Gianni Zanon (c)
Richard Hill	*Scrum-half*	Ivan Francescato
Rob Andrew	*Fly-half*	Diego Dominguez
Chris Oti	*Right Wing*	Marcello Cuttitta
Will Carling (c)	*Centre*	Stefano Barba
Jeremy Guscott	Centre	Fabio Gaetaniello
Rory Underwood	Left Wing	Paolo Vaccari
Jon Webb	*Fullback*	Luigi Troiani
Paul Rendall	*Reserve 1*	Massimo Bonomi

Score: England 36 (J. Guscott 2, R. Underwood, J. Webb tries; J. Webb 4 con, 4 pen) defeated Italy 6 (M. Cuttitta try, D. Dominguez con).

Pool A

England 37–9 USA

Date: October 11, 1991.
Venue: Twickenham, London.
Referee: Les Peard (Wales).

England	Position	USA
Jason Leonard	*Prop*	Lance Manga
John Olver	*Hooker*	Tony Flay
Gary Pearce	*Prop*	Norm Mottram
Wade Dooley	*Lock*	Kevin Swords (c)
Nigel Redman	*Lock*	Chuck Tunnacliffe
Gary Rees	*Flanker*	Rob Farley
Mickey Skinner	*Flanker*	Shawn Lipman
Dean Richards	*Number 8*	Tony Ridnall
Richard Hill	*Scrum-half*	Mark Pidcock
Rob Andrew	*Fly-half*	Chris O'Brien
Nigel Heslop	*Right Wing*	Gary Hein
Will Carling (c)	*Centre*	Kevin Higgins
Simon Halliday	*Centre*	Mark Williams
Rory Underwood	*Left Wing*	Paul Sheehy
Simon Hodgkinson	*Fullback*	Ray Nelson
N/A	*Reserve 1*	Mike de Jong
N/A	*Reserve 2*	Jay Wilkerson

Score: England 37 (R. Underwood 2, W. Carling, N. Heslop, M. Skinner tries;
S. Hodgkinson 4 con, 3 pen) defeated USA 9 (R. Nelson try, M. Williams con, pen).

Pool A

Italy 21–31 New Zealand

Date: October 13, 1991.
Venue: Welford Road, Leicester.
Referee: Kerry Fitzgerald (Australia).

Italy	Position	New Zealand
Massimo Cuttitta	*Prop*	Richard Loe
Giancarlo Pivetta (c)	*Hooker*	Sean Fitzpatrick
Franco Properzi-Curti	*Prop*	Steve McDowell
Giambattista Croci	*Lock*	Ian Jones
Roberto Favaro	*Lock*	Gary Whetton (c)
Alessandro Bottacchiari	*Flanker*	Mark Carter
Massimo Giovanelli	*Flanker*	Alan Whetton
Carlo Checchinato	*Number 8*	Zinzan Brooke
Ivan Francescato	*Scrum-half*	Jason Hewett
Massimo Bonomi	*Fly-half*	Grant Fox
Marcello Cuttitta	*Right Wing*	John Kirwan
Diego Dominguez	*Centre*	Craig Innes
Fabio Gaetaniello	*Centre*	Walter Little
Edgardo Venturi	*Left Wing*	Va'aiga Tuigamala
Paolo Vaccari	*Fullback*	Terry Wright
Giovanni Grespan	*Reserve 1*	Shayne Philpott

Score: New Zealand 31 (Z. Brooke, J. Hewett, C. Innes, V. Tuigamala tries; G. Fox 3 con, 3
pen) defeated Italy 21 (M. Bonomi, M. Cuttitta tries; D. Dominguez 2 con, 3 pen).

Pool B	**Scotland 47–9 Japan**	

Date: October 5, 1991.
Venue: Murrayfield, Edinburgh.
Referee: Ed Morrison (England).

Scotland	Position	Japan
Paul Burnell	*Prop*	Osamu Ota
John Allan	*Hooker*	Masahiro Kunda
David Sole (c)	*Prop*	Masanori Takura
Chris Gray	*Lock*	Toshiyuki Hayashi
Doddie Weir	*Lock*	Ekeroma Tifaga
Finlay Calder	*Flanker*	Hiroyuki Kajihara
John Jeffrey	*Flanker*	Shuji Nakashima
Derek White	*Number 8*	Sinali-Tui Latu
Gary Armstrong	*Scrum-half*	Wataru Murata
Craig Chalmers	*Fly-half*	Katsuhiro Matsuo
Tony Stanger	*Right Wing*	Terunori Masuho
Scott Hastings	*Centre*	Seiji Hirao (c)
Sean Lineen	*Centre*	Eiji Kutsuki
Iwan Tukalo	*Left Wing*	Yoshihito Yoshida
Gavin Hastings	*Fullback*	Takahiro Hosokawa
David Milne	*Reserve 1*	N/A
Douglas Wyllie	*Reserve 2*	N/A

Score: Scotland 47 (C. Chalmers, G. Hastings, S. Hastings, T. Stanger, I. Tukalo, D. White tries, penalty try; G. Hastings 5 con, 2 pen, C. Chalmers 1 pen) defeated Japan 9 (T. Hosokawa try, con, drop-goal).

Pool B	**Ireland 55–11 Zimbabwe**	

Date: October 6, 1991.
Venue: Lansdowne Road, Dublin.
Referee: Keith Lawrence (New Zealand).

Ireland	Position	Zimbabwe
Des Fitzgerald	*Prop*	Adrian Garvey
Steve Smith	*Hooker*	Brian Beattie
Nick Popplewell	*Prop*	Robin Hunter
Neil Francis	*Lock*	Rob Demblon
Donal Lenihan	*Lock*	Michael Martin
Gordon Hamilton	*Flanker*	Chris Botha
Philip Matthews (c)	*Flanker*	Brenden Dawson
Brian Robinson	*Number 8*	Brenton Catterall
Rob Saunders	*Scrum-half*	Andy Ferreira
Ralph Keyes	*Fly-half*	Ralph Kuhn
Keith Crossan	*Right Wing*	Craig Brown
David Curtis	*Centre*	Mark Letcher
Vince Cunningham	*Centre*	Richard Tsimba
Simon Geoghegan	*Left Wing*	David Walters
Jim Staples	*Fullback*	Brian Currin (c)
N/A	*Reserve 1*	William Schultz

Score: Ireland 55 (B. Robinson 4, N. Popplewell 2, D. Curtis, S. Geoghegan tries; R. Keyes 4 con, 5 pen) defeated Zimbabwe 11 (B. Dawson, W. Schultz tries; A. Ferreira 1 pen).

Pool B — Ireland 32–16 Japan

Date: October 9, 1991.
Venue: Lansdowne Road, Dublin.
Referee: L. Colati (Fiji).

Ireland	Position	Japan
John Fitzgerald	Prop	Osamu Ota
Terry Kingston (c)	Hooker	Tsuyoshi Fujita
Gary Halpin	Prop	Masanori Takura
Neil Francis	Lock	Toshiyuki Hayashi
Mick Galwey	Lock	Atsushi Oyagi
Gordon Hamilton	Flanker	Hiroyuki Kajihara
Pat O'Hara	Flanker	Ekeroma Tifaga
Noel Mannion	Number 8	Sinali-Tui Latu
Rob Saunders	Scrum-half	Masami Horikoshi
Ralph Keyes	Fly-half	Katsuhiro Matsuo
Jack Clarke	Right Wing	Terunori Masuho
David Curtis	Centre	Seiji Hirao (c)
Brendan Mullin	Centre	Eiji Kutsuki
Keith Crossan	Left Wing	Yoshihito Yoshida
Jim Staples	Fullback	Takahiro Hosokawa
Vince Cunningham	Reserve 1	Masahiro Kunda
N/A	Reserve 2	Katsufumi Miyamoto

Score: Ireland 32 (N. Mannion 2, P. O'Hara, J. Staples tries; R. Keyes 2 con, 4 pen) defeated Japan 16 (T. Hayashi, H. Kajihara, Y. Yoshida tries; T. Hosokawa 2 con).

Pool B — Scotland 51–12 Zimbabwe

Date: October 9, 1991.
Venue: Murrayfield, Edinburgh.
Referee: Don Reordan (United States).

Scotland	Position	Zimbabwe
Paul Burnell	Prop	Adrian Garvey
Kenny Milne	Hooker	Brian Beattie
Alan Watt	Prop	Alex Nicholls
Damian Cronin	Lock	Michael Martin
Doddie Weir	Lock	Honeywell Nguruve
Graham Marshall	Flanker	Brenden Dawson
Derek Turnbull	Flanker	Darren Muirhead
Derek White	Number 8	Brenton Catterall
Greig Oliver	Scrum-half	Ewan MacMillan
Douglas Wyllie	Fly-half	Craig Brown
Tony Stanger	Right Wing	William Schultz
Scott Hastings	Centre	Mark Letcher
Sean Lineen	Centre	Richard Tsimba
Iwan Tukalo	Left Wing	David Walters
Peter Dods (c)	Fullback	Brian Currin (c)
Craig Chalmers	Reserve 1	Elimon Chimbima
N/A	Reserve 2	Robin Hunter
N/A	Reserve 3	Chris Roberts

Score: Scotland 51 (I. Tukalo 3, S. Hastings, T. Stanger, D. Turnbull, G. Weir, D. White tries; P. Dods 5 con, 2 pen, D. Wyllie drop-goal) defeated Zimbabwe 12 (A. Garvey 2 tries; B. Currin 2 con).

Pool B — Scotland 24–15 Ireland

Date: October 12, 1991.
Venue: Murrayfield, Edinburgh.
Referee: Fred Howard (England).

Scotland	Position	Ireland
Paul Burnell	*Prop*	Des Fitzgerald
John Allan	*Hooker*	Steve Smith
David Sole (c)	*Prop*	Nick Popplewell
Chris Gray	*Lock*	Neil Francis
Doddie Weir	*Lock*	Donal Lenihan
Finlay Calder	*Flanker*	Gordan Hamilton
John Jeffrey	*Flanker*	Philip Matthews (c)
Derek White	*Number 8*	Brian Robinson
Gary Armstrong	*Scrum-half*	Rob Saunders
Craig Chalmers	*Fly-half*	Ralph Keyes
Tony Stanger	*Right Wing*	Keith Crossan
Scott Hastings	*Centre*	David Curtis
Sean Lineen	*Centre*	Brendan Mullin
Iwan Tukalo	*Left Wing*	Simon Geoghegan
Gavin Hastings	*Fullback*	Jim Staples
Graham Shiel	*Reserve 1*	N/A

Score: Scotland 24 (G. Armstrong, G. Shiel tries; G. Hastings 2 con, 3 pen, C. Chalmers 1 drop-goal) defeated Ireland 15 (R. Keyes 4 pen, drop-goal).

Pool B — Japan 52–8 Zimbabwe

Date: October 14, 1991.
Venue: Ravenhill Park, Belfast.
Referee: René Hourquet (France).

Japan	Position	Zimbabwe
Osamu Ota	*Prop*	Adrian Garvey
Masahiro Kunda	*Hooker*	Brian Beattie
Masanori Takura	*Prop*	Alex Nicholls
Toshiyuki Hayashi	*Lock*	Chris Botha
Atsushi Oyagi	*Lock*	Michael Martin
Hiroyuki Kajihara	*Flanker*	Brenden Dawson
Ekeroma Tifaga	*Flanker*	Honeywell Nguruve
Sinali-Tui Latu	*Number 8*	Brenton Catterall
Masami Horikoshi	*Scrum-half*	Ewan MacMillan
Katsuhiro Matsuo	*Fly-half*	Craig Brown
Terunori Masuho	*Right Wing*	William Schultz
Seiji Hirao (c)	*Centre*	Mark Letcher
Eiji Kutsuki	*Centre*	Richard Tsimba
Yoshihito Yoshida	*Left Wing*	David Walters
Takahiro Hosokawa	*Fullback*	Brian Currin (c)
N/A	*Reserve 1*	Gary Snyder

Score: Japan 52 (E. Kutsuki 2, T. Masuho 2, Y. Yoshida 2, M. Horikoshi, K. Matsuo, E. Tifaga tries; T. Hosokawa 5 con, 2 pen) defeated Zimbabwe 8 (H. Nguruve, R. Tsimba tries).

Pool C — Argentina 19–32 Australia

Date: October 4, 1991.
Venue: Stradey Park, Llanelli.
Referee: David Bishop (New Zealand).

Argentina	Position	Australia
Diego Cash	*Prop*	Tony Daly
Ricardo leFort	*Hooker*	Phil Kearns
Federico Mendez	*Prop*	Ewen McKenzie
German Llanes	*Lock*	Troy Coker
Pedro Sporleder	*Lock*	Rod McCall
Mario Carreras	*Flanker*	Willie Ofahengaue
Pablo Garreton (c)	*Flanker*	Simon Poidevin
Jose Santamarina	*Number 8*	John Eales
Gonzalo Camardon	*Scrum-half*	Nick Farr-Jones (c)
Lisandro Arbizu	*Fly-half*	Michael Lynagh
Diego Cuesta Silva	*Right Wing*	David Campese
Hernan Garcia Simon	*Centre*	Tim Horan
Eduardo Laborde	*Centre*	Jason Little
Martin Teran Nougues	*Left Wing*	Rob Egerton
Guillermo Del Castillo	*Fullback*	Marty Roebuck
Mariano Bosch	*Reserve 1*	David Nucifora

Score: Australia 32 (D. Campese 2, T. Horan 2, P. Kearns tries; M. Lynagh 3 con, 2 pen) defeated Argentina 19 (M. Teran Nougues 2 tries; G. Del Castillo 1 con, 1 pen; L. Arbizu 2 drop-goals).

Pool C — Wales 13–16 Western Samoa

Date: October 6, 1991.
Venue: Cardiff Arms Park, Cardiff.
Referee: Patrick Robin (France).

Wales	Position	Western Samoa
Laurence Delaney	*Prop*	Vili Alalatoa
Ken Waters	*Hooker*	Stan To'omalatai
Mike Griffiths	*Prop*	Peter Fatialofa (c)
Phil May	*Lock*	Mark Birtwistle
Kevin Moseley	*Lock*	Mat Keenan
Richie Collins	*Flanker*	Apollo Perelini
Emyr Lewis	*Flanker*	Sila Vaifale
Phil Davies	*Number 8*	Pat Lam
Robert Jones	*Scrurn-half*	Mathew Vaea
Mark Ring	*Fly-half*	Stephen Bachop
Ieuan Evans (c)	*Right Wing*	Brian Lima
Scott Gibbs	*Centre*	Frank Bunce
Mike Hall	*Centre*	To'o Vaega
Arthur Jones	*Left Wing*	Timo Tagaloa
Tony Clement	*Fullback*	Andrew Aiolupo
Garin Jenkins	*Reserve 1*	N/A
Martyn Morris	*Reserve 2*	N/A
Mike Rayer	*Reserve 3*	N/A

Score: Western Samoa 16 (T. Vaega, S. Vaifale tries; M. Vaea con, 2 pen) defeated Wales 13 (I. Evans, A. Jones tries; M. Ring con, 2 pen).

Pool C — Wales 16–7 Argentina

Date: October 9, 1991.
Venue: Cardiff Arms Park, Cardiff.
Referee: René Hourquet (France).

Wales	Position	Argentina
Laurence Delaney	*Prop*	Federico Mendez
Garin Jenkins	*Hooker*	Ricardo leFort
Mike Griffiths	*Prop*	Luis Molina
Paul Arnold	*Lock*	German Llanes
Kevin Moseley	*Lock*	Pedro Sporleder
Emyr Lewis	*Flanker*	Mario Carreras
Richard Webster	*Flanker*	Pablo Garreton (c)
Phil Davies	*Number 8*	Jose Santamarina
Robert Jones	*Scrum-half*	Gonzalo Camardon
Mark Ring	*Fly-half*	Lisandro Arbizu
Ieuan Evans (c)	*Right Wing*	Diego Cuesta Silva
Scott Gibbs	*Centre*	Hernan Garcia Simon
Mike Hall	*Centre*	Eduardo Laborde
Arthur Jones	*Left Wing*	Martin Teran Nougues
Mike Rayer	*Fullback*	Guillermo Del Castillo

Score: Wales 16 (P. Arnold try; M. Ring 3 pen, M. Rayer pen) defeated Argentina 7 (H. Garcia Simon try; G. Del Castillo pen).

Pool C — Australia 9–3 Western Samoa

Date: October 9, 1991.
Venue: Pontypool Park, Pontypool.
Referee: Ed Morrison (England).

Australia	Position	Western Samoa
Dan Crowley	*Prop*	Vili Alalatoa
Phil Kearns	*Hooker*	Stan To'omalatai
Cameron Lillicrap	*Prop*	Peter Fatialofa (c)
Troy Coker	*Lock*	Mark Birtwistle
Steve Cutler	*Lock*	Mat Keenan
Jeff Miller	*Flanker*	Danny Kaleopa
Brendan Nasser	*Flanker*	Junior Paramore
John Eales	*Number 8*	Apollo Perelini
Nick Farr-Jones (c)	*Scrum-half*	Mathew Vaea
Michael Lynagh	*Fly-half*	Stephen Bachop
David Campese	*Right Wing*	Tupo Fa'amasino
Anthony Herbert	*Centre*	Frank Bunce
Tim Horan	*Centre*	To'o Vaega
John Flett	*Left Wing*	Brian Lima
Marty Roebuck	*Fullback*	Andrew Aiolupo
Peter Slattery	*Reserve 1*	Timo Tagaloa

Score: Australia 9 (M. Lynagh 3 pen) defeated Western Samoa 3 (M. Vaea pen).

Pool C — Wales 3–38 Australia

Date: October 12, 1991.
Venue: Cardiff Arms Park, Cardiff.
Referee: Keith Lawrence (New Zealand).

Wales	Position	Australia
Laurence Delaney	*Prop*	Tony Daly
Garin Jenkins	*Hooker*	Phil Kearns
Mike Griffiths	*Prop*	Ewen McKenzie
Paul Arnold	*Lock*	John Eales
Kevin Moseley	*Lock*	Rod McCall
Emyr Lewis	*Flanker*	Jeff Miller
Richard Webster	*Flanker*	Simon Poidevin
Phil Davies	*Number 8*	Willie Ofahengaue
Robert Jones	*Scrum-half*	Peter Slattery
Mark Ring	*Fly-half*	Michael Lynagh (c)
Ieuan Evans (c)	*Right Wing*	David Campese
Scott Gibbs	*Centre*	Tim Horan
Mike Hall	*Centre*	Jason Little
Arthur Jones	*Left Wing*	Rob Egerton
Tony Clement	*Fullback*	Marty Roebuck
David Evans	*Reserve 1*	N/A
Mike Rayer	*Reserve 2*	N/A

Score: Australia 38 (M. Roebuck 2, D. Campese, T. Horan, M. Lynagh, P. Slattery tries; M. Lynagh 4 con, 2 pen) defeated Wales 3 (M. Ring pen).

Pool C — Argentina 12–35 Western Samoa

Date: October 13, 1991.
Venue: Sardis Road, Pontypridd.
Referee: Brian Anderson (New Zealand) injured, replaced by Jim Fleming (Scotland).

Argentina	Position	Western Samoa
Manuel Aguirre	*Prop*	Vili Alalatoa
Mariano Bosch	*Hooker*	Stan To'omalatai
Diego Cash	*Prop*	Peter Fatialofa (c)
Fernando Buabse	*Lock*	Mark Birtwistle
Pedro Sporleder	*Lock*	Mat Keenan
Pablo Garreton (c)	*Flanker*	Apollo Perelini
Francisco Irarrazaval	*Flanker*	Sila Vaifale
Jose Santamarina	*Number 8*	Pat Lam
Gonzalo Camardon	*Scrum-half*	Mathew Vaea
Lisandro Arbizu	*Fly-half*	Stephen Bachop
Diego Cuesta Silva	*Right Wing*	Brian Lima
Hernan Garcia Simon	*Centre*	Frank Bunce
Eduardo Laborde	*Centre*	To'o Vaega
Martin Teran Nougues	*Left Wing*	Timo Tagaloa
Guillermo Angaut	*Fullback*	Andrew Aiolupo
Mario Carreras	*Reserve 1*	N/A
Santiago Meson	*Reserve 2*	N/A

Score: Western Samoa 35 (B. Lima 2, T. Tagaloa 2, S. Bachop, F. Bunce tries; M. Vaea 4 con, pen) defeated Argentina 12 (M. Teran Nougues try; L. Arbizu con, pen, E. Laborde pen).

Pool D
France 30–3 Romania

Date: October 4, 1991.
Venue: Stade de la Méditerranée, Béziers.
Referee: Les Peard (Wales).

France	Position	Romania
Gregoire Lascube	*Prop*	Gheorghe Leonte
Philippe Marocco	*Hooker*	Gheorghe Ion
Pascal Ondarts	*Prop*	Constantin Stan
Jean-Marie Cadieu	*Lock*	Sandu Ciorascu
Olivier Roumat	*Lock*	Sandu Cojocariu
Laurent Cabannes	*Flanker*	Gheorghe Dinu
Eric Champ	*Flanker*	Andrei Guranescu
Abdelatif Benazzi	*Number 8*	Haralambie Dumitras (c)
Fabien Galthie	*Scrum-half*	Daniel Neaga
Didier Camberabero	*Fly-half*	Neculai Nichitean
Patrice Lagisquet	*Right Wing*	Nicolae Racean
Thierry Lacroix	*Centre*	Adrian Lungu
Franck Mesnel	*Centre*	George Sava
Philippe Saint-Andre	*Left Wing*	Catalin Sasu
Serge Blanco (c)	*Fullback*	Marian Dumitru
Jean-Baptiste Lafond	*Reserve 1*	N/A

Score: France 30 (J.-B. Lafond, O. Roumat, P. Saint-Andre tries, penalty try; D. Camberabero con, 4 pen) defeated Romania 3 (N. Nichitean pen).

Pool D
Canada 13–3 Fiji

Date: October 5, 1991.
Venue: Stade Jean Dauger, Bayonne.
Referee: Kerry Fitzgerald (Australia).

Canada	Position	Fiji
Eddie Evans	*Prop*	Epeli Naituvau
David Speirs	*Hooker*	Salacieli Naivilawasa
Dan Jackart	*Prop*	Mosese Taga (c)
Norm Hadley	*Lock*	Samuela Domoni
John Robertsen	*Lock*	Laitia Savai
Al Charron	*Flanker*	Alifereti Dere
Gord MacKinnon	*Flanker*	Laisenia Katonawale
Glen Ennis (c)	*Number 8*	Tamovutoakula
Chris Tynan	*Scrum-half*	Pauliasi Tabulutu
Gareth Rees	*Fly-half*	Waisale Serevi
Steve Gray	*Right Wing*	Tomasi Lovo
John Lecky	*Centre*	Savenaca Aria
Christian Stewart	*Centre*	Noa Nadruku
Pat Palmer	*Left Wing*	Filimoni Seru
Scott Stewart	*Fullback*	Severo Koroduadua
N/A	*Reserve 1*	Dranivesi Baleiwei

Score: Canada 13 (S. Stewart try; G. Rees 3 pen) defeated Fiji 3 (W. Serevi drop-goal).

Pool D

France 33–9 Fiji
Date: October 8, 1991.
Venue: Stade Lesdiguières, Grenoble.
Referee: Derek Bevan (Wales).

France	Position	Fiji
Gregoire Lascube	*Prop*	Mosese Taga (c)
Philippe Marocco	*Hooker*	Dranivesi Baleiwei
Pascal Ondarts	*Prop*	Naibuku Vuli
Jean-Marie Cadieu	*Lock*	Samuela Domoni
Olivier Roumat	*Lock*	Laitia Savai
Laurent Cabannes	*Flanker*	Alifereti Dere
Eric Champ	*Flanker*	Pita Naruma
Abdelatif Benazzi	*Number 8*	Tamovutoakula
Fabien Galthie	*Scrum-half*	Mosese Vosanibole
Didier Camberabero	*Fly-half*	Waisale Serevi
Jean-Baptiste Lafond	*Right Wing*	Tomasi Lovo
Franck Mesnel	*Centre*	Savenaca Aria
Philippe Sella	*Centre*	Kalaveti Naisoro
Philippe Saint-Andre	*Left Wing*	Filimoni Seru
Serge Blanco (c)	*Fullback*	Severo Koroduadua
N/A	*Reserve 1*	Laisenia Katonawale
N/A	*Reserve 2*	Pauliasi Tabulutu
N/A	*Reserve 3*	Peni Volavola

Score: France 33 (J.-B. Lafond 3, P. Sella 2, D. Camberabero, tries; D. Camberabero 3 con, pen) defeated Fiji 9 (P. Naruma try ; S. Koroduadua con, pen).

Pool D

Canada 19–11 Romania
Date: October 9, 1991.
Venue: Stade Municipal, Toulouse.
Referee: Sandy MacNeill (Australia).

Canada	Position	Romania
Eddie Evans	*Prop*	Gheorghe Leonte
Karl Svoboda	*Hooker*	Gheorghe Ion
Dan Jackart	*Prop*	Constantin Stan
Norm Hadley	*Lock*	Sandu Ciorascu
Ron Vanden Brink	*Lock*	Constantin Cojocariu
Bruce Breen	*Flanker*	Gheorghe Dinu
Gord MacKinnon	*Flanker*	Ioan Doja
Glen Ennis	*Number 8*	Haralambie Dumitras (c)
John Graf	*Scrum-half*	Daniel Neaga
Gareth Rees	*Fly-half*	Neculai Nichitean
Pat Palmer	*Right wing*	Nicolae Racean
John Lecky	*Centre*	Nicolae Fulina
Christian Stewart	*Centre*	Adrian Lungu
Scott Stewart	*Left Wing*	Catalin Sasu
Mark Wyatt (c)	*Fullback*	Marian Dumitru
N/A	*Reserve 1*	Tiberiu Brinza
N/A	*Reserve 2*	George Sava
N/A	*Reserve 3*	Gabriel Vlad

Score: Canada 19 (G. Ennis, G. MacKinnon tries; M. Wyatt con, 2 pen; G. Rees drop-goal) defeated Romania 11 (A. Lungu, C. Sasu tries; N. Nichitean pen).

Pool D

Romania 17–15 Fiji

Date: October 12, 1991.
Venue: Stade Municipal des Sports, Brive.
Referee: Owen Doyle (Ireland).

Romania	Position	Fiji
Constantin Stan	*Prop*	Peni Volavola
Gheorghe Ion	*Hooker*	Dranivesi Baleiwei
Gabriel Vlad	*Prop*	Naibuku Vuli
Sandu Ciorascu	*Lock*	Aisake Nadolo
Constantin Cojocariu	*Lock*	Laitia Savai
Gheorghe Dinu	*Flanker*	Alifereti Dere (c)
Micusor Marin	*Flanker*	Tamovutoakula
Haralambie Dumitras (c)	*Number 8*	Max Olsson
Daniel Neaga	*Scrum-half*	Pauliasi Tabulutu
Neculai Nichitean	*Fly-half*	Tomasi Rabaka
Lician Colceriu	*Right Wing*	Filimoni Seru
Nicolae Fulina	*Centre*	Kalaveti Naisoro
Adrian Lungu	*Centre*	Noa Nadruku
Catalin Sasu	*Left Wing*	Tevita Vonolagi
Nicolae Racean	*Fullback*	Opeti Turuva
Ilie Ivancuic	*Reserve 1*	Epeli Naituvau
N/A	*Reserve 2*	Pita Naruma

Score: Romania 17 (H. Dumitras, G. Ion, C. Sasu tries; N. Racean con, N. Nichitean pen) defeated Fiji 15 (O. Turuva 2 pen, drop-goal, T. Rabaka 2 drop-goals).

Pool D

France 19–13 Canada

Date: October 13, 1991.
Venue: Stade Armandie, Agen.
Referee: Stephen Hilditch (Ireland).

France	Position	Canada
Gregoire Lascube	*Prop*	Eddie Evans
Philippe Marocco	*Hooker*	Karl Svoboda
Pascal Ondarts	*Prop*	Dan Jackart
Jean-Marie Cadieu	*Lock*	Norm Hadley
Olivier Roumat	*Lock*	John Robertsen
Laurent Cabannes	*Flanker*	Al Charron
Eric Champ	*Flanker*	Gord MacKinnon
Abdelatif Benazzi	*Number 8*	Glen Ennis
Fabien Galthie	*Scrum-half*	Chris Tynan
Didier Camberabero	*Fly-half*	Gareth Rees
Jean-Baptiste Lafond	*Right Wing*	Steve Gray
Franck Mesnel	*Centre*	Christian Stewart
Philippe Sella	*Centre*	Tom Woods
Philippe Saint-Andre	*Left Wing*	Pat Palmer
Serge Blanco (c)	*Fullback*	Mark Wyatt (c)
Thierry Lacroix	*Reserve 1*	Scott Stewart
Jean-Luc Sadourny	*Reserve 2*	Ron Vanden Brink

Score: France 19 (J.-B. Lafond, P. Saint-Andre tries; D. Camberabero con, pen, T. Lacroix 2 pen) defeated Canada 13 (M. Wyatt try; G. Rees pen, drop-goal, M. Wyatt pen).

Quarter-final Scotland 28–6 Western Samoa

Date: October 19, 1991.
Venue: Murrayfield, Edinburgh.
Referee: Derek Bevan (Wales).

Scotland	Position	Western Samoa
Paul Burnell	*Prop*	Vili Alalatoa
John Allan	*Hooker*	Stan To'omalatai
David Sole (c)	*Prop*	Peter Fatialofa (c)
Chris Gray	*Lock*	Mark Birtwistle
Doddie Weir	*Lock*	Eddie Ioane
Finlay Calder	*Flanker*	Apollo Perelini
John Jeffrey	*Flanker*	Sila Vaifale
Derek White	*Number 8*	Pat Lam
Gary Armstrong	*Scrum-half*	Mathew Vaea
Craig Chalmers	*Fly-half*	Stephen Bachop
Tony Stanger	*Right Wing*	Brian Lima
Scott Hastings	*Centre*	Frank Bunce
Graham Shiel	*Centre*	To'o Vaega
Iwan Tukalo	*Left Wing*	Timo Tagaloa
Gavin Hastings	*Fullback*	Andrew Aiolupo

Score: Scotland 28 (J. Jeffrey 2, A. Stanger tries; G. Hastings 2 con, 4 pen) defeated Western Samoa 6 (M. Vaea 1 pen, S. Bachop 1 drop-goal).

Quarter-final France 10–19 England

Date: October 19, 1991.
Venue: Parc des Princes, Paris.
Referee: David Bishop (New Zealand).

France	Position	England
Gregoire Lascube	*Prop*	Jason Leonard
Philippe Marocco	*Hooker*	Brian Moore
Pascal Ondarts	*Prop*	Jeff Probyn
Jean-Marie Cadieu	*Lock*	Paul Ackford
Olivier Roumat	*Lock*	Wade Dooley
Laurent Cabannes	*Flanker*	Mickey Skinner
Eric Champ	*Flanker*	Peter Winterbottom
Marc Cecillon	*Number 8*	Mike Teague
Fabien Galthie	*Scrum-half*	Richard Hill
Thierry Lacroix	*Fly-half*	Rob Andrew
Jean-Baptiste Lafond	*Right Wing*	Nigel Heslop
Franck Mesnel	*Centre*	Will Carling (c)
Philippe Sella	*Centre*	Jeremy Guscott
Philippe Saint-Andre	*Left Wing*	Rory Underwood
Serge Blanco (c)	*Fullback*	Jon Webb

Score: England 19 (W. Carling, R. Underwood tries; J. Webb con, 3 pen) defeated France 10 (J.-B. Lafond try; T. Lacroix 2 pen).

Quarter-final — Ireland 18–19 Australia

Date: October 20, 1991.
Venue: Lansdowne Road, Dublin.
Referee: Jim Fleming (Scotland).

Ireland	Position	Australia
Des Fitzgerald	*Prop*	Tony Daly
Steve Smith	*Hooker*	Phil Kearns
Nick Popplewell	*Prop*	Ewen McKenzie
Neil Francis	*Lock*	John Eales
Donal Lenihan	*Lock*	Rod McCall
Gordon Hamilton	*Flanker*	Jeff Miller
Philip Matthews (c)	*Flanker*	Simon Poidevin
Brian Robinson	*Number 8*	Willie Ofahengaue
Rob Saunders	*Scrum-half*	Nick Farr-Jones (c)
Ralph Keyes	*Fly-half*	Michael Lynagh
Jack Clarke	*Right Wing*	David Campese
David Curtis	*Centre*	Tim Horan
Brendan Mullin	*Centre*	Jason Little
Simon Geoghegan	*Left Wing*	Rob Egerton
Jim Staples	*Fullback*	Marty Roebuck
N/A	*Reserve 1*	Peter Slattery

Score: Australia 19 (D. Campese 2, M. Lynagh tries; M. Lynagh 2 con, 1 pen) defeated Ireland 18 (G. Hamilton try; R. Keyes con, 3 pen, drop-goal).

Quarter-final — Canada 13–29 New Zealand

Date: October 20, 1991.
Venue: Stade Lille-Metropol, Villeneuve d'Ascq.
Referee: Fred Howard (England).

Canada	Position	New Zealand
Eddie Evans	*Prop*	Richard Loe
David Speirs	*Hooker*	Sean Fitzpatrick
Paul Szabo	*Prop*	Steve McDowell
Norm Hadley	*Lock*	Ian Jones
Ron Vanden Brink	*Lock*	Gary Whetton (c)
Al Charron	*Flanker*	Paul Henderson
Gord MacKinnon	*Flanker*	Alan Whetton
Glen Ennis	*Number 8*	Zinzan Brooke
Chris Tynan	*Scrum-half*	Graeme Bachop
Gareth Rees	*Fly-half*	Grant Fox
Steve Gray	*Right Wing*	John Kirwan
Christian Stewart	*Centre*	Craig Innes
Tom Woods	*Centre*	Bernie McCahill
Scott Stewart	*Left Wing*	Va'aiga Tuigamala
Mark Wyatt (c)	*Fullback*	John Timu

Score: New Zealand 29 (J. Timu 2, Z. Brooke, J. Kirwan, B. McCahill tries; G. Fox 3 con, pen) defeated Canada 13 (A. Charron, C. Tynan tries; G. Rees con, M. Wyatt pen).

Semi-final — Scotland 6–9 England

Date: October 26, 1991.
Venue: Murrayfield, Edinburgh.
Referee: Kerry Fitzgerald (Australia).

Scotland	Position	England
Paul Burnell	Prop	Jason Leonard
John Allan	Hooker	Brian Moore
David Sole (c)	Prop	Jeff Probyn
Chris Gray	Lock	Paul Ackford
Doddie Weir	Lock	Wade Dooley
Finlay Calder	Flanker	Mickey Skinner
John Jeffrey	Flanker	Peter Winterbottom
Derek White	Number 8	Mike Teague
Gary Armstrong	Scrum-half	Richard Hill
Craig Chalmers	Fly-half	Rob Andrew
Tony Stanger	Right Wing	Simon Halliday
Scott Hastings	Centre	Will Carling (c)
Sean Lineen	Centre	Jeremy Guscott
Iwan Tukalo	Left Wing	Rory Underwood
Gavin Hastings	Fullback	Jon Webb

Score: England 9 (J. Webb 2 pen; R. Andrew drop-goal) defeated Scotland 6 (G. Hastings 2 pen).

Semi-final — Australia 16–6 New Zealand

Date: October 27, 1991.
Venue: Lansdowne Road, Dublin.
Referee: Jim Fleming (Scotland).

Australia	Position	New Zealand
Tony Daly	Prop	Richard Loe
Phil Kearns	Hooker	Sean Fitzpatrick
Ewen McKenzie	Prop	Steve McDowell
John Eales	Lock	Ian Jones
Rod McCall	Lock	Gary Whetton (c)
Willie Ofahengaue	Flanker	Mark Carter
Simon Poidevin	Flanker	Alan Whetton
Troy Coker	Number 8	Zinzan Brooke
Nick Farr-Jones (c)	Scrum-half	Graeme Bachop
Michael Lynagh	Fly-half	Grant Fox
David Campese	Right Wing	John Kirwan
Tim Horan	Centre	Craig Innes
Jason Little	Centre	Bernie McCahill
Rob Egerton	Left Wing	John Timu
Marty Roebuck	Fullback	Kieran Crowley

Score: Australia 16 (D. Campese, T. Horan tries; M. Lynagh con, 2 pen) defeated New Zealand 6 (G. Fox 2 pen).

3rd Place Play-off **New Zealand 13–6 Scotland**

Date: October 30, 1991.
Venue: Cardiff Arms Park, Cardiff.
Referee: Stephen Hilditch (Ireland).

New Zealand	Position	Scotland
Richard Loe	*Prop*	Paul Burnell
Sean Fitzpatrick	*Hooker*	John Allan
Steve McDowell	*Prop*	David Sole (c)
Ian Jones	*Lock*	Chris Gray
Gary Whetton (c)	*Lock*	Doddie Weir
Andy Earl	*Flanker*	Finlay Calder
Michael Jones	*Flanker*	John Jeffrey
Zinzan Brooke	*Number 8*	Derek White
Graeme Bachop	*Scrum-half*	Gary Armstrong
Jon Preston	*Fly-half*	Craig Chalmers
John Kirwan	*Right Wing*	Tony Stanger
Craig Innes	*Centre*	Scott Hastings
Walter Little	*Centre*	Sean Lineen
Va'aiga Tuigamala	*Left Wing*	Iwan Tukalo
Terry Wright	*Fullback*	Gavin Hastings
Shayne Philpott	*Reserve 1*	Peter Dods

Score: New Zealand 13 (W. Little try; J. Preston 3 pen) defeated
Scotland 6 (G. Hastings 2 pen).

The Final **England 6–12 Australia**

Date: November 2, 1991.
Venue: Twickenham, London.
Referee: Derek Bevan (Wales).

England	Position	Australia
Jason Leonard	*Prop*	Tony Daly
Brian Moore	*Hooker*	Phil Kearns
Jeff Probyn	*Prop*	Ewen McKenzie
Paul Ackford	*Lock*	John Eales
Wade Dooley	*Lock*	Rod McCall
Mickey Skinner	*Flanker*	Willie Ofahengaue
Peter Winterbottom	*Flanker*	Simon Poidevin
Mike Teague	*Number 8*	Troy Coker
Richard Hill	*Scrum-half*	Nick Farr-Jones (c)
Rob Andrew	*Fly-half*	Michael Lynagh
Simon Halliday	*Right Wing*	David Campese
Will Carling (c)	*Centre*	Tim Horan
Jeremy Guscott	*Centre*	Jason Little
Rory Underwood	*Left Wing*	Rob Egerton
Jon Webb	*Fullback*	Marty Roebuck

Score: Australia 12 (T. Daly try; M. Lynagh con, 2 pen) defeated
England 6 (J. Webb 2 pen).

Rugby World Cup 1995

Tournament Statistics

Score change: The International Rugby Board increased the value of a try from four points to five points in 1992, in an effort to encourage more tries to be scored.

Pool Stage – Final Standings

Pool A							
Team	Wins	Draws	Losses	For	Against	Tries	Points
South Africa	3	0	0	68	26	6	9
Australia	2	0	1	87	41	11	7
Canada	1	0	2	45	50	4	5
Romania	0	0	3	14	97	1	3

• South Africa and Australia advanced to the quarter-finals.

Pool B							
Team	Wins	Draws	Losses	For	Against	Tries	Points
England	3	0	0	95	60	6	9
W. Samoa	2	0	1	96	88	12	7
Italy	1	0	2	69	94	7	5
Argentina	0	0	3	69	87	8	3

• England and Western Samoa advanced to the quarter-finals.

Pool C							
Team	Wins	Draws	Losses	For	Against	Tries	Points
New Zealand	3	0	0	225	45	28	9
Ireland	2	0	1	93	94	13	7
Wales	1	0	2	89	68	9	5
Japan	0	0	3	55	252	8	3

• New Zealand and Ireland advanced to the quarter-finals.

Pool D							
Team	Wins	Draws	Losses	For	Against	Tries	Points
France	3	0	0	114	47	13	9
Scotland	2	0	1	149	27	18	7
Tonga	1	0	2	44	90	6	5
Ivory Coast	0	0	3	29	172	3	3

• France and Scotland advanced to the quarter-finals.

Pool Stage – Results Snapshot

Pool A		
South Africa	27–18	Australia
Canada	34–3	Romania
South Africa	21–8	Romania
Australia	27–11	Canada
Australia	42–3	Romania
South Africa	20–0	Canada

Pool B		
W. Samoa	42–18	Italy
England	24–18	Argentina
W. Samoa	32–26	Argentina
England	27–20	Italy
Italy	31–25	Argentina
England	23–22	W. Samoa

Pool C		
Wales	57–10	Japan
New Zealand	43–19	Ireland
Ireland	50–28	Japan
New Zealand	34–9	Wales
New Zealand	145–17	Japan
Ireland	24–23	Wales

Pool D		
Scotland	89–0	Ivory Coast
France	38–10	Tonga
France	54–18	Ivory Coast
Scotland	41–5	Tonga
Tonga	29–11	Ivory Coast
France	22–19	Scotland

Rugby World Cup 1995: The Finals

Quarter-finals

France 36
Ireland 12

Semi-finals

South Africa 19
France 15

South Africa 42
Western Samoa 14

Final

South Africa 15
New Zealand 12

England 25
Australia 22

New Zealand 45
England 29

New Zealand 48
Scotland 30

Third Place Play-off

France 19
England 9

Detailed Results

Pool A — South Africa 27–18 Australia

Date: May 25, 1995.
Venue: Newlands, Cape Town.
Referee: Derek Bevan (Wales).

South Africa	Position	Australia
Os Du Randt	*Prop*	Dan Crowley
James Dalton	*Hooker*	Phil Kearns
Balie Swart	*Prop*	Ewen McKenzie
Mark Andrews	*Lock*	John Eales
Hannes Strydom	*Lock*	Rod McCall
Ruben Kruger	*Flanker*	Willie Ofahengaue
Francois Pienaar (c)	*Flanker*	David Wilson
Rudolf Straeuli	*Number 8*	Tim Gavin
Joost van der Westhuizen	*Scrum-half*	George Gregan
Joel Stransky	*Fly-half*	Michael Lynagh (c)
Pieter Hendriks	*Right Wing*	David Campese
Hennie le Roux	*Centre*	Dan Herbert
Japie Mulder	*Centre*	Jason Little
James Small	*Left Wing*	Damian Smith
Andre Joubert	*Fullback*	Matthew Pini
Garry Pagel	*Reserves*	N/A

Score: South Africa 27 (P. Hendriks, J. Stransky tries; J. Stransky con, 4 pen, drop-goal) defeated Australia 18 (P. Kearns, M. Lynagh tries; M. Lynagh con, 2 pen).

Pool A — Canada 34–3 Romania

Date: May 26, 1995.
Venue: Boet Erasmus Stadium, Port Elizabeth.
Referee: Colin Hawke (New Zealand).

Canada	Position	Romania
Eddie Evans	*Prop*	Gheorghe Leonte
Mark Cardinal	*Hooker*	Ionel Negreci
Rod Snow	*Prop*	Gabriel Vlad
Glen Ennis	*Lock*	Sandu Ciorascu (c)
Mike James	*Lock*	Constantin Cojocariu
Al Charron	*Flanker*	Alexandru Gealapu
Ian Gordon	*Flanker*	Traian Oroian
Colin McKenzie	*Number 8*	Ovidiu Slusariuc
John Graf	*Scrum-half*	Daniel Neaga
Gareth Rees (c)	*Fly-half*	Neculai Nichitean
Dave Lougheed	*Right Wing*	Lician Colceriu
Steve Gray	*Centre*	Romeo Gontineac
Christian Stewart	*Centre*	Nicolae Racean
Winston Stanley	*Left Wing*	Ionel Rotaru
Scott Stewart	*Fullback*	Gheorghe Solomie
N/A	*Reserves*	Vasile Flutur, Ilie Ivancuic

Score: Canada 34 (A. Charron, C. McKenzie, R. Snow tries; G. Rees 2 con, 4 pen, drop-goal) defeated Romania 3 (N. Nichitean pen).

Pool A   South Africa 21–8 Romania
Date: May 30, 1995.
Venue: Newlands, Cape Town.
Referee: Ken McCartney (Scotland).

South Africa	Position	Romania
Marius Hurter	*Prop*	Gheorghe Leonte
Chris Rossouw	*Hooker*	Ionel Negreci
Garry Pagel	*Prop*	Gabriel Vlad
Krynauw Otto	*Lock*	Sandu Ciorascu
Kobus Wiese	*Lock*	Constantin Cojocariu
Robbie Brink	*Flanker*	Alexandru Gealapu
Ruben Kruger	*Flanker*	Andrei Guranescu
Adriaan Richter (c)	*Number 8*	Tiberiu Brinza (c)
Johan Roux	*Scrum-half*	Vasile Flutur
Hennie leRoux	*Fly-half*	Ilie Ivancuic
Pieter Hendriks	*Right Wing*	Lician Colceriu
Christiaan Scholtz	*Centre*	Romeo Gontineac
Brendan Venter	*Centre*	Nicolae Racean
James Small	*Left Wing*	Gheorghe Solomie
Gavin Johnson	*Fullback*	Vasile Brici
Joel Stransky	*Reserves*	Valere Tufa

Score: South Africa 21 (A. Richter 2 tries; G. Johnson con, 3 pen) defeated Romania 8 (A. Guranescu try, I. Ivancuic pen).

Pool A   Australia 27–11 Canada
Date: May 31, 1995.
Venue: Boet Erasmus Stadium, Port Elizabeth.
Referee: Patrick Robin (France).

Australia	Position	Canada
Tony Daly	*Prop*	Eddie Evans
Phil Kearns	*Hooker*	Karl Svoboda
Mark Hartill	*Prop*	Rod Snow
John Eales	*Lock*	Mike James
Warwick Waugh	*Lock*	Gareth Rowlands
Willie Ofahengaue	*Flanker*	John Hutchinson
Ilie Tabua	*Flanker*	Gord MacKinnon
Tim Gavin	*Number 8*	Al Charron
Peter Slattery	*Scrum-half*	John Graf
Michael Lynagh (c)	*Fly-half*	Gareth Rees (c)
David Campese	*Right Wing*	Dave Lougheed
Tim Horan	*Centre*	Steve Gray
Jason Little	*Centre*	Christian Stewart
Joe Roff	*Left Wing*	Winston Stanley
Matthew Burke	*Fullback*	Scott Stewart
Michael Foley, George Gregan, Ewen McKenzie	*Reserves*	Glen Ennis

Score: Australia 27 (M. Lynagh, J. Roff, I. Tabua tries; M. Lynagh 3 con, 2 pen) defeated Canada 11 (A. Charron try, G. Rees 2 pen).

Pool A — South Africa 20–0 Canada

Date: June 3, 1995.
Venue: Boet Erasmus Stadium, Port Elizabeth.
Referee: David McHugh (Ireland).

South Africa	Position	Canada
Marius Hurter	Prop	Eddie Evans
James Dalton	Hooker	Mark Cardinal
Garry Pagel	Prop	Rod Snow
Hannes Strydom	Lock	Al Charron
Kobus Wiese	Lock	Glen Ennis
Robbie Brink	Flanker	Ian Gordon
Francois Pienaar (c)	Flanker	Gord MacKinnon
Adriaan Richter	Number 8	Colin McKenzie
Johan Roux	Scrum-half	John Graf
Joel Stransky	Fly-half	Gareth Rees (c)
Pieter Hendriks	Right Wing	Dave Lougheed
Christiaan Scholtz	Centre	Steve Gray
Brendan Venter	Centre	Christian Stewart
Gavin Johnson	Left Wing	Winston Stanley
Andre Joubert	Fullback	Scott Stewart
Hennie leRoux, Krynauw Otto, Joost van der Westhuizen	Reserves	John Hutchinson, Chris Michaluk

Score: South Africa 20 (A. Richter 2 tries; J. Stransky 2 con, 2 pen) defeated Canada 0.

Pool A — Australia 42–3 Romania

Date: June 3, 1995.
Venue: Danie Craven Stadium, Stellenbosch.
Referee: Naoki Saito (Japan).

Australia	Position	Romania
Tony Daly	Prop	Gheorghe Leonte
Michael Foley	Hooker	Ionel Negreci
Ewen McKenzie	Prop	Gabriel Vlad
John Eales	Lock	Sandu Ciorascu
Rod McCall (c)	Lock	Constantin Cojocariu
Ilie Tabua	Flanker	Alexandru Gealapu
David Wilson	Flanker	Andrei Guranescu
Tim Gavin	Number 8	Tiberiu Brinza (c)
George Gregan	Scrum-half	Vasile Flutur
Scott Bowen	Fly-half	Ilie Ivancuic
Joe Roff	Right Wing	Lician Colceriu
Dan Herbert	Centre	Romeo Gontineac
Tim Horan	Centre	Nicolae Racean
Damian Smith	Left Wing	Gheorghe Solomie
Matthew Burke	Fullback	Vasile Brici
Daniel Manu, Matthew Pini, Peter Slattery	Reserves	Adrian Lungu, Valere Tufa

Score: Australia 42 (J. Roff 2, M. Burke, M. Foley, D. Smith, D. Wilson tries; M. Burke 2 con, J. Eales 4 con) defeated Romania 3 (I. Ivancuic drop-goal).

Pool B

Argentina 18–24 England

Date: May 27, 1995.
Venue: King's Park, Durban.
Referee: Jim Fleming (Scotland).

Argentina	Position	England
Matias Corral	*Prop*	Jason Leonard
Federico Mendez	*Hooker*	Brian Moore
Patricio Noriega	*Prop*	Victor Ubogu
German Llanes	*Lock*	Martin Bayfield
Pedro Sporleder	*Lock*	Martin Johnson
Rolando Martin	*Flanker*	Ben Clarke
Cristian Viel Temperley	*Flanker*	Tim Rodber
Jose Santamarina	*Number 8*	Steve Ojomoh
Rodrigo Crexell	*Scrum-half*	Dewi Morris
Lisandro Arbizu	*Fly-half*	Rob Andrew
Diego Albanese	*Right Wing*	Rory Underwood
Diego Cuesta Silva	*Centre*	Will Carling (c)
Sebastian Salvat (c)	*Centre*	Jeremy Guscott
Martin Teran Nougues	*Left Wing*	Tony Underwood
Ezequiel Jurado	*Fullback*	Mike Catt
Sebastian Irazoqui	*Reserves*	Neil Back, Phil de Glanville

Score: England 24 (R. Andrew 6 pen, 2 drop-goals) defeated Argentina 18 (L. Arbizu, P. Noriega tries; L. Arbizu 1 con, 2 pen).

Pool B

Italy 18–42 Western Samoa

Date: May 27, 1995.
Venue: Basil Kenyon Stadium, East London.
Referee: Joel Dume (France).

Italy	Position	Western Samoa
Massimo Cuttitta (c)	*Prop*	Peter Fatialofa (c)
Carlo Orlandi	*Hooker*	Tala Leiasamaiva'o
Franco Properzi-Curti	*Prop*	Mike Mika
Roberto Favaro	*Lock*	Lio Falaniko
Pierpaolo Pedroni	*Lock*	Daryl Williams
Orazio Arancio	*Flanker*	Junior Paramore
Julian Gardner	*Flanker*	Sila Vaifale
Carlo Checchinato	*Number 8*	Shem Tatupu
Alessandro Troncon	*Scrum-half*	Tu Nu'uali'itia
Diego Dominguez	*Fly-half*	Darren Kellett
Marcello Cuttitta	*Right Wing*	George Harder
Massimo Bonomi	*Centre*	Tupo Fa'amasino
Ivan Francescato	*Centre*	To'o Vaega
Massimo Ravazzolo	*Left Wing*	Brian Lima
Paolo Vaccari	*Fullback*	Mike Umaga
N/A	*Reserves*	Potu Leavasa

Score: Western Samoa 42 (G. Harder 2, B. Lima 2, D. Kellett, S. Tatupu tries; D. Kellett 3 con, 2 pen) defeated Italy 18 (M. Cuttitta, P. Vaccari tries; D. Dominguez con, pen, drop-goal).

Pool B — Western Samoa 32–26 Argentina

Date: May 30, 1995.
Venue: Basil Kenyon Stadium, East London.
Referee: David Bishop (New Zealand).

Western Samoa	Position	Argentina
George Latu	*Prop*	Matias Corral
Tala Leiasamaiva'o	*Hooker*	Federico Mendez
Mike Mika	*Prop*	Patricio Noriega
Lio Falaniko	*Lock*	German Llanes
Potu Leavasa	*Lock*	Pedro Sporleder
Junior Paramore	*Flanker*	Rolando Martin
Shem Tatupu	*Flanker*	Cristian Viel Temperley
Pat Lam (c)	*Number 8*	Jose Santamarina
Tu Nu'uali'itia	*Scrum-half*	Rodrigo Crexell
Darren Kellett	*Fly-half*	Jose Cilley
George Harder	*Right Wing*	Diego Cuesta Silva
Tupo Fa'amasino	*Centre*	Lisandro Arbizu
To'o Vaega	*Centre*	Sebastian Salvat (c)
Brian Lima	*Left Wing*	Martin Teran Nougues
Mike Umaga	*Fullback*	Ezequiel Jurado
Peter Fatialofa, George Leaupepe, Fata Sini	*Reserves*	N/A

Score: Western Samoa 32 (G. Harder, P. Lam, G. Leaupepe tries; D. Kellett con, 5 pen) defeated Argentina 26 (R. Crexell try, penalty try; J. Cilley 2 con, 4 pen).

Pool B — England 27–20 Italy

Date: May 31, 1995.
Venue: King's Park, Durban.
Referee: Stephen Hilditch (Ireland).

England	Position	Italy
Jason Leonard	*Prop*	Massimo Cuttitta (c)
Brian Moore	*Hooker*	Carlo Orlandi
Graham Rowntree	*Prop*	Franco Properzi-Curti
Martin Bayfield	*Lock*	Mark Giacheri
Martin Johnson	*Lock*	Pierpaolo Pedroni
Neil Back	*Flanker*	Orazio Arancio
Tim Rodber	*Flanker*	Andrea Sgorlon
Ben Clarke	*Number 8*	Julian Gardner
Kyran Bracken	*Scrum-half*	Alessandro Troncon
Rob Andrew (c)	*Fly-half*	Diego Dominguez
Rory Underwood	*Right Wing*	Mario Gerosa
Phil de Glanville	*Centre*	Stefano Bordon
Jeremy Guscott	*Centre*	Ivan Francescato
Tony Underwood	*Left Wing*	Paolo Vaccari
Mike Catt	*Fullback*	Luigi Troiani
N/A	*Reserves*	N/A

Score: England 27 (R. Underwood, T. Underwood tries; R. Andrew con, 5 pen) defeated Italy 20 (M. Cuttitta, P.Vaccari tries; D. Dominguez 2 con, 2 pen).

Pool B   England 44–22 Western Samoa

Date: June 4, 1995.
Venue: King's Park, Durban.
Referee: Patrick Robin (France).

England	Position	Western Samoa
Graham Rowntree	*Prop*	George Latu
Graham Dawe	*Hooker*	Tala Leiasamaiva'o
Victor Ubogu	*Prop*	Mike Mika
Martin Johnson	*Lock*	Lio Falaniko
Richard West	*Lock*	Potu Leavasa
Neil Back	*Flanker*	Junior Paramore
Steve Ojomoh	*Flanker*	Shem Tatupu
Dean Richards	*Number 8*	Pat Lam (c)
Dewi Morris	*Scrum-half*	Tu Nu'uali'itia
Mike Catt	*Fly-half*	Darren Kellett
Ian Hunter	*Right Wing*	George Harder
Will Carling (c)	*Centre*	Tupo Fa'amasino
Phil de Glanville	*Centre*	To'o Vaega
Rory Underwood	*Left Wing*	Brian Lima
Jon Callard	*Fullback*	Mike Umaga
Kyran Bracken, Damian Hopley, John Mallett, Brian Moore, Tim Rodber	*Reserves*	Peter Fatialofa, Saini Lemamea, Fata Sini, Shem Tatupu

Score: England 44 (R. Underwood 2, N. Back tries, penalty try; J. Callard 3 con, 5 pen, M. Catt drop-goal) defeated Western Samoa 22 (F. Sini 2, M. Umaga tries; T. Fa'amasino 2 con, pen).

Pool B   Italy 31–25 Argentina

Date: June 4, 1995.
Venue: Basil Kenyon Stadium, East London.
Referee: Clayton Thomas (Wales).

Italy	Position	Argentina
Massimo Cuttitta (c)	*Prop*	Matias Corral
Carlo Orlandi	*Hooker*	Federico Mendez
Franco Properzi-Curti	*Prop*	Patricio Noriega
Mark Giacheri	*Lock*	German Llanes
Pierpaolo Pedroni	*Lock*	Pedro Sporleder
Orazio Arancio	*Flanker*	Rolando Martin
Andrea Sgorlon	*Flanker*	Cristian Viel Temperley
Julian Gardner	*Number 8*	Jose Santamarina
Alessandro Troncon	*Scrum-half*	Rodrigo Crexell
Diego Dominguez	*Fly-half*	Jose Cilley
Mario Gerosa	*Right Wing*	Diego Cuesta Silva
Stefano Bordon	*Centre*	Lisandro Arbizu
Ivan Francescato	*Centre*	Sebastian Salvat (c)
Paolo Vaccari	*Left Wing*	Martin Teran Nougues
Luigi Troiani	*Fullback*	Ezequiel Jurado

Score: Italy 31 (D. Dominguez, M. Gerosa, P. Vaccari tries; D. Dominguez 2 con, 4 pen) defeated Argentina 25 (J. Cilley, M. Corral, R. Martin tries, penalty try; J. Cilley con, pen).

Pool C — Wales 57–10 Japan

Date: May 27, 1995.
Venue: Free State Stadium, Bloemfontein.
Referee: Efrahim Sklar (Argentina).

Wales	Position	Japan
John Davies	*Prop*	Osamu Ota
Garin Jenkins	*Hooker*	Masahiro Kunda (c)
Mike Griffiths	*Prop*	Kazuaki Takahashi
Derwyn Jones	*Lock*	Bruce Ferguson
Gareth Llewllyn	*Lock*	Yoshihiko Sakuraba
Stuart Davies	*Flanker*	Hiroyuki Kajihara
Hemi Taylor	*Flanker*	Sinali-Tui Latu
Emyr Lewis	*Number 8*	Sione-Tupo Latu Mailangi
Andrew Moore	*Scrum-half*	Masami Horikoshi
Adrian Davies	*Fly-half*	Seiji Hirao
Ieuan Evans	*Right Wing*	Terunori Masuho
Mike Hall (c)	*Centre*	Yukio Motoki
Neil Jenkins	*Centre*	Akira Yashida
Gareth Thomas	*Left Wing*	Lopeti Oto
Tony Clement	*Fullback*	Tsutomu Matsuda
David Evans, Stuart Roy	*Reserves*	N/A

Score: Wales 57 (G. Thomas 3, I. Evans 2, A. Moore, H. Taylor tries; N. Jenkins 5 con, 4 pen) defeated Japan 10 (L. Oto 2 tries).

Pool C — Ireland 19–43 New Zealand

Date: May 27, 1995.
Venue: Ellis Park, Johannesburg.
Referee: Wayne Erickson (Australia).

Ireland	Position	New Zealand
Gary Halpin	*Prop*	Olo Brown
Terry Kingston (c)	*Hooker*	Sean Fitzpatrick (c)
Nick Popplewell	*Prop*	Craig Dowd
Neil Francis	*Lock*	*Ian Jones*
Gabriel Fulcher	*Lock*	Blair Larsen
David Corkery	*Flanker*	Jamie Joseph
Denis McBride	*Flanker*	Josh Kronfeld
Paddy Johns	*Number 8*	Mike Brewer
Michael Bradley	*Scrum-half*	Graeme Bachop
Eric Elwood	*Fly-half*	Andrew Mehrtens
Simon Geoghegan	*Right Wing*	Jonah Lomu
Jonathan Bell	*Centre*	Frank Bunce
Brendan Mullin	*Centre*	Walter Little
Richard Wallace	*Left Wing*	Jeff Wilson
Jim Staples	*Fullback*	Glen Osborne
Maurice Field	*Reserves*	Marc Ellis, Norm Hewitt, Kevin Schuler

Score: New Zealand 43 (J. Lomu 2, F. Bunce, J. Kronfeld, G. Osborne tries; A. Mehrtens 3 con, 4 pen) defeated Ireland 19 (S. Corkery, G. Halpin, D. McBride tries; E. Elwood 2 con).

Pool C — Ireland 50–28 Japan

Date: May 31, 1995.
Venue: Free State Stadium, Bloemfontein.
Referee: Stef Neethling (South Africa).

Ireland	Position	Japan
Nick Popplewell (c)	*Prop*	Osamu Ota
Keith Wood	*Hooker*	Masahiro Kunda (c)
Paul Wallace	*Prop*	Masanori Takura
Neil Francis	*Lock*	Bruce Ferguson
Davy Tweed	*Lock*	Yoshihiko Sakuraba
David Corkery	*Flanker*	Hiroyuki Kajihara
Eddie Halvey	*Flanker*	Sinali-Tui Latu
Paddy Johns	*Number 8*	Sione-Tupo Latu Mailangi
Niall Hogan	*Scrum-half*	Masami Horikoshi
Paul Burke	*Fly-half*	Seiji Hirao
Simon Geoghegan	*Right Wing*	Lopati Oto
Maurice Field	*Centre*	Yukio Motoki
Brendan Mullin	*Centre*	Akira Yashida
Richard Wallace	*Left Wing*	Yoshihito Yoshida
Conor O'Shea	*Fullback*	Tsutomu Matsuda
Anthony Foley, Terry Kingston	*Reserves*	Ko Izawa

Score: Ireland 50 (S. Corkery, N. Francis, S. Geoghegan, E. Halvey, N. Hogan tries, 2 penalty tries; P. Burke 6 con, pen) defeated Japan 28 (S. Hirao 1, K. Izawa 1, S.-T. Latu 1, M. Takura tries; Y. Yoshida 4 con).

Pool C — New Zealand 34–9 Wales

Date: May 31, 1995.
Venue: Ellis Park, Johannesburg.
Referee: Ed Morrison (England).

New Zealand	Position	Wales
Olo Brown	*Prop*	John Davies
Sean Fitzpatrick (c)	*Hooker*	Jonathan Humphreys
Craig Dowd	*Prop*	Ricky Evans
Ian Jones	*Lock*	Derwyn Jones
Blair Larsen	*Lock*	Greg Prosser
Jamie Joseph	*Flanker*	Mark Bennett
Josh Kronfeld	*Flanker*	Gareth Llewllyn
Mike Brewer	*Number 8*	Hemi Taylor
Graeme Bachop	*Scrum-half*	Robert Jones
Andrew Mehrtens	*Fly-half*	Neil Jenkins
Marc Ellis	*Right Wing*	Ieuan Evans
Frank Bunce	*Centre*	Mike Hall (c)
Walter Little	*Centre*	Gareth Thomas
Jonah Lomu	*Left Wing*	Wayne Proctor
Glen Osborne	*Fullback*	Tony Clement
Eric Rush	*Reserves*	N/A

Score: New Zealand 34 (M. Ellis, J. Kronfeld, W. Little tries; A. Mehrtens 2 con, 4 pen, drop-goal) defeated Wales 9 (N. Jenkins 2 pen, drop-goal).

Pool C
Japan 17–145 New Zealand
Date: June 4, 1995.
Venue: Free State Stadium, Bloemfontein.
Referee: George Gadjovich (Canada).

Japan	Position	New Zealand
Osamu Ota	*Prop*	Craig Dowd
Masahiro Kunda (c)	*Hooker*	Norm Hewitt
Kazuaki Takahashi	*Prop*	Richard Loe
Bruce Ferguson	*Lock*	Robin Brooke
Yoshihiko Sakuraba	*Lock*	Blair Larsen
Ko Izawa	*Flanker*	Paul Henderson
Hiroyuki Kajihara	*Flanker*	Kevin Schuler
Sinal-Tui Latu	*Number 8*	Zinzan Brooke
Wataru Murata	*Scrum-half*	Ant Strachan
Keiji Hirose	*Fly-half*	Simon Culhane
Lopeti Oto	*Right Wing*	Eric Rush
Yukio Motoki	*Centre*	Marc Ellis
Akira Yashida	*Centre*	Alama Ieremia
Yoshihito Yoshida	*Left Wing*	Jeff Wilson
Tsutomu Matsuda	*Fullback*	Glen Osborne
Takashi Akatsuka	*Reserves*	Jamie Joseph

Score: New Zealand 145 (M. Ellis 6, E. Rush 3, J. Wilson 3, R. Brooke 2, G. Osborne 2, S. Culhane, C. Dowd, P. Henderson, A. Ieremia, R. Loe tries; S. Culhane, 20 con) defeated Japan 17 (H. Kajihara 2 tries; K. Hirose 2 con, pen).

Pool C
Ireland 24–23 Wales
Date: June 4, 1995.
Venue: Ellis Park, Johannesburg.
Referee: Ian Rogers (South Africa).

Ireland	Position	Wales
Gary Halpin	*Prop*	John Davies
Terry Kingston (c)	*Hooker*	Jonathan Humphreys
Nick Popplewell	*Prop*	Mike Griffiths
Neil Francis	*Lock*	Derwyn Jones
Gabriel Fulcher	*Lock*	Gareth Llewllyn
David Corkery	*Flanker*	Stuart Davies
Denis McBride	*Flanker*	Hemi Taylor
Paddy Johns	*Number 8*	Emyr Lewis
Niall Hogan	*Scrum-half*	Robert Jones
Eric Elwood	*Fly-half*	Adrian Davies
Simon Geoghegan	*Right Wing*	Ieuan Evans
Jonathan Bell	*Centre*	Mike Hall (c)
Brendan Mullin	*Centre*	Neil Jenkins
Richard Wallace	*Left Wing*	Gareth Thomas
Conor O'Shea	*Fullback*	Tony Clement
Eddie Halvey	*Reserves*	Ricky Evans

Score: Ireland 24 (E. Halvey, D. McBride, N. Popplewell tries; E. Elwood 3 con, pen) defeated Wales 23 (J. Humphreys, H. Taylor tries; N. Jenkins 2 con, 2 pen; A. Davies drop-goal).

Pool D — France 38–10 Tonga

Date: May 26, 1995.
Venue: Loftus Versfeld, Pretoria.
Referee: Steve Lander (England).

France	Position	Tonga
Louis Armary	Prop	Saili Feao
Jean-Michel Gonzales	Hooker	Fololisi Masila
Philippe Gallart	Prop	Tu'akalua Fukofuka
Olivier Brouzet	Lock	Willie Lose
Olivier Merle	Lock	Falamani Mafi
Abdelatif Benazzi	Flanker	'Ipolito Fenukitau
Philippe Benetton	Flanker	Feleti Mahoni
Marc Cecillon	Number 8	Mana 'Otai (c)
Aubin Hueber	Scrum-half	Manu Vunipola
Yann Delaigue	Fly-half	'Elisi Vunipola
Emile Ntamack	Right Wing	Alaska Taufa
Thierry Lacroix	Centre	Peneili Latu
Philippe Sella	Centre	Unuoi Va'enuku
Philippe Saint-Andre (c)	Left Wing	Tevita Va'enuku
Jean-Luc Sadourny	Fullback	Sateki Tuipulotu
Laurent Cabannes	Reserves	'Inoke Afeaki, Fe'ao Vunipola

Score: France 38 (T. Lacroix 2, A. Hueber, P. Saint-Andre tries; T. Lacroix 3 con, 3 pen; Y. Delaigue drop-goal) defeated Tonga 10 (T. Va'enuku try; S. Tuipulotu con, pen).

Pool D — Scotland 89–0 Ivory Coast

Date: May 26, 1995.
Venue: Olympia Park, Rustenburg.
Referee: Felise Vito (Western Samoa).

Scotland	Position	Ivory Coast
Paul Burnell	Prop	Ernest Bley
Kevin McKenzie	Hooker	Eduard Angoran
Peter Wright	Prop	Toussaint Djehi
Stewart Campbell	Lock	Gilbert Bado
Doddie Weir	Lock	Amidou Kone
Ian Smith	Flanker	Isimaila Lassissi
Peter Walton	Flanker	Patrice Pere
Rob Wainwright	Number 8	Djakaria Sanoko
Bryan Redpath	Scrum-half	Frederic Dupont
Craig Chalmers	Fly-half	Athananse Dali (c)
Craig Joiner	Right Wing	Paulin Bouazo
Graham Shiel	Centre	Lucien Niakou
Tony Stanger	Centre	Jean Sathiq
Kenny Logan	Left Wing	Celestin N'Gabala
Gavin Hastings (c)	Fullback	Victor Kouassi
N/A	Reserves	Max Brito, Abubacar Camara, Alfred Okou

Score: Scotland 89 (G. Hastings 4, K. Logan 2, P. Walton 2, C. Chalmers, T. Stanger, P. Burnell, P. Wright, G. Shiel tries; G. Hastings 9 con, 2 pen) defeated Ivory Coast 0.

Scotland 41–5 Tonga

Pool D

Date: May 30, 1995.
Venue: Loftus Versfeld, Pretoria.
Referee: Barry Leask (Australia).

Scotland	Position	Tonga
Dave Hilton	*Prop*	Saili Feao
Kenny Milne	*Hooker*	Fe'ao Vunipola
Peter Wright	*Prop*	Tu'akalua Fukofuka
Damian Cronin	*Lock*	Pouvalu Latukefu
Doddie Weir	*Lock*	Willie Lose
Iain Morrison	*Flanker*	'Inoke Afeaki
Rob Wainwright	*Flanker*	'Ipolito Fenukitau
Eric Peters	*Number 8*	Mana 'Otai (c)
Derrick Patterson	*Scrum-half*	Manu Vunipola
Craig Chalmers	*Fly-half*	'Elisi Vunipola
Craig Joiner	*Right Wing*	Alaska Taufa
Scott Hastings	*Centre*	Peneili Latu
Ian Jardine	*Centre*	Unuoi Va'enuku
Kenny Logan	*Left Wing*	Tevita Va'enuku
Gavin Hastings (c)	*Fullback*	Sateki Tuipulotu
Paul Burnell	*Reserves*	Nafe Tufui, Etuini Talaka

Score: Scotland 41 (G. Hastings, S. Hastings, E. Peters tries; G. Hastings con, 8 pen) defeated Tonga 5 (I. Fenukitau try).

France 54–18 Ivory Coast

Pool D

Date: May 30, 1995.
Venue: Olympia Park, Rustenberg.
Referee: Han Moon-Soo (South Korea).

France	Position	Ivory Coast
Laurent Benezech	*Prop*	Toussaint Djehi
Marc de Rougemont	*Hooker*	Achille Niamien
Christian Califano	*Prop*	Jean-Pasca Ezoua
Olivier Brouzet	*Lock*	Djakaria Sanoko
Olivier Roumat	*Lock*	Ble Aka
Laurent Cabannes	*Flanker*	Alfred Okou
Arnaud Costes	*Flanker*	Patrice Pere
Abdelatif Benazzi	*Number 8*	Isimaila Lassissi
Guy Accoceberry	*Scrum-half*	Frederic Dupont
Yann Delaigue	*Fly-half*	Abubacar Camara
Philippe Saint-Andre (c)	*Right Wing*	Max Brito
Thierry Lacroix	*Centre*	Lucien Niakou
Franck Mesnel	*Centre*	Jean Sathiq (c)
William Techoueyres	*Left Wing*	A. Soulama
Sebastian Viars	*Fullback*	Victor Kouassi
Philippe Benetton, Christophe Deylaud	*Reserves*	Eduard Angoran, Ernest Bley, Paulin Bouazo, Amidou Kone

Score: France 54 (T. Lacroix 2, G. Accoceberry, A. Benazzi, A. Costes, P. Saint-Andre, W. Techoueyres, S. Viars tries; C. Deylaud 2 con, T. Lacroix 2 con, 2 pen) defeated Ivory Coast 18 (A. Camara, A. Soulama tries; V. Kouassi con, 2 pen).

Pool D

France 22–19 Scotland

Date: June 3, 1995.
Venue: Loftus Versfeld, Pretoria.
Referee: Wayne Erickson (Australia).

France	Position	Scotland
Laurent Benezech	*Prop*	Dave Hilton
Jean-Michel Gonzales	*Hooker*	Kenny Milne
Christian Califano	*Prop*	Peter Wright
Olivier Merle	*Lock*	Damian Cronin
Olivier Roumat	*Lock*	Doddie Weir
Arnaud Costes	*Flanker*	Iain Morrison
Laurent Cabannes	*Flanker*	Rob Wainwright
Philippe Benetton	*Number 8*	Eric Peters
Guy Accoceberry	*Scrum-half*	Bryan Redpath
Christophe Deylaud	*Fly-half*	Craig Chalmers
Emile Ntamack	*Right Wing*	Craig Joiner
Thierry Lacroix	*Centre*	Scott Hastings
Franck Mesnel	*Centre*	Graham Shiel
Philippe Saint-Andre (c)	*Left Wing*	Kenny Logan
Jean-Luc Sadourny	*Fullback*	Gavin Hastings (c)
Marc Cecillon, Aubin Hueber	*Reserves*	Paul Burnell, Ian Jardine

Score: France 22 (E. Ntamack try; T. Lacroix con, 5 pen) defeated Scotland 19 (R. Wainwright try; G. Hastings con, 4 pen).

Pool D

Tonga 29–11 Ivory Coast

Date: June 3, 1995.
Venue: Olympia Park, Rustenberg.
Referee: Don Reordan (United States).

Tonga	Position	Ivory Coast
Tu'akalua Fukofuka	*Prop*	Ernest Bley
Fe'ao Vunipola	*Hooker*	Eduard Angoran
Etuini Talakai	*Prop*	Toussaint Djehi
Pouvalu Latukefu	*Lock*	Gilbert Bado
Falamani Mafi	*Lock*	Soumalia Kone
'Inoke Afeaki	*Flanker*	Alfred Okou
Willie Lose	*Flanker*	Patrice Pere
Mana 'Otai (c)	*Number 8*	Isimaila Lassissi
Nafe Tufui,	*Scrum-half*	Frederic Dupont
'Elisi Vunipola	*Fly-half*	Abubacar Camara
Peneili Latu	*Right Wing*	Max Brito
Simana Mafile'o	*Centre*	Lucien Niakou
Unuoi Va'enuku	*Centre*	Jean Sathiq (c)
Tevita Va'enuku	*Left Wing*	ASoulama
Sateki Tuipulotu	*Fullback*	Victor Kouassi
Taipa Isitolo, Takau Lutua, Feleti Fakaongo	*Reserves*	Djakaria Sanoko, Athanase Dali, Thierry Kouame Daniel Quansah

Score: Tonga 29 (P. Latukefu, M. 'Otai, S. Tuipulotu tries, penalty try; S. Tuipulotu 3 con, pen) defeated Ivory Coast 11 (A. Okou try; A. Dali 2 pen).

Quarter-final — France 36–12 Ireland

Date: June 10, 1995.
Venue: King's Park, Durban.
Referee: Ed Morrison (England).

France	Position	Ireland
Louis Armary	*Prop*	Gary Halpin
Jean-Michel Gonzales	*Hooker*	Terry Kingston (c)
Christian Califano	*Prop*	Nick Popplewell
Olivier Merle	*Lock*	Neil Francis
Olivier Roumat	*Lock*	Gabriel Fulcher
Abdelatif Benazzi	*Flanker*	David Corkery
Laurent Cabannes	*Flanker*	Denis McBride
Marc Cecillon	*Number 8*	Paddy Johns
Aubin Hueber	*Scrum-half*	Niall Hogan
Christophe Deylaud	*Fly-half*	Eric Elwood
Emile Ntamack	*Right Wing*	Simon Geoghegan
Thierry Lacroix	*Centre*	Jonathan Bell
Philippe Sella	*Centre*	Brendan Mullin
Philippe Saint-Andre (c)	*Left Wing*	Darragh O'Mahony
Jean-Luc Sadourny	*Fullback*	Conor O'Shea
N/A	*Reserves*	Eddie Halvey

Score: France 36 (E. Ntamack, P. Saint-Andre tries; T. Lacroix con, 8 pen) defeated Ireland 12 (E. Elwood 4 pen).

Quarter-final — South Africa 42–14 Western Samoa

Date: June 10, 1995.
Venue: Ellis Park, Johannesburg.
Referee: Jim Fleming (Scotland).

South Africa	Position	Western Samoa
Os Du Randt	*Prop*	George Latu
Chris Rossouw	*Hooker*	Tala Leiasamaiva'o
Balie Swart	*Prop*	Mike Mika
Mark Andrews	*Lock*	Lio Falaniko
Kobus Wiese	*Lock*	Saini Lemamea
Ruben Kruger	*Flanker*	Junior Paramore
Francois Pienaar (c)	*Flanker*	Shem Tatupu
Rudolf Streauli	*Number 8*	Pat Lam (c)
Joost van der Westhuizen	*Scrum-half*	Tu Nu'uali'itia
Hennie leRoux	*Fly-half*	Fata Sini
Gavin Johnson	*Right Wing*	George Harder
Japie Mulder	*Centre*	Tupo Fa'amasino
Christiaan Scholtz	*Centre*	To'o Vaega
Chester Williams	*Left Wing*	Brian Lima
Andre Joubert	*Fullback*	Mike Umaga
Naka Drotske, Krynauw Otto, Adriaan Richter, Brendan Venter	*Reserves*	Peter Fatialofa, Brendan Reidy, Fereti Tuilagi, Sila Vaifale

Score: South Africa 42 (C. Williams 4, M. Andrews, C. Rossouw tries; G. Johnson 3 con, 2 pen) defeated Western Samoa 14 (T. Nu'uali'itia, S. Tatupu tries; T. Fa'amasino 2 con).

Quarter-final **Australia 22–25 England**

Date: June 11, 1995.
Venue: Newlands, Cape Town.
Referee: David Bishop (New Zealand).

Australia	Position	England
Dan Crowley	*Prop*	Jason Leonard
Phil Kearns	*Hooker*	Brian Moore
Ewen McKenzie	*Prop*	Victor Ubogu
John Eales	*Lock*	Martin Bayfield
Rod McCall	*Lock*	Martin Johnson
Willie Ofahengaue	*Flanker*	Ben Clarke
David Wilson	*Flanker*	Tim Rodber
Tim Gavin	*Number 8*	Dean Richards
George Gregan	*Scrum-half*	Dewi Morris
Michael Lynagh (c)	*Fly-half*	Rob Andrew
David Campese	*Right Wing*	Rory Underwood
Tim Horan	*Centre*	Will Carling (c)
Jason Little	*Centre*	Jeremy Guscott
Damian Smith	*Left Wing*	Tony Underwood
Matthew Burke	*Fullback*	Mike Catt
N/A	*Reserves*	Steve Ojomoh

Score: England 25 (T. Underwood try; R. Andrew con, 5 pen, 1 drop-goal) defeated Australia 22 (D. Smith try; M. Lynagh con, 5 pen).

Quarter-final **New Zealand 48–30 Scotland**

Date: June 11, 1995.
Venue: Loftus Versfeld, Pretoria.
Referee: Derek Bevan (Wales).

New Zealand	Position	Scotland
Olo Brown	*Prop*	Dave Hilton
Sean Fitzpatrick (c)	*Hooker*	Kenny Milne
Richard Loe	*Prop*	Peter Wright
Robin Brooke	*Lock*	Damian Cronin
Ian Jones	*Lock*	Doddie Weir
Jamie Joseph	*Flanker*	Iain Morrison
Josh Kronfeld	*Flanker*	Rob Wainwright
Zinzan Brooke	*Number 8*	Eric Peters
Graeme Bachop	*Scrum-half*	Bryan Redpath
Andrew Mehrtens	*Fly-half*	Craig Chalmers
Marc Ellis	*Right Wing*	Craig Joiner
Frank Bunce	*Centre*	Scott Hastings
Walter Little	*Centre*	Graham Shiel
Jonah Lomu	*Left Wing*	Kenny Logan
Jeff Wilson	*Fullback*	Gavin Hastings (c)
N/A	*Reserves*	Stewart Campbell, Ian Jardine

Score: New Zealand 48 (W. Little 2, F. Bunce, S. Fitzpatrick, J. Lomu, A. Mehrtens tries; A. Mehrtens 6 con, 2 pen) defeated Scotland 30 (G. Weir 2, S. Hastings tries; G. Hastings 3 con, 3 pen).

Semi-final — South Africa 19–15 France

Date: June 17, 1995.
Venue: King's Park, Durban.
Referee: Derek Bevan (Wales).

South Africa	Position	France
Os Du Randt	*Prop*	Louis Armary
Chris Rossouw	*Hooker*	Jean-Michel Gonzales
Balie Swart	*Prop*	Christian Califano
Hannes Strydom	*Lock*	Olivier Merle
Kobus Wiese	*Lock*	Olivier Roumat
Ruben Kruger	*Flanker*	Abdelatif Benazzi
Francois Pienaar (c)	*Flanker*	Laurent Cabannes
Mark Andrews	*Number 8*	Marc Cecillon
Joost van der Westhuizen	*Scrum-half*	Fabien Galthie
Joel Stransky	*Fly-half*	Christophe Deylaud
James Small	*Right Wing*	Emile Ntamack
Hennie leRoux	*Centre*	Thierry Lacroix
Japie Mulder	*Centre*	Philippe Sella
Chester Williams	*Left Wing*	Philippe Saint-Andre (c)
Andre Joubert	*Fullback*	Jean-Luc Sadourny
Johan Roux	*Reserves*	N/A

Score: South Africa 19 (R. Kruger try; J. Stransky con, 4 pen) defeated France 15 (T. Lacroix 5 pen).

Semi-final — England 29–45 New Zealand

Date: June 18, 1995.
Venue: Newlands, Cape Town.
Referee: Stephen Hilditch (Ireland).

England	Position	New Zealand
Jason Leonard	*Prop*	Olo Brown
Brian Moore	*Hooker*	Sean Fitzpatrick (c)
Victor Ubogu	*Prop*	Craig Dowd
Martin Bayfield	*Lock*	Robin Brooke
Martin Johnson	*Lock*	Ian Jones
Ben Clarke	*Flanker*	Mike Brewer
Tim Rodber	*Flanker*	Josh Kronfeld
Dean Richards	*Number 8*	Zinzan Brooke
Dewi Morris	*Scrum-half*	Graeme Bachop
Rob Andrew	*Fly-half*	Andrew Mehrtens
Rory Underwood	*Right Wing*	Jonah Lomu
Will Carling (c)	*Centre*	Frank Bunce
Jeremy Guscott	*Centre*	Walter Little
Tony Underwood	*Left Wing*	Jeff Wilson
Mike Catt	*Fullback*	Glen Osborne

Score: New Zealand 45 (J. Lomu 4, G. Bachop, J. Kronfeld tries; A. Mehrtens 3 con, pen, drop-goal, Z. Brooke drop-goal) defeated England 29 (W. Carling 2, R. Underwood 2 tries; R. Andrew 3 con, 1 pen).

3rd Place Play-off   England 9–19 France

Date: June 22, 1995.
Venue: Loftus Versfeld, Pretoria.
Referee: David Bishop (New Zealand).

England	Position	France
Jason Leonard	*Prop*	Laurent Benezech
Brian Moore	*Hooker*	Jean-Michel Gonzales
Victor Ubogu	*Prop*	Christian Califano
Martin Bayfield	*Lock*	Olivier Merle
Martin Johnson	*Lock*	Olivier Roumat
Ben Clarke	*Flanker*	Abdelatif Benazzi
Tim Rodber	*Flanker*	Laurent Cabannes
Steve Ojomoh	*Number 8*	Albert Cigagna
Dewi Morris	*Scrum-half*	Fabien Galthie
Rob Andrew	*Fly-half*	Franck Mesnel
Ian Hunter	*Right Wing*	Emile Ntamack
Will Carling (c)	*Centre*	Thierry Lacroix
Jeremy Guscott	*Centre*	Philippe Sella
Rory Underwood	*Left Wing*	Philippe Saint-Andre (c)
Mike Catt	*Fullback*	Jean-Luc Sadourny
N/A	*Reserves*	Olivier Brouzet

Score: France 19 (E. Ntamack, O. Roumat tries; T. Lacroix 3 pen) defeated England 9 (R. Andrew 3 pen).

The Final   South Africa 15–12 New Zealand

Date: June 24, 1995.
Venue: Ellis Park, Johannesburg.
Referee: Ed Morrison (England).

South Africa	Position	New Zealand
Os Du Randt	*Prop*	Olo Brown
Chris Rossouw	*Hooker*	Sean Fitzpatrick (c)
Balie Swart	*Prop*	Craig Dowd
Hannes Strydom	*Lock*	Robin Brooke
Kobus Wiese	*Lock*	Ian Jones
Ruben Kruger	*Flanker*	Mike Brewer
François Pienaar (c)	*Flanker*	Josh Kronfeld
Mark Andrews	*Number 8*	Zinzan Brooke
Joost van der Westhuizen	*Scrum-half*	Graeme Bachop
Joel Stransky	*Fly-half*	Andrew Mehrtens
James Small	*Right Wing*	Jonah Lomu
Hennie leRoux	*Centre*	Frank Bunce
Japie Mulder	*Centre*	Walter Little
Chester Williams	*Left Wing*	Jeff Wilson
Andre Joubert	*Fullback*	Glen Osborne
Gary Pagel, Rudolf Straeuli, Brendan Venter	*Reserves*	Marc Ellis, Jamie Joseph, Richard Loe, Ant Strachan

Score: South Africa 15 (J. Stransky 3 pen, 2 drop-goal) defeated New Zealand 12 (A. Mehrtens 3 pen, 1 drop-goal) after extra time.

Rugby World Cup 1999
Tournament Statistics

Pool Stage – Final Standings

Pool A							
Team	Wins	Draws	Losses	For	Against	Tries	Points
South Africa	3	0	0	132	35	18	6
Scotland	2	0	1	120	58	15	4
Uruguay	1	0	2	42	97	4	2
Spain	0	0	3	18	122	0	0

- South Africa advanced to the quarter-finals. Scotland advanced to a play-off.

Pool B							
Team	Wins	Draws	Losses	For	Against	Tries	Points
New Zealand	3	0	0	176	28	22	6
England	2	0	1	184	47	22	4
Tonga	1	0	2	48	171	4	2
Italy	0	0	3	35	196	2	0

- New Zealand advanced to the quarter-finals. England advanced to a play-off.

Pool C							
Team	Wins	Draws	Losses	For	Against	Tries	Points
France	3	0	0	108	52	13	6
Fiji	2	0	1	124	68	14	4
Canada	1	0	2	114	82	12	2
Namibia	0	0	3	28	186	4	0

- France advanced to the quarter-finals. Fiji advanced to a play-off.

Pool D							
Team	Wins	Draws	Losses	For	Against	Tries	Points
Wales	2	0	1	118	71	14	4
Argentina	2	0	1	83	51	3	4
Samoa	2	0	1	97	72	11	4
Japan	0	0	3	36	140	2	0

- Wales advanced to the quarter-finals. Argentina and Samoa advanced to a play-off.

Pool E							
Team	Wins	Draws	Losses	For	Against	Tries	Points
Australia	3	0	0	135	31	19	6
Ireland	2	0	1	100	45	12	4
Romania	1	0	2	50	126	5	2
USA	0	0	3	52	135	5	0

- Australia advanced to the quarter-finals. Ireland advanced to a play-off.

Pool Stage – Results Snapshot

Pool A		
Uruguay	27–15	Spain
South Africa	46–29	Scotland
Scotland	43–12	Uruguay
South Africa	47–3	Spain
South Africa	39–3	Uruguay
Scotland	48–0	Spain

Pool B		
England	67–7	Italy
New Zealand	45–9	Tonga
New Zealand	30–16	England
Tonga	28–25	Italy
New Zealand	101–3	Italy
England	101–10	Tonga

Pool C		
Fiji	67–18	Namibia
France	33–20	Canada
France	47–13	Namibia
Fiji	38–22	Canada
Canada	72–11	Namibia
France	28–19	Fiji

Pool D		
Wales	23–18	Argentina
Samoa	43–9	Japan
Wales	64–15	Japan
Argentina	32–16	Samoa
Samoa	38–31	Wales
Argentina	33–12	Japan

Pool E		
Ireland	53–8	USA
Australia	57–9	Romania
Romania	27–25	USA
Australia	23–3	Ireland
Australia	55–19	USA
Ireland	44–14	Romania

Quarter-final Play-offs		
England	45–24	Fiji
Scotland	35–20	Samoa
Argentina	28–24	Ireland

Rugby World Cup 1999: The Finals

Quarter-finals

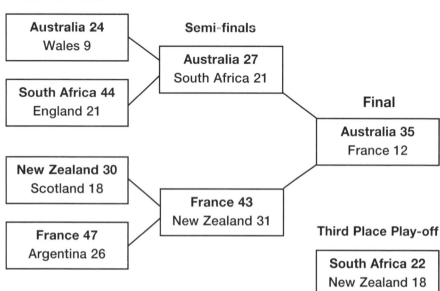

Semi-finals

Quarter-finals

Australia 24
Wales 9

South Africa 44
England 21

New Zealand 30
Scotland 18

France 47
Argentina 26

Semi-finals

Australia 27
South Africa 21

France 43
New Zealand 31

Final

Australia 35
France 12

Third Place Play-off

South Africa 22
New Zealand 18

Detailed Results

Pool A — Spain 15–27 Uruguay

Date: October 2, 1999.
Venue: Netherdale, Galashiels.
Referee: Chris White (England).

Spain	Position	Uruguay
Jordi Camps Riba	Prop	Pablo Lemoine
Fernando de la CallePozo	Hooker	Diego Lamelas
Jose Ignacio Zapatero Ferreras	Prop	Rodrigo Sanchez
Sergio Souto Vidal	Lock	Juan Carlos Bado
Jose Miguel Villau Cabeza	Lock	Mario Lame
Jose Diaz	Flanker	Nicolas Brignoni
Carlos Souto Vidal	Flanker	Martin Panizza
Alberto Malo Navio (c)	Number 8	Diego Ormaechea (c)
Jaime Alonso Lasheras	Scrum-half	Federico Sciarra
Andrei Kovalenco	Fly-half	Diego Aquirre
Rafael Bastide Gutierrez	Right Wing	Pablo Castabile
A. E. Fernandez-Valderam	Centre	Martin Mendaro
Sebastien Loubsens	Centre	Pedro Vecino
Oriol Ripol Fortuny	Left Wing	Martin Ferres
M. A. Frechilla Manrique	Fullback	Alfonso Cardoso
Oscar Astarloa Uriarte, Alfonso Mata Suarez, Diego Zarzosa Pena	Reserves	Francisco de los Santos, Nicolas Grille, Juan Menchaca, Agustin Ponce de Leon, Fernando Sosa Diaz, Guillermo Storace

Score: Uruguay 27 (A. Cardoso, J. Menchaca, D. Ormaechea tries, penalty try; D. Aquirre con, pen, F. Sciarra con) defeated Spain 15 (A. Kovalenco 5 pen).

Pool A — Scotland 29–46 South Africa

Date: October 3, 1999.
Venue: Murrayfield, Edinburgh.
Referee: Colin Hawke (New Zealand).

Scotland	Position	South Africa
George Graham	Prop	Os Du Randt
Gordon Bulloch	Hooker	Naka Drotske
Tom Smith	Prop	Cobus Visagie
Stuart Grimes	Lock	Mark Andrews
Scott Murray	Lock	Albert van den Berg
Budge Pountney	Flanker	Johan Erasmus
Martin Leslie	Flanker	Andre Venter
Gordon Simpson	Number 8	Bobby Skinstad
Gary Armstrong (c)	Scrum-half	Joost van der Westhuizen (c)
Gregor Townsend	Fly-half	Jannie de Beer
Kenny Logan	Right Wing	Deon Kayser
John Leslie	Centre	Robbie Fleck
Alan Tait	Centre	Brendan Venter
Cammie Murray	Left Wing	Pieter Rossouw
Glenn Metcalfe	Fullback	Percy Montgomery
Dave Hilton, Jamie Mayer, Peter Walton, Doddie Weir	Reserves	Ollie le Roux, Krynauw Otto, Breyton Paulse

Score: South Africa 46 (R. Fleck, D. Kayser, O. le Roux, J. van der Westhuizen, B. Venter, A. Venter tries; J. de Beer 5 con, 2 pen) defeated Scotland 29 (M. Leslie, A. Tait tries; K. Logan 2,con, 4 pen, G. Townsend drop-goal).

Pool A — Scotland 43–12 Uruguay

Date: October 8, 1999.
Venue: Murrayfield, Edinburgh.
Referee: Stuart Dickinson (Australia).

Scotland	Position	Uruguay
George Graham	Prop	Pablo Lemoine
Gordon Bulloch	Hooker	Diego Lamelas
Tom Smith	Prop	Rodrigo Sanchez
Stuart Grimes	Lock	Juan Carlos Bado
Scott Murray	Lock	Mario Lame
Budge Pountney	Flanker	Nicolas Brignoni
Martin Leslie	Flanker	Martin Panizza
Gordon Simpson	Number 8	Diego Ormaechea (c)
Gary Armstrong (c)	Scrum-half	Federico Sciarra
Gregor Townsend	Fly-half	Diego Aquirre
Kenny Logan	Right Wing	Pablo Castabile
Jamie Mayer	Centre	Martin Mendaro
Alan Tait	Centre	Pedro Vecino
Cammie Murray	Left Wing	Juan Menchaca
Glenn Metcalfe	Fullback	Alfonso Cardoso
Shaun Longstaff, Dave Hilton, Bryan Redpath, Robbie Russell, Peter Walton	Reserves	Eduardo Berruti, Francisco de los Santos, Nicolas Grille, Agustin Ponce de Leon, Fernando Sosa Diaz, Guillermo Storace, Jose Viana

Score: Scotland 43 (G. Metcalfe, G. Armstrong, M. Leslie, R. Russell, G. Simpson, G. Townsend tries; K. Logan 5 con, pen) defeated Uruguay 12 (D. Aquirre 3 pen, F. Sciarra pen).

Pool A — South Africa 47–3 Spain

Date: October 10, 1999.
Venue: Murrayfield, Edinburgh.
Referee: Paul Honiss (New Zealand).

South Africa	Position	Spain
Adrian Garvey	Prop	Jordi Camps Riba
Chris Rossouw	I looker	Diego Zarzosa Pena
Ollie le Roux	Prop	Jose Ignacio Zapatero Ferreras
Krynauw Otto	Lock	Oscar Astarloa Uriarte
Fritz van Heerden	Lock	Jose Miguel Villau Cabeza
Ruben Kruger	Flanker	Jose Diaz
Andre Vos (c)	Flanker	Carlos Souto Vidal
Anton Leonard	Number 8	Alberto Malo Navio (c)
Werner Swanepoel	Scrum-half	Aratz Gallastegui Sodupe
Jannie de Beer	Fly-half	Aitor Etxeberria de la Rosa
Kaya Malotana	Right Wing	M. A. Frechilla Manrique
Wayne Julies	Centre	Fernando Diez Molina
Pieter Muller	Centre	Alberto Socias Olmos
Stefan Terblanche	Left Wing	Jose Ignacio Inchausti Bravo
Breyton Paulse	Fullback	Francisco Puertas Soto
Naka Drotske, Os Du Randt, Deon Kayser, Bobby Skinstad, Joost van der Westhuizen	Reserves	Fernando de la Calle Pozo, Luis Javier Martinez Villanueva, Alfonso Mata Suarez, Victor Torres Funes, Ferran Velazco Querol

Score: South Africa 47 (A. Vos 2, A. Leonard, P. Muller, B. Skinstad, W. Swanepoel, tries; penalty try; J. de Beer 6 con) defeated Spain 3 (F. Velazco Querol pen).

Pool A
South Africa 39–3 Uruguay

Date: October 15, 1999.
Venue: Hampden Park, Glasgow.
Referee: Peter Marshall (Australia).

South Africa	Position	Uruguay
Os Du Randt	*Prop*	Pablo Lemoine
Naka Drotske	*Hooker*	Diego Lamelas
Cobus Visagie	*Prop*	Rodrigo Sanchez
Mark Andrews	*Lock*	Juan Carlos Bado
Krynauw Otto	*Lock*	Mario Lame
Johan Erasmus	*Flanker*	Nicolas Grille
Andre Venter	*Flanker*	Martin Panizza
Bobby Skinstad	*Number 8*	Diego Ormaechea (c)
Joost van der Westhuizen (c)	*Scrum-half*	Fernando Sosa Diaz
Jannie de Beer	*Fly-half*	Diego Aquirre
Deon Kayser	*Right Wing*	Pablo Castabile
Robbie Fleck	*Centre*	Fernando Paullier
Brendan Venter	*Centre*	Pedro Vecino
Pieter Rossouw	*Left Wing*	Juan Menchaca
Percy Montgomery	*Fullback*	Alfonso Cardoso
Ollie leRoux, Albert van den Berg	*Reserves*	Sebastian Aguirre, Juan Alzueta, Eduardo Berruti, Nicolas Brignoni, Guillermo Storace, Jose Viana

Score: South Africa 39 (A. van den Berg 2, R. Fleck, D. Kayser, J. van der Westhuizen tries; J. de Beer 4 con, 2 pen) defeated Uruguay 3 (D. Aquirre pen).

Pool A
Scotland 48–0 Spain

Date: October 16, 1999.
Venue: Murrayfield, Edinburgh.
Referee: Clayton Thomas (Wales).

Scotland	Position	Spain
Paul Burnell	*Prop*	Victor Torres Funes
Robbie Russell	*Hooker*	Diego Zarzosa Pena
Dave Hilton	*Prop*	Jose Ignacio Zapatero Ferreras
Andy Reed	*Lock*	Oscar Astarloa Uriarte
Doddie Weir	*Lock*	Jose Miguel Villau Cabeza
Cameron Mather	*Flanker*	Jose Diaz
Peter Walton	*Flanker*	Carlos Souto Vidal
Stuart Reid	*Number 8*	Alfonso Mata Suarez
Bryan Redpath (c)	*Scrum-half*	Aratz Gallastegui Sodupe
Duncan Hodge	*Fly-half*	Andrei Kovalenco
Shaun Longstaff	*Right Wing*	M. A. Frechilla Manrique
Jamie Mayer	*Centre*	A. E. Fernandez-Valderam (c)
James McLaren	*Centre*	Sebastien Loubsens
Cammie Murray	*Left Wing*	Jose Ignacio Inchausti Bravo
Chris Patterson	*Fullback*	Francisco Puertas Soto
Ian Fairley, Gregor Townsend	*Reserves*	Fernando de la Calle Pozo, Javier Martine Villanueva, Agustin Malet Raga, Alberto Socias Olmos, Steve Tuineau Iloa, F. V. Querol

Score: Scotland 48 (C. Mather 2, S. Longstaff, D. Hodge, J. McLaren, C. Murray tries, penalty try; D. Hodge 5 con, pen) defeated Spain 0.

Pool B — England 67–7 Italy

Date: October 2, 1999.
Venue: Twickenham, London.
Referee: Andre Watson (South Africa).

England	Position	Italy
Jason Leonard	Prop	Franco Properzi-Curti
Richard Cockerill	Hooker	Alessandro Moscardi
Phil Vickery	Prop	Federico Pucciariello
Danny Grewcock	Lock	Walter Cristofoletto
Martin Johnson (c)	Lock	Mark Giacheri
Neil Back	Flanker	Mauro Bergamasco
Richard Hill	Flanker	Massimo Giovanelli (c)
Lawrence Dallaglio	Number 8	Orazio Arancio
Matt Dawson	Scrum-half	Alessandro Troncon
Jonny Wilkinson	Fly-half	Diego Dominguez
Austin Healey	Right Wing	PaoloVaccari
Phil de Glanville	Centre	Luca Martin
Will Greenwood	Centre	Cristian Stoica
Dan Luger	Left Wing	Nicolas Zisti
Matt Perry	Fullback	Matt Pini
Nick Beal, Martin Corry, Darren Garforth, Phil Greening, Jeremy Guscott, Graham Rowntree	Reserves	Carlo Checchinato, Andrea de Rossi, Francesco Mazzariol, Nicola Mazzucato

Score: England 67 (N. Back, M. Corry, M. Dawson, P. de Glanville, R. Hill, D. Luger, M. Perry, J. Wilkinson tries; J. Wilkinson 6 con, 5 pen) defeated Italy 7 (D. Dominguez try, con).

Pool B — New Zealand 45–9 Tonga

Date: October 3, 1999.
Venue: Ashston Gate, Bristol.
Referee: Derek Bevan (Wales).

New Zealand	Position	Tonga
Carl Hoeft	Prop	Ta'u Fainga'anuku
Anton Oliver	Hooker	Fe'ao Vunipola
Kees Meeuws	Prop	Tevita Taumeopeau
Robin Brooke	Lock	Isi Fatani
Norm Maxwell	Lock	Benhur Kivalu
Josh Kronfeld	Flanker	Hese Fakatou
Reuben Thorne	Flanker	Jonathon Koloi
Taine Randell (c)	Number 8	Va'a Toloke
Justin Marshall	Scrum-half	Sililo Martens
Andrew Mehrtens	Fly-half	'Elisi Vunipola
Tana Umaga	Right Wing	Tauna'holo Taufahema
Christian Cullen	Centre	David Tiueti
Alama Ieremia	Centre	Semi Taupeaafe
Jonah Lomu	Left Wing	Fepiko Tatafu
Jeff Wilson	Fullback	Siua Taumalolo
Craig Dowd, Daryl Gibson, Byron Kelleher, Royce Willis	Reserves	Ngalu Taufo'ou, Isi Tapueluelu, Matt Te Pou, Sione Tuipulotu

Score: New Zealand 45 (J. Lomu 2, B. Kelleher, J. Kronfeld, N. Maxwell tries; A. Mehrtens 4 con, 4 pen) defeated Tonga 9 (S. Taumalolo 3 pen).

Pool B — England 16–30 New Zealand

Date: October 9, 1999.
Venue: Twickenham, London.
Referee: Peter Marshall (Australia).

England	Position	New Zealand
Jason Leonard	*Prop*	Craig Dowd
Richard Cockerill	*Hooker*	Anton Oliver
Phil Vickery	*Prop*	Carl Hoeft
Danny Grewcock	*Lock*	Robin Brooke
Martin Johnson (c)	*Lock*	Norm Maxwell
Neil Back	*Flanker*	Josh Kronfeld
Richard Hill	*Flanker*	Reuben Thorne
Lawrence Dallaglio	*Number 8*	Taine Randell (c)
Matt Dawson	*Scrum-half*	Justin Marshall
Jonny Wilkinson	*Fly-half*	Andrew Mehrtens
Austin Healey	*Right Wing*	Tana Umaga
Phil de Glanville	*Centre*	Christian Cullen
Jeremy Guscott	*Centre*	Alama Ieremia
Dan Luger	*Left Wing*	Jonah Lomu
Matt Perry	*Fullback*	Jeff Wilson
Martin Corry, Darren Garforth, Paul Grayson, Phil Greening, Tim Rodber	*Reserves*	Tony Brown, Greg Feek, Daryl Gibson, Byron Kelleher, Royce Willis

Score: New Zealand 30 (B. Kelleher, J. Lomu, J. Wilson tries; A. Mehrtens 3 con, 3 pen) defeated England 16 (P. de Glanville try; J. Wilkinson con, 3 pen).

Pool B — Italy 25–28 Tonga

Date: October 10, 1999.
Venue: Welford Road, Leicester.
Referee: David McHugh (Ireland).

Italy	Position	Tonga
Andrea Castellani	*Prop*	Ta'u Fainga'anuku
Alessandro Moscardi	*Hooker*	Latiume Maka
Alejandro Moreno	*Prop*	Ngalu Taufo'ou
Carlo Checchinato	*Lock*	Benhur Kivalu
Mark Giacheri	*Lock*	Falamani Mafi
Massimo Giovanelli (c)	*Flanker*	David Edwards
Stefano Saviozzi	*Flanker*	Jonathon Koloi
Carlo Caione	*Number 8*	Kati Tu'ipulotu
Alessandro Troncon	*Scrum-half*	Sililo Martens
Diego Dominguez	*Fly-half*	Brian Wooley
Fabio Roselli	*Right Wing*	Tauna'holo Taufahema
Sandro Ceppolino	*Centre*	Semi Taupeaafe
Cristian Stoica	*Centre*	'Elisi Vunipola (c)
Paolo Vaccari	*Left Wing*	Epi Taione
Matt Pini	*Fullback*	Siua Taumalolo
Andrea Moretti, Nicola Mazzucato	*Reserves*	David Tiueti, Isi Tapueluelu, Matt Te Pou, Isa Fatani

Score: Tonga 28 (I. Fatani, T. Taufahema, S. Tuipulotu tries; S. Tuipulotu 2 con, 2 pen, drop-goal) defeated Italy 25 (A. Moscardi try; D. Dominguez con, 6 pen).

Pool B — New Zealand 101–3 Italy

Date: October 14, 1999.
Venue: McAlpine Stadium, Huddersfield.
Referee: Jim Fleming (Scotland).

New Zealand	Position	Italy
Craig Dowd	*Prop*	Andrea Castellani
Mark Hammett	*Hooker*	Andrea Moretti
Greg Feek	*Prop*	Alejandro Moscardi
Ian Jones	*Lock*	Carlo Checchinato
Royce Willis	*Lock*	Mark Giacheri
Andrew Blowers	*Flanker*	Massimo Giovanelli (c)
Dylan Mika	*Flanker*	Stefano Saviozzi
Taine Randell (c)	*Number 8*	Carlo Caione
Byron Kelleher	*Scrum-half*	Alessandro Troncon
Tony Brown	*Fly-half*	Diego Dominguez
Glen Osborne	*Right Wing*	Paolo Vaccari
Pita Alatini	*Centre*	Sandro Ceppolino
Daryl Gibson	*Centre*	Cristian Stoica
Jonah Lomu	*Left Wing*	Nicolas Zisti
Jeff Wilson	*Fullback*	Matt Pini
Robin Brooke, Christian Cullen, Phys Duggan, Kees Meeuws, Scott Robertson	*Reserves*	Orazio Arancio, Walter Cristofoletto, Francesco Mazzariol, Nicola Mazzucato Alessandro Moscardi, Franco Properzi-Curti

Score: New Zealand 101 (J. Wilson 3, J. Lomu 2, G. Osborne 2, T. Brown, C. Cullen, D. Gibson, M. Hammett, D. Mika, T. Randell, S. Robertson tries; T. Brown 11 con, 3 pen) defeated Italy 3 (D. Dominguez 1 pen).

Pool B — England 101–10 Tonga

Date: October 15, 1999.
Venue: Twickenham, London.
Referee: Wayne Erickson (Australia).

England	Position	Tonga
Graham Rowntree	*Prop*	Ngalu Taufo'ou
Phil Greening	*Hooker*	Fe'ao Vunipola
Phil Vickery	*Prop*	Tevita Taumeopeau
Gareth Archer	*Lock*	Isi Fatani
Martin Johnson (c)	*Lock*	Benhur Kivalu
Richard Hill	*Flanker*	David Edwards
Joe Worsley	*Flanker*	Jonathon Koloi
Lawrence Dallaglio	*Number 8*	Kati Tu'ipulotu
Matt Dawson	*Scrum-half*	Sililo Martens
Paul Grayson	*Fly-half*	'Elisi Vunipola
Austin Healey	*Right Wing*	David Tiueti
Will Greenwood	*Centre*	Salesi Finau
Jeremy Guscott	*Centre*	Fepiko Tatafu
Dan Luger	*Left Wing*	Semi Taupeaafe
Matt Perry	*Fullback*	Sateki Tuipulotu
Nick Beal, Mike Catt, Richard Cockerill, Danny Grewcock	*Reserves*	Ta'u Fainga'anuku, Latiume Maka, Falamani Mafi, Isi Tapueluelu, Va'a Toloke, Sione Tuipulotu

Score: England 101 (P. Greening 2, W. Greenwood 2, J. Guscott 2, A. Healey 2, D. Luger 2, M. Dawson, R. Hill, M. Perry tries; P. Grayson 12 con, 4 pen) defeated Tonga 10 (T. Tiueti try; S. Tuipulotu con, pen).

Pool C — Fiji 67–18 Namibia

Date: October 1, 1999.
Venue: Stade Méditerranée, Béziers.
Referee: David McHugh (Ireland).

Fiji	Position	Namibia
Dan Rouse	*Prop*	Mario Jacobs
Greg Smith (c)	*Hooker*	Hugo Horn
Joeli Veitayaki	*Prop*	Joodt Opperman
Emori Katalau	*Lock*	Heino Senekal
Simon Raiwalui	*Lock*	Pieter Steyn
Alfi Mocelutu Vuivau	*Flanker*	Quinn Hough (c)
Apisai Naevo	*Flanker*	Jaco Olivier
Seta Tawake Naivaluwaqa	*Number 8*	Sean Furter
Jacob Rauluni	*Scrum-half*	Riaan Jantjies
Waisale Serevi	*Fly-half*	Johan Zaayman
Fero Lasagavibau	*Right Wing*	Dirk Farmer
Viliame Satala	*Centre*	Attie Samuelson
Waisake Sotutu	*Centre*	Schalk van der Merwe
Imanueli Tikomaimakogai	*Left Wing*	Deon Mouton
Alfred Uluinayau	*Fullback*	Lean van Dyk
Lawrence Little, Epeli Naituvau, Meli Nakauta, Koli Sewabu	*Reserves*	Andries Blaauw, Herman Lintvelt, Eben Smith, Johannes Theron, Glovin van Wyk, S. J. van Rensburg, F. van Rensburg

Score: Fiji 67 (F. Lasagavibau 2, E. Katalau, A. Mocelutu Vuivau, J. Rauluni, V. Satala, G. Smith, S. Tawake Naivaluwaqa, I. Tikomaimakogai tries; W. Serevi 8 con, 2 pen) defeated Namibia 18 (M. Jacobs, H. Senekal tries; L. van Dyk con, 2 pen).

Pool C — France 33–20 Canada

Date: October 2, 1999.
Venue: Stade Méditerranée, Béziers.
Referee: Brian Campsell (England).

France	Position	Canada
Christian Califano	*Prop*	Rod Snow
Raphael Ibanez (c)	*Hooker*	Pat Dunkley
Franck Tournaire	*Prop*	John Thiel
Abdelatif Benazzi	*Lock*	Mike James
Fabien Pelous	*Lock*	John Tait
Marc Lievremont	*Flanker*	Dan Baugh
Olivier Magne	*Flanker*	John Hutchinson
Christophe Juillet	*Number 8*	Al Charron
Pierre Mignoni	*Scrum-half*	Morgan Williams
Thomas Castaignede	*Fly-half*	Gareth Rees (c)
Xavier Garbajosa	*Right Wing*	Courtney Smith
Richard Dourthe	*Centre*	Scott Bryan
Stephane Glas	*Centre*	Dave Lougheed
Christophe Dominici	*Left Wing*	Winston Stanley
Ugo Mola	*Fullback*	Scott Stewart
Olivier Brouzet, Christophe Lamaison, Lionel Mallier, Emile Ntamack, Cedric Soulette, Stephane Castaignede	*Reserves*	Ryan Banks, Richard Bice, John Graf, Bobby Ross, Mike Schmid

Score: France 33 (T. Castaignede, S. Glas, O. Magne, E. Ntamack tries; R. Dourthe 2 con, 3 pen defeated Canada 20 (M. Williams 2 tries; G. Rees con, pen, B. Ross con, pen).

Pool C

France 47–13 Namibia

Date: October 8, 1999.
Venue: Parc Lescure, Bordeaux.
Referee: Chris White (England).

France	Position	Namibia
Christian Califano	*Prop*	Mario Jacobs
Raphael Ibanez (c)	*Hooker*	Hugo Horn
Franck Tournaire	*Prop*	Joodt Opperman
Olivier Brouzet	*Lock*	Heino Senekal
Fabien Pelous	*Lock*	Pieter Steyn
Marc Lievremont	*Flanker*	Quinn Hough (c)
Olivier Magne	*Flanker*	Thys van Rooyen
Thomas Lievremont	*Number 8*	Sean Furter
Pierre Mignoni	*Scrum-half*	Riaan Jantjies
Christophe Lamaison	*Fly-half*	Johan Zaayman
Philippe Bernat-Sallas	*Right Wing*	Attie Samuelson
Richard Dourthe	*Centre*	Schalk van der Merwe
Stephane Glas	*Centre*	Francois van Rensburg
Emile Ntamack	*Left Wing*	Lean van Dyk
Ugo Mola	*Fullback*	Glovin van Wyk
Abdelatif Benazzi, Arnaud Costes, Marc Dal Maso, Cedric Desbrosse, Xavier Garbajosa, Cedric Soulette, Stephane Castaignede	*Reserves*	Andries Blaauw, Herman Lintvelt, Cliff Loubscher, Eben Smith, Johannes Theron, S. J. van Rensburg

Score: France 47 (U. Mola 3, P. Bernat-Salles, E. Ntamack, P. Mignoni tries; R. Dourthe 4 con, 3 pen) defeated Namibia 13 (A. Samuelson try; L. van Dyk con, 2 pen).

Pool C

Fiji 38–22 Canada

Date: October 9, 1999.
Venue: Parc Lescure, Bordeaux.
Referee: Ed Morrison (England).

Fiji	Position	Canada
Dan Rouse	*Prop*	Rod Snow
Greg Smith (c)	*Hooker*	Pat Dunkley
Joeli Veitayaki	*Prop*	John Thiel
Emori Katalau	*Lock*	Mike James
Simon Raiwalui	*Lock*	John Tait
Ilie Tabua	*Flanker*	Dan Baugh
Seta Tawake Naivaluwaqa	*Flanker*	John Hutchinson
Alfi Mocelutu Vuivau	*Number 8*	Al Charron
Jacob Rauluni	*Scrum-half*	Morgan Williams
Nicky Little	*Fly-half*	Gareth Rees (c)
Fero Lasagavibau	*Right Wing*	Dave Lougheed
Viliame Satala	*Centre*	Scott Bryan
Waisake Sotutu	*Centre*	Kyle Nichols
Marika Vunibaka	*Left Wing*	Winston Stanley
Alfred Uluinayau	*Fullback*	Scott Stewart
Waisale Serevi, Apisai Naevo, Mosese Rauluni, Koli Sewabu	*Reserves*	Mark Cardinal, John Hutchinson, Duane Major

Score: Fiji 38 (V. Satala 2, F. Lasagavibau, M. Vunibaka tries; N. Little 3 con, 3 pen, drop goal) defeated Canada 22 (M. James try; G. Rees con, 4 pen, drop-goal).

Pool C — Canada 72–11 Namibia

Date: October 14, 1999.
Venue: Stade Municipal, Toulouse.
Referee: Andrew Cole (Australia).

Canada	Position	Namibia
Rod Snow	Prop	Joodt Opperman
Mark Cardinal	Hooker	Hugo Horn
John Thiel	Prop	Eben Smith
Mike James	Lock	Heino Senekal
John Tait	Lock	Pieter Steyn
Dan Baugh	Flanker	Quinn Hough (c)
John Hutchinson	Flanker	Thys van Rooyen
Al Charron	Number 8	Sean Furter
Morgan Williams	Scrum-half	Riaan Jantjies
Gareth Rees (c)	Fly-half	Johan Zaayman
Joe Pagano	Right Wing	Attie Samuelson
Dave Lougheed	Centre	Schalk van der Merwe
Kyle Nichols	Centre	Francois van Rensburg
Winston Stanley	Left Wing	Lean van Dyk
Scott Stewart	Fullback	Glovin van Wyk
Ryan Banks, Scott Bryan, Pat Dunkley, John Graf, Bobby Ross, Mike Schmid	Reserves	Andries Blaauw, Herman Lintvelt, Johannes Theron

Score: Canada 72 (K. Nichols 2, R. Snow 2, W. Stanley 2, A. Charron, B. Ross, M. Williams tries; G. Rees 9 con, 3 pen) defeated Namibia 11 (Q. Hough try; L. van Dyk 2 pen).

Pool C — France 28–19 Fiji

Date: October 16, 1999.
Venue: Stade Municipal, Toulouse.
Referee: Paddy O'Brien (New Zealand).

France	Position	Fiji
Christian Califano	Prop	Dan Rouse
Raphael Ibanez (c)	Hooker	Greg Smith (c)
Franck Tournaire	Prop	Joeli Veitayaki
Abdelatif Benazzi	Lock	Emori Katalau
Fabien Pelous	Lock	Simon Raiwalui
Marc Lievremont	Flanker	Ilie Tabua
Olivier Magne	Flanker	Seta Tawake Naivaluwaqa
Christophe Juillet	Number 8	Alfi Mocelutu Vuivau
Stephane Castaignede	Scrum-half	Jacob Rauluni
Christophe Lamaison	Fly-half	Nicky Little
Philippe Bernat-Sallas	Right Wing	Manasa Bari
Richard Dourthe	Centre	Viliame Satala
Emile Ntamack	Centre	Waisake Sotutu
Christophe Dominici	Left Wing	Fero Lasagavibau
Ugo Mola	Fullback	Alfred Uluinayau
Olivier Brouzet, Arnaud Costes, Marc Dal Maso, Fabien Galthie, Xavier Garbajosa	Reserves	Meli Nakauta, Koli Sewabu

Score: France 28 (C. Juillet, C. Dominici tries, penalty try; R. Dourthe 2 con, 2 pen) defeated Fiji 19 (A. Uluinayau try; N. Little con, 4 pen).

Pool D — Wales 23–18 Argentina

Date: October 1, 1999.
Venue: Millennium Stadium, Cardiff.
Referee: Paddy O'Brien (New Zealand).

Wales	Position	Argentina
Peter Rogers	*Prop*	Roberto Grau
Garin Jenkins	*Hooker*	Mario Ledesma Arocena
Dai Young	*Prop*	Mauricio Reggiardo
Craig Quinnell	*Lock*	Alejandro Allub
Chris Wyatt	*Lock*	Ignacio Fernandez Lobbe
Colin Charvis	*Flanker*	Lucas Ostiglia
Brett Sinkinson	*Flanker*	Santiago Phelan
Scott Quinnell	*Number 8*	Gonzalo Longo Elia
Rob Howley (c)	*Scrum-half*	Agustin Pichot
Neil Jenkins	*Fly-half*	Gonzalo Quesada
Dafydd James	*Right Wing*	Diego Albanese
Scott Gibbs	*Centre*	Lisandro Arbizu (c)
Mark Taylor	*Centre*	Eduardo Simone
Gareth Thomas	*Left Wing*	Octavio Bartolucci
Shane Howarth	*Fullback*	Manuel Contepomi
Jason Jones-Hughes	*Reserves*	Gonzalo Camardon, Omar Hasan Jalil, Rolando Martin

Score: Wales 23 (C. Charvis, M. Taylor tries; N. Jenkins 2 con, 3 pen) defeated Argentina 18 (G. Quesada 6 pen).

Pool D — Samoa 43–9 Japan

Date: October 3, 1999.
Venue: Racehorse Ground, Wrexham.
Referee: Andrew Cole (Australia).

Samoa	Position	Japan
Robbie Ale	*Prop*	Shin Hasegawa
Trevor Leota	*Hooker*	Masahiro Kunda
Brendan Reidy	*Prop*	Kohei Oguchi
Sene Ta'ala	*Lock*	Robert Gordon
Lama Tone	*Lock*	Naoya Okubo
Graig Glendinning	*Flanker*	Greg Smith
Junior Paramore	*Flanker*	Yasunori Watanabe
Pat Lam (c)	*Number 8*	Jamie Joseph
Stephen So'oilao	*Scrum-half*	Graeme Bachop
Stephen Bachop	*Fly-half*	Keiji Hirose
Brian Lima	*Right Wing*	Terunori Masuho
Va' aiga Tuigamala	*Centre*	Andrew McCormick
To'o Vaega	*Centre*	Yukio Motoki
Afato So'oalo	*Left Wing*	Daisuke Ohata
Silao Leaega	*Fullback*	Tsutomu Matsuda
Earl Va'a, John Clarke, George Leaupepe, Mike Mika, Opeta Palepoi, Semo Setiti	*Reserves*	Takeomi Ito, Masaaki Sakata, Hiroyuki Tanuma, Patiliai Tuidraki, Akira Yoshida

Score: Samoa 43 (B. Lima 2, A. So'oalo 2, S. Leaega tries; S. Leaega 3 con, 4 pen) defeated Japan 9 (K. Hirose 3 pen).

Pool D — Wales 64–15 Japan

Date: October 9, 1999.
Venue: Millennium Stadium, Cardiff.
Referee: Joel Dume (France).

Wales	Position	Japan
Peter Rogers	*Prop*	Shin Hasegawa
Garin Jenkins	*Hooker*	Masahiro Kunda
Dai Young	*Prop*	Kohei Oguchi
Craig Quinnell	*Lock*	Robert Gordon
Mike Voyle	*Lock*	Naoya Okubo
Brett Sinkinson	*Flanker*	Greg Smith
Martyn Williams	*Flanker*	Yasunori Watanabe
Geraint Lewis	*Number 8*	Jamie Joseph
Rob Howley (c)	*Scrum-half*	Graeme Bachop
Neil Jenkins	*Fly-half*	Keiji Hirose
Jason Jones-Hughes	*Right Wing*	Terunori Masuho
Scott Gibbs	*Centre*	Andrew McCormick
Mark Taylor	*Centre*	Yukio Motoki
Allan Bateman	*Left Wing*	Daisuke Ohata
Shane Howarth	*Fullback*	Tsutomu Matsuda
David Llewellyn, Ben Evans, Jonathan Humphreys, Stephen Jones, Andrew Lewis, Gareth Thomas, Chris Wyatt	*Reserves*	Takeomi Ito, Masaaki Sakata, Hiroyuki Tanuma, Patiliai Tuidraki, Akira Yoshida

Score: Wales 64 (M. Taylor 2, D. Llewellyn, A. Bateman, S. Gibbs, R. Howley, S. Howarth, G. Thomas tries, penalty try; N. Jenkins 8 con, pen) defeated Japan 15 (D. Ohata, P. Tuidraki tries, K. Hirose con, pen).

Pool D — Argentina 32–16 Samoa

Date: October 10, 1999.
Venue: Stradey Park, Llanelli.
Referee: Wayne Erickson (Australia).

Argentina	Position	Samoa
Omar Hasan Jalil	*Prop*	Robbie Ale
Mario Ledesma Arocena	*Hooker*	Trevor Leota
Mauricio Reggiardo	*Prop*	Brendan Reidy
Alejandro Allub	*Lock*	Opeta Palepoi
Ignacio Fernandez Lobbe	*Lock*	Lama Tone
Rolando Martin	*Flanker*	Junior Paramore
Santiago Phelan	*Flanker*	Sene Ta'ala
Gonzalo Longo Elia	*Number 8*	Pat Lam (c)
Agustin Pichot	*Scrum-half*	Stephen So'oilao
Gonzalo Quesada	*Fly-half*	Stephen Bachop
Diego Albanese	*Right Wing*	Brian Lima
Lisandro Arbizu (c)	*Centre*	George Leaupepe
Eduardo Simone	*Centre*	Va' aiga Tuigamala
Octavio Bartolucci	*Left Wing*	Afato So'oalo
Manuel Contepomi	*Fullback*	Silao Leaega
Gonzalo Camardon, Miguel Ruiz, Martin Scelzo	*Reserves*	Isaac Fea'unati, Onehunga Matauiau Esau, Mike Mika, Kalolo Toleafoa, Tanner Vili

Score: Argentina 32 (A. Allub try; G. Quesada 8 pen, drop-goal) defeated Samoa 16 (J. Paramore try; S. Leaega con, 3 pen).

Pool D — Wales 31–38 Samoa

Date: October 14, 1999.
Venue: Millennium Stadium, Cardiff.
Referee: Ed Morrison (England).

Wales	Position	Samoa
Peter Rogers	Prop	Robbie Ale
Garin Jenkins	Hooker	Trevor Leota
Dai Young	Prop	Brendan Reidy
Gareth Llewellyn	Lock	Lio Falaniko
Chris Wyatt	Lock	Lama Tone
Brett Sinkinson	Flanker	Craig Glendinning
Martyn Williams	Flanker	Junior Paramore
Scott Quinnell	Number 8	Pat Lam (c)
Rob Howley (c)	Scrum-half	Stephen So'oialo
Neil Jenkins	Fly-half	Stephen Bachop
Dafydd James	Right Wing	Brian Lima
Scott Gibbs	Centre	George Leaupepe
Mark Taylor	Centre	To'o Vaega
Gareth Thomas	Left Wing	Va' aiga Tuigamala
Shane Howarth	Fullback	Silao Leaega
Ben Evans, Andrew Lewis	Reserves	Terry Fanolua, Earl Va'a, Onehunga Matauiau Esau, Mike Mika, Semo Setiti, Sene Ta'ala

Score: Samoa 38 (S. Bachop 2, L. Falaniko, P. Lam, S. Leaega tries; S. Leaega 5 con, pen) defeated Wales 31 (G. Thomas try, 2 penalty tries; N. Jenkins 2 con, 4 pen).

Pool D — Argentina 33–12 Japan

Date: October 16, 1999.
Venue: Millennium Stadium, Cardiff.
Referee: Stuart Dickinson (Australia).

Argentina	Position	Japan
Omar Hasan Jalil	Prop	Toshikazu Nakamichi
Mario Ledesma Arocena	Hooker	Masahiro Kunda
Mauricio Reggiardo	Prop	Kohei Oguchi
Alejandro Allub	Lock	Robert Gordon
Pedro Sporleder	Lock	Hiroyuki Tanuma
Rolando Martin	Flanker	Naoya Okubo
Santiago Phelan	Flanker	Greg Smith
Ignacio Fernandez Lobbe	Number 8	Jamie Joseph
Agustin Pichot	Scrum-half	Graeme Bachop
Gonzalo Quesada	Fly-half	Keiji Hirose
Diego Albanese	Right Wing	Daisuke Ohata
Lisandro Arbizu (c)	Centre	Andrew McCormick (c)
Eduardo Simone	Centre	Yukio Motoki
Gonzalo Camardon	Left Wing	Patiliai Tuidraki
Ignacio Corleto	Fullback	Tsutomu Matsuda
Felipe Contepomi, Lucas Ostigla, Miguel Ruiz	Reserves	Shin Hasegawa, Takeomi Ito, Naoto Nakamura, Masaaki Sakata

Score: Argentina 33 (D. Albanese, A. Pichot tries; F. Contepomi con, G. Quesada 7 pen) defeated Japan 12 (K. Hirose 4 pen).

Pool E — Ireland 53–8 USA

Date: October 2, 1999.
Venue: Lansdowne Road, Dublin.
Referee: Joel Dume (France).

Ireland	Position	USA
Peter Clohessy	*Prop*	Ray Lehner
Keith Wood	*Hooker*	Tom Billups
Paul Wallace	*Prop*	George Sucher
Jeremy Davidson	*Lock*	Luke Gross
Paddy Johns	*Lock*	Alec Parker
Trevor Brennan	*Flanker*	Dave Hodges
Andy Ward	*Flanker*	Richard Tardits
Dion O'Cuinneagain (c)	*Number 8*	Dan Lyle (c)
Tom Tierney	*Scrum-half*	Kevin Dalzell
David Humphreys	*Fly-half*	Mark Williams
Matt Mostyn	*Right Wing*	Vaea Anitoni
Brian O'Driscoll	*Centre*	Juan Grobler
Kevin Maggs	*Centre*	Tomasi Takau
Justin Bishop	*Left Wing*	Brian Hightower
Conor O'Shea	*Fullback*	Kurt Shuman
Jonathan Bell, Eric Elwood, Eric Miller, Ross Nesdale, Malcolm O'Kelly, Brian O'Meara, Justin Fitzpatrick	*Reserves*	Kirk Khasigian, Tasi Mo'unga, David Niu, Shaun Paga, Mark Scharrenberg

Score: Ireland 53 (K. Wood 4, B. O'Driscoll, J. Bishop tries, penalty try; E. Elwood 2 con, D. Humphreys 4 con, 2 pen) defeated USA 8 (K. Dalzell try, pen).

Pool E — Australia 57–9 Romania

Date: October 3, 1999.
Venue: Ravenhill Park, Belfast.
Referee: Paul Honiss (New Zealand).

Australia	Position	Romania
Andrew Blades	*Prop*	Laurentiu Rotaru
Phil Kearns	*Hooker*	Petru Balan
Richard Harry	*Prop*	Constantin Stan
David Giffin	*Lock*	Tiberiu Brinza
John Eales (c)	*Lock*	Ovidiu Slusariuc
Owen Finegan	*Flanker*	Alin Petrache
David Wilson	*Flanker*	Erdinci Septar
Toutai Kefu	*Number 8*	Catalin Draguceanu
George Gregan	*Scrum-half*	Petre Mitu
Rod Kafer	*Fly-half*	Roland Vusec
Ben Tune	*Right Wing*	Cristian Sauan
Tim Horan	*Centre*	Gabriel Brezoianu
Dan Herbert	*Centre*	Romeo Gontineac (c)
Jason Little	*Left Wing*	Gheorghe Solomie
Matthew Burke	*Fullback*	Mihai Vioreanu
Mark Connors, Dan Crowley, Nathan Grey, Jeremy Paul, Joe Roff, Tiaan Strauss, Chris Whitaker	*Reserves*	Daniel Chiriac, Florin Corodeanu, Nicolae Dragos Dima, Razvan Mavrodin

Score: Australia 57 (T. Kefu 3, J. Roff 2, M. Burke, T. Horan, R. Kafer, J. Little tries; M. Burke 5 con, J. Eales con) defeated Romania 9 (P. Mitu 3 pen).

Pool E — USA 25–27 Romania

Date: October 9, 1999.
Venue: Lansdowne Road, Dublin.
Referee: Jim Fleming (Scotland).

USA	Position	Romania
Ray Lehner	*Prop*	Razvan Mavrodin
Tom Billups	*Hooker*	Petru Balan
George Sucher	*Prop*	Constantin Stan
Luke Gross	*Lock*	Tiberiu Brinza
Alec Parker	*Lock*	Tudor Constantin
Dan Lyle (c)	*Flanker*	Alin Petrache
Tasi Mo'unga	*Flanker*	Erdinci Septar
Rob Lumkong	*Number 8*	Catalin Draguceanu
Kevin Dalzell	*Scrum-half*	Petre Mitu
David Niu	*Fly-half*	Roland Vusec
Vaea Anitoni	*Right Wing*	Cristian Sauan
Juan Grobler	*Centre*	Gabriel Brezoianu
Mark Scharrenberg	*Centre*	Romeo Gontineac (c)
Brian Hightower	*Left Wing*	Gheorghe Solomie
Kurt Shuman	*Fullback*	Mihai Vioreanu
Joe Clayton, Dave Hodges, Kirk Khasigian, Shaun Paga, Tomasi Takau, Richard Tardits	*Reserves*	Daniel Chiriac, Florin Corodeanu, Nicolae Dragos Dima

Score: Romania 27 (G. Solomie 2, T. Constantin, A. Petrache tries; P. Mitu 2 con, 1 pen) defeated USA 25 (B. Hightower, D. Lyle, K. Shuman tries; K. Dalzell 2 con, 2 pen).

Pool E — Ireland 3–23 Australia

Date: October 10, 1999.
Venue: Lansdowne Road, Dublin.
Referee: Clayton Thomas (Wales).

Ireland	Position	Australia
Paul Wallace	*Prop*	Andrew Blades
Keith Wood	*Hooker*	Phil Kearns
Justin Fitzpatrick	*Prop*	Richard Harry
Malcolm O'Kelly	*Lock*	David Giffin
Paddy Johns	*Lock*	John Eales (c)
Trevor Brennan	*Flanker*	Mark Connors
Andy Ward	*Flanker*	David Wilson
Dion O'Cuinneagain (c)	*Number 8*	Toutai Kefu
Tom Tierney	*Scrum-half*	George Gregan
David Humphreys	*Fly-half*	Stephen Larkham
Matt Mostyn	*Right Wing*	Ben Tune
Brian O'Driscoll	*Centre*	Tim Horan
Kevin Maggs	*Centre*	Dan Herbert
Justin Bichop	*Left Wing*	Joe Roff
Conor O'Shea	*Fullback*	Matthew Burke
Jonathan Bell, Bob Casey, Peter Clohessy, Eric Elwood, Eric Miller	*Reserves*	Dan Crowley, Owen Finegan, Nathan Grey Jason Little, Jeremy Paul, Tiaan Strauss

Score: Australia 23 (T. Horan, B. Tune tries; M. Burke 2 con, 2 pen, J. Eales pen) defeated Ireland 3 (D. Humphreys pen).

Pool E — Australia 55–19 USA

Date: October 14, 1999.
Venue: Thomond Park, Limerick.
Referee: Andre Watson (South Africa).

Australia	Position	USA
Dan Crowley	*Prop*	Ray Lehner
Michael Foley	*Hooker*	Tom Billups
Rod Moore	*Prop*	George Sucher
Tom Bowman	*Lock*	Luke Gross
Mark Connors	*Lock*	Alec Parker
Owen Finegan	*Flanker*	Dave Hodges
Tiaan Strauss	*Flanker*	Tasi Mo'unga
Jim Williams	*Number 8*	Rob Lumkong
Chris Whitaker	*Scrum-half*	Kevin Dalzell (c)
Stephen Larkham	*Fly-half*	David Niu
Matthew Burke	*Right Wing*	Vaea Anitoni
Nathan Grey	*Centre*	Juan Grobler
Jason Little (c)	*Centre*	Mark Scharrenberg
Scott Staniforth	*Left Wing*	Brian Hightower
Chris Latham	*Fullback*	Kurt Shuman
Matt Cockbain, David Giffin, Rod Kafer, Joe Roff	*Reserves*	Jesse Coulson, Kirk Khasigian, Marc L'Huillier, Shaun Paga, Eric Reed, Tini Saulala, Tomasi Takau

Score: Australia 55 (S. Staniforth 2, M. Burke, M. Foley, S. Larkham, C. Latham, T. Strauss, C. Whitaker tries; M. Burke 5 con, pen) defeated USA 19 (J. Grobler try; K. Dalzell con, 3 pen, drop-goal).

Pool E — Ireland 44–14 Romania

Date: October 15, 1999.
Venue: Lansdowne Road, Dublin.
Referee: Brian Campsell (England).

Ireland	Position	Romania
Paul Wallace	*Prop*	Razvan Mavrodin
Ross Nesdale	*Hooker*	Petru Balan
Justin Fitzpatrick	*Prop*	Constantin Stan
Malcolm O'Kelly	*Lock*	Tiberiu Brinza
Paddy Johns	*Lock*	Tudor Constantin (c)
Kieron Dawson	*Flanker*	Alin Petrache
Andy Ward	*Flanker*	Erdinci Septar
Dion O'Cuinneagain (c)	*Number 8*	Catalin Draguceanu
Tom Tierney	*Scrum-half*	Petre Mitu
Eric Elwood	*Fly-half*	Roland Vusec
Matt Mostyn	*Right Wing*	Cristian Sauan
Jonathan Bell	*Centre*	Gabriel Brezoianu
Mike Mullins	*Centre*	Romeo Gontineac
Jimmy Topping	*Left Wing*	Gheorghe Solomie
Conor O'Shea	*Fullback*	Mihai Vioreanu
Jeremy Davidson, Gordon D'Arcy, Angus McKeen, Brian O'Meara, Brian O'Driscoll, Keith Wood, Alan Quinlan	*Reserves*	Marius Iacob, Daniel Chiriac, Florin Corodeanu, Nicolae Dragos Dima, Radu Fugigi, Laurentiu Rotaru, Ionut Tofan

Score: Ireland 44 (C. O'Shea 2, D. O'Cuinneagain, T. Tierney, A. Ward tries; E. Elwood 5 con, 2 pen) defeated Romania 14 (D. Sauan try; P. Mitu 3 pen).

Quarter-final Play-off **England 45–24 Fiji**
Date: October 20, 1999.
Venue: Twickenham, London.
Referee: Derek Bevan (Wales).

England	Position	Fiji
Darren Garforth	Prop	Dan Rouse
Phil Greening	Hooker	Greg Smith (c)
Jason Leonard	Prop	Joeli Veitayaki
Gareth Archer	Lock	Emori Katalau
Martin Johnson (c)	Lock	Simon Raiwalui
Neil Back	Flanker	Koli Sewabu
Joe Worsley	Flanker	Seta Tawake Naivaluwaqa
Lawrence Dallaglio	Number 8	Alfi Mocelutu Vuivau
Austin Healey	Scrum-half	Mosese Rauluni
Jonny Wilkinson	Fly-half	Waisale Serevi
Nick Beal	Right Wing	Imanueli Tikomaimakogai
Mike Catt	Centre	Meli Nakauta
Will Greenwood	Centre	Viliame Satala
Dan Luger	Left Wing	Marika Vunibaka
Matt Perry	Fullback	Alfred Uluinayau
Richard Cockerill, Matt Dawson, Phil de Glanville, Paul Grayson, Richard Hill, Tim Rodber, Graham Rowntree	Reserves	Nicky Little, Inoke Male, Epeli Naituvau, Jacob Rauluni, Isaia Rasila, Waisake Sotutu

Score: England 45 (N. Back, N. Beal, P. Greening, D. Luger tries; M. Dawson con, J. Wilkinson con, 7 pen) defeated Fiji 24 (M. Nakauta, V. Satala, I. Tikomaimakogai tries; W. Serevi pen, N. Little 3 con).

Quarter-final Play-off **Scotland 35–20 Samoa**
Date: October 20, 1999.
Venue: Murrayfield, Edinburgh.
Referee: Colin Hawke (New Zealand).

Scotland	Position	Samoa
George Graham	Prop	Polo Asi
Gordon Bulloch	Hooker	Trevor Leota
Tom Smith	Prop	Brendan Reidy
Doddie Weir	Lock	Lio Falaniko
Scott Murray	Lock	Lama Tone
Budge Pountney	Flanker	Craig Glendinning
Martin Leslie	Flanker	Semo Sititi
Gordon Simpson	Number 8	Pat Lam (c)
Gary Armstrong (c)	Scrum-half	Stephen So'oilao
Gregor Townsend	Fly-half	Stephen Bachop
Kenny Logan	Right Wing	Brian Lima
Jamie Mayer	Centre	Terry Fanolua
James McLaren	Centre	To'o Vaega
Cammie Murray	Left Wing	Va' aiga Tuigamala
Glenn Metcalfe	Fullback	Silao Leaega
Paul Burnell, Stuart Grimes, Duncan Hodge, Cameron Mather, Robbie Russell	Reserves	Earl Va'a, Robbie Ale, Onehunga Matauiau Esau, Sene Ta'ala, Filipo Toala

Score: Scotland 35 (M. Leslie, C. Murray tries, penalty try; K. Logan con, 5 pen) defeated Samoa 20 (B. Lima, S. Sititi tries, S. Leaega 2 con, 2 pen).

Quarter-final Play-off Argentina 28–24 Ireland

Date: October 20, 1999.
Venue: Stade Felix Bollaert, Lens.
Referee: Stuart Dickinson (Australia).

Argentina	Position	Ireland
Omar Hasan Jalil	*Prop*	Paul Wallace
Mario Ledesma Arocena	*Hooker*	Keith Wood
Mauricio Reggiardo	*Prop*	Reg Corrigan
Alejandro Allub	*Lock*	Malcolm O'Kelly
Ignacio Fernandez Lobbe	*Lock*	Jeremy Davidson
Rolando Martin	*Flanker*	Kieron Dawson
Santiago Phelan	*Flanker*	Andy Ward
Gonzalo Longo Elia	*Number 8*	Dion O'Cuinneagain (c)
Agustin Pichot	*Scrum-half*	Tom Tierney
Gonzalo Quesada	*Fly-half*	David Humphreys
Diego Albanese	*Right Wing*	Matt Mostyn
Lisandro Arbizu (c)	*Centre*	Brian O'Driscoll
Eduardo Simone	*Centre*	Kevin Maggs
Gonzalo Camardon	*Left Wing*	Justin Bishop
Ignacio Corleto	*Fullback*	Conor O'Shea
Felipe Contepomi, Martin Scelzo	*Reserves*	Bob Casey, Eric Miller, Justin Fitzpatrick

Score: Argenitna 28 (D. Albanese try; G. Quesada con, 7 pen) defeated
Ireland 24 (D. Humphreys 7 pen, drop-goal).

Quarter-final

Wales 9–24 Australia
Date: October 23, 1999.
Venue: Millennium Stadium, Cardiff.
Referee: Colin Hawke (New Zealand).

Wales	Position	Australia
Peter Rogers	*Prop*	Andrew Blades
Garin Jenkins	*Hooker*	Michael Foley
Dai Young	*Prop*	Richard Harry
Craig Quinnell	*Lock*	David Giffin
Chris Wyatt	*Lock*	John Eales (c)
Colin Charvis	*Flanker*	Matt Cockbain
Brett Sinkinson	*Flanker*	David Wilson
Scott Quinnell	*Number 8*	Tiaan Strauss
Rob Howley (c)	*Scrum-half*	George Gregan
Neil Jenkins	*Fly-half*	Stephen Larkham
Dafydd James	*Right Wing*	Ben Tune
Scott Gibbs	*Centre*	Tim Horan
Mark Taylor	*Centre*	Dan Herbert
Gareth Thomas	*Left Wing*	Joe Roff
Shane Howarth	*Fullback*	Matthew Burke
Allan Bateman, Ben Evans, Andrew Lewis, Mike Voyle	*Reserves*	Mark Connors, Owen Finegan, Jason Little, Jeremy Paul

Score: Australia 24 (G. Gregan 2, B. Tune tries; M. Burke 3 con, pen) defeated Wales 9 (N. Jenkins 3 pen).

Quarter-final

England 21–44 South Africa
Date: October 24, 1999.
Venue: Stade de France, Paris.
Referee: Jim Fleming (Scotland).

England	Position	South Africa
Jason Leonard	*Prop*	Os Du Randt
Phil Greening	*Hooker*	Naka Drotske
Phil Vickery	*Prop*	Cobus Visagie
Danny Grewcock	*Lock*	Mark Andrews
Martin Johnson (c)	*Lock*	Krynauw Otto
Neil Back	*Flanker*	Johan Erasmus
Richard Hill	*Flanker*	Andre Venter
Lawrence Dallaglio	*Number 8*	Bobby Skinstad
Matt Dawson	*Scrum-half*	Joost van der Westhuizen (c)
Paul Grayson	*Fly-half*	Jannie de Beer
Nick Beal	*Right Wing*	Deon Kayser
Phil de Glanville	*Centre*	Robbie Fleck
Will Greenwood	*Centre*	Pieter Muller
Dan Luger	*Left Wing*	Pieter Rossouw
Matt Perry	*Fullback*	Percy Montgomery
Mike Catt, Martin Corry, Austin Healey, Jonny Wilkinson	*Reserves*	Ollie le Roux, Stefan Terblanche, Albert van den Berg, Andre Vos

Score: South Africa 44 (P. Rossouw, J. van der Westhuizen tries; J. de Beer 2 con, 5 pen, 5 drop-goal) defeated England 21 (P. Grayson 6 pen, J. Wilkinson pen).

Quarter-final   Scotland 18–30 New Zealand

Date: October 24, 1999.
Venue: Murrayfield, Edinburgh.
Referee: Ed Morrison (England).

Scotland	Position	New Zealand
Paul Burnell	*Prop*	Craig Dowd
Gordon Bulloch	*Hooker*	Anton Oliver
Tom Smith	*Prop*	Carl Hoeft
Doddie Weir	*Lock*	Robin Brooke
Scott Murray	*Lock*	Norm Maxwell
Budge Pountney	*Flanker*	Josh Kronfeld
Martin Leslie	*Flanker*	Reuben Thorne
Gordon Simpson	*Number 8*	Taine Randell (c)
Gary Armstrong (c)	*Scrum-half*	Justin Marshall
Gregor Townsend	*Fly-half*	Andrew Mehrtens
Kenny Logan	*Right Wing*	Tana Umaga
Jamie Mayer	*Centre*	Christian Cullen
Alan Tait	*Centre*	Alama Ieremia
Cammie Murray	*Left Wing*	Jonah Lomu
Glenn Metcalfe	*Fullback*	Jeff Wilson
George Graham, Stuart Grimes, Robbie Russell	*Reserves*	Tony Brown, Daryl Gibson, Mark Hammett, Ian Jones, Kees Meeuws

Score: New Zealand 30 (T. Umaga 2, J. Lomu, J. Wilson tries; A. Mehrtens 2 con, 2 pen) defeated Scotland 18 (B. Pountney, C. Murray tries; K. Logan con, pen, G. Townsend drop-goal).

Quarter-final   Argentina 26–47 France

Date: October 24, 1999.
Venue: Lansdowne Road, Dublin.
Referee: Derek Bevan (Wales).

Argentina	Position	France
Roberto Grau	*Prop*	Cedric Soulette
Mario Ledesma Arocena	*Hooker*	Raphael Ibanez (c)
Mauricio Reggiardo	*Prop*	Franck Tournaire
Alejandro Allub	*Lock*	Abdelatif Benazzi
Ignacio Fernandez Lobbe	*Lock*	Olivier Brouzet
Rolando Martin	*Flanker*	Marc Lievremont
Santiago Phelan	*Flanker*	Olivier Magne
Gonzalo Longo Elia	*Number 8*	Christophe Juillet
Agustin Pichot	*Scrum-half*	Fabien Galthie
Gonzalo Quesada	*Fly-half*	Christophe Lamaison
Diego Albanese	*Right Wing*	Philippe Bernat-Salles
Lisandro Arbizu (c)	*Centre*	Richard Dourthe
Eduardo Simone	*Centre*	Emile Ntamack
Gonzalo Camardon	*Left Wing*	Christophe Dominici
Ignacio Corleto	*Fullback*	Xavier Garbajosa
Agustin Canalda, Manuel Contepomi, Felipe Contepomi, Nicolas Fernandez Miranda, Lucas Ostiglia, Miguel Ruiz, Martin Scelzo	*Reserves*	David Auradou, Arnaud Costes, Marc Dal Maso, Pieter de Villiers, Stephane Glas, Ugo Mola, Stephane Castaignede

Score: France 47 (P. Bernat-Salles 2, X. Garbajosa 2, E. Ntamack tries; C. Lamaison 5 con, 4 pen) defeated Argentina 26 (L. Arbizu, A. Pichot tries; F. Contepomi pen, G. Quesada 2 con, 3 pen).

Semi-final — Australia 27–21 South Africa

Date: October 30, 1999.
Venue: Twickenham, London.
Referee: Derek Bevan (Wales).

Australia	Position	South Africa
Andrew Blades	*Prop*	Os Du Randt
Michael Foley	*Hooker*	Naka Drotske
Richard Harry	*Prop*	Cobus Visagie
David Giffin	*Lock*	Mark Andrews
John Eales (c)	*Lock*	Krynauw Otto
Matt Cockbain	*Flanker*	Johan Erasmus
David Wilson	*Flanker*	Andre Venter
Toutai Kefu	*Number 8*	Bobby Skinstad
George Gregan	*Scrum-half*	Joost van der Westhuizen (c)
Stephen Larkham	*Fly-half*	Jannie de Beer
Ben Tune	*Right Wing*	Deon Kayser
Tim Horan	*Centre*	Robbie Fleck
Dan Herbert	*Centre*	Pieter Muller
Joe Roff	*Left Wing*	Pieter Rossouw
Matthew Burke	*Fullback*	Percy Montgomery
Mark Connors, Owen Finegan, Nathan Grey, Jason Little	*Reserves*	Henry Honiball, Ollie le Roux, Stefan Terblanche, Albert van den Berg, Andre Vos

Score: Australia 27 (M. Burke 8 pen, S. Larkham drop-goal) defeated South Africa 21 (J. de Beer 6 pen, drop-goal) after extra time.

Semi-final — France 43–31 New Zealand

Date: October 31, 1999.
Venue: Twickenham, London.
Referee: Jim Fleming (Scotland).

France	Position	New Zealand
Cedric Soulette	*Prop*	Craig Dowd
Raphael Ibanez (c)	*Hooker*	Anton Oliver
Franck Tournaire	*Prop*	Carl Hoeft
Abdelatlf Benazzi	*Lock*	Robin Brooke
Fabien Pelous	*Lock*	Norm Maxwell
Marc Lievremont	*Flanker*	Josh Kronfeld
Olivier Magne	*Flanker*	Reuben Thorne
Christophe Juillet	*Number 8*	Taine Randell (c)
Fabien Galthie	*Scrum-half*	Byron Kelleher
Christophe Lamaison	*Fly-half*	Andrew Mehrtens
Philippe Bernat-Salles	*Right Wing*	Tana Umaga
Richard Dourthe	*Centre*	Christian Cullen
Emile Ntamack	Centre	Alama Ieremia
Christophe Dominici	*Left Wing*	Jonah Lomu
Xavier Garbajosa	*Fullback*	Jeff Wilson
Olivier Brouzet, Arnaud Costes, Pieter de Villiers, Stephane Glas, Ugo Mola, Stephane Castaignede	*Reserves*	Daryl Gibson, Justin Marshall, Kees Meeuws, Royce Willis

Score: France 43 (P. Bernat-Salles, R. Dourthe, C. Lamaison, C. Dominici tries; C. Lamaison 4 con, 3 pen, 2 drop-goal) defeated New Zealand 31 (J. Lomu 2, J. Wilson tries ; A. Mehrtens 2 con, 4 pen).

3rd Place Play-off   New Zealand 18–22 South Africa

Date: November 4, 1999.
Venue: Millennium Stadium, Cardiff.
Referee: Peter Marshall (Australia).

New Zealand	Position	South Africa
Craig Dowd	Prop	Os Du Randt
Mark Hammett	Hooker	Naka Drotske
Kees Meeuws	Prop	Cobus Visagie
Royce Willis	Lock	Mark Andrews
Norm Maxwell	Lock	Krynauw Otto
Josh Kronfeld	Flanker	Johan Erasmus
Reuben Thorne	Flanker	Andre Venter
Taine Randell (c)	Number 8	Andre Vos
Justin Marshall	Scrum-half	Joost van der Westhuizen (c)
Andrew Mehrtens	Fly-half	Henry Honiball
Tana Umaga	Right Wing	Breyton Paulse
Christian Cullen	Centre	Robbie Fleck
Alama Ieremia	Centre	Pieter Muller
Jonah Lomu	Left Wing	Stefan Terblanche
Jeff Wilson	Fullback	Percy Montgomery
Pita Alatini, Carl Hoeft, Dylan Mika, Anton Oliver	Reserves	Ruben Kruger, Ollie le Roux, Chris Rossouw, Werner Swanepoel, Albert van den Berg

Score: South Africa 22 (B. Paulse try; H. Honiball con, 3 pen, P. Montgomery 2 drop-goal) defeated New Zealand 18 (A. Mehrtens 6 pen).

The Final   Australia 35–12 France

Date: November 6, 1999.
Venue: Millennium Stadium, Cardiff.
Referee: Andre Watson (South Africa).

Australia	Position	France
Andrew Blades	Prop	Cedric Soulette
Michael Foley	Hooker	Raphael Ibanez (c)
Richard Harry	Prop	Franck Tournaire
David Giffin	Lock	Abdelatif Benazzi
John Eales (c)	Lock	Fabien Pelous
Matt Cockbain	Flanker	Marc Lievremont
David Wilson	Flanker	Olivier Magne
Toutai Kefu	Number 8	Christophe Juillet
George Gregan	Scrum-half	Fabien Galthie
Stephen Larkham	Fly-half	Christophe Lamaison
Ben Tune	Right Wing	Philippe Bernat-Salles
Tim Horan	Centre	Richard Dourthe
Dan Herbert	Centre	Emile Ntamack
Joe Roff	Left Wing	Christophe Dominici
Matthew Burke	Fullback	Xavier Garbajosa
Mark Connors, Dan Crowley, Owen Finegan, Nathan Grey, Jason Little, Jeremy Paul, Chris Whitaker	Reserves	Olivier Brouzet, Arnaud Costes, Marc Dal Maso, Pieter de Villiers, Stephane Glas, Ugo Mola, Stephane Castaignede

Score: Australia 35 (O. Finegan, B. Tune try; M. Burke 2 con, 7 pen) defeated France 12 (C. Lamaison 4 pen).

Rugby World Cup 2003
Tournament Statistics

Bonus point rule: The 2003 tournament introduced the bonus point system to Rugby World Cup for the first time. A bonus point was awarded to any team that scored four or more tries in a match, and/or any team that lost a match by seven points or less.

Pool Stage – Final Standings

Pool A							
Team	**Wins**	**Draws**	**Losses**	**For**	**Against**	**Bonus**	**Points**
Australia	4	0	0	273	32	2	18
Ireland	3	0	1	141	55	3	15
Argentina	2	0	2	140	57	3	11
Romania	1	0	3	65	192	1	5
Namibia	0	0	4	28	310	0	0

• Australia and Ireland advanced to the quarter-finals.

Pool B							
Team	**Wins**	**Draws**	**Losses**	**For**	**Against**	**Bonus**	**Points**
France	4	0	0	204	70	4	20
Scotland	3	0	1	102	97	2	14
Fiji	2	0	2	98	112	1	9
USA	1	0	3	86	125	2	6
Japan	0	0	4	79	163	0	0

• France and Scotland advanced to the quarter-finals.

Pool C							
Team	**Wins**	**Draws**	**Losses**	**For**	**Against**	**Bonus**	**Points**
England	4	0	0	255	47	3	19
South Africa	3	0	1	184	60	3	15
Samoa	2	0	2	138	117	2	10
Uruguay	1	0	3	56	255	0	4
Georgia	0	0	4	46	200	0	0

• England and South Africa advanced to the quarter-finals.

Pool D							
Team	**Wins**	**Draws**	**Losses**	**For**	**Against**	**Bonus**	**Points**
New Zealand	4	0	0	282	57	4	20
Wales	3	0	1	132	98	2	14
Italy	2	0	2	76	124	0	8
Canada	1	0	3	54	135	1	5
Tonga	0	0	4	46	178	1	1

• New Zealand and Wales advanced to the quarter-finals.

Pool Stage – Results Snapshot

Pool A		
Australia	24–8	Argentina
Ireland	45–17	Romania
Argentina	67–14	Namibia
Australia	90–8	Romania
Ireland	64–7	Namibia
Argentina	50–3	Romania
Australia	142–0	Namibia
Ireland	16–15	Argentina
Romania	37–7	Namibia
Australia	17–16	Ireland

Pool B		
France	61–18	Fiji
Scotland	32–11	Japan
Fiji	19–18	USA
France	51–29	Japan
Scotland	39–15	USA
Fiji	41–13	Japan
France	51–9	Scotland
USA	39–26	Japan
France	41–14	USA
Scotland	22–20	Fiji

Pool C		
South Africa	72–6	Uruguay
England	84–6	Georgia
Samoa	60–13	Uruguay
England	25–6	South Africa
Samoa	46–9	Georgia
South Africa	46–19	Georgia
England	35–22	Samoa
Uruguay	24–12	Georgia
South Africa	60–10	Samoa
England	111–13	Uruguay

Pool D		
New Zealand	70–7	Italy
Wales	41–10	Canada
Italy	36–12	Tonga
New Zealand	68–6	Canada
Wales	27–20	Tonga
Italy	19–14	Canada
New Zealand	91–7	Tonga
Wales	27–15	Italy
Canada	24–7	Tonga
New Zealand	53–37	Wales

Rugby World Cup 2003: The Finals

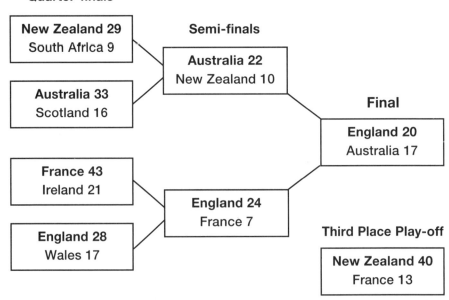

Quarter-finals

| New Zealand 29 |
| South Africa 9 |

| Australia 33 |
| Scotland 16 |

Semi-finals

| Australia 22 |
| New Zealand 10 |

Final

| England 20 |
| Australia 17 |

| France 43 |
| Ireland 21 |

| England 28 |
| Wales 17 |

| England 24 |
| France 7 |

Third Place Play-off

| New Zealand 40 |
| France 13 |

Detailed Results

Pool A — Australia 24–8 Argentina

Date: October 10, 2003.
Venue: Telstra Stadium, Sydney.
Referee: Paul Honiss (New Zealand).

Australia	Position	Argentina
Bill Young	*Prop*	Roberto Grau
Brendan Cannon	*Hooker*	Mario Ledesma
Al Baxter	*Prop*	Omar Hasan
David Giffin	*Lock*	Ignacio Fernandez Lobbe
Nathan Sharpe	*Lock*	Patricio Albacete
George Smith	*Flanker*	Santiago Phelan
Phil Waugh	*Flanker*	Rolando Martin
David Lyons	*Number 8*	Gonzalo Longo
George Gregan (c)	*Scrum-half*	Agustin Pichot (c)
Stephen Larkham	*Fly-half*	Felipe Contepomi
Wendell Sailor	*Right Wing*	Diego Albanese
Elton Flatley	*Centre*	Jose Orango
Matt Burke	*Centre*	Manuel Contepomi
Joe Roff	*Left Wing*	Jose Maria Nunez Piossek
Mat Rogers	*Fullback*	Ignacio Corleto
Daniel Vickerman, Ben Darwin, Matt Giteau, Lote Tuqiri, Jeremy Paul, Chris Whitaker, Matt Cockbain	*Reserves*	Juan Martin Hernandez, Martin Durrand, Mauricio Reggiardo

Score: Australia 24 (J. Roff, W. Sailor tries; E. Flatley con, 4 pen) defeated Argentina 8 (I. Corleto try; F.Contepomi pen).

Pool A — Ireland 45–17 Romania

Date: October 11, 2003.
Venue: Central Coast Stadium, Gosford.
Referee: Jonathan Kaplan (South Africa).

Ireland	Position	Romania
Marcus Horan	*Prop*	Petru Balan
Keith Wood (c)	*Hooker*	Razvan Mavrodin
Reggie Corrigan	*Prop*	Marcei Socaciu
Malcolm O'Kelly	*Lock*	Sorin Socol
Paul O'Connell	*Lock*	Augustin Petrichei
Victor Costello	*Flanker*	George Chiriac
Keith Gleeson	*Flanker*	Ovidiu Tonita
Anthony Foley	*Number 8*	Cristian Petre
Peter Stringer	*Scrum-half*	Lucian Sirbu
David Humphreys	*Fly-half*	Ionut Tofan
Shane Horgan	*Right Wing*	Cristian Sauan
Kevin Maggs	*Centre*	Romeo Gontineac (c)
Brian O'Driscoll	*Centre*	Valentin Maftei
Denis Hickie	*Left Wing*	Gabriel Brezoianu
Girvan Dempsey	*Fullback*	Danut Dumbrava
John Kelly, Ronan O'Gara, Guy Easterby, Alan Quinlan, Donnacha O' Callaghan, Shane Byrne, John Hayes	*Reserves*	Ioan Teodorescu, Mihai Vioreanu, Iulian Andrei, Marius Niculai, Marian Tudori, Petrisor Toderasc, Cezar Popescu

Score: Ireland 45 (D. Hickie 2, V. Costello, S. Horgan, K. Wood tries; D. Humphreys 3 con, 4 pen, R. O'Gara con) defeated Romania 17 (V. Maftei try, penalty try; I. Tofan con, pen, I. Andrie con).

Pool A — Argentina 67–14 Namibia

Date: October 14, 2003.
Venue: Central Coast Stadium, Gosford.
Referee: Nigel Williams (Wales).

Argentina	Position	Namibia
Mauricio Reggiardo	*Prop*	Kees Lensing
Federico Mendez	*Hooker*	Johannes Meyer
Martin Scelzo	*Prop*	Neil du Toit
Pedro Sporleda	*Lock*	Heino Senekal
Rimas Alvarez	*Lock*	Eben Isaacs
Martin Durand	*Flanker*	Schalk van der Merwe
Lucas Ostiglia	*Flanker*	Herman Lintvelt
Pablo Bouza	*Number 8*	Sean Furter (c)
Nicholas Fernandez Miranda (c)	*Scrum-half*	Hakkies Husselman
Gonzalo Quesada	*Fly-half*	Emile Wessels
Diego Albanese	*Right Wing*	Deon Mouton
Juan Fernandez Miranda	*Centre*	Corne Powell
Martin Gaitan	*Centre*	Du Preez Grobler
Hernan Senillosa	*Left Wing*	Melrick Africa
Juan Martin Hernandez	*Fullback*	Jurie Booysen
Felipe Contepomi, Ignacio Fernandez Lobbe, Rodrigo Roncero, Mario Ledesma	*Reserves*	Neil Swanepoel, Vincent Dreyer, Ronaldo Pedro, Jurgens van Lill, Wolfie Duvenhage, Andries Blaauw

Score: Argentina 67 (M. Gaitan 3, P. Bouza, J. Fernandez Miranda, N. Fernandez Miranda, F. Mendez tries, 2 penalty tries; G. Quesada 7 con, pen) defeated Namibia 14 (D. Grobler, H. Husselman tries; E. Wessells 2 con).

Pool A — Australia 90–8 Romania

Date: October 18, 2003.
Venue: Suncorp Stadium, Brisbane.
Referee: Pablo Deluca (Argentina).

Australia	Position	Romania
Bill Young	*Prop*	Petrisor Toderasc
Brendan Cannon	*Hooker*	Razvan Mavrodin
Al Baxter	*Prop*	Silviu Florea
Daniel Vickerman	*Lock*	Sorin Socol
Nathan Sharpe	*Lock*	Cristian Petre
George Smith	*Flanker*	Marius Niculai
Phil Waugh	*Flanker*	Ovidiu Tonita
David Lyons	*Number 8*	George Chiriac
George Gregan (c)	*Scrum-half*	Lucian Sirbu
Stephen Larkham	*Fly-half*	Ionut Tofan
Wendell Sailor	*Right Wing*	Cristian Sauan
Elton Flatley	*Centre*	Romeo Gontineac (c)
Matt Burke	*Centre*	Valentin Maftei
Joe Roff	*Left Wing*	Gabriel Brezoianu
Mat Rogers	*Fullback*	Danut Dumbrava
Stirling Mortlock, Ben Darwin, Matt Giteau, Lote Tuqiri, Jeremy Paul, Justin Harrison, Matt Cockbain	*Reserves*	Ioan Teodorescu, Mihai Vioreanu, Cristian Podea, Bogdan Tudor, Marian Tudori, Marcel Socaciu Cezar Popescu

Score: Australia 90 (M. Rogers 3, M. Burke 2, S. Larkham 2, M. Giteau, S. Mortlock, J. Roff, G. Smith, L. Tuqiri tries; E. Flatley 11 con, pen) defeated Romania 8 (P. Toderasc try; I. Tofan pen).

Pool A

Ireland 64–7 Namibia

Date: October 19, 2003.
Venue: Aussie Stadium, Sydney.
Referee: Andrew Cole (Australia).

Ireland	Position	Namibia
Marcus Horan	*Prop*	Kees Lensing
Keith Wood (c)	*Hooker*	Johannes Meyer
John Hayes	*Prop*	Neil du Toit
Malcolm O'Kelly	*Lock*	Heino Senekal
Paul O'Connell	*Lock*	Archie Graham
Simon Easterby	*Flanker*	Schalk van der Merwe
Alan Quinlan	*Flanker*	Wolfie Duvenhage
Eric Miller	*Number 8*	Sean Furter (c)
Peter Stringer	*Scrum-half*	Hakkies Husselman
Ronan O'Gara	*Fly-half*	Emile Wessels
Shane Horgan	*Right Wing*	Vincent Dreyer
Kevin Maggs	*Centre*	Corne Powell
Brian O'Driscoll	*Centre*	Du Preez Grobler
Denis Hickie	*Left Wing*	Deon Mouton
Girvan Dempsey	*Fullback*	Ronaldo Pedro
John Kelly, Guy Easterby, Simon Best, Shane Byrne	*Reserves*	Melrick Africa, Neil Swanepoel, Morne Schreuder, Herman Lintvelt Jurgens van Lill, Cor van Tonder, Andries Blaauw

Score: Ireland 64 (A. Quinlan 2, E. Miller 2, G. Dempsey, G. Easterby, D. Hickie, M. Horan, S. Horgan, J. Kelly tries; R. O'Gara 7 con) defeated Namibia 7 (C. Powell try; E. Wessells con).

Pool A

Argentina 50–3 Romania

Date: October 22, 2003.
Venue: Aussie Stadium, Sydney.
Referee: Chris White (England).

Argentina	Position	Romania
Rodrigo Roncero	*Prop*	Petrisor Toderasc
Mario Ledesma	*Hooker*	Razvan Mavrodin
Martin Scelzo	*Prop*	Silviu Florea
Pedro Sporleder	*Lock*	Sorin Socol
Patricio Albacete	*Lock*	Cristian Petre
Santiago Phelan (c)	*Flanker*	Marian Tudori
Martin Durand	*Flanker*	Ovidiu Tonita
Pablo Bouza	*Number 8*	George Chiriac
Nicholas Fernandez Miranda	*Scrum-half*	Lucian Sirbu
Juan Fernandez Miranda	*Fly-half*	Ionut Tofan
Diego Albanese	*Right Wing*	Cristian Sauan
Manuel Contepomi	*Centre*	Romeo Gontineac (c)
Martin Gaitan	*Centre*	Valentin Maftei
Jose Maria Nunez Piossek	*Left Wing*	Ioan Teodorescu
Juan Martin Hernandez	*Fullback*	Gabriel Brezoianu
Agustin Pichot, Gonzalo Quesada, Rolando Martin, Omar Hasan	*Reserves*	Vasile Ghioc, Cristian Sauan, Iulian Andrei, Agustin Petrichei, Floran Tatu, Cezar Popescu, Paulica Ion

Score: Argentina 50 (P. Bouza 2, J. Hernandez 2, M. Contepomi, N. Fernandez Miranda, M. Gaitan tries; J. Fernandez Miranda 4 con, pen, G. Quesada 2 con) defeated Romania 3 (I. Tofan pen).

Pool A · Australia 142–0 Namibia

Date: October 25, 2003.
Venue: Adelaide Oval, Adelaide.
Referee: Joel Jutge (France).

Australia	Position	Namibia
Matt Dunning	Prop	Kees Lensing
Jeremy Paul	Hooker	Cor van Tonder
Ben Darwin	Prop	Neil du Toit
Justin Harrison	Lock	Heino Senekal
Nathan Sharpe	Lock	Eben Isaacs
George Smith	Flanker	Shaun van Rooi
David Croft	Flanker	Herman Lintvelt
David Lyons	Number 8	Jurgens van Lill
Chris Whitaker (c)	Scrum-half	Hakkies Husselman
Matt Giteau	Fly-half	Morne Schreuder
Mat Rogers	Right Wing	Vincent Dreyer
Nathan Grey	Centre	Emile Wessells
Stirling Mortlock	Centre	Du Preez Grobler
Lote Tuqiri	Left Wing	Deon Mouton
Chris Latham	Fullback	Ronaldo Pedro
Matt Burke, Morgan Turinui, John Roe, Matt Cockbain, David Giffin	Reserves	Deon Grunschloss, Sean Furter, Schalk van der Merwe, Phillipus Isaacs, Melrick Africa, Neil Swanepoel, Andries Blaauw

Score: Australia 142 (C. Latham 5, M. Giteau 3, L. Tuqiri 3, M. Rogers 2, M. Turinui 2 M. Burke, N. Grey, D. Lyons, S. Mortlock, J. Paul, J. Roe tries, penalty try; M. Rogers 16 con) defeated Namibia 0.

Pool A · Argentina 15–16 Ireland

Date: October 26, 2003.
Venue: Adelaide Oval, Adelaide.
Referee: Andre Watson (South Africa).

Argentina	Position	Ireland
Roberto Grau	Prop	Reggie Corrigan
Federico Mendez	Hooker	Keith Wood (c)
Mauricio Reggiardo	Prop	John Hayes
Ignacio Fernandez Lobbe	Lock	Malcolm O'Kelly
Rimas Alvarez	Lock	Paul O'Connell
Lucas Ostiglia	Flanker	Simon Easterby
Rolando Martin	Flanker	Alan Quinlan
Gonzalo Longo	Number 8	Victor Costello
Agustin Pichot (c)	Scrum-half	Peter Stringer
Gonzalo Quesada	Fly-half	David Humphreys
Diego Albanese	Right Wing	Shane Horgan
Felipe Contepomi	Centre	Kevin Maggs
Jose Orango	Centre	Brian O'Driscoll
Jose Maria Nunez Piossek	Left Wing	Denis Hickie
Ignacio Corleto	Fullback	Girvan Dempsey
Martin Scelzo	Reserves	Ronan O'Gara, Eric Miller, Marcus Horan

Score: Ireland 16 (A. Quinlan try; D. Humphreys con, pen, R. O'Gara 2 pens) defeated Argentina 15 (G. Quesada 3 pen, drop-goal, I. Corleto drop-goal).

Pool A — Namibia 7–37 Romania

Date: October 30, 2003.
Venue: York Park, Launceston.
Referee: Peter Marshall (Australia).

Namibia	Position	Romania
Kees Lensing	Prop	Petru Balan
Johannes Meyer	Hooker	Razvan Mavrodin
Neil du Toit	Prop	Marcel Socaciu
Heino Senekal	Lock	Augustin Petrichei
Eben Isaacs	Lock	Cristian Petre
Schalk van der Merwe	Flanker	George Chiriac
Wolfie Duvenhage	Flanker	Ovidiu Tonita
Sean Furter (c)	Number 8	Sorin Socol
Neil Swanepoel	Scrum-half	Lucian Sirbu
Morne Schreuder	Fly-half	Ionut Tofan
Rudi van Vuuren	Right Wing	Gabriel Brezoianu
Emile Wessells	Centre	Romeo Gontineac (c)
Du Preez Grobler	Centre	Valentin Maftei
Deon Mouton	Left Wing	Ioan Teodorescu
Ronaldo Pedro	Fullback	Danut Dumbrava
Corne Powell, Deon Grunschloss, Jurgens van Lill, Cor van Tonder, Andries Blaauw	Reserves	Mihai Vioreanu, Marian Tudori, Cristian Sauan, Iulian Andrei, Silviu Florea, Popescu, Petrisor Toderasc

Score: Romania 37 (G. Chiriac, A. Petrichei, C. Sauan, L. Sirbu, I. Teodorescu tries; I. Tofan 3 con, 2 pen) defeated Namibia 7 (E. Isaacs try; E. Wessells con).

Pool A — Australia 17–16 Ireland

Date: November 1, 2003.
Venue: Telstra Dome, Melbourne.
Referee: Paddy O'Brien (New Zealand).

Australia	Position	Ireland
Bill Young	Prop	Reggie Corrigan
Brendan Cannon	Hooker	Keith Wood (c)
Ben Darwin	Prop	John Hayes
David Giffin	Lock	Malcolm O'Kelly
Nathan Sharpe	Lock	Paul O'Connell
George Smith	Flanker	Simon Easterby
Phil Waugh	Flanker	Keith Gleeson
David Lyons	Number 8	Anthony Foley
George Gregan (c)	Scrum-half	Peter Stringer
Stephen Larkham	Fly-half	Ronan O'Gara
Wendell Sailor	Right Wing	Shane Horgan
Elton Flatley	Centre	Kevin Maggs
Matt Burke	Centre	Brian O'Driscoll
Wendell Sailor	Left Wing	Simon Best
Mat Rogers	Fullback	Girvan Dempsey
Daniel Vickerman, Al Baxter, Matt Giteau, Lote Tuqiri, Jeremy Paul, Matt Cockbain	Reserves	David Humphreys, Eric Miller, John Kelly, Donnacha O'Callaghan, Marcus Horan

Score: Australia 17 (G. Smith try; E. Flatley 3 pen; G. Gregan drop-goal) defeated Ireland 16 (B. O'Driscoll try; R. O'Gara con, 2 pen, B. O'Driscoll drop-goal).

France 61–18 Fiji

Pool B

Date: October 11, 2003.
Venue: Suncorp Stadium, Brisbane.
Referee: Alain Rolland (Ireland).

France	Position	Fiji
Jean-Jacques Crenca	*Prop*	Richard Nyholt
Raphael Ibanez	*Hooker*	Greg Smith
Jean-Baptiste Poux	*Prop*	Joeli Veitayaki
Fabien Pelous	*Lock*	Ifereimi Rawaqa
Jerome Thion	*Lock*	Api Naevo
Serge Betson	*Flanker*	Sisa Koyamaibole
Olivier Magne	*Flanker*	Kitione Salawa
Imanol Harinordoquy	*Number 8*	Alifereti Doviverata (c)
Fabien Galthié (c)	*Scrum-half*	Mosese Rauluni
Frederik Michalak	*Fly-half*	Nicky Little
Christophe Dominici	*Right Wing*	Vilimoni Delasau
Yanick Jauzion	*Centre*	Seru Rabeni
Tony Marsh	*Centre*	Aisea Tuilevu
Aurelien Rougerie	*Left Wing*	Rupeni Caucaunibuca
Nicolas Brusque	*Fullback*	Norman Ligairi
Pepito Elhorga, Gerald Merceron, Christian Labat, Olivier Brouzet	*Reserves*	Waisale Serevi, Marika Vunibaka, Sami Rabaka, Vulu Maimuri, Kele Leawere, Naca Seru

Score: France 61 (Y. Jauzion 3, C. Dominici 2, I. Harinordoquy, R. Ibanez tries; F. Michalak 4 con, 6 pen) defeated Fiji 18 (R. Caucaunibuca, A. Naevo tries; N. Little con, 2 pen).

Scotland 32–11 Japan

Pool B

Date: October 12, 2003.
Venue: Dairy Farmers Stadium, Townsville.
Referee: Stuart Dickinson (Australia).

Scotland	Position	Japan
Tom Smith	*Prop*	Shin Hasegawa
Rob Russell	*Hooker*	Masao Amino
Bruce Douglas	*Prop*	Masahiko Toyoyama
Scott Murray	*Lock*	Hajime Kiso
Stuart Grimes	*Lock*	Adam Parker
Jason White	*Flanker*	Naoyo Okubo
Jon Petrie	*Flanker*	Takuro Miuchi (c)
Simon Taylor	*Number 8*	Takeomi Ito
Bryan Redpath (c)	*Scrum-half*	Takashi Tsuji
Gordon Ross	*Fly-half*	Keiji Hirose
Chris Paterson	*Right Wing*	Hirotoki Onazawa
James McLaren	*Centre*	Yukio Motoki
Andy Craig	*Centre*	Ruben Parkinson
Kenny Logan	*Left Wing*	Daisuke Ohata
Ben Hinshelwood	*Fullback*	Tsutomu Matsuda
Simon Danielli, Gregor Townsend, Martin Leslie, Ross Beattie, Gavin Kerr	*Reserves*	Toru Kurihara, Andrew Miller, Yuji Sonada, Yasunori Watanabe, Masaaki Sakata

Score: Scotland 32 (C. Paterson 2, S. Danielli, S. Grimes, S. Taylor tries; C. Paterson con, pen, G. Townsend con) defeated Japan 11 (H. Onazawa try; K. Hirose 2 pen).

Pool B — Fiji 19–18 USA

Date: October 15, 2003.
Venue: Suncorp Stadium, Brisbane.
Referee: Joel Jutge (France).

Fiji	Position	USA
Joeli Veitayaki	Prop	Mike MacDonald
Greg Smith	Hooker	Kirk Khasigian
Naca Seru	Prop	Dan Dorsey
Ifereimi Rawaqa	Lock	Alec Parker
Api Naevo	Lock	Luke Gross
Alivereti Mocelutu	Flanker	Kort Schubert
Koli Sewabu	Flanker	David Hodges (c)
Alifereti Doviverata (c)	Number 8	Dan Lyle
Mosese Rauluni	Scrum-half	Kevin Dalzell
Nicky Little	Fly-half	Mike Hercus
Vilimoni Delasau	Right Wing	Riaan van Zyl
Seru Rabeni	Centre	Kain Cross
Aisea Tuilevu	Centre	Phillip Eloff
Marika Vunibaka	Left Wing	David Fee
Alfred Uluinayau	Fullback	Paul Emerick
Sisa Koyamaibole, Vula Maimuri, Richard Nyholt	Reserves	John Buchholz, Kain Cross, Salesi Sika

Score: Fiji 19 (A. Naevo try; N. Little con, 4 pen) defeated USA 18 (K. Schubert, R. van Zyl tries; M. Hercus con, 2 pen).

Pool B — France 51–29 Japan

Date: October 18, 2003.
Venue: Dairy Farmers Stadium, Townsville.
Referee: Alan Lewis (Ireland).

France	Position	Japan
Olivier Milloud	Prop	Shin Hasegawa
Yannick Bru	Hooker	Masaaki Sakata
Jean-Baptiste Poux	Prop	Ryo Yamamura
Fabien Pelous	Lock	Hiroyuki Tanuma
Olivier Brouzet	Lock	Adam Parker
Serge Betson	Flanker	Naoyo Okubo
Olivier Magne	Flanker	Takuro Miuchi (c)
Christian Labit	Number 8	Takeomi Ito
Fabien Galthié (c)	Scrum-half	Yuji Sonada
Frederik Michalak	Fly-half	Andrew Miller
Christophe Dominici	Right Wing	Hirotoki Onazawa
Damien Traille	Centre	Hideki Namba
Tony Marsh	Centre	George Konia
Aurelien Rougerie	Left Wing	Daisuke Ohata
Clement Poitrenaud	Fullback	Toru Kurihara
Gerald Merceron, Sebastien Chabal, David Auradou, Raphael Ibanez, Jean-Jacques Crenca	Reserves	Ryota Asano, Koichi Kubo

Score: France 51 (A. Rougerie 2, J. Crenca, C. Dominici, F. Michalak, F. Pelous tries; F. Michalak 5 con, 3 pen, G. Merceron con) defeated Japan 29 (G. Konia, D. Ohata tries; T. Kurihara 2 con, 5 pen).

Pool B

Scotland 39–15 USA
Date: October 20, 2003.
Venue: Suncorp Stadium, Brisbane.
Referee: Jonathan Kaplan (South Africa).

Scotland	Position	USA
Tom Smith	*Prop*	Mike MacDonald
Gordon Bulloch (c)	*Hooker*	Kirk Khasigian
Gavin Kerr	*Prop*	Dan Dorsey
Nathan Hines	*Lock*	Alec Parker
Stuart Grimes	*Lock*	Luke Gross
Ross Beattie	*Flanker*	Kort Schubert
Jon Petrie	*Flanker*	David Hodges (c)
Simon Taylor	*Number 8*	Dan Lyle
Mike Bair	*Scrum-half*	Kevin Dalzell
Gregor Townsend	*Fly-half*	Mike Hercus
Chris Paterson	*Right Wing*	Riaan van Zyl
Andrew Henderson	*Centre*	Kain Cross
Andy Craig	*Centre*	Phillip Eloff
Simon Danielli	*Left Wing*	David Fee
Glenn Metcalfe	*Fullback*	Paul Emerick
Ben Hinshelwood, Kenny Logan, Bryan Redpath, Martin Leslie, Jason White, Bruce Douglas	*Reserves*	Jason Keyter, Link Wilfley, Kimball Kjar, Jurie Gouws, Oloseti Fifita, Richard Liddington

Score: Scotland 39 (S. Danielli 2, G. Kerr, C. Paterson, G. Townsend tries; C. Paterson 4 con, 2 pen) defeated USA 15 (M. Hercus 5 pen).

Pool B

Fiji 41–13 Japan
Date: October 23, 2003.
Venue: Dairy Farmers Stadium, Townsville.
Referee: Nigel Williams (Wales).

Fiji	Position	Japan
Isaia Rasila	*Prop*	Masahito Yamamato
Greg Smith	*Hooker*	Masaaki Sakata
Naca Seru	*Prop*	Masahiko Toyoyama
Emori Katalau	*Lock*	Hajime Kiso
Api Naevo	*Lock*	Adam Parker
Alivereti Mocelutu	*Flanker*	Naoyo Okubo
Koli Sewabu	*Flanker*	Takuro Miuchi (c)
Alifereti Doviverata (c)	*Number 8*	Takeomi Ito
Sami Rabaka	*Scrum-half*	Takashi Tsuji
Waisele Serevi	*Fly-half*	Andrew Miller
Vilimoni Delasau	*Right Wing*	Hirotoki Onazawa
Seru Rabeni	*Centre*	Yukio Motoki
Epeli Ruivadra	*Centre*	Ruben Parkinson
Aisea Tuilevu	*Left Wing*	Daisuke Ohata
Norman Ligairi	*Fullback*	Tsutomu Matsuda
Marika Vunibaka, Mosese Rauluni, Nicky Little, Sisi Koyamaibole, Vula Maimuri, Gadolo	*Reserves*	Toru Kurihara, Ryota Asano, George Konia, Koichi Kubo, Yuji Sonada, Joeli Veitayaki, Masao Amino, Shin Hasegawa

Score: Fiji 41 (N. Ligairi 2, A. Tuilevu 2, M. Vunibaka tries; N. Little 2 con, 3 pen, W. Serevi pen) defeated Japan 13 (A. Miller try, con, pen, drop-goal).

Pool B

France 51–9 Scotland

Date: October 25, 2003.
Venue: Telstra Stadium, Sydney.
Referee: David McHugh (Ireland).

France	Position	Scotland
Jean-Jacques Crenca	*Prop*	Tom Smith
Raphael Ibanez	*Hooker*	Gordon Bulloch
Sylvain Marconnet	*Prop*	Gavin Kerr
Fabien Pelous	*Lock*	Scott Murray
Jerome Thion	*Lock*	Stuart Grimes
Serge Betson	*Flanker*	Jason White
Olivier Magne	*Flanker*	Cameron Mather
Imanol Harinordoquy	*Number 8*	Simon Taylor
Fabien Galthié (c)	*Scrum-half*	Bryan Redpath (c)
Frederik Michalak	*Fly-half*	Gregor Townsend
Christophe Dominici	*Right Wing*	Chris Paterson
Yanick Jauzion	*Centre*	Andrew Henderson
Tony Marsh	*Centre*	Andy Craig
Aurelien Rougerie	*Left Wing*	Kenny Logan
Nicolas Brusque	*Fullback*	Glenn Metcalfe
Damien Traille, Gerald Merceron, Olivier Brouzet, Patrick Tabacco, Olivier Milloud, Yannick Bru	*Reserves*	James McLaren, Jon Petrie, Nathan Hines, Bruce Douglas, Robbie Russell

Score: France 51 (S. Betson, N. Brusque, F. Galthié, I. Harinordoquy, F. Michalak tries; F. Michalak 4 con, 4 pen, drop-goal, N. Brusque drop-goal) defeated Scotland 9 (C. Paterson 3 pen).

Pool B

Japan 26–39 USA

Date: October 27, 2003.
Venue: Central Coast Stadium, Gosford.
Referee: Steve Walsh (New Zealand).

Japan	Position	USA
Shin Hasegawa	*Prop*	Mike MacDonald
Masao Amino	*Hooker*	Kirk Khasigian
Masahiko Toyoyama	*Prop*	Dan Dorsey
Hajime Kiso	*Lock*	Gerhard Klerck
Adam Parker	*Lock*	Luke Gross
Naoyo Okubo	*Flanker*	Kort Schubert
Takuro Miuchi (c)	*Flanker*	David Hodges (c)
Takeomi Ito	*Number 8*	Dan Lyle
Yuji Sonada	*Scrum-half*	Kevin Dalzell
Andrew Miller	*Fly-half*	Mike Hercus
Toru Kurihara	*Right Wing*	Riaan van Zyl
Yukio Motoki	*Centre*	Salesi Sika
George Konia	*Centre*	Phillip Eloff
Daisuke Ohata	*Left Wing*	David Fee
Tsutomu Matsuda	*Fullback*	Paul Emerick
Hirotoki Onazawa, Takashi Tsuji, Yuya Saito, Masahito Yamamato	*Reserves*	John Buchholz, Kimball Kjar, Jacob Waasdorp, Matthew Wyatt

Score: USA 39 (P. Eloff, M. Hercus, K. Khasigian, R. van Zyl tries; M. Hercus 4 con, 2 pen) defeated Japan 26 (T. Kurihara, D. Ohata tries; T. Kurihara 2 con, 4 pen).

Pool B

France 41–14 USA

Date: October 31, 2003.
Venue: WIN Stadium, Wollongong.
Referee: Paul Honiss (New Zealand).

France	Position	USA
Olivier Milloud	*Prop*	Mike MacDonald
Yannick Bru (c)	*Hooker*	Kirk Khasigian
Jean-Baptiste Poux	*Prop*	Dan Dorsey
David Auradou	*Lock*	Alec Parker
Olivier Brouzet	*Lock*	Luke Gross
Sebastien Chabal	*Flanker*	Kort Schubert
Patrick Tabacco	*Flanker*	David Hodges (c)
Christian Labit	*Number 8*	Dan Lyle
Dmitri Yachvili	*Scrum-half*	Kevin Dalzell
Gerald Merceron	*Fly-half*	Mike Hercus
David Bory	*Right Wing*	Riaan van Zyl
Damien Traille	*Centre*	Salesi Sika
Brian Liebenberg	*Centre*	Phillip Eloff
Pepito Elhorga	*Left Wing*	David Fee
Clement Poitrenaud	*Fullback*	John Buchholz
Sylvain Marconnet	*Reserves*	Matt Sherman, Jason Keyter, Mose Timoteo, Jurie Gouws, Jacob Waasdorp, Matthew Wyatt

Score: France 41 (B. Liebenberg 3, Y. Bru, J. Poux tries; G. Merceron 2 con, 3 pen, D. Yachvili drop-goal) defeated USA 14 (M. Hercus, K. Schubert tries; M. Hercus 2 con).

Pool B

Scotland 22–20 Fiji

Date: November 1, 2003.
Venue: Aussie Stadium, Sydney.
Referee: Tony Spreadbury (England).

Scotland	Position	Fiji
Tom Smith	*Prop*	Isaia Rasila
Gordon Bulloch	*Hooker*	Greg Smith
Bruce Douglas	*Prop*	Joeli Veitayaki
Nathan Hines	*Lock*	Ifereimi Rawaqa
Stuart Grimes	*Lock*	Api Naevo
Ross Beattie	*Flanker*	Vula Maimuri
Cameron Mather	*Flanker*	Koli Sewabu
Simon Taylor	*Number 8*	Alifereti Doviverata (c)
Bryan Redpath (c)	*Scrum-half*	Mosese Rauluni
Chris Paterson	*Fly-half*	Nicky Little
Simon Danielli	*Right Wing*	Aisea Tuilevu
Andrew Henderson	*Centre*	Seru Rabeni
Gregor Townsend	*Centre*	Epeli Ruivadra
Kenny Logan	*Left Wing*	Rupeni Caucaunibuca
Glenn Metcalfe	*Fullback*	Norman Ligairi
Ben Hinshelwood, Jason White, Robbie Russell	*Reserves*	Vilimoni Delasau, Isikeli Nacewa, Jacob Rauluni, Kitione Salawa, Sisi Koyamaibole, Naca Seru

Score: Scotland 22 (T. Smith try; C. Paterson con, 5 pen) defeated Fiji 20 (R. Caucaunibuca 2 tries; N. Little 2 con, 2 pen).

Pool C — South Africa 72–6 Uruguay

Date: October 11, 2003.
Venue: Subiaco Oval, Perth.
Referee: Paddy O'Brien (New Zealand).

South Africa	Position	Uruguay
Lawrence Sephaka	*Prop*	Rodrigo Sanchez
Danie Coetzee	*Hooker*	Diego Lamelas
Richard Bands	*Prop*	Pablo Lemoine
Bakkies Botha	*Lock*	Juan Carlos Bado
Victor Matfield	*Lock*	Juan Alzueta
Joe van Niekerk	*Flanker*	Nicolas Brignoni
Danie Rossouw	*Flanker*	Marcelo Gutierrez
Juan Smith	*Number 8*	Rodrigo Capo
Joost van der Westhuizen (c)	*Scrum-half*	Emiliano Caffera
Louis Koen	*Fly-half*	Sebastian Aquirre
Thinus Delport	*Right Wing*	Emiliano Ibarra
De Wet Barry	*Centre*	Martin Mendaro
Jaque Fourie	*Centre*	Diego Aguirre (c)
Ashwin Willemse	*Left Wing*	Alfonso Cardoso
Werner Greeff	*Fullback*	Joaquin Pastore
Selborne Boome, Derke Hougaard, Neil de Kock, Ricardo Loubscher, John Smit, Hendro Scholtz	*Reserves*	Bernardo Amarillo, Eduardo Berruti, Nicolas Grille, Juan Ramon Menchacca, Hernan Ponte, Juan Andres Perez, Guillermo Storace

Score: South Africa 72 (J. van der Westhuizen 3, B. Botha 2, R. Bands, T. Delport, J. Fourie, W. Greeff, J. Rossouw, H. Scholtz, J. van Niekerk tries; L. Koen 5 con, D. Hougaard con) defeated Uruguay 6 (D. Aguirre 2 pen).

Pool C — England 84–6 Georgia

Date: October 12, 2003.
Venue: Subiaco Oval, Perth.
Referee: Pablo Deluca (Argentina).

England	Position	Georgia
Trevor Woodman	*Prop*	Goderdzi Shvelidze
Steve Thompson	*Hooker*	Akvsenti Giorgadze
Phil Vickery	*Prop*	Aleko Margvelashvili
Martin Johnson (c)	*Lock*	Zurab Mchedlishvili
Ben Kay	*Lock*	Victor Didebulidze
Richard Hill	*Flanker*	Gia Labadze
Neil Back	*Flanker*	Gregoire Yachvili
Lawrence Dallaglio	*Number 8*	George Chkhaidze
Matt Dawson	*Scrum-half*	Irakli Abuseridze
Jonny Wilkinson	*Fly-half*	Paliko Jimsheladze
Ben Cohen	*Right Wing*	Vasil Katsadze (c)
Mike Tindall	*Centre*	Irakli Giorgadze
Will Greenwood	*Centre*	Tedo Zibzibabze
Jason Robinson	*Left Wing*	Malkhaz Urjukashvili
Josh Lewsey	*Fullback*	Besik Khamashuridze
Dan Luger, Paul Grayson, Andy Gomarsall, Lewis Moody, Jason Leonard, Mark Regan	*Reserves*	Badri Khekhelashvili, Merab Kvirikashvili, Irakli Machkhaneli, David Bolgashvili, Vano Nadiradze, Soso Nikolaenko, David Dadunashvili

Score: England 84 (B. Cohen 2, W. Greenwood 2, N. Back, L. Dallaglio, M. Dawson, D. Luger, M. Regan, J. Robinson, S. Thompson, M. Tindall tries; J. Wilkinson 5 con, 2 pen, P. Grayson 4 con) defeated Georgia 6 (P. Jimsheladze pen, M. Urjukashvili pen).

Pool C — Samoa 60–13 Uruguay

Date: October 15, 2003.
Venue: Subiaco Oval, Perth.
Referee: David McHugh (Ireland).

Samoa	Position	Uruguay
Kas Lealamau'a	Prop	Rodrigo Sanchez
John Meredith	Hooker	Diego Lamelas
Jeremy Tomuli	Prop	Pablo Lemoine
Opeta Palepoi	Lock	Juan Carlos Bado
Leo Lafaiali'i	Lock	Juan Alzueta
Peter Poulos	Flanker	Marcelo Gutierrez
Maurie Fa'asavalu	Flanker	Nicolas Grille
Semo Sititi (c)	Number 8	Rodrigo Capo
Steven So'oialo	Scrum-half	Juan Campomar
Earl Va'a	Fly-half	Bernardo Amarillo
Sailosi Tagicakibau	Right Wing	Carlos Baldasarri
Brian Lima	Centre	Martin Mendaro
Terry Fanolua	Centre	Diego Aguirre (c)
Lome Fa'atau	Left Wing	Joaquin Pastore
Tanner Vili	Fullback	Juan Mechaca
Dale Rasmussen, Dominic Feaunati, Denning Tyrell, Kitiona Viliamu, Mahonri Schwalger, Simon Lemalu	Reserves	Jose Viana, Joaquin de Freitas, Nicolas Brignoni, Ignacio Conti, Jan Alvarez, Juan Andres Perez, Juan Machado

Score: Samoa 60 (M. Fa'asavalu 2, B. Lima 2, L. Fa'atau, D. Feaunati, S. Lemalu, O. Palepoi, S. Tagicakibau, T. Vili tries; E. Va'a 3 con, S. Lemalu con, T. Vili con) defeated Uruguay 13 (R. Capo, P. Lemoine tries; D. Aguirre pen).

Pool C — South Africa 6–25 England

Date: October 18, 2003.
Venue: Subiaco Oval, Perth.
Referee: Peter Marshall (Australia).

South Africa	Position	England
Christo Bezuidenhout	Prop	Trevor Woodman
Danie Coetzee	Hooker	Steve Thompson
Richard Bands	Prop	Phil Vickery
Bakkies Botha	Lock	Martin Johnson (c)
Victor Matfield	Lock	Ben Kay
Corné Krige (c)	Flanker	Lewis Moody
Joe van Niekerk	Flanker	Neil Back
Juan Smith	Number 8	Lawrence Dallaglio
Joost van der Westhuizen	Scrum-half	Kyran Bracken
Louis Koen	Fly-half	Jonny Wilkinson
Thinus Delport	Right Wing	Ben Cohen
De Wet Barry	Centre	Mike Tindall
Jorrie Muller	Centre	Will Greenwood
Ashwin Willemse	Left Wing	Jason Robinson
Jaco van der Westhuyzen	Fullback	Josh Lewsey
Werner Greeff, Derke Hougaard, Lawrence Sephaka, John Smit	Reserves	Dan Luger, Joe Worsley, Jason Leonard

Score: England 25 (W. Greenwood try; J. Wilkinson con, 4 pen, 2 drop-goal) defeated South Africa 6 (L. Koen 2 pen).

Pool C

Georgia 9–46 Samoa

Date: October 19, 2003.
Venue: Subiaco Oval, Perth.
Referee: Alain Rolland (Ireland).

Georgia	Position	Samoa
Goderdzi Shvelidze	Prop	Kas Lealamau'a
Akvsenti Giorgadze	Hooker	John Meredith
Soso Nikolaenko	Prop	Jeremy Tomuli
Zurab Mchedlishvili	Lock	Opeta Palepoi
Vano Nadiradze	Lock	Leo Lafaiali'i
Gia Labadze	Flanker	Peter Poulos
Yachvili	Flanker	Maurie Fa'asavalu
Ilia Zedginidze (c)	Number 8	Semo Sititi (c)
Irakli Abuseridze	Scrum-half	Steven So'oialo
Paliko Jimsheladze	Fly-half	Earl Va'a
Vasil Katsadze	Right Wing	Sailosi Tagicakibau
Irakli Giorgadze	Centre	Brian Lima
Tedo Zibzibabze	Centre	Terry Fanolua
Malkhaz Urjukashvili	Left Wing	Ron Fanuatanu
Badri Khekhelashvili	Fullback	Tanner Vili
Besik Khamashuridze, Irakli Machkhaneli, Merab Kvirikashvili, David Bolgashvili, Victor Didebulidze, Aleko Margvelashvili	Reserves	Dale Rasmussen, Dominic Feaunati, Denning Tyrell, Siaosi Vaili, Kitiona Viliamu, Mahonri Schwalger, Simon Lemalu

Score: Samoa 46 (D. Feaunati, B. Lima, S. Sititi, S. So'oialo, S. Tagicakibau, E. Va'a tries; E. Va'a 5 con, 2 pen) defeated Georgia 9 (P. Jimsheladze 2 pen, drop-goal).

Pool C

South Africa 46–19 Georgia

Date: October 24, 2003.
Venue: Aussie Stadium, Sydney.
Referee: Stuart Dickinson (Australia).

South Africa	Position	Georgia
Lawrence Sephaka	Prop	Avtandil Kopaliani
John Smit (c)	Hooker	David Dadunashvili
Faan Rautenbach	Prop	Alexandre Magvelashvili
Bakkies Botha	Lock	Sergo Gujaraidze
Selborne Boome	Lock	Victor Didebulidze
Hendro Scholtz	Flanker	George Tsiklauri
Danie Rossouw	Flanker	David Bolgashvili
Joe van Niekerk	Number 8	George Chkhaidze
Neil de Kock	Scrum-half	Irakli Modebadze
Derke Hougaard	Fly-half	Paliko Jimsheladze
Breyton Paulse	Right Wing	Archil Kavtarashvili
Werner Greeff	Centre	Vasil Katsadze (c)
Jaque Fourie	Centre	Otar Eloshvili
Stefan Terblache	Left Wing	Gocha Khonelidze
Ricardo Loubscher	Fullback	Irakli Machkhaneli
Jorrie Muller, Schalk Burger, Dale Santon	Reserves	Besik Khamashuridze, Merab Kvirikashvili, Ilia Zedginidze, Irakli Abuseridze, Soso Nikolaenko, Akvsenti Giorgadze

Score: South Africa 46 (D. Rossouw 2, B. Botha, S. Burger, J. Fourie, D. Hougaard, J. van Niekerk tries; D. Hougaard 4 con, pen) defeated Georgia 19 (D. Dadunashvili try; P. Jimsheladze con, 3 pen, M. Kvirikashvili pen).

Pool C

England 35–22 Samoa

Date: October 26, 2003.
Venue: Telstra Dome, Melbourne.
Referee: Jonathan Kaplan (South Africa).

England	Position	Samoa
Jason Leonard	*Prop*	Kas Lealamau'a
Mark Regan	*Hooker*	John Meredith
Julian White	*Prop*	Jeremy Tomuli
Martin Johnson (c)	*Lock*	Opeta Palepoi
Ben Kay	*Lock*	Leo Lafaiali'i
Joe Worsley	*Flanker*	Peter Poulos
Neil Back	*Flanker*	Maurie Fa'asavalu
Lawrence Dallaglio	*Number 8*	Semo Sititi (c)
Matt Dawson	*Scrum-half*	Steven So'oialo
Jonny Wilkinson	*Fly-half*	Earl Va'a
Ben Cohen	*Right Wing*	Sailosi Tagicakibau
Mike Tindall	*Centre*	Brian Lima
Stuart Abbott	*Centre*	Terry Fanolua
Iain Balshaw	*Left Wing*	Lome Fa'atau
Jason Robinson	*Fullback*	Tanner Vili
Mike Catt, Lewis Moody, Phil Vickery, Steve Thompson	*Reserves*	Dale Rasmussen, Dominic Feaunati, Denning Tyrell, Kitiona Viliamu, Des Tuiavi'i, Simon Lemalu, Mahonri Schwalger

Score: England 35 (N. Back, I. Balshaw, P. Vickery tries, penalty try; J. Wilkinson 3 con, 2 pen, drop-goal) defeated Samoa 22 (S. Sititi try; E. Va'a con, 5 pen).

Pool C

Georgia 12–24 Uruguay

Date: October 28, 2003.
Venue: Aussie Stadium, Sydney.
Referee: Kelvin Deaker (New Zealand).

Georgia	Position	Uruguay
Goderdzi Shvelidze	*Prop*	Rodrigo Sanchez
David Dadunashvili	*Hooker*	Diego Lamelas
Avtandil Kopaliani	*Prop*	Pablo Lemoine
Zurab Mchedlishvili	*Lock*	Juan Carlos Bado
Sergo Gujaraidze	*Lock*	Juan Alzueta
George Chkhaidze	*Flanker*	Hernan Ponte
Gregoire Yachvili	*Flanker*	Nicolas Grille
Ilian Zedginidze	*Number 8*	Rodrigo Capo
Irakli Modebadze	*Scrum-half*	Juan Campomar
Paliko Jimsheladze	*Fly-half*	Sebastian Aguirre
Archil Kavtarashvili	*Right Wing*	Carlos Baldasarri
Irakli Giorgadze Vasil Katsadze (c)	*Centre*	Martin Mendaro
Tedo Zibzibadze	*Centre*	Diego Aguirre (c)
Malkhaz Urjukashvili	*Left Wing*	Alfonso Cardoso
Irakli Machkhaneli	*Fullback*	Juan Menchaca
Besik Khamashuridze, Merab Kvirikashvili, Ilia Zedginidze, Irakl Abuseridze, Soso Nikolaenko, Akvsenti Giorgadze	*Reserves*	Joaquin Pastore, Bernardo Amarillo, Marcelo Gutierrez, Nicolas Brignoni, Guillermo Storace, Juan Andres Perez, Eduardo Berruti

Score: Uruguay 24 (N. Brignoni, A. Cardoso, D. Lamelas tries; D. Aguirre 2 con, J. Menchaca con, pen) defeated Georgia 12 (M. Kvirikashvili 3 pen, M. Urjukashvili pen).

Pool C — South Africa 60–10 Samoa

Date: November 1, 2003.
Venue: Suncorp Stadium, Brisbane.
Referee: Chris White (England).

South Africa	Position	Samoa
Christo Bezuidenhout	Prop	Kas Lealamau'a
John Smit	Hooker	John Meredith
Faan Rautenbach	Prop	Jeremy Tomuli
Bakkies Botha	Lock	Opeta Palepoi
Victor Matfield	Lock	Leo Lafaiali'i
Corné Krige (c)	Flanker	Peter Poulos
Joe van Niekerk	Flanker	Maurie Fa'asavalu
Juan Smith	Number 8	Semo Sititi (c)
Joost van der Westhuizen	Scrum-half	Steven So'oialo
Derick Hougaard	Fly-half	Earl Va'a
Thinus Delport	Right Wing	Sailosi Tagicakibau
De Wet Barry	Centre	Brian Lima
Jorrie Muller	Centre	Romi Ropati
Ashwin Willemse	Left Wing	Lome Fa'atau
Jaco van der Westhuyzen	Fullback	Tanner Vili
Jaque Fourie, Louis Koen, Neil de Kock, Danie Rossouw, Schalk Burger, Richard Bands, Danie Coetzee, John Smit	Reserves	Dale Rasmussen, Dominic Feaunati, Denning Tyrell, Kitiona Viliamu, Des Tuiavi'i, Tamato Leupolu

Score: South Africa 60 (N. de Kock, J. Fourie, D. Hougaard, J. Muller, J. Smith, J. van der Westhuizen, J. van Niekerk, A. Willemse tries; D. Hougaard 5 con, pen, drop-goal, L. Koen 2 con) defeated Samoa 10 (O. Palepoi try; E. Va'a con, pen).

Pool C — England 111–13 Uruguay

Date: November 2, 2003.
Venue: Suncorp Stadium, Brisbane.
Referee: Nigel Williams (Wales).

England	Position	Uruguay
Jason Leonard	Prop	Eduardo Berruti
Dorian West	Hooker	Diego Lamelas
Phil Vickery (c)	Prop	Pablo Lemoine
Martin Corry	Lock	Juan Carlos Bado
Danny Grewcock	Lock	Juan Miguel Alvarez
Joe Worsley	Flanker	Nicolas Brignoni
Lewis Moody	Flanker	Nicolas Grille
Lawrence Dallaglio	Number 8	Rodrigo Capo
Andy Gomarsall	Scrum-half	Juan Campomar
Paul Grayson	Fly-half	Sebastian Aguirre
Dan Luger	Right Wing	Jose Viana
Mike Catt	Centre	Martin Mendaro
Stuart Abbott	Centre	Diego Aquirre (c)
Iain Balshaw	Left Wing	Alfonso Cardoso
Josh Lewsey	Fullback	Juan Menchaca
Jason Robinson, Will Greenwood, Kyran Bracken, Martin Johnson	Reserves	Emiliano Caffera, Diego Reyes, Marcelo Gutierrez, Juan Alzueta, Guillermo Storace, Juan Andres Perez, Rodrigo Sanchez

Score: England 111 (J. Lewsey 5, I. Balshaw 2, M. Catt 2, A. Gomarsall 2, J. Robinson 2, S. Abbott, W. Greenwood, D. Luger, L. Moody tries; P. Grayson 11 con, M. Catt 2 con) defeated Uruguay 13 (P. Lemoine try; J. Menchaca con, 2 pen).

Pool D — New Zealand 70–7 Italy

Date: October 11, 2003.
Venue: Telstra Dome, Melbourne.
Referee: Andrew Cole (Australia).

New Zealand	Position	Italy
Dave Hewett	Prop	Salvatore Perugini
Kevin Mealamu	Hooker	Carlo Festuccia
Greg Somerville	Prop	Ramiro Martinez
Brad Thorn	Lock	Carlo Checchinato (c)
Chris Jack	Lock	Christian Bezzi
Reuben Thorne (c)	Flanker	Scott Palmer
Richie McCaw	Flanker	Mauro Bergamasco
Jerry Collins	Number 8	Matthew Phillips
Justin Marshall	Scrum-half	Matteo Mazzantini
Carlos Spencer	Fly-half	Francesco Mazzariol
Doug Howlett	Right Wing	Nicola Mazzucato
Daniel Carter	Centre	Matteo Barbini
Tana Umaga	Centre	Andrea Masi
Joe Rokocoko	Left Wing	Mirco Bergamasco
Mils Muliaina	Fullback	Gert Peens
Ma'a Nonu, Leon MacDonald, Rodney So'oialo, Marty Holah, Mark Hammett, Kees Meeuws	Reserves	Gonzalo Canale, Alessandro Troncon, Andrea Benatti, Sergio Parisse, Martin Castrogiovanni,

Score: New Zealand 70 (D. Howlett 2, J. Rokocoko 2, C. Spencer 2, D. Carter, B. Thorn, R. Thorne, L. MacDonald, J. Marshall tries; D. Carter 6 con, C. Spencer pen) defeated Italy 7 (M. Phillips try; G. Peens con).

Pool D — Wales 41–10 Canada

Date: October 12, 2003.
Venue: Telstra Dome, Melbourne.
Referee: Chris White (England).

Wales	Position	Canada
Duncan Jones	Prop	Rod Snow
Robin McBrydo	Hooker	Mark Lawson
Gethin Jenkins	Prop	Jon Thiel
Brent Cockbain	Lock	Colin Yukes
Gareth Llewellyn	Lock	Mike James
Dafydd Jones	Flanker	Al Charron (c)
Martyn Williams	Flanker	Adam van Staveren
Colin Charvis (c)	Number 8	Josh Jackson
Gareth Cooper	Scrum-half	Morgan Williams
Ceri Sweeney	Fly-half	Bob Ross
Gareth Thomas	Right Wing	David Lougheed
Iestyn Harris	Centre	Marco Di Girolamo
Sonny Parker	Centre	Nikyta Witkowski
Mark Jones	Left Wing	Winston Stanley
Kevin Morgan	Fullback	James Pritchard
Mark Taylor, Dwayne Peel, Robert Sidoli, Adam Jones, Huw Bennett, Gethin Jenkins	Reserves	Ryan Smith, Jamie Cudmore, Garth Cooke, Kevin Tkachuk

Score: Wales 41 (C. Charvis, G. Cooper, M. Jones, S. Parker, G. Thomas tries; I. Harris 5 con, 2 pen) defeated Canada 10 (K. Tkachuk try; J. Pritchard con, B. Ross drop-goal).

Pool D — Italy 36–12 Tonga

Date: October 15, 2003.
Venue: Canberra Stadium, Canberra.
Referee: Steve Walsh (New Zealand).

Italy	Position	Tonga
Andrea Lo Cicero	*Prop*	Tonga Lea'aetoa
Fabio Ongaro	*Hooker*	Ephram Taukafa
Martin Castrogiovanni	*Prop*	Heamani Lavaka
Santiago Dellape	*Lock*	Milton Ngauamo
Marco Bortolami	*Lock*	Viliami Vaki
Andrea de Rossi	*Flanker*	Inoke Afeaki
Aaron Persico	*Flanker*	Ipolito Fenukitau
Sergio Parisse	*Number 8*	Benhur Kivalu
Alessandro Troncon	*Scrum-half*	Sililo Martens
Rima Wakarua	*Fly-half*	Sateki Tu'ipulotu
Nicola Mazzucato	*Right Wing*	Tevita Tu'ifua
Manuel Dallan	*Centre*	John Payne
Christian Stoica	*Centre*	Gus Leger
Denis Dallan	*Left Wing*	Sione Fonua
Gonzalo Canale	*Fullback*	Pierre Hola
Mauro Bergamasco, Carlo Checchinato, Carlo Festuccia, Andrea Masi	*Reserves*	Johnny Ngauamo, Stanley Afeaki, Usaia Latu, Sila Va'enuku, Viliami Ma'asi, Kisi Pulu

Score: Italy 36 (D. Dallan 2, M.Dallan tries; R. Wakarua 3 con, 5 pen) defeated Tonga 12 (J. Payne, T. Tu'ifua tries; S. Tu'ipulotu con).

Pool D — New Zealand 68–6 Canada

Date: October 17, 2003.
Venue: Telstra Dome, Melbourne.
Referee: Tony Spreadbury (England).

New Zealand	Position	Canada
Carl Hoeft	*Prop*	Kevin Tkachuk
Mark Hammett	*Hooker*	Aaron Abrams
Kees Meeuws	*Prop*	Garth Cooke
Brad Thorn	*Lock*	Jamie Cudmore
Chris Jack	*Lock*	Ed Knaggs
Reuben Thorne (c)	*Flanker*	Ryan Banks (c)
Marty Holah	*Flanker*	Jim Douglas
Rodney So'oialo	*Number 8*	Jeff Reid
Steve Devine	*Scrum-half*	Ed Fairhurst
Carlos Spencer	*Fly-half*	Jared Barker
Caleb Ralph	*Right Wing*	Sean Fauth
Daniel Carter	*Centre*	Marco Di Girolamo
Ma'a Nonu	*Centre*	John Cannon
Mils Muliaina	*Left Wing*	Matt King
Leon MacDonald	*Fullback*	Quentin Fyffe
Doug Howlett, Richie McCaw, Daniel Braid, Corey Flynn	*Reserves*	Nikyta Witkowski, Ryan Smith, Adam van Staveren, Colin Yukes, Rod Snow

Score: New Zealand 68 (M. Muliaina 4, C. Ralph 2, R. So'oialo 2, K. Meeuws, M. Nonu tries; D. Carter 9 con) defeated Canada 6 (J. Barker 2 pen).

Pool D

Wales 27–20 Tonga
Date: October 19, 2003.
Venue: Canberra Stadium, Canberra.
Referee: Paul Honiss (New Zealand).

Wales	Position	Tonga
Iestyn Thomas	*Prop*	Kisi Pulu
Mefin Davies	*Hooker*	Viliami Ma'asi
Gethin Jenkins	*Prop*	Heamani Lavaka
Gareth Llewellyn	*Lock*	Usaia Latu
Robert Sidoli	*Lock*	Viliami Vaki
Dafydd Jones	*Flanker*	Ipolito Fenukitau
Colin Charvis (c)	*Flanker*	Stanley Afeaki
Alix Popham	*Number 8*	Benhur Kivalu (c)
Gareth Cooper	*Scrum-half*	Sililo Martens
Stephen Jones	*Fly-half*	Pierre Hola
Tom Shanklin	*Right Wing*	Tevita Tu'ifua
Iestyn Harris	*Centre*	John Payne
Mark Taylor	*Centre*	Sukanaivalu Hufanga
Mark Jones	*Left Wing*	Sione Fonua
Rhys Williams	*Fullback*	Sila Va'enuku
Dwayne Peel, Martyn Williams, Chris Wyatt, Huw Bennett, Adam Jones	*Reserves*	Milton Ngauamo, Nisifolo Naufahu, Ephram Taukafa, Tonga Lea'aetoa

Score: Wales 27 (G. Cooper, M. Williams tries; S. Jones con, 4 pen, M. Williams drop-goal) defeated Tonga 20 (P. Hola, B. Kivalu, H. Lavaka tries; P. Hola con, pen).

Pool D

Italy 19–14 Canada
Date: October 21, 2003.
Venue: Canberra Stadium, Canberra.
Referee: Paddy O'Brien (New Zealand).

Italy	Position	Canada
Andrea Lo Cicero	*Prop*	Rod Snow
Fabio Ongaro	*Hooker*	Mark Lawson
Martin Castrogiovanni	*Prop*	Jon Thiel
Santiago Dellape	*Lock*	Colin Yukes
Marco Bortolami	*Lock*	Al Charron (c)
Andreaa de Rossi	*Flanker*	Jamie Cudmore
Aaron Persico	*Flanker*	Jim Douglas
Sergio Parisse	*Number 8*	Ryan Banks
Alessandro Troncon (c)	*Scrum-half*	Morgan Williams
Rima Wakarua	*Fly-half*	Jared Barker
Denis Dallan	*Right Wing*	Dave Lougheed
Manuel Dallan	*Centre*	Marco Di Girolamo
Cristian Stoica	*Centre*	John Cannon
Mirco Bergamasco	*Left Wing*	Winston Stanley
Gonzalo Canale	*Fullback*	Quentin Fyffe
Andrea Masi, Francesco Mazzariol, Matteo Mazzantini, Scott Palmer, Carlo Festuccia, Aaron Persico, Carlo Checchinato	*Reserves*	Josh Jackson, Rod Snow, Kevin Tkachuk

Score: Italy 19 (S. Parisse try; R. Wakarua con, 4 pen) defeated Canada 14 (Q. Fyffe try; J. Barker 3 pen).

Pool D New Zealand 91–7 Tonga

Date: October 24, 2003.
Venue: Suncorp Stadium, Brisbane.
Referee: Pablo Deluca (Argentina).

New Zealand	Position	Tonga
Kees Meeuws	*Prop*	Kisi Pulu
Corey Flynn	*Hooker*	Viliami Ma'asi
Greg Somerville	*Prop*	Heamani Lavaka
Brad Thorn	*Lock*	Usaia Latu
Ali Williams	*Lock*	Viliami Vaki
Reuben Thorne (c)	*Flanker*	Ipolito Fenukitau
Daniel Braid	*Flanker*	Stanley Afeaki
Rodney So'oialo	*Number 8*	Benhur Kivalu (c)
Justin Marshall	*Scrum-half*	Sililo Martens
Carlos Spencer	*Fly-half*	Pierre Hola
Caleb Ralph	*Right Wing*	Tevita Tu'ifua
Daniel Carter	*Centre*	John Payne
Leon MacDonald	*Centre*	Sukanaivalu Hufanga
Doug Howlett	*Left Wing*	Sione Fonua
Mils Muliaina	*Fullback*	Sila Va'enuku
Ben Atiga, Ma'a Nonu, Marty Holah, Richie McCaw, Dave Hewett	*Reserves*	Sateki Tu'ipulotu, Gus Leger, Edward Langi, Milton Ngauamo, Kisi Pulu, Ephram Taukafa, Tonga Lea'aetoa

Score: New Zealand 91 (D. Howlett 2, M. Muliaina 2, C. Ralph 2, D. Braid, D. Carter, C. Flynn, L. MacDonald, K. Meeuws, C. Spencer tries, penalty try; L. MacDonald 12 con, C. Spencer con) defeated Tonga 7 (P. Hola try; S. Tu'ipulotu con).

Pool D Italy 15–27 Wales

Date: October 25, 2003.
Venue: Canberra Stadium, Canberra.
Referee: Andrew Cole (Australia).

Italy	Position	Wales
Andrea Lo Cicero	*Prop*	Duncan Jones
Fabio Ongaro	*Hooker*	Robin McBryde
Martin Castrogiovanni	*Prop*	Adam Jones
Carlo Checchinato	*Lock*	Brent Cockbain
Santiago Dellape	*Lock*	Gareth Llewellyn
Andreaa de Rossi	*Flanker*	Dafydd Jones
Aaron Persico	*Flanker*	Martyn Williams
Sergio Parisse	*Number 8*	Colin Charvis (c)
Alessandro Troncon (c)	*Scrum-half*	Dwayne Peel
Rima Wakarua	*Fly-half*	Ceri Sweeney
Denis Dallan	*Right Wing*	Gareth Thomas
Andrea Masi	*Centre*	Iestyn Harris
Cristian Stoica	*Centre*	Sonny Parker
Nicola Mazzucato	*Left Wing*	Mark Jones
Gonzalo Canale	*Fullback*	Kevin Morgan
Francesco Mazzariol, Scott Palmer, Mauro Bergamasco, Cristian Bezzi, Matthew Phillips, Carlo Festuccia, Salvatore Perugini	*Reserves*	Rhys Williams, Dwayne Peel, Stephen Jones, Gareth Cooper, Rob Sidoli, Jonathan Thomas, Gethin Jenkins

Score: Wales 27 (Dafydd Jones, M. Jones, S. Parker tries; I. Harris 3 con, 2 pen) defeated Italy 15 (R. Wakarua 5 pen).

Pool D — Canada 24–7 Tonga

Date: October 29, 2003.
Venue: WIN Stadium, Wollongong.
Referee: Alain Rolland (Ireland).

Canada	Position	Tonga
Rod Snow	*Prop*	Tonga Lea'aetoa
Mark Lawson	*Hooker*	Ephram Taukafa
Garth Cooke	*Prop*	Heamani Lavaka
Al Charron (c)	*Lock*	Milton Ngauamo
Mike James	*Lock*	Inoke Afeaki
Jamie Cudmore	*Flanker*	Nisifolo Naufahu
Adam van Staveren	*Flanker*	Sione Tu'Amoheloa
Josh Jackson	*Number 8*	Benhur Kivalu (c)
Morgan Williams	*Scrum-half*	Sililo Martens
Bob Ross	*Fly-half*	Pierre Hola
Winston Stanley	*Right Wing*	Sione Fonau
Marco Di Girolamo	*Centre*	John Payne
Nikyta Witkowski	*Centre*	Johnny Ngauamo
Sean Fauth	*Left Wing*	Pila Fifita
Quentin Fyffe	*Fullback*	Gus Leger
James Pritchard, Ryan Smith, Ed Fairhurst, Jeff Reid, Colin Yukes, Aaron Abrams, Kevin Tkachuk	*Reserves*	David Palu, Sukanaivalu Hufanga, Viliami Vaki, Ipolito Fenukitau, Usaia Latu, Kafalosi Tonga, Viliami Ma'asi

Score: Canada 24 (A. Abrams, S. Fauth tries; J. Pritchard con, B. Ross 4 pen) defeated Tonga 7 (I. Afeaki try; P. Hola con).

Pool D — New Zealand 53–37 Wales

Date: November 2, 2003.
Venue: Telstra Stadium, Sydney.
Referee: Andre Watson (South Africa).

New Zealand	Position	Wales
Dave Hewett	*Prop*	Iestyn Thomas
Keven Mealamu	*Hooker*	Robin McBryde
Greg Somerville	*Prop*	Adam Jones
Brad Thorn	*Lock*	Brent Cockbain
Ali Williams	*Lock*	Rob Sidoli
Reuben Thorne (c)	*Flanker*	Jonathan Thomas
Richie McCaw	*Flanker*	Colin Charvis (c)
Jerry Collins	*Number 8*	Alix Popham
Justin Marshall	*Scrum-half*	Gareth Cooper
Carlos Spencer	*Fly-half*	Stephen Jones
Doug Howlett	*Right Wing*	Tom Shanklin
Aaron Mauger	*Centre*	Sonny Parker
Leon MacDonald	*Centre*	Mark Taylor
Joe Rokocoko	*Left Wing*	Shane Williams
Mils Muliaina	*Fullback*	Garan Evans
Rodney So'oialo, Kees Meeuws	*Reserves*	Gareth Thomas, Ceri Sweeney, Dwayne Peel, Dafydd Jones, Chris Wyatt, Gethin Jenkins, Mefin Davies

Score: New Zealand 53 (D. Howlett 2, J. Rokocoko 2, L. MacDonald, A. Mauger, C. Spencer, A. Williams tries; L. MacDonald 5 con, pen) defeated Wales 37 (C. Charvis, S. Parker, M. Taylor, S. Williams tries; S. Jones 4 con, 3 pen).

Quarter-final   New Zealand 29–9 South Africa

Date: November 8, 2003.
Venue: Telstra Dome, Melbourne.
Referee: Tony Spreadbury (England).

New Zealand	Position	South Africa
Dave Hewett	*Prop*	Christo Bezuidenhout
Keven Mealamu	*Hooker*	John Smit
Greg Somerville	*Prop*	Faan Rautenbach
Chris Jack	*Lock*	Bakkies Botha
Ali Williams	*Lock*	Victor Matfield
Reuben Thorne (c)	*Flanker*	Corné Krige (c)
Richie McCaw	*Flanker*	Danie Rossouw
Jerry Collins	*Number 8*	Juan Smith
Justin Marshall	*Scrum-half*	Joost van der Westhuizen
Carlos Spencer	*Fly-half*	Derick Hougaard
Doug Howlett	*Right Wing*	Thinus Delport
Aaron Mauger	*Centre*	De Wet Barry
Leon MacDonald	*Centre*	Jorrie Muller
Joe Rokocoko	*Left Wing*	Ashwin Willemse
Mils Muliaina	*Fullback*	Jaco van der Westhuyzen
Daniel Carter, Caleb Ralph, Steve Devine, Marty Holah, Brad Thorn, Mark Hammett, Kees Meeuws	*Reserves*	Jaque Fourie, Louis Koen, Neil de Kock, Schalk Burger, Selborne Boome, Richard Bands, Danie Coetzee

Score: New Zealand 29 (L. MacDonald, K. Mealamu, J. Rokocoko tries; L. MacDonald con, 3 pen, A. Mauger drop-goal) defeated South Africa 9 (D. Hougaard 3 pen).

Quarter-final   Australia 33–16 Scotland

Date: November 8, 2003.
Venue: Suncorp Stadium, Brisbane.
Referee: Steve Walsh (New Zealand).

Australia	Position	Scotland
Bill Young	*Prop*	Tom Smith
Brendan Cannon	*Hooker*	Gordon Bulloch
Ben Darwin	*Prop*	Bruce Douglas
Justin Harrison	*Lock*	Nathan Hines
Nathan Sharpe	*Lock*	Stuart Grimes
George Smith	*Flanker*	Jason White
Phil Waugh	*Flanker*	Cameron Mather
David Lyons	*Number 8*	Simon Taylor
George Gregan (c)	*Scrum-half*	Bryan Redpath (c)
Stephan Larkham	*Fly-half*	Chris Paterson
Wendell Sailor	*Right Wing*	Kenny Logan
Elton Flatley	*Centre*	Andrew Henderson
Stirling Mortlock	*Centre*	Gregor Townsend
Lote Tuqiri	*Left Wing*	Simon Danielli
Mat Rogers	*Fullback*	Glenn Metcalfe
Joe Roff, Matt Giteau, Daniel Vickerman, Chris Whitaker, Brendan Cannon, Matt Cockbain, Al Baxter, Jeremy Paul	*Reserves*	Ben Hinshelwood, James McLaren, Jon Petrie, Scott Murray, Gordan McIlwham, Robbie Russell

Score: Australia 33 (G. Gregan, D. Lyons, S. Mortlock tries; E. Flatley 3 con, 4 pen) defeated Scotland 16 (R. Russell try; C. Paterson con, 2 pen, drop-goal).

Quarter-final ## France 43–21 Ireland

Date: November 9, 2003.
Venue: Telstra Dome, Melbourne.
Referee: Jonathan Kaplan (South Africa).

France	Position	Ireland
Jean-Jacques Crenca	*Prop*	Reggie Corrigan
Raphael Ibanez	*Hooker*	Keith Wood (c)
Sylvain Marconnet	*Prop*	John Hayes
Fabien Pelous	*Lock*	Malcolm O'Kelly
Jerome Thion	*Lock*	Paul O'Connell
Serge Betsen	*Flanker*	Simon Easterby
Olivier Magne	*Flanker*	Keith Gleeson
Imanol Harinordoquy	*Number 8*	Victor Costello
Fabien Galthie (c)	*Scrum-half*	Peter Stringer
Frederik Michalak	*Fly-half*	Ronan O'Gara
Christophe Dominici	*Right Wing*	John Kelly
Yanick Jauzion	*Centre*	Kevin Maggs
Tony Marsh	*Centre*	Brian O'Driscoll
Aurelien Rougerie	*Left Wing*	Shane Horgan
Nicolas Brusque	*Fullback*	Girvan Dempsey
Brain Leibenberg, Patrick Tabacco, Yannick Bru, Pepito Elhorga, Olivier Magne, Olivier Milloud	*Reserves*	David Humphreys, Eric Miller, John Kelly, Donnacha Callaghan, Marcus Horan

Score: France 43 (J. Crenca, C. Dominici, I. Harinordoquy, O. Magne tries; F. Michalak 4 con, 5 pen) defeated Ireland 21 (B. O'Driscoll 2, K. Maggs tries; D. Humphreys 3 con).

Quarter-final ## England 28–17 Wales

Date: November 9, 2003.
Venue: Suncorp Stadium, Brisbane.
Referee: Alain Rolland (Ireland).

England	Position	Wales
Jason Leonard	*Prop*	Iestyn Thomas
Steve Thompson	*Hooker*	Robin McBryde
Phil Vickery	*Prop*	Adam Jones
Martin Johnson (c)	*Lock*	Brent Cockbain
Ben Kay	*Lock*	Rob Sidoli
Lewis Moody	*Flanker*	Dafydd Jones
Neil Back	*Flanker*	Colin Charvis (c)
Lawrence Dallaglio	*Number 8*	Jonathan Thomas
Matt Dawson	*Scrum-half*	Gareth Cooper
Jonny Wilkinson	*Fly-half*	Stephen Jones
Ben Cohen	*Right Wing*	Shane Williams
Mike Tindall	*Centre*	Iestyn Harris
Will Greenwood	*Centre*	Mark Taylor
Dan Luger	*Left Wing*	Mark Jones
Jason Robinson	*Fullback*	Gareth Thomas
Mike Catt, Stuart Abbott, Kyran Bracken, Trevor Woodman	*Reserves*	Ceri Sweeney, Dwayne Peel, Martyn Williams, Gareth Llewellyn, Gethin Jenkins, Mefin Davies

Score: England 28 (W. Greenwood try; J. Wilkinson con, 6 pen, drop-goal) defeated Wales 17 (C. Charvis, S. Jones, M. Williams tries; I. Harris con).

Semi-final — Australia 22–10 New Zealand

Date: November 15, 2003.
Venue: Telstra Stadium, Sydney.
Referee: Chris White (England).

Australia	Position	New Zealand
Bill Young	Prop	Dave Hewett
Brendan Cannon	Hooker	Keven Mealamu
Ben Darwin	Prop	Greg Somerville
Justin Harrison	Lock	Chris Jack
Nathan Sharpe	Lock	Ali Williams
George Smith	Flanker	Reuben Thorne (c)
Phil Waugh	Flanker	Richie McCaw
David Lyons	Number 8	Jerry Collins
George Gregan (c)	Scrum-half	Justin Marshall
Stephan Larkham	Fly-half	Carlos Spencer
Wendell Sailor	Right Wing	Doug Howlett
Elton Flatley	Centre	Aaron Mauger
Stirling Mortlock	Centre	Leon MacDonald
Lote Tuqiri	Left Wing	Joe Rokocoko
Mat Rogers	Fullback	Mils Muliaina
Joe Roff, Nathan Grey, Matt Cockbain, David Giffin, Al Baxter, Jeremy Paul	Reserves	Byron Kelleher, Marty Holah, Brad Thorn, Kees Meeuws

Score: Australia 22 (S. Mortlock try; E. Flatley con, 5 pen) defeated New Zealand 10 (R. Thorne try; L. MacDonald con, pen).

Semi-final — France 7–24 England

Date: November 16, 2003.
Venue: Telstra Stadium, Sydney.
Referee: Paddy O'Brien (New Zealand).

France	Position	England
Jean-Jacques Crenca	Prop	Trevor Lewsey
Raphael Ibanez	Hooker	Steve Thompson
Sylvain Marconnet	Prop	Phil Vickery
Fabien Pelous	Lock	Martin Johnson (c)
Jerome Thion	Lock	Ben Kay
Serge Betsen	Flanker	Richard Hill
Olivier Magne	Flanker	Neil Back
Imanol Harinordoquy	Number 8	Lawrence Dallaglio
Fabien Galthie (c)	Scrum-half	Matt Dawson
Frederik Michalak	Fly-half	Jonny Wilkinson
Christophe Dominici	Right Wing	Jason Robinson
Yanick Jauzion	Centre	Mike Catt
Tony Marsh	Centre	Will Greenwood
Aurelien Rougerie	Left Wing	Ben Cohen
Nicolas Brusque	Fullback	Josh Lewsey
Clement Poitrenaud, Gerald Merceron, Christian Labit, Olivier Milloud	Reserves	Mike Tindall, Kyran Bracken, Lewis Moody, Jason Leonard, Dorian West

Score: England 24 (J. Wilkinson 5 pen, 3 drop-goal) defeated France 7 (S. Betsen try; F. Michalak con).

3rd Place Play-off   # New Zealand 40–13 France
Date: November 20, 2003.
Venue: Telstra Stadium, Sydney.
Referee: Chris White (New Zealand).

New Zealand	Position	France
Dave Hewett	*Prop*	Sylvain Marconnet
Keven Mealamu	*Hooker*	Yannick Bru (c)
Greg Somerville	*Prop*	Jean-Baptiste Poux
Chris Jack	*Lock*	David Auradou
Ali Williams	*Lock*	Thibault Privat
Reuben Thorne (c)	*Flanker*	Sebastian Chabal
Richie McCaw	*Flanker*	Patrick Tabacco
Jerry Collins	*Number 8*	Christian Labit
Steve Devine	*Scrum-half*	Dmitri Yachvili
Carlos Spencer	*Fly-half*	Gerald Merceron
Doug Howlett	*Right Wing*	David Bory
Aaron Mauger	*Centre*	Damien Traille
Leon MacDonald	*Centre*	Tony Marsh
Joe Rokocoko	*Left Wing*	Pepito Elhorga
Mils Muliaina	*Fullback*	Clement Poitrenaud
Daniel Carter, Caleb Ralph, Marty Holah, Brad Thorn, Mark Hammett, Carl Hoeft	*Reserves*	Nicolas Brusque, Brian Leibenberg, Frederic Michalak, Olivier Magne, Fabien Pelous, Jacques Crenca, Raphael Ibanez, Jean-Baptiste Poux

Score: New Zealand 40 (C. Jack, M. Holah, D. Howlett, M. Muliaina, B. Thorn, J. Rokocoko tries; D. Carter 4 con, L. MacDonald con) defeated France 13 (P. Elhorga try; D. Yachvili con, pen, drop-goal).

The Final   # Australia 17–20 England
Date: November 22, 2003.
Venue: Telstra Stadium, Sydney.
Referee: Andre Watson (South Africa).

Australia	Position	England
Bill Young	*Prop*	Trevor Woodman
Brendan Cannon	*Hooker*	Steve Thompson
Al Baxter	*Prop*	Phil Vickery
Justin Harrison	*Lock*	Martin Johnson (c)
Nathan Sharpe	*Lock*	Ben Kay
George Smith	*Flanker*	Richard Hill
Phil Waugh	*Flanker*	Neil Back
David Lyons	*Number 8*	Lawrence Dallaglio
George Gregan (c)	*Scrum-half*	Matt Dawson
Stephan Larkham	*Fly-half*	Jonny Wilkinson
Wendell Sailor	*Right Wing*	Jason Robinson
Elton Flatley	*Centre*	Mike Tindall
Stirling Mortlock	*Centre*	Will Greenwood
Lote Tuqiri	*Left Wing*	Ben Cohen
Mat Rogers	*Fullback*	Josh Lewsey
Joe Roff, Matt Cockbain, David Giffin, Jeremy Paul, Matt Dunning	*Reserves*	Iain Balshaw, Mike Catt, Lewis Moody, Jason Leonard

Score: England 20 (J. Robinson try; J. Wilkinson 4 pen, drop-goal) defeated Australia 17 (L. Tuqiri try, E. Flatley 4 pen) after extra time.

Rugby World Cup 2007
Tournament Statistics

Third Place Incentive: In an effort to give more incentive to the smaller nations, the IRB announced that the third placed team from each pool would automatically qualify for Rugby World Cup 2011. Previously only the quarter-finalists were granted automatic qualification.

Pool Stage – Final Standings

Pool A							
Team	**Wins**	**Draws**	**Losses**	**For**	**Against**	**Bonus**	**Points**
South Africa	4	0	0	189	47	3	19
England	3	0	1	108	88	2	14
Tonga	2	0	2	89	96	1	9
Samoa	1	0	3	69	143	1	5
USA	0	0	4	61	142	1	1

- South Africa and England advanced to the quarter-finals.

Pool B							
Team	**Wins**	**Draws**	**Losses**	**For**	**Against**	**Bonus**	**Points**
Australia	4	0	0	215	41	4	20
Fiji	3	0	1	114	136	3	15
Wales	2	0	2	168	105	4	12
Japan	0	1	3	64	210	1	3
Canada	0	1	3	51	120	0	2

- Australia and Fiji advanced to the quarter-finals.

Pool C							
Team	**Wins**	**Draws**	**Losses**	**For**	**Against**	**Bonus**	**Points**
New Zealand	4	0	0	309	35	4	20
Scotland	3	0	1	116	66	2	14
Italy	2	0	2	85	117	1	9
Romania	1	0	3	40	161	1	5
Portugal	0	0	4	48	209	1	1

- New Zealand and Scotland advanced to the quarter-finals.

Pool D							
Team	**Wins**	**Draws**	**Losses**	**For**	**Against**	**Bonus**	**Points**
Argentina	4	0	0	143	33	2	18
France	3	0	1	188	37	3	15
Ireland	2	0	2	64	82	1	9
Georgia	1	0	3	50	111	1	5
Namibia	0	0	4	30	212	0	0

- Argentina and France advanced to the quarter-finals.

Pool Stage – Results Snapshot

Pool A		
England	28–10	USA
South Africa	59–7	Samoa
Tonga	25–15	USA
South Africa	36–0	England
Tonga	19–15	Samoa
South Africa	30–25	Tonga
England	44–22	Samoa
Samoa	25–21	USA
England	36–20	Tonga
South Africa	64–15	USA

Pool B		
Australia	91–3	Japan
Wales	42–17	Canada
Fiji	35–31	Japan
Australia	32–20	Wales
Fiji	29–16	Canada
Wales	72–18	Japan
Australia	55–12	Fiji
Canada	12–12	Japan
Australia	37–6	Canada
Fiji	38–34	Wales

Pool C		
New Zealand	76–14	Italy
Scotland	56–10	Portugal
Italy	24–18	Romania
New Zealand	108–13	Portugal
Scotland	42–0	Romania
Italy	31–5	Portugal
New Zealand	40–0	Scotland
Romania	14–10	Portugal
New Zealand	85–8	Romania
Scotland	18–16	Italy

Pool D		
Argentina	17–12	France
Ireland	32–17	Namibia
Argentina	33–3	Georgia
Ireland	14–10	Georgia
France	87–10	Namibia
France	25–3	Ireland
Argentina	63–3	Namibia
Georgia	30–0	Namibia
France	64–7	Georgia
Argentina	30–15	Ireland

Rugby World Cup 2003: The Finals

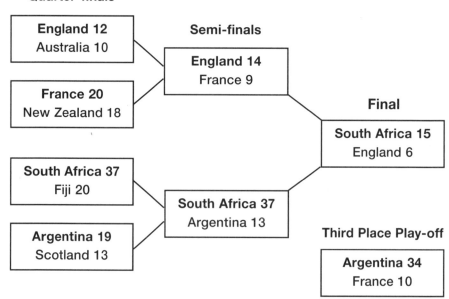

Quarter-finals

England 12
Australia 10

France 20
New Zealand 18

South Africa 37
Fiji 20

Argentina 19
Scotland 13

Semi-finals

England 14
France 9

South Africa 37
Argentina 13

Final

South Africa 15
England 6

Third Place Play-off

Argentina 34
France 10

Detailed Results

Pool A — England 28–10 USA

Date: September 8, 2007.
Venue: Stade Felix Bollaert, Lens.
Referee: Jonathan Kaplan (South Africa).

England	Position	USA
Andrew Sheridan	Prop	Mike MacDonald
Mark Regan	Hooker	Owen Lentz
Phil Vickery (c)	Prop	Chris Osentowski
Simon Shaw	Lock	Alec Parker
Ben Kay	Lock	Mike Mangan
Joe Worsley	Flanker	Louis Stanfill
Tom Rees	Flanker	Todd Clever
Lawrence Dallaglio	Number 8	Henry Bloomfield
Shaun Perry	Scrum-half	Chad Erskine
Olly Barkley	Fly-half	Mike Hercus (c)
Jason Robinson	Right Wing	Takudzwa Ngwenya
Mike Catt	Centre	Vahafolau Esikia
Jamie Noon	Centre	Paul Emerick
Josh Lewsey	Left Wing	Salesi Sika
Mark Cueto	Fullback	Chris Wyles
George Chuter, Matt Stevens, Martin Corry, Lewis Moody, Peter Richards, Andy Farrell, Mathew Tait	Reserves	Blake Burdette, Matekitonga Moeakiola, Alec Parker, Inaki Basauri, Valenese Malifa

Score: England 28 (O. Barkley, T. Rees, J. Robinson tries; O. Barkley 2 con, 3 pen) defeated USA 10 (M. Moeakiola try; M. Hercus con, pen).

Pool A — South Africa 59–7 Samoa

Date: September 9, 2007.
Venue: Parc des Princes, Paris.
Referee: Paul Honiss (New Zealand).

South Africa	Position	Samoa
Os du Randt	Prop	Justin Va'a
John Smit (c)	Hooker	Mahonri Schwalger
C.J. van der Linde	Prop	Census Johnston
Bakkies Botha	Lock	Joe Tekori
Victor Matfield	Lock	Kane Thompson
Schalk Burger	Flanker	Daniel Leo
Juan Smith	Flanker	Semo Sititi (c)
Danie Rossouw	Number 8	Henry Tuilagi
Fourie du Preez	Scrum-half	Junior Polu
Butch James	Fly-half	Eliota Fuimaono-Sapolu
Bryan Habana	Right Wing	Alesana Tuilagi
Jean de Villiers	Centre	Jerry Meafou
Jaque Fourie	Centre	Gavin Williams
J.P. Pietersen	Left Wing	Lome Fa'atau
Percy Montgomery	Fullback	David Lemi
Bismarck du Plessis, Brendon Botha, Johannes Muller, Wickus van Heerden, Enrico Januarie, Andre Pretorius, Francois Steyn	Reserves	Tanielu Fuga, Kas Lealamanua, Alfie Vaeluaga, Justin Purdie, Elvis Seveali'i, Loki Crichton, Brian Lima

Score: South Africa 59 (B. Habana 4, P. Montgomery 2, J. Fourie, J.P. Pietersen tries; P. Montgomery 5 con, 3 pen) defeated Samoa 7 (G. Williams try; con).

Pool A — USA 15–25 Tonga

Date: September 12, 2007.
Venue: Stade de la Mosson, Montpellier.
Referee: Stuart Dickinson (Australia).

USA	Position	Tonga
Mike MacDonald	Prop	Soane Tonga'uiha
Owen Lentz	Hooker	Aleki Lutui
Chris Osentowski	Prop	Kisi Pulu
Alec Parker	Lock	Lisiate Fa'aoso
Mike Mangan	Lock	Paino Hehea
Louis Stanfill	Flanker	Hale T Pole
Todd Clever	Flanker	Nili Latu (c)
Henry Bloomfield	Number 8	Finau Maka
Chad Erskine	Scrum-half	Soane Havea
Mike Hercus (c)	Fly-half	Pierre Hola
Takudzwa Ngwenya	Right Wing	Joseph Vaka
Vahafolau Esikia	Centre	Epeli Taione
Albert Tuipulotu	Centre	Sukanaivalu Hufanga
Salesi Sika	Left Wing	Tevita Tu'ifua
Chris Wyles	Fullback	Vungakoto Lilo
Blake Burdette, Inaki Basauri, Matekitonga Moeakiola, Philip Eloff	Reserves	Sione Tu'ipulotu, Aisea Havili, Lotu Filipine, Viliami Vaki, Toma Toke, Isileli Tupou, Ephraim Taukafa

Score: Tonga 25 (F. Maka, J. Vaka, V. Vaki tries; P. Hola 2 con, 2 pen) defeated USA 15 (M. MacDonald, L. Stanfill tries; M. Hercus con, pen).

Pool A — England 0–36 South Africa

Date: September 14, 2007.
Venue: Stade de France, Paris.
Referee: Joel Jutge (France).

England	Position	South Africa
Andrew Sheridan	Prop	Os du Randt
Mark Regan	Hooker	John Smit (c)
Matt Stevens	Prop	Brendon Botha
Simon Shaw	Lock	Bakkies Botha
Ben Kay	Lock	Victor Matfield
Martin Corry (c)	Flanker	Wickus van Heerden
Tom Rees	Flanker	Juan Smith
Nick Easter	Number 8	Danie Rossouw
Shaun Perry	Scrum-half	Fourie du Preez
Mike Catt	Fly-half	Butch James
Paul Sackey	Right Wing	Bryan Habana
Andy Farrell	Centre	Francois Steyn
Jamie Noon	Centre	Jacque Fourie
Josh Lewsy	Left Wing	J.P. Pietersen
Jason Robinson	Fullback	Percy Montgomery
Andy Gomarsall, Lewis Moody, Steve Borthwick, George Chuter, Matthew Tait, Perry Freshwater, Peter Richards	Reserves	Johannes Muller, Ruan Pienaar, C.J. van der Linde, Bismarck de Plessis, Andre Pretorius, Bobby Skinstad, Wynand Olivier

Score: South Africa 36 (J.P. Pietersen 2, J. Smith tries; P. Montgomery 3 con, 4 pen, F. Steyn pen) defeated England 0.

Pool A — Samoa 15–19 Tonga

Date: September 16, 2007.
Venue: Stade de la Mosson, Montpellier.
Referee: Jonathan Kaplan (South Africa).

Samoa	Position	Tonga
Kas Lealamanua	Prop	Soane Tonga'uiha
Mahonri Schwalger	Hooker	Ephraim Taukafa
Census Johnston	Prop	Kisi Pulu
Joe Tekori	Lock	Inoke Afeaki
Kane Thompson	Lock	Paino Hehea
Daniel Leo	Flanker	Hale T Pole
Ulia Ulia	Flanker	Nili Latu (c)
Semo Sititi (c)	Number 8	Finau Maka
Steve So'oialo	Scrum-half	Enele Taufa
Loki Crichton	Fly-half	Pierre Hola
Alesana Tuilagi	Right Wing	Joseph Vaka
Seilala Mapusua	Centre	Epeli Taione
Elvis Seveali'i	Centre	Sukanaivalu Hufanga
Sailosi Tagicakibau	Left Wing	Tevita Tu'ifua
Gavin Williams	Fullback	Vungakoto Lilo
Muliufi Salanoa, David Lemi, Junior Polu, Tanielu Fuga, Leo Lafaiali'i, Justin Purdie, Lolo Lui, Census Johnston	Reserves	Sione Tu'ipulotu, Aisea Havili, Lotu Filipine, Viliami Vaki, Toma Toke, Isileli Tupou, Ephraim Taukafa

Score: Tonga 19 (E. Taione try; P. Hola con, 4 pen) defeated Samoa 15 (G. Williams 5 pen).

Pool A — South Africa 30–25 Tonga

Date: September 22, 2007.
Venue: Stade Felix Bollaert, Lens.
Referee: Wayne Barnes (England).

South Africa	Position	Tonga
Gurthro Steenkamp	Prop	Soane Tonga'uiha
Gary Botha	Hooker	Aleki Lutui
C.J. van der Linde	Prop	Kisi Pulu
Bakkies Botha	Lock	Paino Hehea
Albert van den Berg	Lock	'Emosi Kauhenga
Wickus van Heerden	Flanker	Viliami Vaki
Danie Rossouw	Flanker	Nili Latu (c)
Bobby Skinstad (c)	Number 8	Finau Mak
Enrico Januarie	Scrum-half	Sione Tu'ípulotu
Andre Pretorius	Fly-half	Pierre Hola
J.P. Pietersen	Right Wing	Joseph Vaka
Wayne Julies	Centre	Epeli Taione
Wynand Olivier	Centre	Sukanaivalu Hufanga
Ashwin Willemse	Left Wing	Tevita Tu'ifua
Ruan Pienaar	Fullback	Vungakoto Lilo
Juan Smith, Bryan Habana, Brendon Botha, Percy Montgomery, Francois Steyn	Reserves	Inoke Afeaki, Lotu Filipine, Ephraim Taukafa, Soane Havea, 'Emosi Kauhenga, Aisea Havili, Isileli Tupou

Score: South Africa 30 (R. Pienaar 2, J. Smith, B. Skinstad tries; A. Pretorius con, P. Montgomery con, pen, F. Steyn pen) defeated Tonga 25 (K. Pulu, S. Hufanga, V. Vaki tries; P. Hola 2 con, 2 pen).

Pool A — England 44–22 Samoa

Date: September 22, 2007.
Venue: Stade de la Beaujoire, Nantes.
Referee: Alan Lewis (Ireland).

England	Position	Samoa
Andrew Sheridan	Prop	Kas Lealamanua
George Chuter	Hooker	Mahonri Schwalger
Matt Stevens	Prop	Census Johnston
Simon Shaw	Lock	Joe Tekori
Ben Kay	Lock	Kane Thompson
Martin Corry (c)	Flanker	Daniel Leo
Joe Worsley	Flanker	Semo Sititi (c)
Nick Easter	Number 8	Henry Tuilagi
Andy Gomarsall	Scrum-half	Junior Polu
Jonny Wilkinson	Fly-half	Eliota Fuimaono-Sapolu
Mark Cueto	Right Wing	Alesana Tuilagi
Olly Barkley	Centre	Brain Lima
Matthew Tait	Centre	Seilala Mapusua
Paul Sackey	Left Wing	David Lemi
Josh Lewsey	Fullback	Loki Crichton
Perry Freshwater, Steve Borthwick, Lewis Moody, Dan Hipkiss	Reserves	Fosi Palaamo, Steve So'oialo, Alfie Vaeluaga, Jerry Meafou, Lolo Lui, Justin Purdie

Score: England 44 (M. Corry 2, P. Sackey 2 tries; J. Wilkinson 3 con, 4 pen, 2 drop-goals) defeated Samoa 22 (J. Polu try; L. Crichton con, 5 pen).

Pool A — Samoa 25–21 USA

Date: September 26, 2007.
Venue: Stade Geoffroy-Guichard, St-Etienne.
Referee: Wayne Barnes (England).

Samoa	Position	USA
Kas Lealamanua	Prop	Mike MacDonald
Mahonri Schwalger	Hooker	Owen Lentz
Census Johnston	Prop	Chris Osentowski
Leo Lafaiali'i	Lock	Alec Parker
Kane Thompson	Lock	Hayden Mexted
Semo Sititi (c)	Flanker	Louis Stanfill
Justin Purdie	Flanker	Todd Clever
Alfie Vaeluaga	Number 8	Fifita Mounga
Junior Polu	Scrum-half	Chad Erskine
Eliota Fuimaono-Sapolu	Fly-half	Mike Hercus (c)
Alesana Tuilagi	Right Wing	Salesi Sika
Seilala Mapusua	Centre	Vahafolau Esikia
Elvis Seveali'i	Centre	Philip Eloff
Lome Fa'atau	Left Wing	Takudzwa Ngwenya
Loki Crichton	Fullback	Chris Wyles
David Lemi, Joe Tekori, Ulia Ulia, Naama Leleimalefaga, Lolo Lui, Steve Soòialo, Silao Vaisola Sefo	Reserves	Blake Burdette, Mark Aylor, Matekitonga Moeakiola, Albert Tuipulotu

Score: Samoa 25 (L. Fa'atau, A. Tuilagi, K. Thompson tries; L. Crichton 2 con, 2 pen) defeated USA 21 (T. Ngwenya, L. Stanfill tries; M. Hercus con, 3 pen).

Pool A — England 36–20 Tonga

Date: September 28, 2007.
Venue: Parc des Princes, Paris.
Referee: Alain Rolland (Ireland).

England	Position	Tonga
Andrew Sheridan	Prop	Soane Tonga'uiha
George Chuter	Hooker	Aleki Lutui
Matt Stevens	Prop	Kisi Pulu
Steve Borthwick	Lock	Viliami Vaki
Ben Kay	Lock	Lisiate Fa'aoso
Martin Corry (c)	Flanker	Hale T Pole
Lewis Moody	Flanker	Nili Latu (c)
Nick Easter	Number 8	Finau Maka
Andy Gomarsall	Scrum-half	Sione Tui'pulotu
Jonny Wilkinson	Fly-half	Pierre Hola
Mark Cueto	Right Wing	Joseph Vaka
Olly Barkley	Centre	Epeli Taione
Matthew Tait	Centre	Sukanaivalu Hufanga
Paul Sackey	Left Wing	Tevita Tu'ifua
Josh Lewsey	Fullback	Vungakoto Lilo
Andy Farrell, Phil Vickery, Lawrence Dallaglio, Dan Hipkiss, Lee Mears, Peter Richards	Reserves	Taufa'ao Filise, Hudson Tonga'uiha, Maama Molitika, Ephraim Taukafa, Inoke Afeaki, Aisea Havili, Paino Hehea

Score: England 36 (P. Sackey 2, M. Tait, A. Farrell tries; J. Wilkinson 2 con, 2 pen, 2 drop-goals) defeated Tonga 20 (S. Hufanga, H.T. Pole tries; P. Hola 2 con, 2 pen).

Pool A — South Africa 64–15 USA

Date: September 30, 2007.
Venue: Stade de la Mosson, Montpellier.
Referee: Tony Spreadbury (England).

South Africa	Position	USA
Os du Randt	Prop	Mike MacDonald
John Smit (c)	Hooker	Owen Lentz
Brendon Botha	Prop	Chris Osentowski
Albert van den Berg	Lock	Alec Parker
Victor Matfield	Lock	Mike Mangan
Wickus van Heerden	Flanker	Louis Stanfill
Juan Smith	Flanker	Todd Clever
Schalk Burger	Number 8	Dan Payne
Fourie du Preez	Scrum-half	Chad Erskine
Butch James	Fly-half	Mike Hercus (c)
Bryan Habana	Right Wing	Salesi Sika
Francois Steyn	Centre	Vahafolau Esikia
Jacque Fourie	Centre	Philip Eloff
Akona Ndungane	Left Wing	Takudzwa Ngwenya
Percy Montgomery	Fullback	Chris Wyles
C.J. van der Linde, J.P. Pietersen, Bakkies Botha, Andre Pretorius, Ruan Pienaar, Bobby Skinstad, Bismarck du Plessis, Albert van den Berg	Reserves	Mark Aylor, Matekitonga Moeakiola, Todd Clever, Henry Bloomfield, Mike Petri, Blake Burdette, Valenese Malifa, Thretton Palamo

Score: South Africa 64 (J. Fourie 2, B. Habana 2, S. Burger, F. Steyn, C.J. van der Linde, F. du Preez, J. Smith tries; P. Montgomery 6 con, pen, B. James 2 con) defeated USA 15 (T. Ngwenya, C. Wyles tries; M. Hercus con, pen).

Pool B   Australia 91–3 Japan

Date: September 8, 2007.
Venue: Stade Gerland, Lyon.
Referee: Alan Lewis (Ireland).

Australia	Position	Japan
Matt Dunning	Prop	Masahito Yamamoto
Stephen Moore	Hooker	Taku Inokuchi
Al Baxter	Prop	Ryo Yamamura
Nathan Sharpe	Lock	Takanori Kumagae
Daniel Vickerman	Lock	Luatangi Samurai Vatuvei
Rocky Elsom	Flanker	Yasunori Watanabe
George Smith	Flanker	Takamichi Sasaki (c)
Wycliff Palu	Number 8	Hajime Kiso
George Gregan	Scrum-half	Yuki Yatomi
Stephen Larkham	Fly-half	Kosei Ono
Lote Tuqiri	Right Wing	Hirotoki Onozawa
Matt Giteau	Centre	Nataniela Oto
Stirling Mortlock (c)	Centre	Koji Tair
Adam Ashley-Cooper	Left Wing	Tomoki Kitagwa
Chris Latham	Fullback	Tatsuya Kusumi
Guy Shepherdson, Hugh McMeniman, Berrick Barnes, Drew Mitchell, Adam Freier, Stephen Hoiles, Mark Gerrard	Reserves	Hare Makiri, Yasunori Watanabe

Score: Australia 91 (R. Elsom 3, C. Latham 2, B. Barnes 2, D. Mitchell 2, G. Smith, A. Ashley-Cooper, N. Sharpe, A. Freier tries; S. Mortlock 7 con, 2 pen, M. Giteau 3 cons) defeated Japan 3 (K. Ono pen).

Pool B   Wales 42–17 Canada

Date: September 9, 2007.
Venue: Stade de la Beaujoire, Nantes.
Referee: Alain Rolland (Ireland).

Wales	Position	Canada
Gethin Jenkins	Prop	Rod Snow
Matthew Rees	Hooker	Pat Riordan
Adam Jones	Prop	Jon Thiel
Ian Gough	Lock	Luke Tait
Alun-Wyn Jones	Lock	Mike James
Jonathan Thomas	Flanker	Jamie Cudmore
Martyn Williams	Flanker	Dave Biddle
Alix Popham	Number 8	Sean-Michael Stephen
Dwayne Peel (c)	Scrum-half	Morgan Williams (c)
James Hook	Fly-half	Ander Monro
Shane Williams	Right Wing	James Pritchard
Sonny Parker	Centre	Dave Spicer
Tom Shanklin	Centre	Craig Culpan
Mark Jones	Left Wing	Dth van der Merwe
Kevin Morgan	Fullback	Mike Pyke
Colin Charvis, Stephen Jones, Gareth Thomas, Thomas Rhys Thomas, Michael Owen, Michael Phillips, Duncan Jones	Reserves	Mike Pletch, Dan Pletch, Aaron Carpenter, Jamie Cudmore, Ryan Smith, Colin Yukes, Mike Burak, Ed Fairhurst

Score: Wales 42 (S. Williams 2, A.-W. Jones, S. Parker, C. Charvis tries; S Jones 4 con, J. Hook 3 pen) defeated Canada 17 (J. Cudmore, C. Culpan, M. Williams tries; J. Pritchard con).

Pool B — Japan 31–35 Fiji

Date: September 12, 2007.
Venue: Municipal Stadium, Toulouse.
Referee: Marius Jonker (South Africa).

Japan	Position	Fiji
Tatsukichi Nishiura	*Prop*	Graham Dewes
Yuji Matsubara	*Hooker*	Sunia Koto
Tomokazu Soma	*Prop*	Henry Qiodravu
Hitoshi Ono	*Lock*	Kele Leawere
Luke Thompson	*Lock*	Wame Lewaravu
Hare Makiri	*Flanker*	Semisi Naevo
Philip O'Reilly	*Flanker*	Akapusi Qera
Takuro Miuchi (c)	*Number 8*	Sisa Koyamaibole
Tomoki Yoshida	*Scrum-half*	Mosese Rauluni (c)
Bryce Robins	*Fly-half*	Nicky Little
Kosuke Endo	*Right Wing*	Isoa Neivua
Shotaro Onishi	*Centre*	Seremaia Bai
Yuta Imamura	*Centre*	Seru Rabeni
Christian Loaman	*Left Wing*	Vilimoni Delasau
Go Aruga	*Fullback*	Kameli Ratuvou
Yuki Yatomi, Hirotoki Onozawa, Koji Taira, Ryo Yamamura	*Reserves*	Norman Ligairi, Aca Ratuva, Jone Railomo, Netani Talei

Score: Fiji 35 (A. Qera 2, S. Rabeni, R. Lewaravu tries; N. Little 3 con, 3 pen) defeated Japan 31 (L. Thompson 2, T. Soma tries; T. Soma 2 con, S. Onishi 4 pen).

Pool B — Wales 20–32 Australia

Date: September 15, 2007.
Venue: Millennium Stadium, Cardiff.
Referee: Steve Walsh (New Zealand).

Wales	Position	Australia
Gethin Jenkins	*Prop*	Matt Dunning
Matthew Rees	*Hooker*	Stephen Moore
Adam Jones	*Prop*	Guy Shepherdson
Ian Gough	*Lock*	Nathan Sharpe
Alun-Wyn Jones	*Lock*	Daniel Vickerman
Colin Charvis	*Flanker*	Rocky Elsom
Martyn Williams	*Flanker*	George Smith
Jonathan Thomas	*Number 8*	Wycliff Palu
Dwayne Peel	*Scrum-half*	George Gregan
Stephen Jones	*Fly-half*	Berrick Barnes
Shane Williams	*Right Wing*	Lote Tuqiri
Sonny Parker	*Centre*	Matt Giteau
Tom Shanklin	*Centre*	Stirling Mortlock (c)
Mark Jones	*Left Wing*	Drew Mitchell
Gareth Thomas (c)	*Fullback*	Chris Latham
Alix Popham, Kevin Morgan, James Hook, Duncan Jones, Thomas Rhys Thomas, Michael Owen, Michael Phillips	*Reserves*	Scott Staniforth, Phil Waugh, Stephen Hoiles, Adam Freier, Al Baxter, Mark Chisholm, Julian Huxley

Score: Australia 32 (C. Latham 2, M. Giteau, S. Mortlock tries; S. Mortlock 2 con, pen, M. Giteau con, B. Barnes drop-goal) defeated Wales 20 (J. Thomas, S. Williams tries; S. Jones pen, J. Hook 2 con, pen)

Pool B

Fiji 29–16 Canada

Date: September 16, 2007.
Venue: Millennium Stadium, Cardiff.
Referee: Tony Spreadbury (England).

Fiji	Position	Canada
Graham Dewes	*Prop*	Rod Snow
Sunia Koto	*Hooker*	Pat Riordan
Jone Railomo	*Prop*	Jon Thiel
Kele Leawere	*Lock*	Mike Burak
Ifereimi Rawaqa	*Lock*	Mike James
Semisi Naevo	*Flanker*	Jamie Cudmore
Akapusi Qera	*Flanker*	Dave Biddle
Sisa Koyamaibole	*Number 8*	Sean-Michael Stephen
Mosese Rauluni (c)	*Scrum-half*	Morgan Williams (c)
Nicky Little	*Fly-half*	Ryan Smith
Isoa Neivua	*Right Wing*	James Pritchard
Seremaia Bai	*Centre*	Dave Spicer
Seru Rabeni	*Centre*	Craig Culpan
Vilimoni Delasau	*Left Wing*	Dth van der Merwe
Kameli Ratuvou	*Fullback*	Mike Pyke
Netani Talei, Henry Qiodravu, Maleli Kunavore, Vereniki Sauturaga, Norman Ligairi	*Reserves*	Colin Yukes, Dan Pletch, Luke Tait, Aaron Carpenter

Score: Fiji 29 (K. Ratuvou 2, K. Leawere, V. Delasau tries; N. Little 3 con, pen) defeated Canada 16 (R. Smith try; J. Pritchard con, 3 pen).

Pool B

Wales 72–18 Japan

Date: September 20, 2007.
Venue: Millennium Stadium, Cardiff.
Referee: Joel Jutge (France).

Wales	Position	Japan
Duncan Jones	*Prop*	Tatsukichi Nishiura
Thomas Rhys Thomas	*Hooker*	Yuji Matsubara
Chris Horsman	*Prop*	Tomokazu Soma
Will James	*Lock*	Hitoshi Ono
Alun-Wyn Jones	*Lock*	Luke Thompson
Colin Charvis	*Flanker*	Yasunori Watanabe
Martyn Williams	*Flanker*	Hare Makiri
Alix Popham	*Number 8*	Takuro Miuchi (c)
Michael Phillips	*Scrum-half*	Tomoki Yoshida
Stephen Jones (c)	*Fly-half*	Bryce Robins
Shane Williams	*Right Wing*	Hirotoki Onozawa
James Hook	*Centre*	Shotaro Onishi
Jamie Robinson	*Centre*	Yuta Imamura
Dafydd James	*Left Wing*	Kosuke Endo
Kevin Morgan	*Fullback*	Christian Loamanu
Ian Evans, Ceri Sweeney, Gareth Cooper, Michael Owen, Huw Bennett, Gareth Jenkins, Tom Shanklin	*Reserves*	Koji Taira, Ryota Asano, Tatsuya Kusumi, Ryo Yamamura, Chulwon Kim, Hajime Kiso, Tatsukichi Nishiura, Taku Inokuchi

Score: Wales 72 (M. Williams 2, S. Williams 2, A.-W. Jones, J. Hook, T.R. Thomas, K. Morgan, M. Phillips, D. James, G. Cooper tries; S. Jones 5 con, pen, C. Sweeney 2 con) defeated Japan 18 (K. Endo, H. Onozawa tries; B. Robins con, S. Onishi 2 pen).

Pool B — Australia 55–12 Fiji

Date: September 23, 2007.
Venue: Stade de la Mosson, Montpellier.
Referee: Nigel Owens (Wales).

Australia	Position	Fiji
Matt Dunning	Prop	Alefoso Yalayalatabua
Stephen Moore	Hooker	Vereniki Sauturaga
Guy Shepherdson	Prop	Henry Qiodravu
Mark Chisholm	Lock	Isoa Domolailai
Daniel Vickerman	Lock	Ifereimi Rawaqa
Rocky Elsom	Flanker	Netani Talei
Phil Waugh	Flanker	Aca Ratuva
Wycliff Palu	Number 8	Jone Qovu
George Gregan (c)	Scrum-half	Jone Danunivucu
Berrick Barnes	Fly-half	Waisea Luveniyali
Lote Tuqiri	Right Wing	Isoa Neivua
Matt Giteau	Centre	Seremaia Bai (c)
Adam Ashley-Cooper	Centre	Maleli Kunavore
Drew Mitchell	Left Wing	Vilimoni Delasau
Chris Latham	Fullback	Norman Ligairi
Hugh McMeniman, Adam Freier, Greg Holmes, Sam Cordingley, Scott Staniforth, Stephen Hoiles, Julian Huxley	Reserves	Seru Rabeni, Mosese Rauluni, Wame Lewaravu, Jone Railomo, Sisa Koyamaibole, Gabiriele Lovobalavu

Score: Australia 55 (D. Mitchell 3, M. Giteau 2, A. Ashley-Cooper, S. Hoiles tries; M. Giteau 4 con, 3 pen, B. Barnes drop-goal.) defeated Fiji 12 (I. Neivua, A. Ratuva tries; S. Bai con).

Pool B — Canada 12–12 Japan

Date: September 25, 2007.
Venue: Stade Chaban Delmas, Bordeaux.
Referee: Jonathan Kaplan (South Africa).

Canada	Position	Japan
Rod Snow	Prop	Tatsukichi Nishiura
Pat Riordan	Hooker	Yuji Matsubara
Jon Thiel	Prop	Tomokazu Soma
Mike Burak	Lock	Hitoshi Ono
Mike James	Lock	Luke Thompson
Colin Yukes	Flanker	Hare Makiri
Adam Kleeberger	Flanker	Philip O'Reilly
Aaron Carpenter	Number 8	Takuro Miuchi (c)
Morgan Williams (c)	Scrum-half	Tomoki Yoshida
Ryan Smith	Fly-half	Bryce Robins
James Pritchard	Right Wing	Christian Loamanu
Dave Spicer	Centre	Shotaro Onishi
Craig Culpan	Centre	Yuta Imamura
Dth van der Merwe	Left Wing	Kosuke Endo
Mike Pyke	Fullback	Go Aruga
Dan Pletch, Mike Webb, Scott Franklin, Mike Pletch, Justin Mensah-Coker, Josh Jackson	Reserves	Chulwon Kim, Ryo Yamamura, Luatangi Samurai Vatuvei, Koji Taira, Hirotoki Onozawa, Hajime Kiso

Score: Canada 12 (P. Riordan, D. van der Merwe tries; J. Pritchard con.) drew with Japan 12 (K. Endo, K. Taira tries; S. Onishi con).

Pool B — Australia 37–6 Canada

Date: September 29, 2007.
Venue: Stade Chaban Delmas, Bordeaux.
Referee: Chris White (England).

Australia	Position	Canada
Greg Holmes	Prop	Rod Snow
Adam Freier	Hooker	Pat Riordan
Al Baxter	Prop	Jon Thiel
Nathan Sharpe	Lock	Luke Tait
Mark Chisholm	Lock	Mike James
Hugh McMeniman	Flanker	Colin Yukes
George Smith (c)	Flanker	Dave Biddle
David Lyons	Number 8	Sean-Michael Stephen
Sam Cordingley	Scrum-half	Morgan Williams (c)
Julian Huxley	Fly-half	Ander Monro
Drew Mitchell	Right Wing	James Pritchard
Adam Ashley-Cooper	Centre	Derek Daypuck
Lote Tuqiri	Centre	Mike Pyke
Cameron Shepherd	Left Wing	Justin Mensah-Coker
Chris Latham	Fullback	Dth van der Merwe
Stephen Hoiles, Sean Hardman, Phil Waugh, George Gregan	Reserves	Aaron Carpenter, Mike Webb, Dan Pletch, Mike Pletch, Mike Burak, Nick Trenkel, Ed Fairhurst

Score: Australia 37 (D. Mitchell 2, A. Baxter, A. Freier, G. Smith, C. Latham tries; C. Shepherd 2 con, J. Huxley pen) defeated Canada 6 (J. Pritchard 2 pen).

Pool B — Wales 34–38 Fiji

Date: September 29, 2007.
Venue: Stade de la Beaujoire, Nantes.
Referee: Stuart Dickinson (Australia).

Wales	Position	Fiji
Gethin Jenkins	Prop	Graham Dewes
Matthew Rees	Hooker	Sunia Koto
Chris Horsman	Prop	Jone Railomo
Alun-Wyn Jones	Lock	Kele Leawere
Ian Evans	Lock	Ifereimi Rawaqa
Colin Charvis	Flanker	Semisi Naevo
Martyn Williams	Flanker	Akapusi Qera
Alex Popham	Number 8	Sisa Koyamaibole
Dwayne Peel	Scrum-half	Mosese Rauluni (c)
Stephen Jones	Fly-half	Nicky Little
Shane Williams	Right Wing	Isoa Neivua
James Hook	Centre	Seremaia Bai
Tom Shanklin	Centre	Seru Rabeni
Mark Jones	Left Wing	Vilimoni Delasau
Gareth Thomas (c)	Fullback	Kameli Ratuvou
Thomas Rhys Thomas, Michael Phillips, Ian Gough, Duncan Jones, Michael Owen	Reserves	Sireli Bobo, Henry Qiodravu, Norman Ligairi, Aca Ratuva, Vereniki Sautauraga, Jone Daunivucu

Score: Fiji 38 (V. Delasau, K. Leawere, A. Qera, G. Dewes tries; N.Little 3 con, 4 pen) defeated Wales 34 (A. Popham, M .Williams, M. Jones, G. Thomas, S. Williams tries; J. Hook con, S. Jones 2 con, pen).

Pool C — New Zealand 76–14 Italy

Date: September 8, 2007.
Venue: Stade Velodrome, Marseille.
Referee: Wayne Barnes (England).

New Zealand	Position	Italy
Tony Woodcock	Prop	Salvatore Perugini
Keven Mealamu	Hooker	Fabio Ongaro
Carl Hayman	Prop	Martin Castrogiovanni
Chris Jack	Lock	Santiago Dellapè
Ali Williams	Lock	Marco Bortolami (c)
Jerry Collins	Flanker	Alessandro Zanni
Richie McCaw (c)	Flanker	Mauro Bergamasco
Rodney So'oialo	Number 8	Sergio Parisse
Byron Kelleher	Scrum-half	Alessandro Troncon
Dan Carter	Fly-half	Roland de Marigny
Sitiveni Sivivatu	Right Wing	Marko Stanojevic
Luke McAlister	Centre	Mirco Bergamasco
Mils Muliaina	Centre	Andrea Masi
Doug Howlett	Left Wing	Kaine Robertson
Leon MacDonald	Fullback	David Bortolussi
Jerry Collins, Neemia Tialata, Brendon Leonard, Anton Oliver, Isaia Toeava, Chris Masoe, Aaron Mauger, Sione Lauaki	Reserves	Andrea Lo Cicero, Manoa Vosawai, Carlo Festuccia, Valerio Bernabò, Ezio Galon, Paul Griffen

Score: New Zealand 76 (D. Howlett 3, R. McCaw 2, S. Sivivatu 2, J. Collins 2, M. Muliaina, C. Jack tries; D. Carter 7 con, pen, L. McAlister 2 con) defeated Italy 14 (M. Stanojevic, Mirco Bergamasco tries; D. Bortolussi con, R. de Marigny con).

Pool C — Scotland 56–10 Portugal

Date: September 9, 2007.
Venue: Stade Geoffroy-Guichard, St-Etienne.
Referee: Steve Walsh (New Zealand).

Scotland	Position	Portugal
Allan Jacobsen	Prop	Rui Cordeiro
Scott Lawson	Hooker	Joaquim Ferreira
Euan Murray	Prop	Ruben Spachuck
Nathan Hines	Lock	Gonçalo Uva
Scott Murray	Lock	David Penalva
Jason White (c)	Flanker	Juan Severino Somoza
Allister Hogg	Flanker	João Uva
Simon Taylor	Number 8	Vasco Uva (c)
Mike Blair	Scrum-half	José Pinto
Dan Parks	Fly-half	Duarte Cardoso Pinto
Simon Webster	Right Wing	Pedro Carvalho
Rob Dewey	Centre	Diogo Mateus
Marcus di Rollo	Centre	Federico Sousa
Sean Lamont	Left Wing	David Mateus
Rory Lamont	Fullback	Pedro Leal
Gavin Kerr, Hugo Southwell, Chris Paterson, Scott MacLeod, Kelly Brown, Rory Lawson, Ross Ford	Reserves	Miguel Portela, João Correia, Paulo Murinello, Juan Manuel Muré, Pedro Cabral, Diogo Coutinho, Luis Pissarra

Score: Scotland 56 (R. Lamont 2, S. Lawson, R. Dewey, H. Southwell, K. Brown, D. Parks, R. Ford tries; D. Parks 5 con, C. Paterson 5 con) defeated Portugal 10 (P. Carvalho try; D.C. Pinto con, pen).

Pool C

Italy 24–18 Romania

Date: September 12, 2007.
Venue: Stade Velodrome, Marseille.
Referee: Tony Spreadbury (England).

Italy	Position	Romania
Andrea Lo Cicero	*Prop*	Petrisor Toderasc
Carlo Festuccia	*Hooker*	Marius Tincu
Martin Castrogiovanni	*Prop*	Bogdan Balan
Santiago Dellapè	*Lock*	Sorin Socol (c)
Marco Bortolami (c)	*Lock*	Cristian Petre
Josh Sole	*Flanker*	Florin Corodeanu
Mauro Bergamasco	*Flanker*	Alexandru Manta
Sergio Parisse	*Number 8*	Ovidiu Tonit
Paul Griffen	*Scrum-half*	Lucian Sirbu
Ramiro Pez	*Fly-half*	Ionut Dimofte
Andrea Masi	*Right Wing*	Gabriel Brezoianu
Mirco Bergamasco	*Centre*	Romeo Gontineac
Gonzalo Canale	*Centre*	Csaba Gal
Kaine Robertson	*Left Wing*	Catalin Fercu
David Bortolussi	*Fullback*	Iulian Dumitras
Valerio Bernabò, Ezio Galon, Alessandro Troncon, Manoa Vosawai	*Reserves*	Razvan Mavrodin, Cezar Popescu, Cosmin Ratiu, Dan Vlad, Valentin Calafeteanu, Alexandru Manta

Score: Italy 24 (S. Dellapè try, penalty try; R. Pez con, 3 pen, D. Bortolussi pen) defeated Romania 18 (A. Manta, M. Tincu tries; I. Dimofte con, 2 pen).

Pool C

New Zealand 108–13 Portugal

Date: September 15, 2007.
Venue: Stade Gerland, Lyon.
Referee: Chris White (England).

New Zealand	Position	Portugal
Neemia Tialata	*Prop*	Andre Silva
Andrew Hore	*Hooker*	João Correia
Greg Somerville	*Prop*	Ruben Spachuck
Chris Jack	*Lock*	Marcello D'Orey
Ali Williams	*Lock*	Gonçalo Uva
Jerry Collins (c)	*Flanker*	Diogo Coutinho
Chris Masoe	*Flanker*	Paulo Murinello
Sione Lauaki	*Number 8*	Vasco Uva (c)
Brendon Leonard	*Scrum-half*	Luis Pissarra
Nick Evans	*Fly-half*	Gonçalo Malheiro
Joe Rokocoko	*Right Wing*	Pedro Carvalho
Aaron Mauger	*Centre*	Diogo Mateus
Conrad Smith	*Centre*	Miguel Portela
Isaia Toeava	*Left Wing*	António Aguilar
Mils Mulianina	*Fullback*	Pedro Leal
Leon MacDonald, Carl Hayman, Rodney So'oialo, Andrew Ellis, Anton Oliver, Tony Woodcock, Keven Mealamu	*Reserves*	David Penalva, Duarte Cardoso Pinto, Rui Cordeiro, José Pinto, Tiago Girao, João Uva, Joaquim Ferreira

Score: New Zealand 108 (J. Rokocoko 2, A. Mauger 2, C. Smith 2, I. Toeava, C. Masoe, J. Collins, A. Williams, B. Leonard, N. Evans, C. Hayman, A. Ellis, L. MacDonald, A. Hore tries; N. Evans 14 con) defeated Portugal 13 (R. Cordeiro try; G. Malheiro drop-goal, D.C. Pinto con, pen).

Pool C — Scotland 42–0 Romania

Date: September 18, 2007.
Venue: Murrayfield, Edinburgh.
Referee: Nigel Owens (Wales).

Scotland	Position	Romania
Gavin Kerr	Prop	Petrisor Toderasc
Ross Ford	Hooker	Marius Tincu
Euan Murray	Prop	Bogdan Balan
Nathan Hines	Lock	Sorin Socol (c)
Jim Hamilton	Lock	Cristian Petre
Jason White (c)	Flanker	Florin Corodeanu
Allister Hogg	Flanker	Alexandru Manta
Simon Taylor	Number 8	Ovidiu Tonita
Mike Blair	Scrum-half	Lucian Sirbu
Dan Parks	Fly-half	Ionut Dimofte
Chris Paterson	Right Wing	Gabriel Brezoianu
Rob Dewey	Centre	Romeo Gontineac
Simon Webster	Centre	Csaba Gal
Sean Lamont	Left Wing	Catalin Fercu
Rory Lamont	Fullback	Iulian Dumitras
Craig Smith, Scott McCleod, Chris Cusiter, Hugo Southwell, Scott Lawson, Kelly Brown, Nikki Walker	Reserves	Razvan Mavrodin, Valentin Calafeteanu, Ionut Tofan, Alexandru Tudori, Cosmin Ratiu, Silviu Florea, Florin Vlaicu

Score: Scotland 42 (A. Hogg 3, R. Lamont 2, C. Paterson tries; C. Paterson 6 con) defeated Romania 0.

Pool C — Italy 31–5 Portugal

Date: September 19, 2007.
Venue: Parc des Princes, Paris.
Referee: Marius Jonker (South Africa).

Italy	Position	Portugal
Andrea Lo Cicero	Prop	Rui Cordeiro
Leonardo Ghiraldini	Hooker	João Correia
Martin Castrogiovanni	Prop	Ruben Spachuck
Carlo Del Fava	Lock	Gonçalo Uva
Marco Bortolami (c)	Lock	David Penalva
Sergio Parisse	Flanker	Tiago Girão
Mauro Bergamasco	Flanker	João Uva
Manoa Vosawai	Number 8	Vasco Uva (c)
Alessandro Troncon	Scrum-half	José Pinto
Roland de Marigny	Fly-half	Duarte Cardoso Pinto
Matteo Pratichetti	Right Wing	António Aguilar
Andrea Masi	Centre	Diogo Mateus
Gonzalo Canale	Centre	Federico Sousa
Pablo Canavosio	Left Wing	David Mateus
David Bortolussi	Fullback	Pedro Cabral
Silvio Orlando, Matias Aguero, Salvatore Perugini, Paul Griffen	Reserves	Diogo Gama, Andre Silva, Juan Manuel Muré, Gonçalo Foro, Paulo Murinello, Luis Pissarra, Duarte Figueiredo

Score: Italy 31 (A. Masi 2, M. Bergamasco tries; D. Bortolussi 2 con, 4 pen) defeated Portugal 5 (D. Penalva try).

Pool C Scotland 0–40 New Zealand
Date: September 23, 2007.
Venue: Murrayfield, Edinburgh.
Referee: Marius Jonker (South Africa).

Scotland	Position	New Zealand
Alasdair Dickinson	*Prop*	Tony Woodcock
Scott Lawson	*Hooker*	Anton Oliver
Craig Smith	*Prop*	Carl Hayman
Scott Macleod	*Lock*	Reuben Thorne
Scott Murray (c)	*Lock*	Ali Williams
Kelly Brown	*Flanker*	Chris Masoe
John Barclay	*Flanker*	Richie McCaw (c)
David Callam	*Number 8*	Rodney So'oialo
Chris Cusiter	*Scrum-half*	Byron Kelleher
Chris Paterson	*Fly-half*	Dan Carter
Simon Webster	*Right Wing*	Sitiveni Sivivatu
Andrew Henderson	*Centre*	Luke McAlister
Marcus di Rollo	*Centre*	Conrad Smith
Nikki Walker	*Left Wing*	Doug Howlett
Hugo Southwell	*Fullback*	Leon MacDonald
Dan Parkes, Gavin Kerr, Fergus Thomson, Rory Lawson, Craig Smith, Rob Dewey, Jim Hamilton	*Reserves*	Nick Evans, Brendon Leonard, Andrew Hore, Sione Lauaki, Neemia Talata, Isaia Toeava, Chris Jack

Score: New Zealand 40 (D. Howlett 2, R. McCaw, B. Kelleher, A. Williams, D. Carter tries; D. Carter 2 con, 2 pen.) defeated Scotland 0.

Pool C Romania 14–10 Portugal
Date: September 25, 2007.
Venue: Municipal Stadium, Toulouse.
Referee: Daniel Santamans (France).

Romania	Position	Portugal
Cezar Popescu	*Prop*	Rui Cordeiro
Razvan Mavrodin	*Hooker*	Joaquim Ferreira (c)
Bogdan Balan	*Prop*	Ruben Spachuck
Cosmin Ratiu	*Lock*	Gonçalo Uva
Cristian Petre	*Lock*	David Penalva
Alexandru Manta	*Flanker*	Diogo Coutinho
Florin Corodeanu	*Flanker*	João Uva
Ovidiu Tonita (c)	*Number 8*	Tiago Girão
Valentin Calafeteanu	*Scrum-half*	José Pinto
Dan Dumbrava	*Fly-half*	Duarte Cardoso Pinto
Catalin Fercu	*Right Wing*	Pedro Carvalho
Romeo Gontineac	*Centre*	Federico Sousa
Ionut Dimofte	*Centre*	Miguel Portela
Catalin Nicolae	*Left Wing*	António Aguilar
Iulian Dumitras	*Fullback*	Pedro Leal
Maruis Tincu, Sorin Socol, Paulica Ion, Lucian Sirbu, Valentin Ursache	*Reserves*	João Correira, Gonçalo Malheiro, Juan Manuel Muré, Luis Pissarra, Paulo Murinello, Salvador Palha

Score: Romania 14 (M. Tincu, F. Corodeanu tries; V. Calafeteanu con, D. Dumbrava con) defeated Portugal 10 (J. Ferreira try; D.C. Pinto con, G. Malheiro pen).

New Zealand 85–8 Romania

Pool C

Date: September 29, 2007.
Venue: Municipal Stadium, Toulouse.
Referee: Joel Jutge (France).

New Zealand	Position	Romania
Neemia Tialata	*Prop*	Bogdan Balan
Keven Mealamu	*Hooker*	Marius Tincu
Greg Somerville	*Prop*	Silviu Florea
Reuben Thorne	*Lock*	Sorin Socol (c)
Keith Robinson	*Lock*	Cristian Petre
Jerry Collins (c)	*Flanker*	Florin Corodeanu
Chris Masoe	*Flanker*	Alexandru Manta
Sione Lauaki	*Number 8*	Ovidiu Tonita
Andrew Ellis	*Scrum-half*	Lucian Sirbu
Luke McAlister	*Fly-half*	Ionut Dimofte
Sitiveni Sivivatu	*Right Wing*	Gabriel Brezoianu
Aaron Mauger	*Centre*	Romeo Gontineac
Isaia Toeava	*Centre*	Csaba Gal
Joe Rokocoko	*Left Wing*	Stefan Ciuntu
Nick Evans	*Fullback*	Iulian Dumitras
Doug Howlett, Chris Jack, Richie McCaw, Brendon Leanard, Conrad Smith, Andrew Hore	*Reserves*	Cosmin Ratiu, Razvan Mavrodin, Paulica Ion, Florin Vlaicu, Valentin Calafeteanu, Valentin Ursache, Catalin Robert Dascalu

Score: New Zealand 85 (J. Rokocoko 3, S. Sivivatu 2, I. Toeava 2, C. Masoe, A. Mauger, A. Hore, D. Howlett, C. Smith, N. Evans tries; L. McAlister 4 con, N. Evans 6 con) defeated Romania 8 (M. Tincu try; F. Vlaicu pen).

Scotland 18–16 Italy

Pool C

Date: September 29, 2007.
Venue: Stade Geoffroy-Guichard, St-Etienne.
Referee: Jonathan Kaplan (South Africa).

Scotland	Position	Italy
Gavin Kerr	*Prop*	Salvatore Perugini
Ross Ford	*Hooker*	Carlo Festuccia
Euan Murray	*Prop*	Martin Castrogiovanni
Nathan Hines	*Lock*	Santiago Dellapè
Jim Hamilton	*Lock*	Carlo Del Fava
Jason White (c)	*Flanker*	Josh Sole
Allister Hogg	*Flanker*	Mauro Bergamasco
Simon Taylor	*Number 8*	Sergio Parisse
Mike Blair	*Scrum-half*	Alessandro Troncon (c)
Dan Parks	*Fly-half*	Ramiro Pez
Chris Paterson	*Right Wing*	Andrea Masi
Rob Dewey	*Centre*	Mirco Bergamasco
Simon Webster	*Centre*	Gonzalo Canale
Sean Lamont	*Left Wing*	Kaine Robertson
Rory Lamont	*Fullback*	David Bortolussi
Hugo Southwell, Andrew Henderson, Craig Smith, Kelly Brown, Scott Macleod, Chris Cusiter	*Reserves*	Andrea Lo Cicero, Fabio Ongaro, Ezio Galon

Score: Scotland 18 (C. Paterson 6 pen) defeated Italy 16 (A. Troncon try; D. Bortolussi con, D. Bortolussi 3 pen.).

Pool D   France 12–17 Argentina
Date: September 7, 2007.
Venue: Stade de France, Paris.
Referee: Tony Spreadbury (England).

France	Position	Argentina
Olivier Milloud	*Prop*	Rodrigo Roncero
Raphael Ibanez (c)	*Hooker*	Mario Ledesma Arocena
Pieter de Villiers	*Prop*	Juan Martin Scelzo
Fabien Pelous	*Lock*	Ignacio Fernandez Lobbe
Jerome Thion	*Lock*	Patricio Albacete
Serge Betsen	*Flanker*	Lucas Ostiglia
Remy Martin	*Flanker*	Juan Martin Fernandez Lobbe
Imanol Harinordoquy	*Number 8*	Juan Manuel Leguizamon
Pierre Mignoni	*Scrum-half*	Agustin Pichot (c)
David Skrela	*Fly-half*	Juan Martin Hernandez
Aurelien Rougerie	*Right Wing*	Horacio Agulla
Damien Traille	*Centre*	Felipe Contepomi
Yannick Jauzion	*Centre*	Manuel Contepomi
Christophe Dominici	*Left Wing*	Lucas Borges
Cedric Heymans	*Fullback*	Ignacio Corleto
Frederic Michalak, Dimitri Szarzewski, Sebastien Chabal, Julien Bonnaire, Jean-Baptiste Elissalde	*Reserves*	Rimas Alverez Kairelis, Hernan Senillosa, Santiago Gonzales Bonorino, Martin Durrand

Score: Argentina 17 (I. Corleto try; F. Contepomi 4 pen) defeated France 12 (D. Skrela 4 pen).

Pool D   Ireland 32–17 Namibia
Date: September 9, 2007.
Venue: Stade Chaban Delmas, Bordeaux.
Referee: Joel Jutge (France).

Ireland	Position	Namibia
Marcus Horan	*Prop*	Kees Lensing (c)
Rory Best	*Hooker*	Hugo Horn
John Hayes	*Prop*	Jane du Toit
Donnacha O'Callaghan	*Lock*	Wacca Kazombiaze
Paul O'Connell	*Lock*	Nico Esterhuize
Simon Easterby	*Flanker*	Jacques Nieuwenhuis
David Wallace	*Flanker*	Heino Senekal
Denis Leamy	*Number 8*	Jacques Burger
Peter Stringer	*Scrum-half*	Eugene Jantjies
Ronan O'Gara	*Fly-half*	Emile Wessels
Denis Hickie	*Right Wing*	Heini Bock
Gordan D'Arcy	*Centre*	Piet van Zyl
Brian O'Driscoll (c)	*Centre*	Bratley Langenhoven
Andrew Trimble	*Left Wing*	Ryan Witbooi
Girvan Dempsey	*Fullback*	Tertius Losper
Simon Best, Jerry Flannery, Neil Best, Paddy Wallace, Geordan Murphy	*Reserves*	Michael Mackenzie, Johnny Redelinghuys, Jurie van Tonder, Tinus du Plessis, Johannes Meyer, Melrick Africa

Score: Ireland 32 (S. Easterby, A. Trimble, J. Flannery, B. O'Driscoll tries, penalty try; R. O'Gara 2 con, pen) defeated Namibia 17 (J. Nieuwenhuis, P. van Zyl tries; E. Wessels 2 con, pen).

Pool D	**Argentina 33–3 Georgia**

Date: September 11, 2007.
Venue: Stade Gerland, Lyon.
Referee: Nigel Owens (Wales).

Argentina	Position	Georgia
Marcos Ayerza	*Prop*	David Khinchagashvili
Mario Ledesma Arocena	*Hooker*	Akvsenti Giorgadze
Santiago Gonzalez Bonorino	*Prop*	David Zirakashvili
Rimas Alvarez Kairelis	*Lock*	Ilia Zedginidze (c)
Patricio Albacete	*Lock*	Mamuka Gorgodze
Martin Durand	*Flanker*	Giorgi Chkhaidze
Juan Martin Fernandez Lobbe	*Flanker*	Grigol Labadze
Juan Manuel Leguizamon	*Number 8*	Besso Udesiani
Nicolas Fernandez Miranda	*Scrum-half*	Irakli Abuseridze
Juan Martin Hernandez	*Fly-half*	Merab Kvirikashvili
Federico Martin Aramburu	*Right Wing*	Besiki Khamashuridze
Felipe Contepomi (c)	*Centre*	Irakli Giorgadze
Gonzalo Tiesi	*Centre*	Malkhaz Urjukashvili
Lucas Borges	*Left Wing*	Irakli Machkhaneli
Ignacio Corleto	*Fullback*	Pavle Jimsheladze
Esteban Lozada, Hernan Senillosa, Omar Hasan Jalil, Martin Schusterman, Esteban Lozada, Alberto Vernet Basualdo, Federico Todeschini	*Reserves*	Avtandil Kopaliani, Zviad Maisuradze, Giorgi Shkinin, Goderdzi Shvelidze, Bidzina Samkharadze, Victor Didebulidze, Revaz Gigauri

Score: Argentina 33 (L. Borges 2, P. Albacete, F. Aramburu tries; F. Contepomi con, 3 pen, J.M. Hernandez con) defeated Georgia 3 (M. Kvirikashvili pen).

Pool D	**Ireland 14–10 Georgia**

Date: September 15, 2007.
Venue: Stade Chaban Delmas, Bordeaux.
Referee: Wayne Barnes (England).

Ireland	Position	Georgia
Marcus Horan	*Prop*	Mamuka Magrakvelidze
Rory Best	*Hooker*	Goderdzi Shvelidze
John Hayes	*Prop*	Avtandil Kopaliani
Donnacha O'Callaghan	*Lock*	Ilia Zedginidze (c)
Paul O'Connell	*Lock*	Mamuka Gorgodze
Simon Easterby	*Flanker*	Ilia Maisuradze
David Wallace	*Flanker*	Rati Urushadze
Denis Leamy	*Number 8*	Giorgi Chkhaidze
Peter Stringer	*Scrum-half*	Bidzina Samkharadze
Ronan O'Gara	*Fly-half*	Merab Kvirikashvili
Denis Hickie	*Right Wing*	Giorgi Elizbarashvili
Gordan D'Arcy	*Centre*	Davit Kacharava
Brian O'Driscoll (c)	*Centre*	Malkhaz Urjukashvili
Shane Horgan	*Left Wing*	Giorgi Shkinin
Girvan Dempsey	*Fullback*	Otar Barkalaia
Simon Best, Jerry Flannery, Neil Best, Isaac Boss	*Reserves*	Levan Datunashvili, Irakli Machkhaneli, David Khinchagashvili, Akvsenti Giorgadze, Otar Eloshvili, Zviad Maisuradze, Irakli Abuseridze

Score: Ireland 14 (R. Best, G. Dempsey tries; R. O'Gara 2 con) defeated Georgia 10 (G. Shkinin try; M. Kvirikashvili con, peni).

Pool D — France 87–10 Namibia

Date: September 16, 2007.
Venue: Municipal Stadium, Toulouse.
Referee: Alain Rolland (Ireland).

France	Position	Namibia
Jean-Baptiste Poux	*Prop*	Kees Lensing (c)
Dimitri Szarzewski	*Hooker*	Hugo Horn
Pieter de Villiers	*Prop*	Jane du Toit
Sebastien Chabal	*Lock*	Wacca Kazombiaze
Lionel Nallet	*Lock*	Nico Esterhuize
Yannick Nyanga	*Flanker*	Jacques Burger
Thierry Dusautoir	*Flanker*	Michael Mackenzie
Julien Bonnaire	*Number 8*	Jacques Nieuwenhuis
Jean-Baptiste Elissalde (c)	*Scrum-half*	Jurie van Tonder
Frederic Michalak	*Fly-half*	Emile Wessels
Cedric Heymans	*Right Wing*	Heini Bock
Damien Traille	*Centre*	Piet van Zyl
David Marty	*Centre*	Bratley Langenhoven
Vincent Clerc	*Left Wing*	Ryan Witbooi
Clement Poitrenaud	*Fullback*	Tertius Losper
Nicolas Mas, Yannick Jauzion, Imanol Harinordoquy, Raphael Ibanez, Fabien Pelous, Lionel Beauxis, Aurelien Rougerie	*Reserves*	Lu-Wayne Botes, Eugene Jantjies, Tinus du Plessis, Johnny Redelinghuys, Herman Lindvelt, Johannes Meyer, Melrick Africa, Kees Lensing

Score: France 87 (V. Clerc 3, S. Chabal 2, L. Nallet 2, C. Heymans, D. Marty, T. Dusautoir, J. Bonnaire, J.-B. Elissalde, R. Ibanez tries; J.-B. Elissalde 11 con) defeated Namibia 10 (B. Langenhoven try; T. Losper con, E. Wessels drop-goal).

Pool D — France 25–3 Ireland

Date: September 21, 2007.
Venue: Stade de France, Paris.
Referee: Chris White (England).

France	Position	Ireland
Olivier Milloud	*Prop*	Marcus Horan
Raphael Ibanez (c)	*Hooker*	Jerry Flannery
Pieter de Villiers	*Prop*	John Hayes
Sebastien Chabel	*Lock*	Donnacha O'Callaghan
Jerome Thion	*Lock*	Paul O'Connell
Serge Betsen	*Flanker*	Simon Easterby
Thierry Dusautoir	*Flanker*	David Wallace
Julien Bonnaire	*Number 8*	Denis Leamy
Jean-Baptiste Elissalde	*Scrum-half*	Eoin Reddan
Frederic Michalak	*Fly-half*	Ronan O'Gara
Cedric Heymans	*Right Wing*	Andrew Trimble
Damien Traille	*Centre*	Gordan D'Arcy
David Marty	*Centre*	Brian O'Driscoll (c)
Vincent Clerc	*Left Wing*	Shane Horgan
Clement Poitrenaud	*Fullback*	Girvan Dempsey
Lionel Nallet, Dimitri Szarzewski, Yannick Nyanga, Aurelien Rougerie, Yannick Jauzion, Jean-Baptiste Poux, Lionel Beauxis	*Reserves*	Frankie Sheahan, Malcolm O'Kelly, Neil Best, Simon Best

Score: France 25 (V. Clerc 2 tries; J. Elissalde 5 pen.) defeated Ireland 3 (R. O'Gara drop-goal).

Pool D — Argentina 63–3 Namibia

Date: September 22, 2007.
Venue: Stade Velodrome, Marseille.
Referee: Stuart Dickinson (Australia).

Argentina	Position	Namibia
Rodrigo Roncero	Prop	Johnny Redelinghuys
Alberto Vernet Basualdo	Hooker	Johannes Meyer
Omar Hasan Jalil	Prop	Marius Visser
Carlos Ignacio Fernandez Lobbe	Lock	Wacca Kazombiaze
Patricio Albacete	Lock	Nico Esterhuize
Lucas Ostiglia	Flanker	Michael Mackenzie
Juan Martin Fernandez Lobbe	Flanker	Jacques Burger
Juan Manuel Leguizamon	Number 8	Tinus Du Plessis
Agustin Pichot (c)	Scrum-half	Eugene Jantjies
Felipe Contepomi	Fly-half	Morne Schreuder
Horacio Agulla	Right Wing	Melrick Africa
Manuel Contepomi	Centre	Corne Powell (c)
Gonzalo Tiesi	Centre	Du Preez Grobler
Hernan Senillosa	Left Wing	Deon Mouton
Ignacio Corleto	Fullback	Heini Bock
Nicolas Fernandez Miranda, Gonzalo Longo Elía, Federico Todeschini, Federico Serra Miras, Rimas Alvarez Kairelis, Juan Martin Scelzo	Reserves	Herman Lindvelt, Hugo Horn, Kees Lensing, Piet Van Zyl, Bradley Langenhoven, Heino Senekal, Jurie Van Tonder

Score: Argentina 63 (J.M. Leguizamon 2, R. Roncero, M. Contepomi, F. Contepomi, G. Tiesi, I. Corleto, F. Todeschini tries, penalty try; F. Contepomi 4 con, 2 pen, F. Todeschini 2 con) defeated Namibia 3 (M. Schreuder pen).

Pool D — Georgia 30–0 Namibia

Date: September 26, 2007.
Venue: Stade Felix Bollaert, Lens.
Referee: Steve Walsh (New Zealand).

Georgia	Position	Namibia
Goderdzi Shvelidze	Prop	Kees Lensing (c)
Akvsenti Giorgadze	Hooker	Hugo Horn
David Zirakashvili	Prop	Marius Visser
Levan Datunashvili	Lock	Wacca Kazombiaze
Mamuka Gorgodze	Lock	Heino Senekal
Grigol Labadze	Flanker	Jacques Nieuwenhuis
Rati Urushadze	Flanker	Jacques Burger
Giorgi Chkhaidze	Number 8	Tinus du Plessis
Irakli Abuseridze (c)	Scrum-half	Jurie van Tonder
Merab Kvirikashvili	Fly-half	Morne Schreuder
Giorgi Shkinin	Right Wing	Bratley Langenhoven
Irakli Giorgadze	Centre	Corne Powell
Davit Kacharava	Centre	Piet van Zyl
Irakli Machkhaneli	Left Wing	Ryan Witbooi
Malkhaz Urjukashvili	Fullback	Heini Bock
Victor Didebulidze, Besiki Khamashuridze, Besso Udesiani, David Khinchagashvili, Bidzina Samkharadze, Revaz Gigauri, Avtandil Kopaliani	Reserves	Jane du Toit, Nico Esterhuize, Eugene Jant ies, Johnny Redelinghuys, Melrick Africa, Johannes Myer, Domingo Kamonga

Score: Georgia 30 (A. Giorgadze, I. Machkhaneli, D. Kacharava tries; M. Kvirikashvili 3 con, 3 pen) defeated Namibia 0.

Pool D — France 64–7 Georgia

Date: September 30, 2007.
Venue: Stade Velodrome, Marseille.
Referee: Alan Lewis (Ireland).

France	Position	Georgia
Olivier Milloud	Prop	Mamuka Magrakvelidze
Sebastian Bruno	Hooker	Akvsenti Giorgadze
Jean-Baptiste Poux	Prop	David Zirakashvili
Lionel Nallet	Lock	Victor Didebulidze
Jerome Thion	Lock	Zurab Mtchedlishvili
Serge Betsen (c)	Flanker	Ilia Maisuradze
Yannick Nyanga	Flanker	Rati Urushadze
Julien Bonnaire	Number 8	Giorgi Chkhaidze
Pierre Mignoni	Scrum-half	Irakli Abuseeridze (c)
Lionel Beauxis	Fly-half	Merab Kvirikashvili
Christophe Dominici	Right Wing	Besiki Khamashuridze
Yannick Jauzion	Centre	Irakli Giorgadze
David Marty	Centre	Revaz Gigauri
Aurelien Rougerie	Left Wing	Malkhaz Urjukashvili
Clement Poitrenaud	Fullback	Otar Barkalaia
Jean-Baptiste Elissalde, Fabien Pelous, Dimitri Szarzewski, David Skrela, Nicolas Mas, Remy Martin, Vincent Clerc	Reserves	Bidzina Sankharadze, Goderdzi Shvelidze, Levan Datunashvili, Zviad Maisuradze, Avtandil Kopaliani, Otar Eloshvili, Giorgi Elizbarashvili

Score: France 64 (C. Dominici 2, C. Poitrenaud, Y. Nyanga, S. Bruno, L. Nallet, J. Bonnaire, R. Martin, L. Beauxis tries; L. Beauxis 5 con, 3 pen) defeated Georgia 7 (Z. Maisuradze try; M. Urjukashvili con).

Pool D — Ireland 15–30 Argentina

Date: September 30, 2007.
Venue: Parc des Princes, Paris.
Referee: Paul Honiss (New Zealand).

Ireland	Position	Argentina
Marcus Horan	Prop	Rodrigo Roncero
Jerry Flannery	Hooker	Mario Ledesma Arocena
John Hayes	Prop	Juan Martin Scelzo
Donnacha O'Callaghan	Lock	Carlos Ignacio Fernandez Lobbe
Paul O'Connell	Lock	Patricio Albacete
Simon Easterby	Flanker	Lucas Borges
David Wallace	Flanker	Juan Martin Fernandez Lobbe
Denis Leamy	Number 8	Gonzalo Longo Elia
Eoin Reddan	Scrum-half	Agustin Pichot (c)
Ronan O'Gara	Fly-half	Juan Martin Hernandez
Denis Hickie	Right Wing	Horacio Agulla
Gordan D'Arcy	Centre	Felipe Contepomi
Brian O'Driscoll (c)	Centre	Manuel Contepomi
Shane Horgan	Left Wing	Lucas Borges
Geordan Murphy	Fullback	Ignacio Corleto
Neil Best, Malcolm O'Kelly, Rory Best, Isaac Boss, Gavin Duffy	Reserves	Rimas Alvarez Kairelis, Martin Durand, Hernan Senillosa, Omar Hasan Jalil, Alberto Vernet Basualdo

Score: Argentina 30 (L. Borges, H. Agulla tries; F. Contepomi con, 3 pen, J.M. Hernandez 3 drop-goal) defeated Ireland 15 (B. O'Driscoll, G. Murphy tries; R. O'Gara con, pen).

Quarter-final	Australia 10–12 England

Date: October 6, 2007.
Venue: Stade Velodrome, Marseille.
Referee: Alain Rolland (Ireland).

Australia	Position	England
Matt Dunning	*Prop*	Andrew Sheridan
Stephen Moore	*Hooker*	Mark Regan
Guy Shepherdson	*Prop*	Phil Vickery (c)
Nathan Sharpe	*Lock*	Simon Shaw
Daniel Vickerman	*Lock*	Ben Kay
Rocky Elsom	*Flanker*	Martin Corry
George Smith	*Flanker*	Lewis Moody
Wycliff Palu	*Number 8*	Nick Easter
George Gregan	*Scrum-half*	Andy Gomarsall
Berrick Barnes	*Fly-half*	Jonny Wilkinson
Lote Tuqiri	*Right Wing*	Josh Lewsey
Matt Giteau	*Centre*	Mike Catt
Stirling Mortlock (c)	*Centre*	Matthew Tait
Adam Ashley-Cooper	*Left Wing*	Paul Sackey
Chris Latham	*Fullback*	Jason Robinson
Hugh McMeniman, Phil Waugh, Al Baxter, Drew Mitchell, Adam Freier, Stephen Hoiles	*Reserves*	Peter Richards, George Chuter, Matt Stevens, Toby Flood, Joe Worsley, Lawrence Dallaglio

Score: England 12 (J. Wilkinson 4 pen) defeated Australia 10 (L. Tuqiri try; S. Mortlock con, pen).

Quarter-final	New Zealand 18–20 France

Date: October 6, 2007.
Venue: Millennium Stadium, Cardiff.
Referee: Wayne Barnes (England).

New Zealand	Position	France
Tony Woodcock	*Prop*	Olivier Milloud
Anton Oliver	*Hooker*	Raphael Ibanez (c)
Carl Hayman	*Prop*	Pieter de Villiers
Keith Robinson	*Lock*	Fabien Pelous
Ali Williams	*Lock*	Jerome Thion
Jerry Collins	*Flanker*	Serge Betsen
Richie McCaw (c)	*Flanker*	Thierry Dusautoir
Rodney So'oialo	*Number 8*	Julien Bonnaire
Byron Kelleher	*Scrum-half*	Jean-Baptiste Elissalde
Dan Carter	*Fly-half*	Lionel Beauxis
Sitiveni Sivivatu	*Right Wing*	Cedric Heymans
Luke McAlister	*Centre*	Yannick Jauzion
Mils Muliaina	*Centre*	David Marty
Joe Rokocoko	*Left Wing*	Vincent Clerc
Leon MacDonald	*Fullback*	Damien Traille
Chris Jack, Nick Evans, Andrew Hore, Brendon Leonard, Chris Masoe, Isaia Toeava	*Reserves*	Imanol Harinordoquy, Jean-Baptiste Poux, Sebastian Chabal, Dimitri Szarzewski, Frederic Michalak, Christophe Dominici

Score: France 20 (T. Dusautoir, Y. Jauzion tries; L. Beauxis con, 2 pen, J.-B. Elissalde con) defeated New Zealand 18 (L. McAlister, R. So'oialo tries; D. Carter con, 2 pen).

Quarter-final	**South Africa 37–20 Fiji**	

Date: October 7, 2007.
Venue: Stade Velodrome, Marseille.
Referee: Alan Lewis (Ireland).

South Africa	Position	Fiji
Os du Randt	*Prop*	Graham Dewes
John Smit (c)	*Hooker*	Sunia Koto
Jannie du Plessis	*Prop*	Henry Qiodravu
Bakkies Botha	*Lock*	Kele Leawere
Victor Matfield	*Lock*	Ifereimi Rawaqa
Schalk Burger	*Flanker*	Semisi Naevo
Juan Smith	*Flanker*	Akapusi Qera
Danie Rossouw	*Number 8*	Sisa Koyamaibole
Fourie du Preez	*Scrum-half*	Mosese Rauluni (c)
Butch James	*Fly-half*	Seremaia Bai
Bryan Habana	*Right Wing*	Sireli Bobo
Francois Steyn	*Centre*	Seru Rabeni
Jaque Fourie	*Centre*	Kameli Ratuvou
J.P. Pietersen	*Left Wing*	Vilimoni Delasau
Percy Montgomery	*Fullback*	Norman Ligairi
Wickus van Heerden, Gurthro Steenkamp, Johannes Muller	*Reserves*	Jone Railomo, Gabiriele Lovobalavu, Aca Ratuva, Bill Godolo, Warne Lewaravu

Score: South Africa 37 (J. Fourie, J. Smit, J.P. Pietersen, J. Smith, B. James tries; P. Montgomery 3 con, pen, F. Steyn pen) defeated Fiji 20 (V. Delasau, S. Bobo tries; S. Bai 2 con, 2 pen).

Quarter-final	**Argentina 19–13 Scotland**	

Date: October 7, 2007.
Venue: Stade de France, Paris.
Referee: Joel Jutge (France).

Argentina	Position	Scotland
Rodrigo Roncero	*Prop*	Gavin Kerr
Mario Ledesma Arocena	*Hooker*	Ross Ford
Martin Scelzo	*Prop*	Euan Murray
Carlos Ignacio Fernandez Lobbe	*Lock*	Nathan Hines
Patricio Albacete	*Lock*	Jim Hamilton
Lucas Ostiglia	*Flanker*	Jason White (c)
Juan Martin Fernandez Lobbe	*Flanker*	Allister Hogg
Gonzalo Longo Elia	*Number 8*	Simon Taylor
Agustin Pichot (c)	*Scrum-half*	Mike Blair
Juan Martin Hernandez	*Fly-half*	Dan Parks
Horacio Agulla	*Right Wing*	Chris Paterson
Felipe Contepomi	*Centre*	Rob Dewey
Manuel Contepomi	*Centre*	Simon Webster
Lucas Borges	*Left Wing*	Sean Lamont
Ignacio Corleto	*Fullback*	Rory Lamont
Rimas Alvarez Kairelis, Juan Manuel Leguizamon, Omar Hasan Jalil, Hernan Senillosa	*Reserves*	Andrew Henderson, Chris Cusiter, Scott Macleod, Craig Smith, Kelly Brown, Scott Lawson, Hugo Southwell

Score: Argentina 19 (G. Longo try; F. Contepomi con, 3 pen, J. Hernandez drop-goal) defeated Scotland 13 (C. Cusiter try; C. Paterson con, pen, D. Parks pen).

Semi-final   # England 14–9 France

Date: October 13, 2007.
Venue: Stade de France, Paris.
Referee: Jonathan Kaplan (South Africa).

England	Position	France
Andrew Sheridan	*Prop*	Olivier Milloud
Mark Regan	*Hooker*	Raphael Ibanez (c)
Phil Vickery (c)	*Prop*	Pieter de Villiers
Simon Shaw	*Lock*	Fabien Pelous
Ben Kay	*Lock*	Jerome Thion
Martin Corry	*Flanker*	Serge Betsen
Lewis Moody	*Flanker*	Thierry Dusautoir
Nick Easter	*Number 8*	Julien Bonnaire
Andy Gomarsall	*Scrum-half*	Jean-Baptiste Elissalde
Jonny Wilkinson	*Fly-half*	Lionel Beauxis
Josh Lewsey	*Right Wing*	Cedric Heymans
Mike Catt	*Centre*	Yannick Jauzion
Matthew Tait	*Centre*	David Marty
Paul Sackey	*Left Wing*	Vincent Clerc
Jason Robinson	*Fullback*	Damien Traille
Dan Hipkiss, Joe Worsley, Matt Stevens, George Chuter, Toby Flood, Lawrence Dallaglio, Peter Richards	*Reserves*	Sebastien Chabal, Dimitri Szarzewski, Frederic Michalak, Christophe Dominici, Jean-Baptiste Poux, Imanol Harinordoquy

Score: England 14 (J. Lewsey try; J. Wilkinson 2 pen, drop-goal.)
defeated France 9 (L. Beauxis 3 pen).

Semi-final   # South Africa 37–13 Argentina

Date: October 14, 2007.
Venue: Stade de France, Paris.
Referee: Steve Walsh (New Zealand).

South Africa	Position	Argentina
Os du Randt	*Prop*	Rodrigo Roncero
John Smit (c)	*Hooker*	Mario Ledesma Arocena
C.J. van der Linde	*Prop*	Martin Scelzo
Bakkies Botha	*Lock*	Carlos Ignacio Fernandez Lobbe
Victor Matfield	*Lock*	Patricio Albacete
Schalk Burger	*Flanker*	Lucas Ostiglia
Juan Smith	*Flanker*	Juan Martin Fernandez Lobbe
Danie Rossouw	*Number 8*	Gonzalo Longo Elia
Fourie du Preez	*Scrum-half*	Agustin Pichot (c)
Butch James	*Fly-half*	Juan Martin Hernandez
Bryan Habana	*Right Wing*	Horacio Agulla
Francois Steyn	*Centre*	Felipe Contepomi
Jaque Fourie	*Centre*	Manuel Contepomi
J.P. Pietersen	*Left Wing*	Lucas Borges
Percy Montgomery	*Fullback*	Ignacio Corleto
Johannes Muller, Jannie du Plessis, Bobby Skinstad, Bismarck du Plessis, Wynand Olivier, Andre Pretorius, Ruan Pienaar	*Reserves*	Omar Hasan Jalil, Rimas Alvarez Kairelis, Juan Manuel Leguizamon, Gonzalo Tiesi

Score: South Africa 37 (B. Habana 2, D. Rossouw, F. du Preez tries; P. Montgomery 4 con, 3 pen) defeated Argentina 13 (M. Contepomi try; F. Contepomi con, 2 pen).

3rd Place Play-off   # France 10–34 Argentina
Date: October 19, 2007.
Venue: Parc des Princes, Paris.
Referee: Paul Honiss (New Zealand)

France	Position	Argentina
Jean-Baptiste Poux	*Prop*	Rodrigo Roncero
Raphael Ibanez (c)	*Hooker*	Alberto Vernet Basualdo
Nicolas Mas	*Prop*	Omar Hasan Jalil
Lionel Nallet	*Lock*	Rimas Alvarez Kairelis
Jerome Thion	*Lock*	Patricio Albacete
Yannick Nyanga	*Flanker*	Martin Durand
Thierry Dusautoir	*Flanker*	Juan Martin Fernandez Lobbe
Imanol Harinordoquy	*Number 8*	Gonzalo Longo Elia
Jean-Baptiste Elissalde	*Scrum-half*	Agustin Pichot (c)
Frederic Michalak	*Fly-half*	Juan Martin Hernandez
Christophe Dominici	*Right Wing*	Horacio Agulla
David Marty	*Centre*	Felipe Contepomi
David Skrela	*Centre*	Manuel Contepomi
Aurelien Rougerie	*Left Wing*	Federico Martin Aramburu
Clement Poitrenaud	*Fullback*	Ignacio Corleto
Sebastien Bruno, Remy Martin, Pierre Mignoni, Sebastien Chabal, Vincent Clerc, Lionel Beauxis	*Reserves*	Hernan Senillosa, Juan Manuel Leguizamon, Marcos Ayerza, Esteban Lozada, Eusebio Guinazu

Score: Argentina 34 (F. Contepomi 2, O. Hasan, F. M. Aramburu, I. Corleto tries; F. Contepomi 3 con, pen) defeated France 10 (C. Poitrenaud try; L. Beauxis con, J. Elissalde pen).

The Final   # England 6–15 South Africa
Date: October 20, 2007.
Venue: Stade de France, Paris.
Referee: Alain Rolland (Ireland).

England	Position	South Africa
Andrew Sheridan	*Prop*	Os du Randt
Mark Regan	*Hooker*	John Smit (c)
Phil Vickery (c)	*Prop*	C.J. van der Linde
Simon Shaw	*Lock*	Bakkies Botha
Ben Kay	*Lock*	Victor Matfield
Martin Corry	*Flanker*	Schalk Burger
Lewis Moody	*Flanker*	Juan Smith
Nick Easter	*Number 8*	Danie Rossouw
Andy Gomarsall	*Scrum-half*	Fourie du Preez
Jonny Wilkinson	*Fly-half*	Butch James
Mark Cueto	*Right Wing*	Bryan Habana
Mike Catt	*Centre*	Francois Steyn
Matthew Tait	*Centre*	Jaque Fourie
Paul Sackey	*Left Wing*	J.P. Pietersen
Jason Robinson	*Fullback*	Percy Montgomery
Matt Stevens, Dan Hipkiss, Toby Flood, George Chuter, Joe Worsley, Lawrence Dallaglio, Peter Richards	*Reserves*	Bismarck du Plessis, Wickus van Heerden

Score: South Africa 15 (P. Montgomery 4 pen, F. Steyn pen) defeated England 6 (J. Wilkinson 2 pen).